Countdown to Catastrophe

Palestine 1948

a daily chronology

Hugh Humphries
in collaboration with Ross Campbell

Published by Scottish Friends of Palestine

 Published in 2000 by
Scottish Friends of Palestine
2000

"no settlement can be just and complete if recognition is not accorded to the right of the Arab refugee to return to the home from which he was dislodged by the hazards and strategy of the armed conflict between Arabs and Jews in Palestine. . . . . It would be an offence against the principles of elemental justice if these innocent victims of the conflict were denied the right to return to their homes while Jewish immigrants flow into Palestine, and, indeed, at least offer the threat of permanent replacement of the Arab refugees who have been rooted in the land for centuries."

Count Folke Bernadotte, UN Special Mediator to Palestine
Progress Report, GAOR, 3rd Sess., Supp No. 11 at 14, UN Doc A/648 (1948)

acknowledgement
This book could not have been published without assistance from the The League of Arab States, London Mission. Scottish Friends of Palestine acknowledge this assistance and express their gratitude.

ISBN 0 9521210 2 6

This chronology, and the detail contained therein, would not have been possible without the able assistance of my collaborator, Ross Campbell. It was Ross who trawled the pages of the many volumes of books and journals, cross-referencing the events with the dates. No detail was too small, if it could be chronologically identified. I am indebted to his enthusiasm and patience.

Any errors or opinion expressed are my responsibility.

In researching the many newspapers and books outlining the events of 1948, both Ross and myself learned much of which we had previously been unaware. In particular, the tenacity with which the Palestinian people clung to their land, until terror forced them to seek refuge elswhere. Like anybody in such circumstances, few could believe that the events unfolding around them throughout 1948 were the result of military and strategic intent, designed to dispossess them of their heritage forever.

Of the many accounts recorded for that fateful year, one which made a lasting impact, was that of Palestinian youths, towards the end of March, in earnest conversation in the courtyard of the Church of the Holy Sepulchre. With the noise of military activity, from the Bethlehem area, in the background, The Scotsman correspondent recorded their hesitation. Should they join the congregation in the Church or find a vantage point to observe the military action? At the toss of a coin it was decided. Forget their religious devotions for the rest of the day. Go and enjoy the action.

Before long what appeared as a game to the youths, turned into a nightmare which resulted in the outright expulsion or flight 750 000 men, women and children, the young, the sick and the elderly.

This book is dedicated to those same people.

Hugh Humphries

Contents

Glossary

Arab Liberation Army (ALA) - a force of about 5 000 men, mostly Syrian and Iraqi irregulars, organised in December 1947 to help the Palestinians

Ben Gurion, David - Chairman of the Jewish Agency, Israel's first prime minister and first minister of defence

Eshkol, Levi - the treasurer of the Haganah

Haganah (Defence) - left wing Zionist paramilitary force and eventual Israeli regular army; 35 000 members in May 1947

Irgun (Irgun Zvai Leumi) - National Military Organisation; 3 000 to 5 000 members

Jewish Agency - the pre-state government of the Yishuv

Jewish National Fund - established in 1901 as the land acquisition and administrative arm of the World Zionist Organisation (Land bought through the JNF could be neither sold nor mortgaged, remaining in perpetual trust for Jewish people)

Machnes, Gad - Director General, Minority Affairs Ministry

Mapai - Israeli socialist Zionist party, forerunner of the Israeli Labour Party

Mapam - a Soviet inclined breakaway group from Mapai of which the majority of the Haganah commanders were members (re-absorbed into Mapai in 1948)

Meir (Myerson), Golda - Director of the Jewish Agency's Political Department in Jerusalem and eventual prime minister

Palmach (Shock Troops) - commandos in the Haganah; 2 200 members

Sharett (Shertok), Moshe - Director of the Political Department of the Jewish Agency, Israel's first foreign minister and an eventual prime minister

Shalom Shitrit,Bechor - Minister of Minority Affairs and Police (1948 -)

Stern Gang or LHI (Lohamei Herut Yisrael) - Fighters for the Freedom of Israel; 200 to 300 members

Yishuv (Settlement) - Jewish community in Palestine prior to the founding of the state of Israel; 650 000 at the beginning of 1948

Zionism - an ideology which advocates the in-gathering of Jews throughout the world, with their eventual destination being the land of Palestine

Zisling, Aharon - Minister of Agriculture (1948 - 9)

Introduction

On November 29th 1947 the United Nations General Assembly, in its wisdom, adopted Resolution 181 which resulted in the eventual partition of the land of Palestine. From that point onwards both the British presence and control over events in Palestine dwindled until the British Mandate came to an end on 15 May 1948.

During this period of time, and beyond, the Jewish Zionist colonisers, who from the time of the Balfour Declaration had firmly entrenched themselves on the land, fought a bitter battle against both the British and Palestinian Arab presence in Palestine. It resulted in the eventual permanent expulsion of approximately 750 000 Palestinians from their land, the destruction and demolition of over 400 Palestinian villages. This took place together with the plunder and acquisition of Arab houses, private property, bank accounts and business concerns. Actions which were given a legal gloss in the immediate aftermath of the foundation of the Israeli state.

Throughout 1998 Israel celebrated her achievements together with the 50th anniversary of her "independence". At the same time the Palestinian nation commemorated the 50th anniversary of al-Nakba - the catastrophe. Hundreds of thousands remembered the day they were either driven from their homes or fled their homes to escape the fighting and the threat of death. Many, 50 years previously, thought they were leaving only for a few days, to return after the fighting receded. Few, if any, thought that it would turn out to be an interminable exile, with their homes either being demolished or occupied by strangers.

This aspect of the struggle to establish and enlarge the State of Israel was ignored by Israel and her friends. They chose to ignore the catastrophe which the Zionist state invited, and continues to invite, on the heads of the Palestinian people. Actions, which by any definition of the word, can only be summed up as "genocide". At that point of time, with the ending of World War II, the Palestinians became the "victims of the victims."

Many people, even in Israel, are ignorant of the foundations of the Israeli state. [**See** "By Dint of Whitewash not Confusion: The Portrayal of the Arab-Israeli Conflict in Israeli History and Civics Textbooks, 1955-95" Eli Podeh Gitelson Peace Publn. 1997 (Hebrew)]. Many friends of Israel are likewise ignorant. Many simply do not understand why the Middle East has turned out to be the cauldron we saw yesterday, see to-day and, despite peace efforts, predict for tomorrow.

For the Palestinian people who either live under a still brutal military occupation, as refugees in surrounding Arab states or as citizens in their adopted country, the events of 1998 must have rekindled any latent anger. During 1998 the sanctity of UN resolutions was trumpeted throughout the media, world wide, with regard to Iraq. If the same resolve, with regard to UN resolutions, had been observed over the past 50 years in the pursuit of Palestinian rights then the Middle East would be a totally different place today.

The substance of this chronology is based on research carried out for the production of daily e mails sent out by Scottish Friends of Palestine throughout 1998. The e mails catalogued those events that affected both the land and the people of Palestine fifty years earlier.

The chronology should be regarded as "an invitation" to the reader to find out more about the Palestinian people, the land and the history of both. By no stretch of the imagination is it exhaustive.

To understand current events there must be an understanding and appreciation of those past events which affected hundreds of thousands of innocent Palestinians. The reality of the catastrophic events which overtook the Palestinian nation during 1948 is the mirror image of the "independence" achieved by the State of Israel during that year. Without the catastrophe there would have been no Israeli 50th anniversary celebrations during 1998. There would be no Palestinian refugees, now about 5 000 000 in number, waiting for their rights to be acknowledged. And, to this day, Israel continues to pretend that the refugees do not exist and that she is not responsible, in any way, for their situation. She considers that they certainly have no claims on the land from which they were expelled over half a century ago.

This book, it is hoped, contributes to the understanding of past events thus helping pave the the way for that elusive, well overdue, measure of justice for the Palestinian people.

Comment on sources and structure

The detail in the daily chronologies is based on information extracted from contemporary newspaper reports together with the research and debate initiated from the 1980s onward. Israeli historian, Benny Morris, was amongst the first to delve into Israeli archives and publish his findings. His work was, and continues to be, a milestone in the understanding of the events which overtook the Palestinian nation in 1948.

However Morris' work has not been without its controversy and critics. The debate which it subsequently generated focused on the position taken by Morris that the catastrophe which overtook the Palestinian people was a result of military necessity. Others questioned this viewpoint, arguing that the expulsion of the Palestinian people was the result of deliberate political policy and strategy.

The daily chronologies have been constructed to illustrate the extent of the destruction of historic Palestine - its villages, towns and cities together with the dispossession and expulsion of its people. The political developments, both domestic and international - particularly at the United Nations Security Council - have been charted as the year progressed. The development in Zionist thinking and strategy has likewise been charted.

The principal sources used were The Scotsman and The Times. It should be noted that both The Scotsman and The Telegraph shared correspondents in Palestine and surrounding area. So, for most of the year, three newspapers were effectively covered.

The spread and content between The Scotsman and The Times was interesting. In general The Scotsman's coverage was more wide ranging, both in the geographical sense and in the detail provided. Towards the end of 1948 The Times, on the balance, gave more coverage to political developments internationally.

In both papers a disproportionate amount of space was given to coverage of events in and around Jerusalem. Events in population centres would be featured for the day it happened and the aftermath only appearing in general discourse concerning the plight of refugees. If there was awareness of events in outlying areas, it was rarely reported. There was very little awareness in the media of the discrete miltary operations which were carried out a various points in time, throughout the year, by the Zionist forces. Even now the Israeli Defence Forces Archives, and others, refuse to de-classify those documents relating to the expulsion and massacres of Palestinian Arab civilians or prisoners of war from 1948 onwards.

Walid Khalidi's impressive *All that Remains* - a 600 page documentation of the destruction of Palestinian villages in 1948 - was used extensively. Likewise the research of Benny Morris, in particular the direct quotes of many of the Zionist hierarchy, was used.

In general each daily chronology has been constructed to give the events as they happened "on the ground" at the beginning of the account for that day. Political development or comment is found towards the end of that day's account.

Where events have been outlined with no annotation then, in most cases, referral should be made to The Scotsman, The Telegraph or *All that Remains* for the complete account. Where the detail has been extracted from newspapers the reader should be mindful that there is at least a 24 hour delay in the report appearing in print. For example, if you want to check out events for 15 May, reference should be made to the edition for 16 May. If a "special feature" from a newspaper has been used, then reference should be made to the date in question.

Although care was taken in attaching events to the correct date this did not always prove to be possible. For a number of reasons.

Events which took place over the weekend would be reported in the Monday edition, sometimes with no attempt to identify the precise day, Saturday or Sunday. When attacking Palestinian villages, the favoured strategy used by the Haganah, the Irgun and the Stern Gang was to attack at or before dawn when the villagers were sleeping and any defenders off guard. At times there can be confusion as to which side of midnight the attack took place.

Any delay in the recording of the event and the event itself, particularly if it took place in an outlying area, could result in a discrepancy in the date. Israeli archives might give one date, Palestinian memory another. It was not uncommon for Zionist forces to re-visit a village, weeks later, to "complete business." This could also complicate the dating of an event.

With regard to the writing of Arabic place names, they have mostly been reproduced as per written copy. No attempt has been made to standardise the spelling. So the villages of Deir Yassin, Ein Karim, Al (or "al") Dawayima can appear as Deyr Yasin, Ayn Karem and Ad Dawaimeh.

Throughout the chronology the words "settlement" and "colony" are interchangeable. "Settlement" has a precise definition when used by in international bodies such as the United Nations so, strictly speaking, the word "settlement" should always read "colonial settlement ."

The Irgun and Stern Gang were terrorist organisations. The Haganah was the official "defence" body which acted on behalf of Palestine's Jewry. However when the activities of the Haganah are compared with those of the Irgun and Stern Gang, there is little to differentiate between them. All were expert in terrorising the Palestinian civil population. In the end the temptation to prefix the names of these bodies with the word "terrorist" was resisted

Finally, there was one important change made to the recording of contemporary reports of events in Palestine. The newspaper reports always made reference to the actions of the "Jews" when referring to Palestine's Zionist Jewish community. However it was felt to be important to acknowledge the fact that not all Jews are Zionists, just as all Zionists are not Jews. Where the reports clearly made reference to the actions or words of Zionist Jews then, throughout the book, the word "Jew" has been replaced by "Zionist."

At the time of the passing of the partition resolution on Palestine, 29 November 1947, the reality, on the ground, was that Jewish Zionist colonists owned less than 7% of the land of Palestine. This despite the fact that partition passed control of 55% of the land into the colonisers' hands. Subsequent events were aimed at changing this 7% ownership and enlarging the 55% allocated by the United Nations - by any means possible.

As history eventually recorded, the quotation from Theodore Herzl, the founding father of Zionism,

"He who desires the end, desires the means."[1]

was to be prophetic. Few realised that the events on the eve of the New Year, in the Palestinian port of Haifa, were a harbinger of a things to come during 1948.

On 30 December 1947 a gang from the Irgun, threw a bomb into a crowd of Palestinian Arabs from Haifa oil refinery. Six were killed and a number wounded. Retaliatory action was swift. Within hours Arab workers from the refinery attacked and killed 39 of their Jewish colleagues at the oil plant.

It is worth recording some of the comments of leading Zionists at the time.

Gad Machnes, an expert on Arab affairs and eventual director general of the Israeli Ministry of Minority Affairs, observed

"The Arabs were not ready when they began disturbances. Moreover, much of the Arab public did not want them."[2]

However Machnes had no hesitation in recommending that Arab resistance should be met with "strength and brutality" directed at everyone, including women and children, together with the killing of Arab political leaders.

Yosef Nahmani, a director of the Jewish National Fund in Eastern Galilee, expressed his emotions in his diary

> "This incident depressed me greatly. After all, the Arabs [in Haifa] had declared a truce and why cause the death of innocent people and again ignite the Arabs, so that they will have no choice except to respond against the Jews . . ."[3]

On the eve of 1948, Wednesday 31 December 1947, the Irgun threatened fresh vengeance against Arabs. A British policeman, a Jewish doctor and a Jewish newsvendor were shot dead in Jerusalem. A few days earlier an Arab doctor had been shot dead in in Bethlehem.

With emotions running high the Mandate authorities asked the Jewish Agency to use its influence to ensure that captains of ships approaching Palestine with illegal Zionist immigrants divert to Cyprus. Mrs Golda Myerson (the future Israeli prime minister, Golda Meir) and her escort were stopped and their car searched. The female escort was found in possession of a Sten gun and arrested. However this was the start of the Mandate government's instruction to military personnel to abstain from searching cars and removing "defensive" weapons, so the escort was freed.

As it was, the army had plenty with which to occupy its time. With three trains being plundered during the course of the day, manpower was being diverted to guard communications, post offices and the courts. Few troops were available to act as a buffer between the Palestinian Arab and the Zionist Jew.

And so began the year of 1948.

January

> *.... if it was not for the open [Zionist military] preparations which had a provocative nature the drift into war could have been averted.*
>
> Gad Machnes, Director General, Israeli Ministry of Minority Affairs

As the year unfolded, the Zionist penchant for use of figurative language to describe its various "Military Operations", against both civilian populations and those who resisted them militarily, became clear. It also became clear that these operations could be aptly described in the vogue words of the nineties as "ethnic cleansing" or, when the extent of the eventual devastation of Palestinian society became obvious, "genocide."

And it was right at the start (if not before) that the intentions of the Zionists were aired. Perhaps not in the public but certainly behind closed doors. Yosef Weitz recorded in his diary

> "Is it not now the time to be rid of them ? Why continue to keep in our midst these thorns at a time when they pose a danger to us ?"[4]

Yosef Weitz, director of the Jewish National Fund, was responsible for "local evictions and expulsion operations" against Palestinians and for allocating land to Jewish colonial settlements. From January to March 1948 Weitz was responsible for expelling the local Palestinian population from Ramot- Menashe, Beit Shean Valley and Western Galilee.

As director of the Jewish National Fund, Weitz served on the Population Transfer Committee of the Jewish Agency. In a report he wrote that the 'transfer' of the Arab population from Jewish areas

> "does not serve only one aim - to diminish the Arab population. It also serves a second purpose by no means less important, which is to evacuate the land now cultivated by Arabs and thus release it for Jewish settlement."[5]

Dr Yacov Thon, who served on the same Committee and was, ironically, a founding member of an 'ultra-liberal' group which sought reconciliation and accommodation with the Arabs revealed his intentions at secret committee meetings

> "Without transferring the Arab peasants to neighbouring lands, we will not be able to bring into our future state a large new population. In short without transfer there can be no Jewish immigration."[5]

These sentiments were shared by Irgun leader and Israeli prime-minister to-be, Menachem Begin

> "My greatest worry in those months was that the Arabs might accept the United Nations plan. Then we would have the ultimate tragedy, a Jewish state so small that it could not absorb all the Jews of the world".[6]

As a terrorist leader Begin was well placed to ensure that the Palestinian Arab would never reach agreement with the Zionists. He was also well placed to facilitate their 'transfer' elsewhere.

By mid-January units of the Arab Liberation Army from Syria were in action in Palestine, with little success. Their efforts in the face of the determined Zionists -members of both the Haganah and the Irgun had been trained under the British - were never going to achieve much at this stage. And as long as Palestine was still being governed under the British Mandate, the armies of the surrounding Arab states were loathe to break international law and intervene.

The perception of the struggle ahead by the two major protagonists was always going to be a major determinant of the final outcome.

A number of quotes from Aluf Ygal Yadin, Israel's first chief of operations clearly outlined the Zionist position

> "We had made an intelligence survey. We went through every village in Palestine, and estimated its character, whether it meant trouble or not; and we had a map in which the strategic characters of every Arab village and the quality of its inhabitants were indicated. We had a library of files with the details. We made an air-photographic survey of most of the country;we used to hire a plane at £4 an hour. **We knew in the early months of the trouble that the Palestine Arabs had nobody to organise them properly**,but we had not taken account of the British. The moment we brought up a platoon the British would come and arrest our men. We could have taken Jaffa quite easily, but the British stopped us. **If not for the British we could have quelled the Arab riot in one month.**"

> "We had in November 1947 30 000 members of the Hagana and about 3 000 in the Palmach."

> "In the Air Force we had six or seven obsolete reconnaissance planes. We bought the remains of twenty Austers from the British. We used them as bombers. There were two men in each plane. One man carried

> on his knees home-made bombs weighing 50 kilos, and dropped them over the target. They had a good moral effect, because before 15th May the Arabs had no planes."[7]

> And the Palestinian Arab reality

> "Suddenly, overnight there grew a black market in light armaments, mostly the type which were useless in actual combat.. People used there own money to buy arms; Uncle Ibrahim bought himself a Colt .45, Ali a Walther .38, Mousa a 8mm Beretta. The prices they paid were exorbitant, not only by the standard of 1946 and 1947, but even by today's. They handled the guns with affection, cleaning them too often."

> "There was no one to tell them that the war in the making would demand different arms, organised bodies of men and military training. Their conception of training was to own a gun, perhaps a small hand gun, and to be able to use it, not to prepare for war. Even their wives remembered the names of their guns and recited their husbands' exaggerated claims of their effectiveness."[8]

> and, the formation of the Holy Strugglers, the Mufti of Jerusalem's militia:

> "Practically everyone offered their services, but Ibrahim had no uniforms for them let alone arms and he had no clear idea of where their salaries would come from."

> "They brought with them ill-fitting second hand uniforms and rusty arms consisting of the discarded light equipment left behind in the Western Desert during the Second World War - Italian, German British, American, Canadian and other makes. Ibrahim was also allocated a certain amount of cash each month, which he distributed to his volunteers more in line with need than in accordance with rank and competence - in fact there were no ranks beyond commander and deputy commander."[9]

Even during the early part of the conflict it was apparent, as historians and researchers subsequently revealed, that the Zionist forces were prepared for aggressive action leading to the expansion of the nascent state of Israel. The Palestinians, meanwhile, were not aware of, or ready to cope with, the impending onslaught.

Gad Machnes, although blaming the Mufti of Jerusalem for starting riots the previous month, commented

> " .... if it was not for the open [Zionist military] preparations which had a provocative nature the drift into war could have been averted."[10]

Evidence suggests that the Zionist leaders ignored their own 'Arab experts'. Israeli historian, Uri Milstein, concluded that it was known that "the Palestinian Arabs were divided and thus the majority among them did not want war."[10]

However conflict was very much on the Zionist agenda.

On 5 December , six days after the partition resolution, Ben Gurion was found to have ordered "immediate action to expand Jewish settlement in three areas assigned to the Arab state." [Author's note: the Negev, south-east Palestine (Etzion) and western Galilee]. These settlements would function as forward bases during the predicted hostilities.[11]

These actions gave a clear indication that Ben Gurion had no intention of respecting the boundaries created by the partition resolution. He would never have sent Jewish settlers to live in areas under permanent Arab rule. Clearly conflict for the purpose of enlarging the new state and cleansing it of the indigenous population was very much in mind.

Two weeks later Ben Gurion made it quite clear what was intended, and expected of, the Zionist fighters and terrorists

> "In each attack, a decisive blow should be struck, resulting in the destruction of houses and the expulsion of the population."[11]

And the political leadership of the Zionist movement knew they could proceed with their plans in defiance of British and Arab opposition. The nucleus of the Haganah and the terrorist Irgun Zvei Leumi were British trained. There were some 27 000 experienced Jewish veterans who had served with the British army, some of whom formed the commando units, the Palmach.[12]

In contrast only about 12 000 Palestinian Arabs had served with the British.

January 1

David Ben Gurion, Chairman of the Jewish Agency, met to assess the attack (on Dec.18th) on the village of Khisas [pop 530 incl. 40 Jews] close to the intersection of the borders of Lebanon, Syria and Palestine. Members of the Haganah , under night cover, attacked with bullets and grenades.The death toll was reported as ten dead, including five children. A Haganah spokesman said that it was "unfortunate" that small sleeping children should have fallen victim to"that kind of attack". However as Israeli historian Benny Morris observed, use of "excessive force" was, in the long run, fruitful.

In the early hours of the morning Zionist forces attacked the village of Balad al-Shaykh [pop. 4 120] at the foot of Mount Carmel outside Haifa. At the end of half an hour's fighting 17 Palestinians, including one woman, were dead; 33 were injured including eight women and nine children. Jewish casualties were three dead and two wounded.

It was reported that the Jewish workers at various work places within Haifa, including the refinery, were demanding Jewish guards for protection. However the authorities were quite clear that the deaths of the 38 Jewish workers (some sources referred to 41 deaths) had not been premeditated. They vehemently denied that the Arab guards at the refinery had removed dinner knives, scissors etc from entering Jewish workers.

It was also clear that most Jews in Haifa were not prepared to face the fact that provocation had taken place when the Irgun had thrown the bomb two days earlier.

At least 12 Jews and four Arabs were injured in bomb throwing and shooting incidents in Haifa. The resolve of the Arab population in and around Haifa was seriously damaged by these incidents.

A group of gunmen in battledress, believed to be Zionists, crashed through an Arab roadblock in Jaffa, raking the street with automatic weapons. Ten Arabs were wounded. Earlier, four Arabs and two Jews were killed with 31 Arabs wounded when Zionists attacked a Palestinian village near Haifa.

The Haganah claimed to have 'executed' a German and a Pole 'found guilty of collaborating with the enemy'. The bodies of two men were subsequently found on the outskirts of Rehavia, a Jewish residential suburb of Jerusalem.

The Government's instructions to British forces to abstain from searching cars and removing defensive weapons came into effect.

The ship *United Nations* ran aground north of Haifa with 700 visaless Jews. Only 13 were detained, with the rest being able to prove that they were "Palestine citizens."

January 2

On the day that all Jewish employees failed to turn up for work at

Sarafand, the largest British military base in the Middle East, 12 bombs were discovered at the base by Palestinian employees.

In West Jerusalem, British armoured cars machine gunned snipers on rooftops and behind windows. Heavy street battles raged between Arab, Jew and police. Fourteen people, including three British soldiers died. Two died as a result of Arab sniper fire, the other by an unknown gunman. Zionist forces attempted to blow up the Moslem Supreme Council building.

Heavy fighting was reported around Safad, in northern Galilee. Zionist forces were reported to have blown up Palestinian houses.

The wives of British officials were urged to leave Palestine as soon as possible.

The Scotsman printed an article which was very optimistic of the Arab future in the impending conflict, despite the acknowledged facts that there was no central authority ready to take over, at partition, essential services such as water, supply of food and other essentials. Food was in short supply, with bread prices up by seven or eight times the amount a few months previously

There was a very pessimistic outlook for the Jews and Zionists, although their ambition was acknowledged. Alternative roads were being built to avoid Arab areas, and there were 16 hill-top forts to keep open the road from Tel Aviv to Jerusalem. They had a "fantastic number of Sten Guns" and small arms, a few mortars, 18 "elderly cars" and a dozen training aircraft together with a healthy bank balance for the purchase of heavier weapons.

The Haganah now claimed to have 70 000 members under arms, with the Palmach numbering about 3 000. The latter had been trained with "European armies"and was considered to be a "strike force" with appropriate military organisation. There was also the "Irgun who, it is believed, are proposing to collaborate in face of the common enemy. There is also the small, crazy, and more or less insignificant Stern Gang."

January 3

Forty Zionist militia attacked the village of Ghwway Abu Shusha [pop. 1240], near Tiberias, at 3am. Two villagers, including a woman, were killed as were three of the attackers.

An attack was launched on the village of Ayn al-Zaytun close to Safad [pop. 820]. One villager was killed with four houses fire bombed.

January 4

Members of the terrorist Stern Gang bombed a crowded public square in Jaffa. Up to 30 people were reported dead with about 98 wounded using a lorry loaded with more than just oranges. A technique well rehearsed when fighting the British.

On this occasion two terrorists in Arab disguise, who had been foiled on a previous occasion, parked the lorry amongst buildings in central Jaffa. The blast destroyed the old Turkish Government House, the Central Police Station and a corner of Barclay's Bank. Government House contained two rooms used by the Jaffa Arab National Committee. Premises in the building were also used as a social welfare society, for feeding children and for the destitute. Many of the children were amongst the casualties.

British soldiers who rushed to the scene to help rescue efforts were stoned by Arab crowds for the reason that they believed the British to be responsible since the Stern Gang terrorists were in the uniform of the Royal Irish Fusiliers.

In Jerusalem the Haganah blew up some houses alleged to be the source of sniper fire.

It was reported that the situation in the Old City of Jerusalem was a cause for concern. The British authorities appealed to the religious heads in the city to support an appeal urging the citizens to desist from violent acts. The Muslim leadership had agreed, but a reply was awaited from the Christian Patriarchs and Chief Rabbis. While it was acknowledged that the various religious communities within the Old City had relatively harmonious relations - including the Jews who were known as 'lukewarm Zionists' - the Haganah had installed themselves in the City about a month earlier. With the passing of the partition resolution sniping and more serious violence had followed.

A U.S. ship was discovered carrying 26 cases of TNT bound for Palestine. The discovery was made when one box labelled "Industrial Machinery" fell and broke open.

January 5

The Haganah admitted blowing up the the Palestinian owned Semiramis Hotel in Jerusalem. Twenty six men, women and children who had taken refuge in the hotel were killed, along with the Spanish Consul. A variety of excuses were offered for this particular atrocity including the unsubstantiated claim that it housed the HQ of the Nejada resistance group. The Haganah alleged that the hotel had not been accepting guests for some time and any non-Arab casualties must have been cooperating with the "Arab gangs." In reality the hotel was housing, amongst other people, 16 relatives of the owner, one of Jerusalem's leading Christian families. His two maiden sisters, who were amongst the dead, had left their homes "for greater safety."

A British report called the atrocity "wholesale murder of innocent people". However it had its effect. The hotel was situated in the Katamon district of West Jerusalem, populated by mainly Christian Palestinians some Muslims and British residents. Some residents of Katamon fled the fighting, their homes being dynamited soon after.

> "One of my most vivid memories of that wretched time was the Haganah attack on the Semiramis Hotel.......It so happened that there was a torrential thunderstorm that night, and when the explosion came, it was almost like another clap of thunder. ...... My brother and I were terrified, and I can remember my mother dragging us from our beds onto the floor and pressing us against the wall. I did not understand that it was an explosion and kept asking if the glow in the sky was the sun rising. The exact events are blurred in my memory, but what remains vivid is the terror of my parents and the fear that began to grip me as I saw it."
>
> *The 1948 Exodus: a family story - Ghada Karmi*

Even at that juncture, there was awareness of Zionist intent, as recorded by a young Palestinian, Hala Sakakini. In recording that the people were simply "panic-stricken", provoking images of European refugees during the war, efforts were made to restrain the flight from Katamon. "This is just what the Jews want you to do; you leave and they occupy your houses and then one day you will find that Qatamon has become another Jewish quarter!"[13]

The Jewish Agency complained that British soldiers were effectively acknowledging the legitimacy of Arab road blocks by showing identity documents on demand. The response to the allegation was to be found in the practice of the Zionist terrorists who used British Army uniforms while perpetrating their outrages. The soldiers probably found it easier to continue with their work of providing humanitarian assistance to both parties by showing their documents rather than provoking hostility by dismantling the road block.

A British sergeant was killed at an Arab road block in Haifa.

The illegal Haganah radio station, Voice of Israel, claimed that three houses had been blown up in a village near Tiberias. Eight people were claimed killed.

January 6

At 2am Royal Engineers rescued a mother and her dead baby from the debris of the Semiramis Hotel. The Palestine Government issued a strong denial that the Semiramis Hotel had been used as a base for "marauding gangs" as alleged by the Haganah. The latter's reaction at being accused of "dastardly and wholesale murder of innocent people" was to feign indignation at the Government statement, questioning why they had not reacted to "similar murders by Arabs."

An army lieutenant and a British police officer were shot dead during an attempt to disarm an Arab mourner at a funeral procession on the Acre Haifa road. A British policeman was killed in Jaffa.

Two hundred British soldiers were reported to have demolished Palestinian road blocks around Tulkarem, warning that they would shoot to prevent them being rebuilt.

Two female members of the Haganah were each fined £400 or three years in prison for "unlawfully carrying two Sten guns and six hand grenades." It was a common practice for the women to carry the weapons since only those found carrying the weapons were arrested. This tactic avoided the arrest of the male fighters.

The Arab Higher Executive Committee approved the formation of what effectively amounted to a shadow Government for Palestine.

January 7

Following the attack by the Palmach, six days earlier, on the village of Balad al-Shayk near Haifa, the village was partially evacuated. Some reports indicated the massacre of more than 60 people.
[Author's note: Balad al-Shaykh contains the tomb of Sheikh Izz al-Din al-Qassan who was killed by the British in 1935. The military wing of the Islamic Resistance Movement, Hamas, is named after the Sheikh.]

Fifteen Palestinians were killed and 41 (including a British sergeant and two British policemen) wounded in two bombings carried out by the Irgun at Jaffa Gate, Jerusalem. The terrorists, driving an armoured car given to the Jewish settlement police, and taken earlier from a Jewish garage, wearing stolen police caps threw or rolled a bomb into the patrons of an Arab cafe, drove a further distance and flung out another bomb. Before the armoured car crashed, the terrorists sprayed onlookers with Sten gun fire.The bombers, believed to be the Irgun, were either caught or shot dead. It was believed that the attack was a token protest at the Arab hold over Jaffa Gate, which cut off Jewish access to the Old City. Later the Irgun issued a statement saying that it was determined to destroy all Arab road-blocks leading to the Old City or any area in Palestine.

Two British soldiers were shot and wounded elsewhere in Jerusalem. In the Sheikh Jarrah quarter, to the north of the city, armed Jews and Arabs faced each other with two Jews being killed and three wounded. With all Jewish and Arab employees staying away, the work of the main post office and the courts had almost ground to a halt.

There was no progress to report in the attempt to get all religious leaders to sign a general appeal for the Old City to be free from violence.

The Scotsman reported that "The Arabs have far to go before they can catch up with the well armed Jewish forces who have the big advantage that in the hidden factories in Tel Aviv and Petakh Tiqva home made rifles and sten gun copies from British samples are being turned out by the hundreds."

It was estimated that 500 people had been killed since the passing of the partition resolution at the end of November.

January 8

The reportedly 80 000 strong Haganah organisation announced a policy of "aggressive self-defence." The policy of shoot and bomb first then ask questions later was described as "new." A term which certainly belied its activities to date and which completely avoided any mention of the various pre-planned military operations which were to descend upon the Palestinian civilian population, with such devastating consequences, in the coming months.

With the Palmach "strike force", at the forefront the policy of "aggressive self-defence" The Scotsman commented that with the "violent, bloody attacks upon apparently inoffensive Arabs . . . any sympathy the Jews had won was dissipated with the smoke of the burnt out Arab villages." Apparently "This masterpiece of humbug is on the lips af all

Jews. It was concocted in the inner sanctum of the Jewish Agency and thus legalises any act of wanton murder committed in its name."

Fifteen people were killed during the course of the day, including one British policeman. More than 1 000 Jews were reported to be besieged in the Jewish Quarter of the Old City of Jerusalem. Throughout the city there were continual bursts of machine gun and pistol fire, with the army ferreting out snipers. Eighty Irgun gunmen raided a first-aid clinic to remove a wounded comrade.

The first convoy of Iraqi volunteers, consisting of 90 commandos, left Baghdad en route to Palestine.

For the first time, the question of a Palestine "security force" was raised at the United Nations. With France due to take over the Chair of the Security Council next month the idea of a force akin to the French Foreign Legion was mooted.

American Zionist Jews were reported to be preparing a campaign to have the US arms embargo lifted. The intention was to ask for arms to be provided on a lend-lease basis. A propaganda campaign had been started to persuade the American public that Britain was to blame for events in Palestine, with the American Zionist Emergency Council at the forefront. It was reported that £200 000 was to be despatched to the Jewish Labour Group in Palestine which claimed to provide more than 70% of the manpower for the Haganah.

January 9

A group of Zionists from Yavne attacked 'Wadi Sukrayr' (Suqrir) [pop. 390] to the north of Gaza. A counter-attack was launched by the police. Eight Arabs and 12 Haganah scouts were reported killed. A Haganah intelligence report, dated two days later, recommended that

"the village should be destroyed completely and some males from the village should be murdered."

This was the first operational proposal by the Haganah to demolish and level a village.[14]

The first attack on an isolated Zionist settlement took place at Kefar Szold, a kibbutz in the north of Palestine, by a unit of the Arab Liberation Army from Syria.

The Scotsman reported that a total of three Zionist settlements were attacked by about 600 fighters from this "Arab band" which had crossed the border from Syria that morning. British troops and aircraft dispersed the attackers, but not before the waterworks controlling the marshes of the Huleh were blown up.

The village of Khisas contributed to the Arab firepower. Recently the Haganah had attacked the village. Their calling card had been one house blown up leaving five children dead. The Haganah claimed that the British troops fought side by side with the Arabs. Three Jewish deaths were recorded.

A three cornered Arab-British-Jewish fight took place in southern Palestine when an Arab force of about 100 fighters besieged the colony of Ramat Rachel. Twelve Jews and eight Arabs were reported killed. One British police officer was injured.

In Jerusalem the police ordered the evacuation of the Jewish hospital, on the Arab-Jewish border, in the Old City.

The Stern Gang threatened that those newspaper correspondents who had accepted "Press cards" from the Arab Higher Committee would be considered to have "forfeited privileges and immunity." The demand for such cards came from the substantial American press corp in the area, one of whom had been "molested" in Transjordan by Arabs.

An illegal shipment of 5 200 combat knives and tons of surplus army explosives, destined for Zionist forces in Palestine, were seized in New Jersey. Three lorry loads of demolition charges were seized in Ulster County, en route to the business associate of a "Zionist leader."

Members of the British Administration were told to make domestic arrangements for leaving Palestine at a months notice.

January 11

Zionist forces demolished the strategically important Bridge of Jacob's Daughters over the River Jordan. It was part of the transit route from Syria to Palestine which was used by Syrian fighters a few days previously.

The settlement of Kfar Uriah, on the Jerusalem Jaffa railway, was attacked by Arab forces. Zionist sources spoke of 10 Jewish fatalities in a fight lasting hours. Arab casualties were unknown. Eventually British armoured cars drove off the attackers.

The FBI uncovered a fund of £194 000 for purchase of explosives in the USA in support of the Zionist cause while investigating a shipment of 199 tons of cyclonite, an explosive considerably more explosive than TNT. A statement issued by the Jewish Agency made great play of the fact that arms were required for "defence" but made no effort to explain why explosives, particularly suitable for demolition work, would be used for "defence" purposes.

At a meeting with Ben Gurion, Arab affairs adviser, Ezra Danin, while commenting on the effectiveness of the Arab forces in controlling the main roads and the use of retaliation against local villages to combat this, advised that

> "our friends among the Arabs inform us that a severe blow, with a high rate of casualties to the Arabs would increase Arab fear and would render external Arab intervention ineffective."

Ten days earlier Gad Machnes had advised Ben Gurion along the same lines

> "we need a cruel and brutal retaliating policy, we have to be accurate in time, place and number of dead. If we know that a family is guilty, we should be merciless and kill the women and the children as well, otherwise the reaction is useless. While the forces are in action, there is no room for checking who is guilty and who is not."[15]

While Elias Sasson, director of the Arab Division of the Jewish Agency's Political Department observed of the main towns and the rural hinterland

> "Hunger, high prices, and poverty are rampant in a frightening degree. There is fear and terror everywhere. The flight is painful. from house to house, from neighbourhood to neighbourhood, from city to city, from village to village, and from Palestine to the neighbouring countries."[16]

January 12

Three Palestinian Arabs were killed and seven British soldiers wounded in a village outside Jerusalem while trying to uncover snipers.

In a robbery attributed to the Stern Gang, a branch of Barclay's bank in Gaza was raided by 20 armed Zionists. A British soldier on guard duty was clubbed and his rifle stolen.

Two Jews were killed and one British soldier wounded when Jewish owned lorries were ambushed in Haifa.

Moshe Shertok, head of the Jewish Agency's Political Department, accused British troops of "crippling Jewish defences." The Agency intended to ask the U.N. to authorise a Jewish militia of up to 20 000 men, together with financial aid, to enforce partition.

The Scotsman printed a feature on the training of Palestinian Arab guerrillas, with "fierce hill-men with assorted pistols, long curved knives and rifles slung over their shoulders" ready for their marching orders. Interestingly, the language adopted to describe the scene could have been taken from events a couple of decades or so later. There was the "triangle of terror" in Samaria, which description was accorded to the "militant" Arab towns of Nablus, Tulkarem and Jenin.

January 13

The body of a Pole, believed to have been "executed" by a Zionist firing squad was found in Tel Aviv, bound and gagged.

Haganah "black squads"(bomb squads) attacked the Sheikh Jarrah Arab quarter on the outskirts of Jerusalem, gaining control of the northern approaches to the city, reportedly "wiping out"out the Arab quarter. In the Kidron area they torched or blew up 25 Arab houses.

In this action, one of the heaviest attacks to date, a mortar bombardment rained down on the densely built houses with road approaches being mined to hinder Arab reinforcements. Zionist forces positioned in an adjacent Jewish community, swept the area with machine gun fire.

Hussein al-Khalidi, leader of the Jerusalem National Committee wrote of the situation in the city "There are no people, no discipline, no arms, and no ammunition . . . . the economy is destroyed . . . . there is no flour, no food . . . Jerusalem is emptying out."[17]

Most of the houses on the periphery of the village of Lifta [pop. 1 050] were demolished. (Most of the villagers had left following a terrorist attack by the Stern Gang on 28 Dec.1947 when a bus load of terrorists had halted outside the village coffee shop, spraying the patrons with machine gun fire and throwing grenades. Six were killed.) In the end the western part of the city was secured by evicting the residents of the villages of Romena and Sheikh Badr.To the south of the city, Arab forces besieged the Jewish colony of Kfar Etzion.

A Jewish bus terminus in Haifa was bombed. The deaths of six Jews and two British was reported.

A number of Arab attacks on Jewish settlements were reported. In northern Palestine, in the Hulah area, British troops came to the rescue of settlers at Lahavoth. One settler was killed near Haifa. A Jewish convoy was ambushed between Jerusalem and Hebron with two Jewish fatalities. Once again, British troops gave assistance to the Zionists with the convoy completing its journey under British protection.

On the outskirts of Haifa one Jewish land labourer was killed and another attacked. British troops intervened, inflicting casualties amongst the Arab assailants, with one believed dead. Two bodies were found close to Palestinian villages, one Jewish, one unidentified.

In Jaffa, four Palestinian Arabs, including a four year old girl, were shot dead with seven wounded. Sniping on the Jerusalem-Jaffa road resumed, according to reports.

There were reports that 15 February could be "D Day" for the Arabs to "sweep Zionism from Palestine."

January 14

Four settlements north of Hebron were attacked by Arab raiders. It was believed that there was no pre-planned military strategy involved. Apparently it was led by a Palestinian fighter, sentenced to life imprisonment 10 years previously, who had escaped from Acre prison when it had earlier been attacked by Zionist forces. The Arab Higher Executive and the British Assistant District Commissioner were called to intercede.

Zionist sources claimed that 100 of the attackers had been blown up on surrounding mine fields. Arab sources put their own dead at about 12 and claimed to have killed defenders

A number of street murders and attempted murders took took place in Jerusalem with Jews, and one British officer with a Jewish wife, being the victims. The latter two were killed by attackers. Some Jews leaving their property in the area of the King David Hotel were confronted by Arabs demanding identity papers. On refusing, one woman was abducted, to be found later lying in the street injured. A British officer who went looking for her was shot and injured.

Explosions could be heard to the north of the city, the result of Zionist mortar fire.The Sheikh Jarrah area was subject to a mortar bombardment described as "one of the heaviest attacks of the present disorders." Observers on Mount Scopus watched mortars crashing through the roofs of the houses in this densely built-up and populated area. The approach roads to the area had been mined to hinder Arab and British reinforcements from reaching the scene.

With religious leaders having no success in trying to bring peace to the city, the Haganah and political spokesmen spoke of trouble to come if the Arab "siege" was not lifted and Jews allowed free access in and out of Jerusalem.

An attack was made on the car of the Iraqi consulate-general on the road between Hebron and Jerusalem. It was felt that it could have been a case of mistaken identity since it was only Arab forces that were active in the area.

In Haifa, Palestinians planted a bomb in a post office van resulting in the death of six Jews.

The Times posed the $64 000 question:

> "Are there any prospects of settlement in Palestine after Britain's abandonment of the mandate and subsequent withdrawal ?"

The article pointed out that "Jewish extremists" realised that they had much to gain by striking quickly, before the Arabs could organise themselves. Such action could sway or force the hands of the more "moderate Zionist". Arab objection to partition and the projected boundaries was only one factor making for war. The other was the belief that the Zionists would not be satisfied with their allotted State and would aim at the acquisition of all Palestine and also Transjordan.

The Scotsman featured an article on the Zionist colonies in northern Palestine. The first settlement in Eastern Galilee was established in 1918, part of an "obviously deliberate Jewish policy which placed these isolated Jewish settlements in the heart of Arab Palestine." The settlements now "bulged with sturdy young men and women, hand-picked Haganah detachments" perceived to be doing a good job on land allegedly "neglected for centuries."

A Czech arms deal, worth over $12 million, was concluded with the Haganah. Arms purchased included 24 500 rifles, 5 000 light machine guns, 200 medium machine guns, 54 million rounds of ammunition, 25 Meserschmitts.[18]

January 15

The aftermath of the van explosion the previous day in Haifa brought life to a standstill, with firing intensifying as daylight arrived. The British military installed outposts on rooftops and upper storeys thus bringing sniping, by Arab forces, to a virtual halt.

An Arab bus was fired upon, resulting in one dead passenger and six injured. Some passengers returned fire, with two - armed with a Tommy gun - escaping from the police. At the same time, on the eastern side of Haifa a Jewish bus was fired upon resulting in two dead and one injured.

During the day Haifa came to a standstill as buses and cars fell victim to sniper fire. Jews and Arabs battled for control of the road that led from the Jewish area to the main business quarter. One report put the Arab deaths at ten, Jewish deaths at five.

One Arab was killed and three were seriously wounded by British troops who came to the assistance of a Zionist convoy on the outskirts of Beersheba. A British soldier was shot dead by an unknown gunman in Tel Aviv.

In the Hebron area an RAF Spitfire was fired upon by a plane believed to have come from the Jewish flying club in Palestine. The Spitfire was on patrol over Hebron where British troops were evacuating wounded Jews and Arabs.

Jerusalem was the focus of much fighting. Military estimates pointed to as many as 500 members of the Haganah, together with the Irgun and Stern Gang, operating under one command in the city. The 1 500 Jewish residents in the Jewish Quarter of the Old City, in a state of semi-seige, were subject to incessant sniper fire but refused to evacuate. The occasional grenade was to be seen bringing down a flimsy house in spirals of dust.

Jaffa Gate was patrolled by Palestine Police and regular troops. Both only intervene, it was reported, once trouble starts. This would seem not to have satisfied the Jewish Agency with its daily complaints and demands that British troops should rescue the besieged Jews. The

Scotsman reported that British troops do regularly penetrate Arab barricades to ensure that food gets into the city. They bring out the aged, the sick, women with new-born babies. They even take in doctors, nurses and those residents trapped outside.

The role of British forces in protecting Jewish convoys was reported. Escorting food convoys to Jerusalem was now a regular feature. The RAF was now being used to protect potash convoys from Jericho to Jerusalem.

At the Security Council, Britain reaffirmed its position that British troops would not be involved in enforcing partition. As if in anticipation of a Jewish Agency demand that the UN take appropriate military steps to enforce the resolution, the Philippines drafted a reqest to the Security Council. It asked that an international military force be available to the Palestine Commission to support its task in enforcing partition once the British withdrew.

January 16

A British report to the UN estimated 1 974 deaths or injuries between 30 November (the day after the UN partition resolution was passed) and 10 January. Those killed included 295 Arabs, 262 Jews and 30 British. Increasingly British forces were being called upon to protect Jewish convoys travelling to outlying areas, with the RAF playing an increasingly important role. Jewish convoys conveying potash between Jerusalem and Jericho had the protection of a single plane. Six spitfires together with tanks and other ground support dispersed an Arab force of up to 3 000 who had surrounded four settlements in the Hebron area.

On the road to Mount Scopus a vehicle carrying mostly Jewish members of the Palestine Police Band was attacked and crashed. It caused one death and two injuries. On the same road an armour plated Jewish bus was attacked with two passengers being injured.

The Haganah blew up three Palestinian houses in Haifa as a reprisal for bombing of the Jewish bus terminal two days earlier.

In the first house eight children between the ages of 18 months and 12 years were slaughtered. One woman, aged 25 years, was killed. Four men and three children were injured. It was alleged that this house was a "centre for Arab gangsters". In the second house five Palestinians were killed with five reported yet to be recovered from the rubble. In the third house there were no reported casualties.

Further attacks resulted in the destruction of a bus garage and 19 buses together with a number of Arab homes.

During the course of the day, in attacks attributed to Arab assailants, two British soldiers were shot, one fatally. Two others were stabbed by Arab attackers in Haifa. A goods train was held up and robbed by presumed Arab assailants. A policeman was killed when his bus came under fire. Eleven Zionists, in possession of armaments ranging from pistols to grenades, were arrested by police.

One Zionist was arrested in Haifa following sniping from the area. Three Zionists travelling in an armoured bus were arrested when they were found in possession of pistols and grenades.

Eighty heavily armed Zionists from Hebron settlements were ambushed as they set out to carry out (dawn) raids on nearby Palestinian villages. Mules, Bren guns, Tommy guns and rifles were captured. A further battle developed when a similar raiding party from Kfar Etzion settlement was also ambushed. Palestine Police reported that 100 Zionist fighters had attacked the village of Surif, reputed to be the HQ of Arab guerrilla leader, Abdul Kader Husseini.

Former RAF pilot, Ezer Weizmann, nephew of the Zionist leader,Dr Weizmann, was arrested when he admitted firing upon the Spitfire the previous day.

Zionist sources claimed to have killed 82 Palestinian Arabs in the previous 24 hours.

January 17

Thirty five Haganah fighters and four Arab fighters were reported dead in the proximity of the settlement of Kfar Etzion near the village of Surif, 12 miles south-west of Jerusalem. Reports varied, with the Zionists claiming that their forces were ambushed while on their way by foot to reinforce the settlement. In total, two Zionist parties were ambushed. Later in the day a further Zionist force of about 100 men was reported to have attacked Surif, the HQ of the Arab guerrilla leader, Abdul Kader Husseini.

A Zionist convoy travelling from Jaffa was ambushed outside Jerusalem. One Jewish death was reported, one missing and nine wounded.

The Palestinian village of Dayr Aban [pop. 2 100] was surrounded by force of at least 100 Zionists. There was no record of casualties resulting from what was described as a "punitive expedition."

January 18

The town of Salama, near Tel-Aviv, [pop 6 730] was attacked by the 3rd Battalion of the Alexandroni Brigade (three houses were blown up). The Arab Liberation Militia sent 20 reinforcements to join the 30 strong village militia. The operational orders for the assault force read

"The aim is to attack the northern part of the village of Salama.... to cause deaths, blow up houses and to burn everything possible."[19]

An estimated force of 80 Zionists attacked the village of Kuwaykat [pop. 1 050] close to Acre.

By the 18th, the situation in Jaffa was described thus

> "there is no work. Whoever could leave, has left, there is fear everywhere, and there is no safety. Robbery and theft are common."[20]

A convoy was sniped and ambushed on the Jaffa-Jerusalem road, two Jews were killed including the Haganah chief, Maale Hashiman. The Haganah blew up four house near the suburb of Holan, and houses at two points in the Jaffa area.

The Haganah policy of brutal reprisals resulted in the "temporary evacuation" of the semi-Bedouin community of Mansurat al Kheit on the River Jordan.

A 100 strong Haganah party, searching for the 35 dead as a result of the ambush days earlier, clashed with Arab forces near Beit Jamal. There were conflicting reports of casualties. The dead included the first American to be killed in the conflict. The bodies were eventually brought to the settlement by British troops.

One British soldier was shot dead, by assailants believed to be Arab,while travelling by truck along the Acre-Safad road.

In Haifa most Arab and Jewish businesses had closed by 2pm. Buses with armour plated or netted windows had started to run again between the upper Jewish and lower Arab parts of the town.

A Haganah General Staff directive, underpinning the now common strategy of dynamiting Arab houses during "retaliatory" strikes was issued. Targeted for destruction were those alleged to be "houses serving as concentration points, supply depots and training sites."

January 19

The Haganah attacked the villages of Shafa Amr (Haifa area) and Tamra (in the Nazareth district). In the case of Tamra, an attack force of about 200 killed two Palestinians and wounded three seriously, including a 10 year old boy.

The Irgun were prevented from perpetrating a potentially devastating car bomb attack in the Old City of Jerusalem. A car packed with gelignite and rivets, connected to a timer, tried to enter the city at JaffaGate driven by Jewish bus driver dressed as an Arab and carrying false identity papers. He successfully passed through the checkpoint but was recognised by an Arab bus driver.

The burnt and dismembered body of a Yemenite Jew, believed to be the driver was found later at Jaffa Gate.

In Haifa, Arabs demanded the withdrawal of three busloads of Jewish workers from Consolidated Oil Refineries, thus renewing the stalemate which has prevented resumption of production for the past three weeks.

Four Stern Gang members, including a girl, were sentenced to life imprisonment for taking part in illegal military training, carrying and firing the arms during a raid in October.

It was stated that the four settlements in the Hebron area were in constant danger due to their isolated position.

As two new contingents of Arab volunteers arrived in Damascus, the first British civil servants to leave Palestine - architects, engineers etc - readied for departure.

The Arab Higher Committee refused an invitation to appear before the UN Palestine Commission. The Committee was "determined to persist in rejection of partition and in refusal to recognise the United Nations resolution ."

January 20

A combined force of Palestinians and the ALA, estimated at about 500 fighters, attacked the colony of Yehyam in western Galilee. British troops came to the rescue.

The village of Lubya [pop. 2 350] situated to the west of Tiberias was attacked by Zionist raiders during the night. One villager was reported dead as a result of the attack.

At Jehiam, Upper Galilee, a force of 100 Zionists fortified in a crusader castle, were under siege by an Arab force of about 500. Nine Zionists were killed in what proved to be a well planned attack on this isolated settlement, before being relieved by British troops and police.

In Jerusalem, the relative calm of the previous few days, while religious leaders met to consider the position of Jerusalem, was shattered. The Haganah fired upon members of the Highland Light Infantry as they evacuated inmates of a Jewish home for the aged. One soldier was seriously injured, three less so. One Zionist was killed and three injured in the return fire.

Lord Montagu of Beaulieu suggested, in the House of Lords, that the United Nations should obtain a solemn pledge from the "new Jewish State" that it had no further territorial ambitions in the Middle East.[21]

It was stated that no searches for arms were now being made except when there was evidence of misuse. Zionist 'self defence' organisations would not be obstructed while they acted in purely defensive roles.

At the UN, the Palestine Commission discussed, for the first time, the possibility of sending troops to Palestine. In the absence of UN observers, discussion centred on the feasibility of using press reports as a basis for despatching any such troops.

January 21

It was reported that a second contingent of ALA volunteers arrived in Palestine. Britain informed the UN Palestine Commission that it was not possible to comply with the UN request that a major seaport be opened to speed up the transfer of Zionist immigrants to Palestine. The policy of 1 500 immigrants per month was reaffirmed.

January 22

Golda Meyerson left for New York on a mission of "mobilising American Jewry to give political, moral and financial assistance" to the Zionist endeavours in Palestine.[22] Her primary mission was to obtain arms.

Meanwhile, Arab forces attacked a convoy outside Jaffa at the village of Yazur. The deaths of seven Jewish policemen escorting the convoy was reported. Half an hour later another attack took place on the convoy by a passing vehicle. Three Arabs were reported killed in this exchange with six wounded.(About a month previously, on 18 December, Zionist militia, disguised as British soldiers, had entered the village, threw bombs at the coffee house, killing six villagers.) The site of the village is now a suburb of Tel Aviv.

Ten miles outside Jerusalem, another convoy was attacked resulting in the death of one Jew, with another seriously injured.

In Jaffa, a Zionist sniper shot one Palestinian Arab dead and wounded four others. Later, snipers opened fire on a lorry carrying Arab passengers. One woman and two men were killed. Seven were seriously injured, including five children.

A group of workers from the village of Hamama were attacked by settlers from Nitzanim settlement. Fifteen workers were wounded.

January 23

By this date, commentators were able to affirm that while the two main Zionist terrorist groups - the Irgun and Stern Gang - on occasion would conduct their own operations, in general, together with the official Jewish defence force Haganah, they were all obeying Jewish Agency orders. It was further observed that the Haganah had developed into an efficient, strong well-disciplined, fighting machine which would retaliate viciously and methodically after any Arab attack.

January 25

Golda Meyerson, in an address to the AGM of the Council of Jewish Federations and Welfare Funds in Chicago asked for American Jews to supply up to $30 million immediately.[23]

British armoured cars interrupted an Arab attack on a convoy outside Jerusalem. Ten Jews and two Arabs were reported killed.

January 26

An attack by the Haganah destroyed the village of Sukreir in the Gaza district.

Explosions ripped through various empty premises in Jerusalem, including a booby trapped house in the Jewish quarter where a soldier was injured.

Seven Arabs were reported killed in night attacks near Tel Aviv and Jaffa.

A government directive that all US cargo ships have to be examined was enacted when the US ship, the *Exford*, was directed to Haifa for examination of her cargo.

January 27

An uneasy week long truce in the coastal plane area was broken when Arab forces attacked a convoy and Zionists attacked two Palestinian police officers driving children to school.

At midnight, Zionist attackers penetrated the outskirts of the village of Bayt'Affa [pop.700] north-east of Gaza. An attempt was made to mine some outlying houses but the attackers were detected by village guards. A two hour fight ensued before the raiders withdrew to the nearby settlement of Negba.

An American merchant ship was refused leave to enter Tel Aviv harbour and ordered to Haifa, in conformity with US government instructions to its merchant marine, in order that it could be searched by the Mandate authorities.

It was reported that Czech arms were being supplied to Arab guerrilla fighters; Egypt had supplied several thousand rifles to the exiled Mufti of Jerusalem, according to Egyptian sources.

The Scotsman's Special Correspondent gave an outline of the situation facing King Abdullah of Transjordan, as a delegation from that country arrived in Britain to try and revise the two year old Treaty of Friendship. The Treaty stated that only British troops could be stationed on Transjordan soil, and no other. However the situation had changed drastically from two years ago.

With partition looming and conflict well established, there could soon be a need for states such as Iraq, Saudi Arabia - with no contiguous borders with Palestine - to base troops in Transjordan. Then there was the question of the future of the 10 000 strong Transjordan Frontier Force commonly known as the Arab Legion.

With some 300 000 unruly Bedouin tribespeople within the borders of Transjordan, this British trained and financed police force, together with its British advisers, had proven to be successful in providing state security - not to mention stability in this important area of the Middle East. Officially part of the British Imperial Forces, the Arab Legion was financed to the tune of over one million pounds by Britain. At least two of its brigades were used for guard duty within Palestine.

January 28

A third contingent of 400 ALA volunteers arrived in Palestine.

By this date, 25 Jewish families had moved into Palestinian homes in the looted village of Shaykh Badr, on the outskirts of Jerusalem (now the site of Israel's parliament, the Knesset). This followed pressure brought to bear on the Jewish families by housing committees formed by the Haganah and the Jewish Agency.

If they resisted being moved, then ". . . . sanctions were imposed on them like cutting off support given them by the Social Department of the Community Committee, and when that did not work they were forcibly loaded onto trucks and transferred to Shaykh Badr."[24]

January 29

A Zionist force of five armoured cars was beaten off, with no reported casualties, when it attacked the village of Burayr [pop. 2 740] to the north-east of Gaza.

Zionist terrorists shot and killed two British policemen in Ben Yehuda Street, in the Jewish section of Jerusalem. Police thwarted Arab raids on two trains. However a third was more successful with 40 tons of freight and some arms being captured.

The UN Palestine Commission unanimously agreed to the formation of a Jewish militia in Palestine. It was ready to consider a similar arrangement for the Arabs. Britain told the Commission that she could not allow the formation of such a militia prior to the termination of the Mandate.

The US Consulate-General warned US citizens that the US government "strongly disapproves" of any interference or participation by them in foreign armed forces. Citizens fighting in the armed services of Jews or Arabs would lose their passports and their right to protection. Naturalised citizens would lose their American citizenship.

January 30

Shooting took place around the King David Hotel in Jerusalem. Sniping and sporadic machine gun fire brought traffic to a halt until British armoured cars moved in.The Haganah blew up a house in the Katamon quarter of the city. British sappers eventually rescued the Palestinian occupants.

Yazur village, outside Jaffa, was besieged by Zionist forces. One house was destroyed, with its owner being killed. Arab snipers claimed three Jewish victims, including a woman, in the Manshieh quarter of the Tel Aviv-Jaffa boundary.

January 31

The Jewish owned *Palestine Post* building was devastated by a bomb, with 20 people injured. It was reported that Arab underground forces in the Jerusalem area claimed responsibility while Jewish Agency sources blamed the British.

The UK government formally complained to Bulgaria over its assistance in unauthorised Jewish immigration which contravened the laws of Palestine.

The Royal Navy intercepted a schooner carrying 280 unauthorised Central European Jews destined for Palestine. It was diverted to Cyprus.

Britain amplified its refusal to countenance any militia in Palestine until the Mandate came to an end. It was stated that the Palestine Commission, itself, would not be welcome until two weeks before the Mandate was terminated. Britain would not be responsible for its safety should it arrive earlier. The administration would not be handed over piecemeal, but in its entirety at the end of the Mandate. The Arab Legion would be withdrawn and no British personnel would be loaned to the Commission.

It was at the end of the month that Ben Gurion issued orders to the newly appointed Haganah commander in western Jerusalem. In this area some Arab families had already fled the conflict, paricularly from mixed Arab-Jewish neighbourhoods. The commander was ordered to "settle Jews in every house in abandoned, half-Arab neighbourhoods, such as Romema."[25]

Notes

1 Theodore Herzl, *Diaries* III, p.77
2 Benny Morris, *Falsifying the Record*, (Journal of Palestine Studies, Spring 1995) p.51
3 *ibid* p.53
4 Norman Finkelstein, *Myths, Old and New*, (JoPS, Autumn 1991) p.78
5 Michael Palumbo, *The Palestinian Catastrophe*, p.4
6 *ibid* p.34
7 Harry Sacher, *Israel, the establishment of a state*, p.217
8 Said Aburish, *Children of Bethany*, p.95
9 *ibid* p.105
10 Palumbo, p.36
11 *ibid* p.40
12 Ilan Pappe, *The Making of the Arab-Israeli Conflict 1947-1951*, p.50
13 Nathan Krystall,*The De-Arabisation of West Jerusalem 1947-50* (JoPS, Winter 1998) p.7
14 Benny Morris, *The birth of the Palestinian refugee problem. 1947-1949*. p.32
15 Pappe, p.82
16 Morris, p.30
17 Krystall, p.7
18 Walid Khalidi, *Before their Diaspora*, p.316
19 Walid Khalidi, *All that Remains*, p.256
20 Morris, p.47
21 The Times 21/1/48
22 The Times 23/1/48
23 Henry Cattan, *Palestine, the Arabs and Israel*, p.219
24 Krystall, p.9
25 Morris, p.190

February

In view of the Zionist desire to reduce the number of Arabs in the proposed Jewish state it follows that orders to expel Arabs......were interpreted liberally by most Haganah officers.

"The Palestinian Catastrophe" Michael Palumbo

In the initial stages of the conflict the Arab forces were relatively successful. With little organisation, few modern weapons, with little knowledge of the size and strength of forces facing them, they performed well in the "battle of the convoys", disrupting the Zionist supply lines between their population centres and outlying colonies.

In contrast the Zionists were largely fighting a defensive war. However organisation was a strength and, latterly, it was turned to their distinct advantage. This was typified by the Haganah setting up an office in the US, during February, under the name "Land and Labor" for recruitment of professional military personnel.[1]

Ultimately, the Zionist intelligence service had correct assessments of the disarray, weakness and confusion existing on the Palestinian side and were able to make a fair estimate of the internal conflicts and feuding between the various factions. Telephone conversations between local leaders and the Arab Higher Committee were intercepted. [2]

From the beginning of February onwards, observers noted a relative trickle of Palestinian Arabs leaving their homes to seek safety elsewhere.

On 4 February the British High Commisioner noted that "throughout the Arab middle class there is a steady exodus of those who can afford to leave the country."[3]

> Israeli historian, Rony Gabbay, recorded
> "According to Jewish sources some 30 000 persons [note: 4% of the eventual total], members of well-to-do families in Jerusalem and Haifa, together with the inhabitants of some villages in the Sharon greatly affected by the disturbances and riots departed for neighbouring Arab countries between January to March 1948." [3]

By the end of the month all Jerusalem's neighbourhoods, with the exception of the Jewish Quarter in the Arab dominated Old City, were exclusively Arab or Jewish. There was next to no communication between them.

However when it came to outright expulsion of the population the claim that only "hostile" Arabs were subject to expulsion was refuted by the observation and evidence of the U.N. and neutral observers. They reported that in many cases "considerable brutality" was used to "cleanse" Palestinian villages of their residents - who offered no resistance. It was up to each commander to decide which Arabs were "hostile".

In the words of author and researcher, Michael Palumbo,

> "In view of the Zionist desire to reduce the number of Arabs in the proposed Jewish state it follows that orders to expel Arabs......were interpreted liberally by most Haganah officers."[3]

During February, as historians subsequently revealed, Ben Gurion made it abundantly clear that he was determined to acquire Palestinian owned land and get rid of the owners. The White Paper of 1939 had almost completely blocked Jewish land purchases, suffocating any development and blocking any regional development of Jewish controlled areas. The implication of the partition resolution was that the proposed Zionist state was allocated some 55% of Palestine.The vast majority of this was Palestinian owned.

Ben Gurion's answer, when asked about the absence of Jewish owned land in strategic areas of Palestine, made it quite clear that the Zionists intended outright war. And this war would entail the dispossession and expulsion of the Palestinian people.

> "The war will give us the land, the concepts of 'ours' and 'not ours' are only concepts for peacetime, and during the war they lose all meaning."

And later, when advising to forget "conventional notions" of acquiring land

> "......In the Negev we will not buy land. We will conquer it. You are forgetting that we are at war."[4]

That Ben Gurion knew what was happening, desired what was happening and encouraged what was happening throughout Palestine, was made evident by instructions to the new Officer-in-Command of the Haganah in Jerusalem, David Shaltiel. On 5 February Ben Gurion instructed Shaltiel to conquer Arab districts and to settle Jews in the abandoned and conquered districts.

In this period a number of Palestinian Arab villages in the Coastal Plain (the Sharon) were emptied of their inhabitants. These Palestinian communities were isolated and close to Zionist communities.This was the area between Tel Aviv and Hadera where Jews were in the majority and, according to the partition resolution, was to be the core of the Jewish State. The desertion of the area by its Palestinian residents was mainly through fear. They had witnessed or heard of the activities of the Haganah, the Irgun and the Stern Gang.

February was the month that the UN Palestine Commission reported to the Security Council of the impossibility of its task without the backing from some international force to shore up its authority. The five members, dubbed "The Five Lonely Pilgrims" by the Commission's chairman, Czech born Karel Liscicky, unknown and undistinguished in international circles, were to oversee the birth of the UN's creation.

Liscicky, on the basis of his UNESCO experience, was the only member to have first hand experience of Palestine. He was the only one who had studied the problem of partition in any detail. It was reported that he was embarrased to be considered an expert by the other members of the Commission whose knowledge, initially, of Palestine was considered abysmal.

Whereas Liscicky had cut his teeth during the declining years of the League of Nations, the fore-runner of the United Nations, the vice-chairman, Raul de Medina was a young diplomat more at home in the "more leisurely merry-go-round of diplomacy in Washington" than his own country, Bolivia.

The remaining three members were not diplomats. The Danish member was Per Federspiel, regarded as having a "liberal" political outlook with British sympathies. The only non-English speaking member was, paradoxically, of Welsh descent. Named Morgan, he was a Panamanian former Minister of Education who was critical of Britain. Finally there was Senator Francisco of the Philippines. A lawyer, Francisco was regarded as being more used to dealing with meticulous, well checked over memoranda and resolutions instead of the fluctuating and frightening task into which all five members had been thrust.[5]

February 1

At the village of Al Kabri [pop 5 360] north of Acre a Zionist group attempted to blow up the house of the village leader, an ally of the Mufti. This action resulted in the villagers blocking Jewish traffic en route to the Lebanon.

Palestinian forces planted a bomb at the offices of the *Palestine Post* in Jerusalem. The lorry bomb, parked in the heart of "Jewish" Jerusalem, virtually demolished the building while most of the editorial staff were taking a break in a nearby cafe. One report stated that 20 Jewish civilians were killed, others spoke of about 20 being injured but with no deaths reported officially.

With windows being shattered within a radius of half a mile, it was reported to be Palestine's biggest blast since the Zionists blew up the King David Hotel in July 1946, killing 91 people.

A British cruiser intercepted a schooner with its cargo of illegal Jewish immigrants. They were to be transhipped from Haifa to internment camps in Cyprus.

At the Security Council, on the eve of the Palestine Commission's request for an International Police Force to help implement the partition resolution, a new "crescendo of Jewish pressure" was reported. Three targets were in the Zionists' sights. British firmness in not relinquishing any power before 15 May. British determination not to free any port to assist Jewish immigration before the same date nor to declare to any party their evacuation plans. Britain was accused of a plot to sabotage and destroy the embryonic "Jewish State".

February 2

The Palestine Commission stated that their task was not practicable if Britain was only prepared to allow them to operate in Palestine two weeks before the end of the Mandate. A collapse of security and administrative services was predicted. The Palestine Government, in response, pointed out that since the partition resolution had been passed in the General Assembly, the situation had deteriorated. It was pointed out that the arrival of members of the Commission would probably provoke the Palestinians into further violence, since they were violently opposed to the partition of their land.

Britain's chief permanent delegate at the U.N., Sir Alexander Cadogan, stated

> "The Jewish story that the Arabs were attackers and the Jews the attacked is not in present circumstances tenable.
> The Arabs are determined to show that they will not submit tamely to the United Nations plan of partition, while the Jews are trying to consolidate the advantages gained at the General Assembly by a succession of drastic operations designed to intimidate and cure the Arabs of any desire for further conflict."[6]

Within the United States it was reported that the government was increasingly wary of being involved in the conflict in Palestine. For domestic reasons - keep Palestine out of domestic politics. For international reasons - the U.S., as a supporter of partition, must be see to be as bipartisan as possible. Neutrality was also seen to be important in view of the concern over oil supplies from the Middle East.

February 3

The 'Arab an Nuseirat Bedouin fled their Zionist dominated area, to the north of Tel - Aviv, after an attack by the Haganah.

Two Arab prisoners escaped from Jerusalem central prison in the confusion following an attack by Arab raiders who bombed and raked the building with gunfire. One British constable was wounded.

Ex-soldier Henry Dickson appeared in front of a military court charged with soliciting serving soldiers to sell firearms to Arabs.

Two British policemen were shot dead and a third wounded following an attack, presumed to be carried out by Zionists, in Rehovoth, a Jewish township outside Tel Aviv.

In Haifa, one British policeman was killed and another seriously injured when Arab assailants opened fire. Their rifles were stolen. Arab Legion troops returned fire on a convoy of Jewish buses killing one woman and wounding ten.

Later, in eastern Haifa, four Jews were killed and eight injured when an armoured bus and other buses were fired upon. Four Arabs were killed, victims of a car bomb, in the same area. Several buildings and houses were severely damaged including that of Haifa National Reform Society, a welfare organisation for Palestinian youth. Elsewhere in Haifa bombing and shooting incidents claimed one Arab and two Jewish victims.

The Jewish Agency petitioned the Palestine Commission, accusing Arab States of trying to defeat the 'partition scheme' by force.

> "The world is faced, says the Agency, with an attempt to hold up the Charter to mockery and violation. Its success would spell everlasting discredit to the U.N."

The Agency also formally appealed to the Security Council for action to counter an "Arab plot to overthrow by force" the U.N.'s decision to partition Palestine.

February 4

British paratroopers and Guardsmen fought with a large Arab force in northern Palestine, near Lake Tiberias. One dead and 11 wounded was reported. Other sources indicated 12 Arabs dead, six captured with the rest forced to retreat back over the Syrian border following the three hour battle.

Shooting was reported from Jerusalem, the Gaza-Bersheeba road and Jaffa Tel-Aviv area. On the Jaffa-Haifa road one British soldier was killed and three wounded when an army convoy fought its way through three roadblocks on the Jerusalem Hebron road.

South of Haifa sections of the railway were sabotaged. The Jaffa-Jerusalem railway was likewise sabotaged in several places

February 5

Twelve Arabs were killed and 21 wounded following a battle with the police and soldiers.The Arab irregulars had attacked a Jewish truck near Haifa.

February 6

Al Manshiyya [pop. 810] situated 2km to the east of Acre was attacked by a number of Zionists armed with automatic weapons. They were repulsed by the village defenders. There was no mention of casualties.

Mansurat al Khayt [pop. 200] came under attack from a group of 50 Zionists. Supported by cover fire from automatic weapons they succeeded in blowing up one house. One villager was reported wounded. [At the end of the war the village was in the demilitarised zone; by 1956 all the villagers had been expelled.]

An attack by a contingent of ALA forces on the colonial settlement of Ein Zeitim was broken up by British troops.

The Arab Higher Committee sent the UN a formal declaration of war in "self-defence"against "any force going to Palestine to partition the country". The document made clear that the UN decision to partition the country was "null and void" because of "pressure put by the US delegation and Government on certain nations." Siam (Thailand), Haiti, the Philipinnes, Liberia, Cuba and Colombia were included amongst those pressurised to vote for the resolution.[7]

The Committee refused to acknowledge the moral authority of the partition resolution for which votes were recruited by "nothing short of political blackmail." It reminded the Secretary-Genral that the Assembly refused to test the legality of the proceedings in the International Court of Justice. [8]

February 7

British troops demolished two buildings in the village of Dayr Ayyub (in which lay, according to tradition, the tomb of the prophet Ayyub or Job). The buildings were allegedly the vantage point used to fire upon Zionist convoys passing through the village.

At a meeting of Mapai leaders, Ben Gurion summarised the situation

> "From your entry into Jerusalem through Lifta-Romena, through Mahane Yehuda, King George Street and Mea Shearim - there are no strangers [i.e. Arabs]. One hundred per cent Jews. Since Jerusalem's destruction in the days of the Romans - it hasn't been so Jewish as it is now. In many Arab districts in the west - one sees not one Arab. I do not assume that this will change.

He added

> "what had happened in Jerusalem . . . could well happen in great parts of the country - if we hold on . ." [9]

At the same meeting the purchase of Arab land was discussed and dismissed by Ben Gurion.

February 8

Estimates of 15 000 uniformed and equipped Syrian trained troops from two Arab states were published. With between 300 - 500 fighters arriving weekly the appearance was that of troops, some more ready for offensive action rather than defensive action. The former took the form of Syrian trained forces in American styled uniforms. The latter, untrained local militia, usually with no uniform and armed with a wide array of weapons. Ammunition was on sale in tobacco shops in Arab towns, rifles, pistols and grenades could be bought in the bazaars.

Secret "bomb schools" were reported to be operating throughout Palestine operated by "outside volunteer" explosive experts.

British paratroopers came under heavy fire when they broke up a battle between the warring parties in Haifa. In retaliatory fire, three of the Arab forces were reported killed.

In Tel Aviv, an armed Zionist gang held up a British owned store. The loot was driven away on a stolen lorry.

Ben Gurion amplified his plans for any land captured in the Negev. It would be sold to the Jewish National Fund. Such a strategy would be a source of millions of pounds.When it was pointed out that they were no longer in the Middle Ages and that armies do not steal land, that after the war the Bedouin will return to their land, the reply was to forget "conventional notions."[10]

February 9

British forces blew up a house in Tel Aviv, considering it to be the source of gunfire aimed at a nearby police station. The demolition damaged an adjoining synagogue which, on examination, proved to have reinforced walls. Further examination revealed ladders giving access to windows with strategic views of the surrounding area, four sten guns with magazines and grenades were found. A Jewish freelance photographer was shot in the arm when four Zionist gunmen entered his shop in Tel Aviv.

Zionist forces blew up a Palestinian owned building in the new commercial centre of Jerusalem. One Jewish death and two serious injuries resulted from the ambush of an armoured bus near Lake Huleh.

Villagers from Arab Caesarea began to evacuate their homes out of fear of Zionist actions.

The UN Palestine Commission appealed to Britain to allow it to take preliminary steps in the establishment of local Arab and Jewish militia

February 10

British troops, in their first act of deployment as infantrymen since the partition resolution was adopted in November, took action to prevent fighting between Zionist and Arab forces in the Jewish Montefiore section of Jerusalem.

The six hour battle started when police responded to sniper fire. It intensified as both Haganah and Arab positions on the rooftops and the Old City walls opened fire. In the Jewish quarter of Yemin Moshe, mortar barrages from the British brought the fighting to a halt. The deaths of six

Arabs and one Jew was reported. Two British soldiers were wounded, with one dying later.

South of Haifa, Zionist terrorist forces killed seven Palestinian Arabs with five wounded. It happened when a party of 12 Palestinians were returning to the village of Tireh, near Tulkarm.
According to The Scotsman

> "...they were taken from their lorry by a party of Jews and marched into an orange grove near an RAF camp in Central Palestine."
> "The Arabs were forced to march into orange groves alongside the road and mowed down by gunfire."

In Haifa itself, one Jew was killed in Khamra Square, with both Jews and Arabs wounded.

Arab sources reported the action of a convoy approaching the village of al Maghar and firing upon the residents. No casualty figures were given.

The Jewish Agency lodged objections to 35 of the 45 articles of the draft statute for the projected international city of Jerusalem. The articles were to be presented to the Trusteeship Council for approval.

The first monthly progress report from the Palestine Commission to the Security Council complained of an Arab 'attempt to alter by force' the UN partition plan. The Security Council agreed to examine the need for armed forces or an international police force.

The British government warned the Palestine Commission that the food position in Palestine was "very serious."

February 11

The 'Arab Shudki Bedouin fled their Zionist dominated neighbourhood in the Coastal Plains after the Irgun attacked their encampment.

The *Yerushalayim ha-Nezurah* carrying 679 illegal immigrants was intercepted off the coast of Palestine.

Altogether 25 incidents were reported throughout Palestine.

February 12

Zionist forces launched attacks on the villages of Yazur [pop. 4 030] near

Jaffa and Abu Kabir, a suburb of Jaffa. Using machine guns and mortars the attack lasted from midnight until dawn, with five people wounded and seven houses destroyed.

British troops skirmished with a 'superior' Arab force, possibly the ALA, near the village of al Mansura, north of Safad. One British soldier was killed with no report of Arab casualties.

An Arab bus en route from al Hula to Safad was ambushed by Zionist forces. A mine was detonated under the bus. This, together with simultaneous gunfire and firebombs, killed five passengers with five wounded.

Haifa was the scene of a variety of incidents. A Palestinian Arab was shot dead by assailants in the eastern part of the city; the body of a Jewish resident of Tel Amal was found on the outskirts of the city. A Jewish bus was attacked with six wounded and at Carmel railway station shots were fired which killed two Arabs and wounded four.

Forty miles to the south of Haifa, electricty repair men, together with a military/police escort, came under fire as they were repairing a cable. One Jewish worker was shot dead, another seriously wounded.

Following the shooting of a Jewish woman in Talbiyeh, a Haganah loudspeaker van toured the area ordering the remaining Palestinian residents to leave or else 'they and their property would be blown up.' Despite the van and its occupants being arrested, a British report commented that 'the Arabs did evacuate.' [11]

Irish Guards clashed with a force of 50 Syrian Arabs in northern Palestine. The day long clash resulted in the death of two British soldiers.

February 13

The Jewish Agency accused British troops with being accessories to the killing of four Jewish guards in Jerusalem. The four had been arrested for carrying arms and had later been found dead, with bullet wounds, outside St Stephen's Gate in the Arab quarter of the city. A British Army sergeant-major was placed under arrest.

However the Arab Higher Committee sources denied that the British army had anything to do with the deaths. It was claimed that the four Zionists, dressed as Arabs and found to be heavily armed, had been stopped in a lane leading to the HQ of the Muslim Brotherhood in the Old City.

This was followed by a Haganah order that Jews should refuse to submit to being arrested or searched by British security forces unless in the presence of Jewish police.

In Haifa, a British sergeant was shot dead by Arab assailants. A British corporal investigating the death was wounded by gunmen.

The day's total deaths included 13 Jews, 12 Arabs and two Britons.

February 14

Ben Gurion issued orders to the Haganah commander in Jerusalem for the conquest of the whole city and its suburbs.

A Zionist convoy exchanged fire with villagers as it passed through Burayr, near Gaza. The next day a contingent of British troops forcibly removed a barrier at the entrance to the village. This resulted in two villagers being wounded.

February 15

An ALA uniformed unit attacked the colonial settlements of Tirat Zvi and two others in the Jordan Valley. The Arab forces, who had been training in the area, attacked with three inch mortars.The Haganah were apparently waiting for them and repulsed them after a five hour battle. British units units eventually arrived to disperse the attackers.

At least 35 Arabs and one Jew were reported killed.

Two bridges were blown up over tributaries of the River Jordan on the Syrian-Palestine border. Initial reports indicated that Arab forces were responsible with a possible onslaught on Zionist settlements in the northern "finger" of Palestine in the offing. However, Zionist forces were more likely to be responsible for attempts to blow up three bridges in northern Palestine, since this hindered movement into Palestine.

Under cover of automatic fire, Zionist forces planted two bombs beside the home of Haj Amin al Husseini, Mufti of Jerusalem. One room was demolished. Also in the city, an Arab passerby and his donkey were shot dead as he passed a Jewish quarter.

A Palmach force from the 3rd battalion raided the village of Sa'Sa' in northern Galilee with orders "to blow up 20 houses and kill the largest number of fighters". In the event the forces, under the command of Moshe Kelman, planted bombs during a night raid and succeeded in perpetrating a massacre of six adult villagers and five small children.

Three houses were destroyed and 11 badly damaged.[12]

In Gaza, two British NCOs were fired upon and wounded.A gang of armed Zionists, dressed in British Army uniforms, raided a military camp between Haifa and Tel Aviv and stole a large quantity of army rations. Four British soldiers were wounded in Haifa when gun fire was exchanged between an Arab Legion sentry and a Jewish bus.

Jewish sources reported that the abandoned Jewish Maccabi quarter in no-mans land between Jaffa and Tel Aviv had been set on fire by Arab attackers.

The Stern Gang warned members of foreign consulates in Jerusalem, by letter, that they would be treated as "foes and spies" if they, in the eyes of the terrorists, were deemed to have exploited diplomatic immunity to help the Palestinians. Unnamed members of the Consular Corps from Syria, the Lebanon, Iraq, Egypt, the Yemen and Saudi Arabia were accused of abusing their diplomatic immunity.

The Gang also threatened the rulers of those Middle Eastern countries where anti-Zionist demonstrations had taken place. Snipers were accused of using mosques as vantage points They were now to be regarded as legitimate targets for the terrorists.

The Bedouin tribes 'Arab ar Rumeilat and 'Arab Hawitat evacuated their encampments in the Coastal plain.

The village of Arab Caesarea was captured with most of the remaining villagers fleeing or being expelled[13].

The secretary-general of the Arab League stated that regular armies of the Arab states had no intention of intervening in the Palestinian struggle. They regarded the situation as a civil war where the Zionists were attempting to seize part of Palestine. Regular Arab armies would intervene, he said, only if foreign armies invaded the country and tried to enforce partition.

February 16

Arab Legion troops clashed with Zionist forces in Haifa resulting in the death of three Jewish passengers of a car following a Jewish armoured bus. Haifa police reported that the armoured bus first fired on the troops, killing one of their number.

In an 8 hour clash in northern Palestine, at three settlements, the death of 60 Arab fighters (newspaper sources reported 18 dead) was claimed by a

Haganah spokesman. It was reported that a force of 400 uniformed Arabs armed with three inch mortars had attacked the settlements in the Galilean hills.

Two Palestinians were shot dead. One near St John's hospital in Jerusalem, the other in eastern Haifa.

The British Government stated that food supplies would be adequate until the end of the mandate, but not beyond.

The UN Palestine Commission called for 'prompt action' by the Security Council on the problem of 'providing that armed assistance which alone would enable the Commission to discharge its responsibilities' by keeping Jew and Arab apart when Britain renounces the Mandate. It was argued that unless steps were taken, British withdrawal from Palestine would initiate 'a period of uncontrolled, widespread strife and bloodshed'.

The Commission felt that it could not maintain law and order, implement partition without an adequate military force at its disposal. The absence of such a force would make it impossible to establish boundaries "Certain elements of the Jewish community continue 'to commit irresponsible acts of violence which worsen the security situation.' "

The Commission was of the opinion that a 'Jewish militia' was essential for implementing partition but should not be used for actions outwith the border of the proposed Jewish state or used for retaliatory actions.

Particular concern was expressed over the future of Jerusalem, conceived as a demilitarised enclave within the proposed Arab state. It was observed that

> "The United Nations would be dealt a severe blow if its efforts to to maintain the sacred character of the city and preserve it as a possible centre of peace and harmony should end in a sanguinary struggle."
>
> "This would be a catastrophic conclusion to the era of international concern for that territory."[14]

The first public evidence of American anxiety was revealed when President Truman sent a letter to the Kings of Iraq and Saudi Arabia urging them not to use violence in resisting the partition of Palestine.

In counselling the U.S. to adopt "as a member of the United Nations a really neutral attitude towards Arabs and towards implementation of Palestine partition" the Iraqi Minister for Education, Mohamed Alshabibi pointed out "Many responsible American leaders give direct and strong support to the Zionist cause. They even insist on implementation of partition by force of American troops. Such an attitude cannot but create the reaction in Arab countries."[14]

February 17

The Irgun carried out an attack on Fajja [pop. 1 750] near Jaffa. Some of the villagers fled as a result of the attack, the start of a process of terrorising the villagers by both the Irgun and the Haganah.

On the day that the Security Council began work on the Palestine Commission's proposals, The Times printed a revealing article on how the partition resolution on Palestine was being viewed three months on:

The commission's report appeared to leave open two possibilities to the Council. One was to produce an international army and push the partition scheme through . . . The other to refer the plan back to the General Assembly in special session for revision on the ground that it could not be executed because of Arab opposition. Neither, it was feared, could be effective before 16 May, when, as the commission expected, "complete chaos will descend upon Palestine."

Washington was seen to have given out little that did not beg the question. The United Nations policy for Palestine had been, and would continue to be, largely of the United States making, "which points to a continuing indecision."

"By and large, few observers have any doubt now that the Assembly made a grave mistake in conceding a Jewish claim bound to provoke strong Arab resistance . . ."

And commenting on the logical extension of the partition resolution, that UN member states should now consider giving physical backing to partition:

"But, recalling the hesitations of many members who voted for the partition scheme, one may assume the widespread feeling in their ranks, that they would prefer to be more certain of the justice of the particular United Nations cause which is being resisted."

February 18

The Haganah called up men and women aged 25 to 35 for military service.

Six Palestinian Arabs were killed and 32 wounded following a terrorist explosion in Ramleh Market place. In Haifa, two Arabs were shot dead and one seriously wounded. An Armenian resident was shot dead while standing on a hotel balcony. One Jew was shot but not seriously injured.

Mr Creech Jones, Secretary of State for the Colonies, reminded the Palestine Commission that at the time of the passing of the partition resolution, the General Assembly had been informed by Britain that there was no use in the resolution being passed unless the means of implementation and, if necessary, enforcement were provided.

The Arab Higher Committee posed the question of why Palestine should be selected for enforcement of UN recommendations when the United Nations was being defied by both Korea and the Balkans.

February 19

In Baysan district, a battle took place around the settlement of Tirat Tzvi. At the same time Zionist forces attempted to encircle the nearby village of Farwana. They only managed to blow up three empty houses.

A Haganah convoy was ambushed near Manara in Tiberius district, resulting in the death of three members of the convoy. British troops eventually rescued the convoy.

It was reported that a British convoy stopped in the village of Beit Daja to arrest a man carrying a rifle. The villagers opened fire on the soldiers. In the ensuing battle two villagers were killed and three wounded. One soldier was killed when "he jumped from his truck with a Bren machine-gun in his arms and ran into the village with his gun blazing."

In Jerusalem a British soldier was shot dead and another wounded when shot from behind while window shopping in Jerusalem.Their weapons were stolen. The Irgun claimed responsibility "in reprisal for the destruction of Jewish property in Jerusalem by the British."[15] Further British casualties were reported.

A British policeman was shot and seriously wounded in the Jewish quarter of Jerusalem. A Jewish girl was killed near Tel Aviv.

In Haifa, the head of the Muslim community, Sheikh Mohammed Nimr al Khatib, was shot and seriously wounded by four assailants, believed to be Zionists. In Lower Haifa a Jewish bus was fired upon. Four Jewish passengers were killed and a British policeman injured when Zionist and Arab gunmen raced through the the streets blazing away with Tommy guns at passing traffic.The body of a blindfolded Jewish victim of the violence was found in Haifa with bullet wounds to head and chest.

The Royal Navy intercepted a refugee ship with 700 illegal immigrants off the Palestine coast.

Britain warned the Palestine Commission against creating a Jewish only militia, warning of Arab reaction. It was stressed that Britain was not prepared to negotiate with any "shadow government" the Commission may intend to set up before the end of the mandate.

The United States denied allegations, commonly voiced by many Arab states, that she had exerted extreme pressure on delegations and Governments to vote for the partition resolution.

February 20

Using tanks and armoured vehicles a Zionist force attacked the village of Yazur [pop. 4,030] to the west of Jaffa which had previously been pounded by mortar fire. An ice factory and two houses were demolished. One villager was killed with four wounded.

Clashes took place between Arab irregulars fighting on behalf of the Palestinians and the Haganah. A Jewish convoy was attacked near the village of Menara resulting in three Jewish deaths

A two masted schooner docked at Haifa, with 705 illegal immigrants, for transfer to Cyprus.The *Independence* arrived in Tel Aviv carrying 280 illegal immigrants, volunteers under oath to the Haganah. In Tel Aviv 10 terrorists from the Stern Gang robbed the Palestine Government Veterinary Department, escaping with equipment which they said would be turned "over to the Jewish State when the British withdrew".

The Haganah subjected the Arab central area of Haifa to battleground conditions with mortar bombardments, killing six and wounding 36 Palestinian civilians. It was both started by and followed by heavy street fighting. Initially vicious street fighting then sniping and hit-and-run firing from speeding cars with windows being smashed and groups of Palestinian residents being terrorised and forced to flee for cover - accompanied by mortar shells crashing through roofs and exploding inside homes.

Heavy firing preceded the arrival of British police and paratroopers who engaged both sides with Bren gun fire in order to silence groups of snipers on the roofs and behind windows.

Other population centres were targets for the mortar shells. Including the Eastern Railway Station, the city's market place and the police station. In general Haifa, Palestine's principal port and oil town - with the Jewish area strategically overlooking the low lying Arab areas round the harbour, railways and oil refineries - was the country's chief troublespot with scores of dead and wounded from street fighting.

In Jerusalem, 12 Zionist terrorists escaped from Central Prison. Among those who escaped through a tunnel were leaders of the terrorist Irgun and Stern Gang, including the former deputy of the late Abraham Stern, founder of the Gang, who had eight years to serve of a 15 year sentence.

Arab snipers in Jaffa and Jerusalem killed two Jews. A further three were killed when a convoy was attacked near Safad. In Safad itself, sporadic firing resulted in the death of one Arab. A British soldier was killed by an Arab land mine near Beit Dajan.

The remaining 20 villagers of Arab Caesarea were expelled from their villages after it was surrounded by a Palmach unit and their houses destroyed. This action had been preceded by a Haganah General Staff decision to destroy the houses, which were mostly Jewish property. Thirty houses were eventually blown up, six were left intact due to the shortage of explosives.

Yet it is worth noting the Palestinians of Caesarea had

> 'done all in their power to keep the peace in their village and around it... The villagers supplied agricultural produce to the Jewish market in Haifa and Hadera."

Caesarea was the first pre-planned, organised expulsion of an Arab community by the Haganah in 1948.[13]

The Scotsman's special correspondent reported that

> "Again there have been clear indications that the Arabs do not wish or intend this 'struggle' to begin before the British leave."

In observing that many Palestinians are business people she commented on some of the problems that would face them

"The business life of the Arab community is practically at a standstill. People are not buying anything but daily necessities. . . What is going to happen to the Palestine pound when the mandate ends ? As the Arabs refuse to recognise partition . . . they will not be in a position to negotiate financial agreements. So their currency position will be utterly chaotic."

February 21

The trial of Scot Henry Martin Dickson, a former staff-sergeant in the Black Watch, from Coatbridge, Glasgow, re-commenced in Jerusalem Military Court. He was said to have approached two British soldiers and offered them "a little present" if they consented to being gagged and tied up while arms were being removed from their camp at Asluj in southern Palestine.

Dickson was editor and founder of an English-language weekly, the Arab World Review, the first edition of which had been seized the previous year because of an alleged breach of the censorship regulations. Dickson was eventually found guilty and sentenced to five years imprisonment.

February 22

Terrorists, using the well tried Irgun strategy of dressing up as British soldiers, parked an armoured convoy of three stolen lorries and an armoured car in the middle of a Haganah 'security zone' on Ben Yehuda Street, Jerusalem at 6.45am. The lorries exploded, with the perpetrators escaping in the armoured car, devastating this business/shopping area. A reported 57 Jewish civilians were killed with at least 100 wounded. Blame for this atrocity, which one report indicated was reminiscent of the London blitz, was laid at two doors, with proof of neither.

The Arab commander for the Jerusalem area, Abdul Kader Husseini claimed that it was in reprisal for a similar atrocity perpetrated by the Zionists at Ramleh, the week before when a "basket bomb" had killed six and wounded 32. He said that Arab commandos, trained in Syria, had been used. This was denied by the Arab Higher Committee in Cairo.

The Jewish community were convinced that the hand of the British were behind it. It was pointed out that foreign military advisers, mostly European exiles, were training the Arab guerilla forces. Since December, there had been reports of British volunteers enlisting to fight with the Palestinians.

In the aftermath, during subsequent rioting and reprisals, 10 British soldiers and police were murdered and at least eight wounded.

The day's carnage was not limited to the victims of this particular atrocity. Amongst reprisal victims was a military chaplain, who was seriously wounded, and his three companions killed following an attack near the Jewish Agency building. One British soldier was shot dead and his friend seriously wounded when a Zionist terrorist walked into the hospital in which they were receiving treatment, and shot them. Five soldiers were killed and six injured when a lorry bomb was detonated in the Street of the Prophets. A Jewish child and adult were also killed. Jerusalem residents were advised, officially, not to go to the Jewish shopping area.

Three Arabs were killed by mortar bombs in the Arab quarter of Northern Jerusalem

Mehahem Beigin [Author's note: the same Menachem Begin who became a prime minister of Israel] "commander in chief" of the Irgun called for reprisals against the British. He appealed to world Jewry - especially US Zionists - to declare economic war on Britain.

The Jewish Agency sent a demand to the Palestine Government and British militia HQ for immediate withdrawal of British troops and British police from "Jewish areas" of Jerusalem unless accompanied on security duties by Jewish police.

Thirty Irgun terrorists, disguised as British soldiers, occupied Barclay's Bank in Tel Aviv. They drove up in lorries, stopped traffic and surrounded the premises with barbed wire. However keys could not be found so the the robbery was only partial successful.

Fighting in the Beisan area stopped when 80 British armoured cars drove in between the Arab lines and the concentration of 1 200 Haganah fighters.

Excluding the casualties arising from the morning atrocity in Ben Yehuda Street, it was officially calculated that 42 people had been killed during the day with 96 injured. Both figures were the highest since "partition disturbances" began three months previously.

The Times reported on the strength of the Zionist lobby within US politics, a comment which would not be out of place as we begin the 21st century.

Referring to a political victory in the Bronx by Senator Taft, achieved with the support of the Jewish vote, it observed the Zionists, were becoming daily more arrogant in their pressure on American policy. They were no longer content to accept words. They wanted action, and with Senator Taft appearing to promise it "President Truman can offer no less, if he is to have any hope of keeping their votes."

February 23

Following the devastation in Ben Yehuda Street, reprisals against the British continued. In response to the Palestine Government's statement that it was not prepared to surrender any part of the responsibility for law and order, Zionists laid electrically detonated mines across the approach roads to Jerusalem. Four vehicles were blown up, causing injuries, but no fatalities.

Abdul Kader Husseini, the "veteran Arab guerrilla leader" claimed resonsibility for the Ben Yehuda Street bombing, stating that it was in retaliation for the previous week's basket bomb explosion in Ramleh. Hussein Khalidi, secretary of the Arab Higher Executive, did not comment on responsibility for the explosion but stated that the Arabs had not started

"....this game which could only produce bloodshed and destruction."[16]

In general there was no official comment from the Arabs with regard to responsibility. Any comment made reference to the one fact that Zionist spokesmen studiously ignored, namely that whoever was responsible was largely copying the methods of Zionist terrorists.

The Jewish Agency was single-minded in blaming the British, citing the presence of alleged English drivers of the trucks and armoured cars.

The Irgun and Stern Gang leaders ordered the killing of all British soldiers and police found within the city.The Irgun attacked the Syrian Orphanage building, situated near "Jewish Jerusalem." The mortar attack on a small detachment of the Royal Army Pay Corps lasted two hours with no casualties. The Jewish Hadassah hospital came under heavy fire from Arab positions. It was claimed that Zionist forces based in the hospital or the adjacent Hebrew University had fired a mortar barrage at the Mufti's house.

A Palestinian Arab was shot dead by British troops as he tried to steal from an army camp, in the Latrun, which had yet to be evacuated.

The "High Command" of the Arab militia, who eventually claimed responsibility for the previous day's carnage, issued a communique stating

"Unless the Jews adhere to the rules of war, we shall continue indiscriminate reprisals on a bigger scale."

A meeting of the Arab League ended with members agreeing to withold cooperation in developing oil concessions from any country that might advocate "forceful imposition of a Zionist State in Palestine."

Zionist assertions that the Arabs were the aggressors were met with cries of hypocrisy. "It was the Zionists who were the attackers, who were armed and organised . . . who had . . their supplies of arms and money, their powerful supporters abroad. It was the Jewish villages in Palestine that were fortified and the Jewish people who had practiced military training not the Arabs. It was the Jews who had bought and stolen and smuggled and manufactured arms for years, while the Arabs were being disarmed by the mandatory Power. . . . but it was the Jews whose howls rose to heaven, and who painted the false picture of helpless Jews faced by deadly Arabs." [17]

The village of al Abbasiyya, to the east of Jaffa, received the attention -yet again- of the Zionist forces. Earlier, on 13 December (the Jewish holy day of Chanukka), the Irgun had perpetrated a terrorist attack, blowing up houses, cars, opening fire on villagers at the local cafe, flinging grenades - resulting in nine deaths including a five year old child and a 26 year old woman.This time, two villagers were killed when a Jewish Settlement Police car sped through the town with a grenade being flung at passers-by.

The Arab Higher Committee claimed complete control over a triangular area of central Palestine hills where a 30 000 "volunteer army" was ready to go into battle at 48 hours notice.

Zionist and Arab forces attacked British headquarters in various parts of Jerusalem.The city was reported to be a place of fear and hatred with the British making strenuous efforts to prevent further civil disorder. The police only patrolled the main road leading from the city and treated the predominantly Jewish areas as no-go areas. The city resounded to the sound of gunfire throughout the day. Three mortar bombs landed in the middle of the city, near the women's clinic of the Government hospital which, due to circumstances, was almost empty. A British policeman was shot and wounded in the Sheikh Jarrah Quarter.

The fight to control key roads continued. The Arab forces mined the road to Mount Scopus and the Hadassah Hospital, firing on almost every armed bus. The Zionist forces retaliated by making it impossible for Arabs to travel from Jaffa Gate to the suburbs in the south of the city. From the

Jewish enclave of Yemin, the Haganah fired upon all Arab traffic. When a Jewish bus passed an Arab bus, they shot at each other.

Three former Jewish policemen and two Arabs were killed during an incident near the village of Lubya, Tiberias.
The US view on any international armed force to keep the peace in Palestine was presented to the Security Council. Its purpose would be to keep the peace, not to enforce partition. For the first time, the US delegate indicated that American government was not prepared to stand four-square behind the General Assembly's plan to partition Palestine between Arab and Jew.

February 25

A group of Zionists attacked two Arab police guards, killing one of them, during a raid on the British military court in Jerusalem. Incendiary bombs were left but failed to go off. Allegations that arms and munitions were being stored under the Haram es- Sharif which contains the Dome on the Rock and El Aksa mosque were denied. An inspection made at the invitation of the Haram's director confirmed the presence only of a few worshippers.

The 'Arab Hijazi Bedouin tribe evacuated their land for fear of Zionist attack.

Clare Hollingworth, Special Correspondent for The Scotsman, quoted a spokesman from the Jewish Agency on the general belief that the British was responsible for the Ben Yehuda Street bombing

"We have in our minds no doubt that British personnel perpetrated the outrage."

With no proof ever being offered to substantiate this, and with Arab organisations claiming full responsibility (although denied by the Arab Higher Committee), a further comment from a 'senior Jewish official' was perhaps the pointer towards the true position of the Zionists

"We Jews dare not believe Sunday's explosion was the work of the Arabs. This would cause panic within certain sections of the community."

[Author's note: With hindsight, this was a prescient comment. Before long, many "Ben Yehudas"were being carried out within the Palestinian community by Zionist forces intent on precipitating the very panic they feared within their own community.]

February 26

A Zionist gang equipped with mortars, machine guns and grenades carried out a dawn raid on Bet Daja[pop. 3 840] near Jaffa. Three villagers were killed and four wounded.

The village of Jaba, to the south of Haifa, was subject to a raid by a large force of Zionist troops. Arriving in two armoured buses, they raided a house, smashed up the interior then moved on.

An Arab contingent carried out an attack on Hadassah hospital

Increasing tensions between the Irgun group and the Haganah resulted in 16 wounded after a street battle in Tel Aviv.Apparently the Irgun's efforts to raise funds "by extortion" clashed with the launching of a Haganah defence fund campaign.

February 27

The Jewish Agency stated its intention of going ahead to set up a state with or without the backing of an international force.

Lieut. Gen. Sir Allan G. Cunningham, High Commissioner for Palestine announced he would rule by decree on 1 March to facilitate British withdrawal.

February 28

The village of Salameh suffered its second attack in two months. The attack, by a force of about 250 Zionists, killed three Palestinians, at the expense of six of their own dead.

The deaths of seven Arabs and one Jew, in "intercommunal fighting", was reported.

A ship carrying about 1 000 illegal immigrants to Palestine was intercepted.

A Zionist cross border raid on the Syrian town of Banias was reported.

February 29

The Cairo - Haifa train was blown up during the morning. Thirty British soldiers were killed and 35 wounded when three electrically detonated mines blew three of the four military carriages of the train off the tracks as it drew out of Rehovoth station situated in a Jewish area. A fourth mine containing 100 lbs of ammonal was discovered later.

As was usual, the first coaches had been allocated for military use, soldiers coming home from leave in this case - mainly from the King Own Scottish Borders and the Irish Guards. Such was the blast of the explosion that craters 20 feet deep were left with the effects being felt 3 miles away. The home of the Zionist leader, Dr Weizmann, one mile from the blast, suffered damage.

With the use of mines being a Zionist tactic and with Arab forces content, largely, to loot trains, blame was always going to be laid at the Zionist door. Eventually the Stern Gang claimed responsibility, claiming that it was part of their retaliation for the Ben Yehuda Street explosion.

In Haifa, a car bomb killed five Arabs and injured 25 others. This happened when the chief clerk of Haifa municipality took his car to a garage, near a police vehicle repair depot, because the steering was faulty. The car then blew up.

An attack on a Zionist colony near Tulkarm was repulsed with the help of the Army. It was stated that four Iraqi Arabs were wounded.

A delayed action barrel bomb blew up a Jewish house at Beit Dajan, near Jaffa, injuring one person. It had been rolled off an Arab lorry.

Following a lull in hostilities, possibly due to bad weather, explosions and firing could be heard in Jerusalem. The British army used two pounder shells to silence Zionist snipers, the first time that guns of this calibre had been used in the city.

Armed Irgun robbers held up employees of the Public Works Department. They escaped with with heavy building equipment and several lorries. At the same time, members of the Stern Gang robbed the Jerusalem municipality offices in the Jewish Mahameh Yehuda quarter.

Outside Jaffa, a British patrol was alleged to have disarmed a Haganah unit based in a factory, thus leaving them to the mercy of nearby Arab forces. The bodies of ten Zionists were later found. Reports indicated that Zionist sources believed that the act of disarming was in retaliation for the train atrocity. British police and army spokesmen insisted that their arms had not been taken away.

The illegal immigrants, 982 in number, from the Haganah ship, *Builders and Fighters*, docked at Haifa. They were transferred to a Royal Navy ship for transport to Cyprus.

Notes

1 Walid Khalidi, *Before their Diaspora*, p.316
2 Ilan Pappe, *The making of the Arab-Israeli Conflict 1947-1951*, p.82
3 Michael Palumbo, *The Palestinian Catastrophe*, p.41
4 Norman Finkelstein, *Myths, Old and New*,(Journal of Palestine Studies, Autumn 1991) p.76
5 The Scotsman 9/2/48
6 The Times 3/2/48
7 Henry Cattan, *Palestine, the Arabs and Israel*, p.221
8 The Times 6/2/48
9 Finkelstein, p.76
10 Benny Morris, *The birth of the Palestinian Refugee Problem, 1947-1949* p.170
11 *ibid* p.52
12 Walid Khalidi, *All that Remains*, p.496
13 Morris, p.54
14 The Scotsman 17/2/48
15 The Scotsman 20/2/48
16 The Scotsman 24/2/48
17 The Times 24/2/48

March

Outwardly, he continued until very late in the day to pay requisite lip service to the grand humanist-socialist ideals . . . . on the ground, however, he made sure that what he wanted got done, and he carefully avoided leaving tracks; his name rarely adorns an actual expulsion directive.

Benny Morris commenting on David Ben Gurion

Initially, any debate on the catastrophe which befell the Palestinian people and the refusal of the Israelis to allow refugees to return was plagued by Zionist mythology and propaganda. There was the much discredited, but much trumpeted, claim that Palestine was "a land without people for a people without land." Similarly discredited, but still to be heard from certain Zionist supporters, was the claim that Palestinian leaders urged their people to flee, that radio broadcasts urged likewise.

Why, even if these claims were to be true, this should then entitle Israel to refuse the Palestinian refugees the right to return to their homes, and totally ignore subsequent UN resolutions taking the same position, has yet to be explained to the satisfaction of the international community.

Subsequent debate has focused on whether the Palestinian people fled of their own accord and hence, according to Zionist logic, forfeited the right - forever - to return to their land and their homes. Zionism has always blamed those who were invaded and ignored, quite conveniently, those who carried out the invasion and eventual occupation.

Or were they expelled as part of a deliberate policy? It is only in the past decade or so that historians and researchers have tried to find an answer to this question.

As some historians and biographers of David Ben Gurion, Israel's first prime minister and leader of the Yishuv (Israel's pre-state "government" under the Jewish Agency) openly concede (or at least point out, even if some are not comfortable with the obvious conclusion), most of Ben Gurion's spoken or written intentions were made with one eye to the future.

In the sense that he was aware that history was in the making. That diaries, letters would one day be published. That transcripts, minutes of meetings would be scrutinised by tomorrow's historians and biographers.

Little that he wrote indicated his intention that the Palestinian people should be forcibly removed from their land. You have to go back some ten years earlier, to 1937, to find this sentiment expressed in a letter to his son. When asked what should happen to Palestinian villagers, evicted from their villages,

more often than not his reply was indicated by a shrug of the shoulders or wave of the hand - as in the case of the callous, inhumane expulsions from Lydda-Ramleh area.[1] After a while the army commanders no longer found the need to consult on this issue.
Israeli historian, Benny Morris, observed when commenting on Ben Gurion

> "Outwardly, he continued until very late in the day to pay requisite lip service to the grand humanist-socialist ideals . . . . on the ground, however, he made sure that what he wanted got done, and he carefully avoided leaving tracks; his name rarely adorns an actual expulsion directive."[2]

However the reality of Zionist preparations for the creation of a "Jewish" state was that as early as February 1945, even before the end of World WarII, a series of military master plans had been drawn up by the Haganah (which was under control of the Jewish Agency) in anticipation of open warfare leading to a state.

Plans A, B and C followed. The last of these, adopted in May 1946, called for retaliation or countermeasures, not always aimed at the perpetrators of a particular action, but at those deemed to have assisted in any way. In other words, collective punishment and destruction. It was planned that that such measures should be as immediate as possible, affecting large areas. All means should be used - leaflets, loud speaker vans, radio broadcasts - to ensure that the victims knew why they had been chosen. It was regarded as essential to retaliate in such a way as to undermine Palestinian sense of security.[3]

By December 1947 the Haganah National Command was pushing for the adoption of an "aggressive defence strategy" - Plan Dalet or Plan D. This was adopted on 10 March although it had been envisaged as far back as 1944.[4]

Prior to the implementation of Plan D the Haganah set up the "Committee for Abandoned Arab Property". It was composed of Haganah intelligence officers and Jewish National Fund land purchasing agents and was entrusted with the disposal of all Arab possessions that fell into Zionist hands. Its creation at such an early stage raises the issue of Zionist intentions in the coming months.

Effectively this was a first coat of legal gloss on eventual Israeli looting of Palestinian homes, businesses and property. A situation which continues to this day and, after 50 years, remains to be addressed by the international community.

By the beginning of March, despite explosions of mines in built up Arab areas and "repeated and merciless raids against sleeping Arab villages"[5], carried out in conformity with Plan C, only about 10 out of an eventual 500 or so villages had been taken by Zionist forces. A relatively insignificant number of Palestinians had left their homes.

By mid-March Zionism was in crisis. Even the US government had, to all intents and purposes, backtracked on partition.[5] With this as a backdrop, Plan D was launched in order to achieve

> "control of the area given to us by the U.N. *in addition to areas occupied by us which were outside these borders* and the setting up of forces to counter the possible invasion of Arab armies after May 15."[5]

Plan D constituted

> "a strategic-ideological anchor and basis for expulsions by front,district, brigade and battalion commanders . . . and it gave commanders, *post facto,* a formal, persuavive covering note to explain their actions." [6]

An extract from Plan Dalet, 10th March 1948:

General Section

4] Mounting operations against enemy population centres located inside or near our defensive system in order to prevent them being used as bases by an active armed force. These operations can be divided into the following categories:

Destruction of villages (setting fire to, blowing up, and planting mines in the debris) especially those population centres which are difficult to control continuously.

Mounting combing and control operations according to the following guidelines- encirclement of the village and conducting a search inside it. In the event of resistance, the armed force must be wiped out and the population must be expelled outside the border of the state . . .[7]

And there were the armaments to help bring the plan to fruition.

By March 1948 the local Zionist factories in Palestine were producing 100 sub-machine guns per day (increased to 200 per day in the first week in April), 400 000 rounds of 0.9mm ammunition per month. Production of 150 000 Mills grenades and 30 000 shells of 3inch mortars per month was reported. The factories also produced a favourite weapon of the Zionist fighter, flame throwers. There were anti-tank guns and the Little David or Davidka, a heavy mortar which was the Zionist weapon *par excellence*.

Zionist historians have described the Davidka in relatively benign terms as a device which "tossed a lump of explosive for some 300 yards." The reality was that it propelled a shell containing 60lbs of TNT usually into built up population centres where the blast not only killed and maimed but the noise terrorised men, women and children into a frenzy of fear and panic.[8]

All this contrasted vividly with the provision of armaments in the Palestinian sector.

In a letter to her family on 22 February, a Miss D.A. Norman commented:
"The Old City is even fuller of ammunition than food and every shop of whatever kind seems to have its quota. Bullets are 7½d each and big ones 1s6d. Bombs are 6s or 9s according as you choose French or English. Revolvers and guns are a terrific price ranging from £10-£100."[9]

March 1

By this date the mainly Christian, and wealthier, areas of Haifa such as "Old Carmel"and Wadi Nisnas were "almost completely empty" with the flight of people "...less marked in the eastern part of the town, where the poorer classes . . . are concentrated." While the wealthier Palestinians had more recourse to 'safe havens' than the poor and were prepared, in the face of terrorist/miltary action, to take advantage of this, some Israeli historians[10] have pointed out their belief that other factors may have been at work. Many Arabs, it is alleged may have been fearful of their employment/career prospects under Jewish domination, where Zionist labour ideology and lack of Hebrew could have had adverse impact.

An attempt was made, with Arab forces believed to be responsible, on the life of Lt-General GHA MacMillan, GOC British Troops in Palestine when his car was blown up by an electrically detonated mine on the Jaffa-Jerusalem Road. The car, with no passenger, was blown to bits as it passed Bab Eivad a notorious spot for Arab attacks.

A Jewish Agency spokesman deplored acts of terrorism. The statement was regarded as a pointer to differences which had emerged between the Haganah, the Jewish Agency's "defence force", and the terrorist Irgun and Stern Gang. It was observed that the Agency wished to conserve its forces for the struggle with the Arabs and avoid clashes with the British. It accused the "extremists" of opening a 'second front' by deliberately and consistently attacking British troops and the police.

Following the terrorist attack on the Cairo-Haifa train, the previous day, a proclamation from the military HQ in Jerusalem stated that the British

Army was prepared to use "powerful weapons" impartially to stop fighting between Jews and Arabs. "The object will be to stop the fighting at once with the minimum loss of life. ... The Army will now intervene at every opportunity."[11]

The explosion at Rehovoth provoked a strong and revealing statement from the Palestine Government. An official statement was issued condemning the Jewish Agency's policy of condoning terrorism. The most strongly worded denunciation of the Jewish community to date.[12]

No retaliatory action was threatened but:

> "The Government, mindful of the duties of the security forces to maintain law and order and confronted with the deliberate policy of the Jewish Agency to render their task as difficult as possible, desires now to bring once more to the serious attention of the Yishuv the fact that the continuance of indiscriminate murder and of condoned terrorism can lead only to forfeiture by the community of all rights in the eyes of the world to be numbered among the civilised peoples."

It was pointed out that during the previous year the government had "invited the Agency and Vaad Leumi to call upon the Jewish community to help to find and arrest terrorists as part of the ordinary legal moral duty of the citizens and institutions of any civilised State. This invitation was declined by the Agency on the grounds that it was contrary to Jewish political interests. Since then the outrages had increased in number and barbarity . . ."[13]

The statement listed the crimes of which members of the "Jewish community" were guilty:

> "The hanging of the two sergeants; the numerous occasions when innocent members of the security forces have been treacherously 'shot from behind', the deliberate demolition of buildings with the certain consequence of death and injury to women and children; the planned killing of certain foreign nationals; the intentional shooting of British personnel in hospital; armed robberies and extortion; and, finally, the Rehovoth outrage."

The statement then proceeded to castigate the leaders of the Jewish community for failing to take any steps against those responsible for "political reasons", for the "calculated innuendoes, falsehoods, and propaganda directed against the British members of the security forces who are in fact every day protecting Jewish property and saving hundreds of Jewish lives even at risk of their own."

The Jewish Agency's declaration that it was all for law and order had to be stood against the facts "for many years this international body has been breaking the laws of Palestine and other countries in which it has

operated." The Jewish Agency, the statement continued, refused to put forward any Jewish witnesses to give evidence in the various bombings which had taken place.

Last November the Government had withdrawn its forces from the Tel Aviv area on the understanding that the Agency would establish a civil guard to deal with terrorist incidents in the area. This had never happened and and "terrorists openly and freely continue to murder and rob the Jews themselves."

The Scotsman's correspondent stated that "there is probably no single member of the non-Jewish community in Palestine who does not agree with every word of this plain-speaking statement." [14]

The British Police HQ in Jerusalem released casualty figures in the Holy Land since the UN voted for partition. Since 30th November 1947 the deaths amounted to 674 Arabs, 579 Jews, 74 Army, 18 British police; with over 3 000 wounded.

March 2

The village of al Manara [pop 490] was attacked by the Haganah. The villagers were expelled with some houses being destroyed. Leaflets were distributed warning residents not to return because the village had been mined. Being close to the town of Tiberias, this action demoralised the townspeople since they felt more isolated now that their route to the south had been severed.

British troops joined forces with the Haganah to break up an Arab contingent in Bab al Wad. British six-pounder artillery was sited in strategic positions in Jerusalem for use against sniper positions. Eight acres of orange grove, used to shelter the terrorists responsible for the Rehovoth atrocity, were uprooted by British troops.

A large Jewish convoy took 10 hours to complete a 45 mile journey to Jerusalem from Tel-Aviv due to battles with Arab forces.

The Jewish Agency reacted angrily to the previous day's statement from the Palestine Government. The US delegate to the Security Council indicated that the US favours the implementation of partition by "peaceful measures"only.

It was announced that certain mail services, international money order and insured services in Palestine were discontinued.

March 3

With the Haganah still active in the Tiberias area, the historic village of al 'Ubaydiyya [pop 870], identified as the ancient Canaanite town of Bayt Shamash (Joshua 19:22) felt increasingly isolated and vulnerable to Zionist attacks. The villagers were reported to have left for safety in the Nazareth area following the attack on al Manara the previous day.

Numerous clashes took place throughout Palestine, particularly at Safad, in the Galilee district, where Arab forces were on the offensive.In Jerusalem, a group of armed Arabs held up a police station in the Old City and escaped with 70 rifles and 10 000 rounds of ammunition.

On the Sharon Plain where there was a strong presence of Zionist colonies in the midst of a few Palestinian villages, whose residents had slowly abandoned or had been forced out of their homes, Arab forces withdrew after mortar attacks on a number of the colonies.

And, once again, the terrorist activities of the Stern Gang were at the forefront. This time in Haifa where they claimed responsibility for an army truck detonated in front of the Salem building. Eighteen Palestinian Arab deaths were reported with at least 40 others seriously wounded. Among the dead were two Palestine police constables and five women.The 400lb lorry bomb demolished a seven storey block of shops and flats when the Zionists, dressed as British soldiers, parked the lorry in front of the building. Until two days previously, the building had been used a military observation post, although Zionist sources alleged that it had been the regional HQ of Arab "terrorist" activities under the direction of Syrian and Iraqi officers and contained an ammunition dump.

Subsequent shooting resulted in the death of two Jews, one a five year old girl.

Six Arabs who were captured by the British while attacking a convoy in February appeared in court charged with carrying and discharging firearms. The six Syrians were given the option of a fine or imprisonment on both charges.

A Haganah radio broadcast laid the blame for the Ben Yehuda Street explosion on the British League of ex-Servicemen, which had issued a written statement claiming responsibility. The League was one of the

British fascist groups which joined Sir Oswald Mosely's Union Party at the beginning of the year.

L. Stein, president of the Anglo-Jewish Association, referred to the "heavy burden of guilt" that lay on the shoulders of the "murder gangs" and those who, although they may condemn terrorism, did nothing effective towards stamping it out. The measures proclaimed by the Jewish Agency failed to "arrest the succession of shameful events which had disgraced the Jews of Palestine and dishonoured the Jewish name."

In his address to the Association's council he referred to the "wild and incredible charges" made against Britain without a shred of evidence.[15]

The representatives of 11 Christian communities in the Holy land, representing about 150 000 Palestinian Christians issued a joint statement from the Old City of Jerusalem. It blamed the partition plan for the "lamentable situation in which the Holy Land, the cradle of peace, is now placed." It appealed to all those in power to revoke the plan.[16]

At the Security Council, Canada and China proposed that a last ditch effort should be made at conciliation between Arab and Jew before the Council talked of enforcement measures.

March 4

Numerous incidents were reported throughout Palestine.

A Haganah party (described in one report as a "punitive party") mining a road near Baytuniyah, seven miles northwest of Jerusalem, was engaged by armed passengers in an Arab bus, the intended target. The fighting attracted the attention of Arab forces in the area, resulting in the death of 17 Zionists and one British officer who tried to rescue one of the Zionists. Two were reported to have been taken prisoner.

An army convoy was attacked by Arab forces on the Ramallah-Latrun road. One soldier and two of the attackers were reported killed. In Haifa, Arab snipers killed one Jew and wounded an army officer who came to his aid.

Special correspondent, Clare Hollingworth, of The Scotsman reported on a visit to the heart of the hill country in Palestine where in the "Arab Triangle" formed by the towns of Nablus, Jenin and Tulkarm about 5 000 volunteer soldiers had encamped. The only large territory left in Palestine where "the Arabs can feel entirely safe from Jewish eyes."

In her previous visit to the area, six weeks earlier, she had been continually stopped at unauthorised check points by "ragged bands of self-appointed Arab guards brandishing a curious assortment of antique arms." All this had changed.

For the first time since the beginning of December she spent three days without hearing a single shot.The only soldiers to be seen were members of the official Arab guards - modelled on the British Home guard - and municipal police who were on duty at the approaches to towns and villages and at tracks leading to camps of the Arab Army of Liberation, known as the "volunteers". These were mainly drawn from Iraq, Syria and Transjordan.

Their organisation and discipline were observed to be "surprisingly excellent." There was a complete absence of "hooliganism" which marked the early days of partition conflict. Looting was reported to have been stopped.

There was no sign of hostility towards the British, only "utmost friendliness" was met. One of the first instructions issued to both the Arab Guards and the volunteers was "Protect Britishers and their property with your lives." It was obvious that the Arabs were keen for the date of British departure to arrive so that martial law could be proclaimed and hostilities commence.

An inkling of municipal concerns, no doubt repeated throughout Arab Palestine, was given in the report. The Mayor of Nablus, Suleiman Bey Toukan CBE, expressed concern over future finances. The total income in rates and taxes in Nablus, per month, was £6 000. The municipal hospital alone cost £4 000 per month to run. The Palestine Government had always subsidised health services, schools and purchases of seeds and grain.Where was the money to come from when the British departed? Particularly since Nablus' population had swollen from 25 000 to 30 000 with refugees from Jaffa and other threatened Arab towns - not to mention the "volunteers".

Evacuation plans for all British policemen were announced. The police will be evacuated by 21 May, their wives and children by 28 March.

March 5

Two Arab Liberation Army units of 360 volunteers arrived in Jaffa to aid resistance.

The Haganah attacked and captured the village of Biyar 'Adas [pop 300] in Jaffa district following an attack by the ALA on Migdal. The dawn attack resulted in the death of 15 Arabs with the villagers being expelled.

A light aircraft was used, for the first time, by Zionist forces to protect a convoy on theTel-Aviv Jerusalem road.One British soldier was killed and another wounded during an Arab attack on military transport on the Ramallah-Latrun road. Two Arabs were believed to have been killed.

A three hundred pound bomb, abandoned in a post office in the Jewish quarter of Haifa, was disposed off by the Royal Engineers.

March 6

The Haganah declared a general mobilisation of any Jews of military age in Palestine, including American citizens.

In a precursor of what was to come, with regard to Israel's respect for the authority of the United Nations, Dr Abba Silver, chairman of the American section of the Jewish Agency's Executive stated that the Agency fully respected the authority of the United Nations but reserved the right to take "all necessary measures" which, in the Agency's view, was merited by the situation.

Members of the UN Secretariat arrived in Jerusalem accompanied by an appeal from the High Commissioner, General Sir Alan Cunningham, for the safety of its members.There was little freedom for them to carry out their task, being housed in a "zone within a zone" and being unable to move about except within heavily armoured and guarded cars. The Arab Higher Executive commented that they had arrived at an "unfavourable moment".

In what, with hindsight, was a rather bizarre action, Jerusalem newspapers carried large advertisements for "immediate sale by tender", prior to their evacuation, several army camps and two airfields which had cost millions of pounds to construct. Situated within territory allocated to the proposed Arab state was Sarafand, the largest army base in the Middle East, and the two airfields. With the certainty that the financial situation of the Zionists, compared to that of the Arabs, would ensure future Jewish owners, it was on the cards that the sale would provoke further conflict.

A Syrian spokesman cited an official Arab source that the Arabs now controlled all of Eastern Palestine, from Safad to Hebron.

About 1 000 British troops and 500 policemen with their families departed from Haifa to Britain, following the evacuation announcement on 4 March.

March 7

The US Consulate-General in Jerusalem issued a verbal protest against the inclusion of Americans in the Haganah mobilisation scheme.

Five Haifa Palestinians, including a woman and two boys were killed by an explosion as they walked down from Jewish Hadar Hacarmel to the Arab quarter in lower Haifa.

It was reported that both Zionist and Arabs had reached an advanced stage of preparation for the impending conflict. The Zionist organisation seemed to be superior with a planned 80 000 people on full time duty including 20 000 for the "front line."

In contrast, there were no reliable figures for the Arab capability. Despite it being technically illegal for unauthorised people to carry arms, it was stated that thousands of Palestinians and Jews were being armed and trained. Arab shops were openly selling hand-grenades, rifles, revolvers and ammunition.

Reuters reported that the "Jewish Fighting Forces" - the Haganah and the terrorist Irgun and Stern Gang had reached "full agreement" for a united front against the Arabs. This gave an estimated combined front line strength of 40 000 men and women. This merger brought the right-wing Zionist Revisionist Party into the fold. It was now willing to take part in the Provisional Jewish Government for Palestine.

The entire Jewish owned diamond polishing industry of Palestine closed down. This was one of the industries on which Zionist economists based their hopes for the livliehood of a future Jewish state. Of the four official reasons two were an interesting reflection of the state of the prevailing situation in Palestine. The 2 500 workers in the 34 diamond cutting plants walked out as a result of "hold-ups by dissident underground organisations" and the theft of £200 000 worth of diamonds since 1944.

March 8

Zionist sources indicated that the discussions on a merger between the Haganah and the Irgun was, at present, unlikely to be successful. The stumbling block did not appear to be the acknowledged terrorist nature of the Irgun. The latter, apparently, were not prepared to accept complete subordination under the Haganah.

Three and half tons of arms were discovered at two secret dumps in Marseilles - all part of the French move to uncover arms supplies to Palestine. This followed the seizure of five tons of arms a few days earlier in Paris. This latter cache was believed to be destined for use by the terrorist Irgun with the French police satisfied that the arms came from Communist sources.

Britain informed the Palestine Commission that she would not allow any militia to be formed or equipped on Palestine soil before 15 May. Likewise stocks of arms would not be allowed prior to this date unless the Commission could guarantee the security of such stocks.

March 9

The Haganah issued a final call for Palestine Jews between the ages of 17 - 25 to register for active service. The Irgun described as "misleading" reports of a merger with the Haganah.

The 120 Britons, mostly from religious orders, who decided to stay in Jerusalem when the British depart started on their preparations to withstand a siege.

At a meeting of the Security Council the Russians made it clear that they opposed a US move to try and bring about conciliation in Palestine by further consultations. The Russians were of the opinion that the Security Council should enforce the partition plan adopted by the General Assembly.

March 10

Lydda railway station was set on fire by the Haganah.

Arab forces attacked Neve Ya'aqov on the Ramallah road, north of Jerusalem. One result of this particular clash was the detention by the police of three Britons in a police armoured car following a chase through the surrounding hill country. The three were thought to be "absentees" from the Palestine police (part of the 233 British deserters still at large since 1946). Investigators were of the opinion that the three deserters had joined forces with the Arabs in the hope of avenging the deaths of those comrades gunned down by the Zionist terrorists.

A further contingent of 2 500 British troops was evacuated from Palestine.

Plan Dalet was finalised by the Haganah.

Twenty nine Labour MPs and one Communist voted against the second reading of the Palestine Bill in parliament. The amendment, that it "failed to provide for the independence of Jewish and Arab States", was rejected. It was made clear during the debate that it was felt that the Palestine Commission might not be in a position to take up the reins of power on 15 May . The Security Council and the relevant UN bodies had yet to make suitable arrangements.

While Britain had up to 1 August to effect a complete withdrawal, British troops would only be taking action necessary to secure their own safety and departure from Palestine.

March 11

A car stolen from the US Consul-General in Jerusalem was parked in the courtyard adjacent to the Jewish Agency HQ, "the most carefully guarded Jewish estblishment in Palestine" by its Arab driver. It exploded, wrecking offices, killing 12 and injuring 106.

The offices included those of the Jewish National Council and the Jewish National Fund which "directs finances of colonisation schemes in Palestine". Among the dead was Leib Yaffa, 74, managing director of the JNF and one of the five living participants of the first Zionist conference held 50 years previously. Jewish Agency executive members were in Tel-Aviv and so escaped the blast.

It became clear that Jewish opinion had been shocked by the "Arab terrorist efficiency" in penetrating, and perpetrating such a devastating attack on, the Agency building. Those responsible had made their way through numerous road blocks, a ten foot high fence of coiled barbed wire - essentially an "exagerrated copy of the defences the British had erected round the King David Hotel" after it had been blown up by Zionist terrorists. The driver had walked into the building, then came out and climbed into a taxi which left the scene minutes before the blast.

A British soldier was killed and five seriouly wounded by Arab attackers. It was believed that they were in the vicinity of a Zionist convoy.

During this week the Haganah started a recruitment campaign for men aged between 26 and 35 years of age.

March 12

Arab gunmen hijacked Ethiopia's consular car at Damascus Gate.The Jewish Agency announced that all British military and police vehicles entering Jewish zones in Jerusalem must submit to being searched by "Jewish security squads". Consular cars and vehicles would be similarly treated, despite their status of diplomatic immunity. The British response was to compromise and accept this Zionist dictat.

Americans who, hitherto, had freedom to wander about the Jewish zones found themselves harassed with their cars being subject to rough scrutiny and search.

Haganah demolition squads were in action blowing up houses in the Jaffa suburb of Abu Kebir.

Arab forces attacked the Maccabi quarter on the Tel Aviv-Jaffa border with fire bombs and mortars.With 40 wooden houses ablaze, the Haganah launched a strong counter attack.

The Palmach's 3rd Brigade carried out an attack on the village of Al Huseiniya in Upper Galilee. Five houses were blown up.

Reports indicated that the executive of the Jewish Agency ratified an agreement - subject to approval of those members abroad - which brought the Haganah and the terrorist Irgun under a single command as a unified force. It was agreed that the two bodies would pool men and "war materials" with the Irgun reserving the right, with Haganah approval, to take individual action against the British forces "if necessary". British sources believed the Irgun to be as big as the Palmach, the commando "striking force".[17]

March 13

The Zionists continued to demolish houses in the Katamon area of Jerusalem. Twelve houses were blown up in the northern Galilee village of al Husayniyah [pop 340]. The early morning raid was carried out by 50 members of the Palmach's 3rd Battalion under the cover of heavy fire. Fifteen villagers were killed and 20 wounded before the Zionists withdrew.

There was widespread shooting in Jaffa.

A further 2 000 British troops and 200 civilians departed to Britain from Haifa.

March 14

The area near the village of al Husayniyah was placed under a seven day road curfew following yesterday's raid.

Zionist retaliatory actions, leading to the death of at least 60 Palestinian men, women and children by the end of the day was accompanied by news headlines such as "Jews Attack", "Haganah and Stern Gang in Action", "Many Arabs Killed"

Atrocities and incidents were reported from Safad in the north to Gaza in the south, combined with flare-ups in Jerusalem.With conflicting reports of deaths, a 24 hour battle raged around the colony of Gath near Gaza, with perhaps 37 Arabs and seven Zionists killed.

An attack on the village of 'Ayn Ghazal [pop 2 170] resulted in the demolition of four houses, the death of one Palestinian woman with five men wounded.

Under cover of a hailstorm and heavy supporting firepower, a Haganah squad carried out a night attack in the vicinity of Abu Kebir between Jaffa and Tel-Aviv. The five hour attack resulted in the demolition of 15 houses and the deaths of 20 Palestinians, including, it was believed, women and children. The squad then moved on to the Manieh quarter of Jaffa and blew up four houses.

At the village of al Faluja [pop 4 670] a Zionist supply convoy entered battle with the villagers. Three Jews and "scores" of Arabs were also wounded as the Haganah escorted convoy fought its way through the village.

Later in the day a Haganah demolition squad entered the village and blew up 10 houses including the three storey town hall and the post office.[Author's note: al Faluja held out until the Armistice agreement of 1949. The terms of the agreement were violated two months later when the villagers were coerced into leaving their homes and village.]

Zionist forces blew up a road bridge on the Haifa-Jenin road and repelled Arab forces attacking their supply convoy at Gaza.

It was reported that the British army was being increasingly drawn into the conflict in order to stop the open warfare between the Zionists and Arabs. The firing which "disturbs" Jerusalem every night was joined by the heavier noise Army "two pounders" and automatic fire. Shooting was increasingly in evidence in the Jewish Montefiore quarter of the city, and in a semi-circle which included Katamon where the Stern Gang, with members dressed as British soldiers, was blowing up the houses.

Slowly but surely this wealthy area of Palestinian owned Jerusalem was being razed to the ground.

With the rapprochement between the Haganah and the Irgun, it was reported that the latter had gained Jerusalem as its fief. It was observed that "military extremism", as a counter to Arab resistance, was in the ascendancy. The Stern Gang announced that they intended to start broadcasting in English.

Three former British constables, arrested the previous week in Arab dress while driving an unnumbered armoured car near Jerusalem, were put into an identity parade. Jewish witnesses of the Ben Yehuda Street explosion failed to identify them.

In contrast to the Zionist leadership which operated from within Palestine, it was observed that few members of the Arab Higher Executive were seen in Palestine. Further newspaper comment argued that the Arab side of the conflict, in organising mainly from abroad, gave the Palestine Government little opportunity to deal with them formally.

The Jewish Agency criticised Britain for "an unexpected dereliction of duty in allowing the violation of Palestine's frontiers." At the same time, Arab states were blamed for fomenting strife in Palestine "where the bulk of the Arab population has shown little disposition for conflict."

March 15

The Haganah demolished 14 houses and damaged 10 others in the villages of al Ghubayya and al Fawaqa, to the south east of Haifa. There were no casualties since the villagers had fled following attacks a few days earlier. The New York Times commented that "In what appears to be a new strategy: concentration on the destruction of property . . . the Haganah has in the last three days carried out five such 'punitive' operations."

The village of Wadi al Hawarith, to the north west of Tulkarm (whose ancestors, from the Haritha tribe, can trace their settlement in the area back to the 16th century) was "emptied".

Haganah reports indicate that this was "organised by the Arab leadership." Israeli historian, Benny Morris, found otherwise. He blamed it upon "a combined effect of physical and psychological warfare."[18]

A British constable was killed and two soldiers wounded when they investigated a suspicious light seen in a Jewish house in Haifa. The house was booby-trapped and blew up.

Diary entry for Sir Henry Gurney, Chief Secretary of the Palestine Government:

"On this wet and cheerless day in Jerusalem - it was snowing this morning - all is quiet, because in this weather both sides prefer to remain indoors. But the nightly battle begins regularly about 8 o' clock, and it continues sporadically till dawn. Two nights ago our windows were blown in by some monstrous explosions when some more Arab houses just outside the Zone were destroyed by Jews.

There is little sleep to be had .."[19]

However the UN team in Jerusalem continued to meet in a "sinister" vacuum. Together with the Consular Corps, plans for a neutral zone in the city were discussed.

Zionist sources complained that the British military were discriminating against the Jews, while overlooking alleged Arab illegal activities.

At the Security Council, where the idea of a truce was put to the warring parties, the representative of the Arab Higher Committee pointed out that tinkering with the detail of partition would produce no lasting benefit Peace in Palestine could be guaranteed only by the formation of one independent state for the whole of Palestine.

March 16

Palestinian irregulars blocked of the road to "Zionist colonies" in the Negev at the the village of Bureir in the Gaza district.

The Haganah filed a report on it actions at the village of al Husayniyya three days earlier, allegedly in retaliation for an earlier land mine incident. It claimed that, excluding women and children, more than 30 Arab adults had been killed with the village abandoned and the residents fleeing across the border. Other reports indicate that this was the second visitation, by the Palmach, in pursuit of "retaliatory" action.

The Irgun declared that they would spend the rest of their lives "hounding down" the sponsors of a suggestion made in the House of Commons that convicted Zionist terrorists should serve out the remainder of their sentences in other parts of the British Commonwealth once the Mandate comes to an end. Apparently the suggestion was regarded as "the most barbaric in British history."

Haganah radio alleged that former Nazis had involved themselves with various aspects of the Arab resistance movement in Palestine.

The Arab states indicated that they were prepared to support a truce as long as it was not used to further the partition of Palestine.

March 17

Haganah forces attacked an Arab convoy near the settlement of Kiryat Motzkin on the Acre-Haifa road when it attempted to force its way through a road block on its way to Haifa. The town's commander of its Arab forces, Mohammed bin Hammad al Huneiti, was killed. The assault on one of the lorries precipitated a massive explosion which killed ten Arabs and injured seven. Thirty Zionists were wounded as were two passing British soldiers.

This event seriously undermined the town's morale and was believed to the reason behind peace overtures from the Haifa Arab community two weeks later.

The last villagers from Jammasin, on the Sharon Plain, abandoned their village out of "general fear."

Arab forces carried out a morning attack on the colony of Ein Keshet near Nazareth.Two Jews were killed with the attackers suffering a number of casualties.

Hostilities took an ugly turn with religious and health institutions being implicated in the conflict. Arab reports spoke of a mosque at Qastel village, eight miles to the west of Jerusalem, being blown up by the Haganah. Several other buildings were demolished. Allegations were also made that the Jewish hospital and university on Mount Scopus in Jerusalem were being used for military purposes.

March 18

Palestinian irregulars attacked a Haganah convoy at the village of Artuf, near Latrun, west of Jerusalem. The deaths of at least eight Zionists were reported.

In Haifa a British soldier was shot dead and a British official of the Palestine railways seriously wounded by unknown gunmen operating in the same area.

Using light automatic weapons and heavy machine guns, an Arab force ambushed a Jewish car and its British escort when they hit a landmine on the road from Haifa to Acre.The soldiers were escorting employees from the Palestine Electric Company who were on their way to carry our repairs to army barracks. Five soldiers and three Jews were killed with no known Arab casualties. It took place at the site of the previous day's attack on the Arab convoy when a lorry with explosives blew up.

For the first time, arms were openly for sale in the Jewish areas of Jerusalem. The Jewish agency imposed a two percent "Defence Tax" on all purchases of consumer goods from Jewish traders throughout Palestine.

British trained Arab Legion troops of the Transjordan Army took over security control in two major all-Arab districts of Palestine "under the authority of the Arab League". These were the first troops of a neighbouring Arab state army to move into Palestine in their own uniform.

US President Truman had a secret meeting with Chaim Weizmann at the White House. He pledged support for a Jewish state on 15 May.

March 19

It was reported that the area to the north and east of Haifa continued to be "disturbed" with Zionist and Arab forces taking turns to ambush each other. Two Arab lorries were forced off the road to the north of Haifa with the thirteen occupants forced to leave the vehicles and line up at the side of the road. About 50 waiting Zionists then opened fire killing nine in cold blood, with only one escaping uninjured.

In Haifa itself, a British constable was shot dead trying to rescue the Jewish driver of an armoured truck caught under heavy fire. A police armoured car and an Army car eventually got the driver to safety. An employee of Cable and Wireless was wounded by a sniper as he entered the police HQ in Haifa. In lower Haifa the army blew up an unoccupied house which had earlier been booby-trapped, resulting in the death of a British policeman.

In the Beisan district five Jewish labourers were shot dead while working in a quarry. A variety of assaults on the Palestinian population in and around Tiberius and Safed, with loss of life, were reported.

Local villagers guided police to the site of ten dead Haganah combatants, part of a convoy which had been ambushed the previous day at the foot of the hills west of Jerusalem. The villagers indicated that "strangers" had carried out the attack.

In a complete reversal of its position on partition, US called upon the Security Council to suspend action on the planned partition of Palestine. A call was made for a special session of the General Assembly to work on trusteeship solution.

The announcement appeared to take everybody by surprise. There was "utter consternation" at the Jewish Agency with Ben Gurion declaring that a Jewish state is not dependent on the UN partition decision, but on Jewish Zionist military superiority.The Syrians articulated the position of the Arab States, declaring that at last the United States recognised that the U.N. had no power to partition any country.

The Russians were taken aback while American domestic reaction, at Congress level, created a storm of protest. Senator Klein's rhetoric reached a crescendo when he declared that the decision was the "most terrible sell-out of the common people since Munich."

March 20

An Israeli military intelligence report[20] made it clear that the coastal area near Tel Aviv, which had a heavy concentration of Zionist settlements and was seen as as the core of the planned "Jewish state", should be cleansed of its Arab residents. With increasing attacks on the area, villages were abandoned out of fear. Umm Khalid was one such village to suffer this fate. Famed for its watermelons, it was the site of the crusader Lombard Castle of Roger.

The Secretary-General of the Arab League stated that the Arabs would accept a truce and a limited trusteeship for Palestine if the Zionists would agree to do the same. Ben Gurion rejected Palestine trusteeship "even for the shortest time." He asserted that a Jewish state existed and would "find a way to live in friendship with the Arab peoples."[21]

March 21

Two Arabs dressed in European clothes drove a lorry loaded with explosives into a Haganah road block at the corner of Harbour Street, Haifa. The drivers abandoned the vehicle as it careered down the street before crashing into a lorry in this warehouse area, the busiest district in Haifa.Three minutes later, during which time the thronging crowds had melted away into side roads and alleys, the lorry exploded, creating an inferno in the car park. Six Jews were killed and 14 seriously wounded. Two warehouses were set on fire, a dozen buildings damaged together with wrecked cars and lorries.

Over the weekend the US government's decision against the implementation of the partition scheme provoked an angry response from Ben Gurion "America has surrendered to the terror of the Arab gangs who were armed by the British Foreign Office and who invaded Palestine under its auspices."[22]

Troops from the Highland Light Infantry were positioned with armoured cars and weapon carriers at strategic points in Jerusalem in reaction to the American statement, fearing Zionist attempts to carry out a putsch in the City.

The Executive of the Jewish Agency held an emergency meeting to consider the situation.The bitter denunciation of the American move was matched by a noticeable wave of pro-Russian sentiment. Dr Silver of the American section of the Jewish Agency said that if the Holy Land was to be administered as a UN Trusteeship, it would place the American Government in the "position of fighting Jews in Palestine."[22]

Meanwhile, from Beirut, Azzam Pasha the Secretary-General of the Arab League itemised terms for a truce acceptable to the Arab States. These included the disarmament of the Haganah, the deportation of terrorists, cessation of the immigration to Palestine of those elements destined for the Zionist fighting forces. The League would also cooperate in any solution designed to bring about a single Palestinian state based on the principles of democracy.

Settlers from Kfar Darom, near the Gaza Strip, were reported to be harvesting Arab wheat crops. This was the first documented case of such an incident. It ceased following attacks by Arab irregulars and eventual intervention by the British army who ordered both sides to halt their activities.

March 22

Haifa was the scene of further Zionist action, presumably in response to the bombing of the Jewish dock/warehouse area on Sunday. Police reports indicated that Zionists dressed in army uniform drove two 3-ton lorries loaded with explosives into Iraq Street, near the Arab market in the dock area. The drivers jumped into an accompanying jeep to escape the exploding lorries which devastated this densely populated part of Haifa.

While some paratroopers rushed up bulldozers to help the hundreds of Palestinian digging in the rubble, others manned armoured vehicles and, along with two-pounder guns, strived to keep Arab reaction under control.

The search took place by torchlight with the British being refused entry to the area for three hours. Five bodies were removed in the immediate aftermath. However, estimates put the number dead at 50, with 20 seriously injured.

While this was going on, a mortar fired from the Jewish sector of the city and aimed atthe police HQ in Haifa, killed two policemen. For the first time in this port town, a 25 pounder gun was used by the British against an attack on British forces.

Several hundred Arab fighters waged an attack against the settlement of Hartuv, west of Jerusalem. Further to the west, two Zionist armoured cars were disabled by a mine. The 16 occupants were surrounded and with reinforcements unable to get through, it was presumed they were killed. Reports indicated that Palestine was reminiscent of pioneer days with besieging forces attacking modern stockades throughout the country.

In Jerusalem the British residential security zone was increasingly in the line of fire from both sides. The Belgian Consulate was hit by a two inch shell. Two soldiers were killed and three wounded in the City. To the north, another was shot and seriously wounded while escorting a potash convoy. The Palestine Railways chief clerk died as a result of being shot in the head four days earlier.

The Haganah destroyed the village of Jebalya, near Jaffa.

The British foreign secretary, Ernest Bevin, placed proposals for Transjordan annexation of the West Bank, in place of Palestinian Arab statehood, before the British cabinet for approval.[23]

Throughout the day there was angry reaction to the American representative at the Security Council withdrawing US support for partition. A Stern Gang radio broadcast accused the Americans of "treachery".

March 23

Before dawn a task force of British infantry, tanks and 25 pounders was reported to have moved to the west from Jerusalem to take "punitive action" against a force of Arab fighters attacking the isolated colony of Har Tuv 13 miles from Jerusalem. By the time they arrived, the attackers had been forewarned and had disappeared. It was reported that 600 British troops moved into the neighbouring village of 'Artuf and two others but "almost all the villagers had been evacuated before the occupation."[23]

Zionist sources reported the deaths of nine Arabs during an attack on traffic on the Hebron- Beersheba area. A further 14 deaths were reported in clashes between Tel-Aviv and Haifa.

In Jerusalem, an explosion rocked the Jewish area of Yemen Moshe when a lorry was run into a Haganah post at the back of the King David Hotel, demolishing 30 to 40 small houses. The Haganah claimed that only 15 people were slightly wounded. However, one British soldier was killed by a ricochet bullet in the head.

In an attempt to ensure food supplies for at least two months licenses were issued to Jewish and Arab chambers of commerce for the import of certain foodstuffs.

March 24

Fighting between Arab and Zionist intensified. Arab guerrillas tightened their hold on two main roads linking Jerusalem to the rest of Palestine. A battle at the settlement of Neve Yaacob was stopped by a combination of forces under General MacMillan GOC Palestine and those of the Arab Legion under Brigadier John Glubb Pasha. Both arrived at the battle scene after the ambush of a Zionist convoy resulted in the death of 14 Zionists with 10 wounded. A temporary truce was enforced while jeeps transported the victims to hospital.

Earlier reports indicated a similar attack on a 60 vehicle convoy by 200 Arab guerrillas near Bab El Wad. The convoy was forced to stop when the first four heavy armour plated cars were mined. British gunners and infantry rushed to the scene with the assistance of a spotter plane flying overhead. With Arab sniper fire still holding up the convoy, it was reported that 12 Zionists were killed and 30 wounded.

In Jerusalem, on the road to Mount Scopus, a Jewish bus was mined resulting in 11 passengers killed. Arab mortar shells fell in the Jewish Yemen Moshe quarter of the city.

Two bombs were thrown at an Arab bus on the Nazareth road near Haifa, resulting in the death of two Palestinians with two seriously wounded. Five Palestinian labourers were shot dead and six seriously wounded when fired upon from the Zionist colony of Kiryat Motzkin. The chief clerk of the Egyptian Consulate was shot dead in Lower Haifa.

The Haganah destroyed the Bedouin hamlets near Yevniel, Tiberias.

The colony of Atarot, north of Jerusalem, was attacked by Palestinian guerrillas.

Three young British constables were found guilty of unauthorised carrying of firearms and ammunition for which they were sentenced to ten years in prison. A seven year sentence was to run concurrently for possession of an armoured car. They were found not guilty of firing at a Zionist colony. A Palestinian Arab temporary constable was sentenced to seven and three years in prison on related charges.

March 25

Battle-ready troops and a platoon of Bren-gun carriers were in action in Jerusalem during the night to prevent renewed Arab attacks on Yemin Moshe. Mortar and sniper fire had been directed onto the quarter following a lorry bomb in the same area two days ago.

The Jewish Agency requested of the Palestine Comission that Scandinavian forces stationed in N Germany be called upon to maintain law and order in Jerusalem. 10 000 Norwegian and Danish troops were envisaged after British withdrawal. The Agency alleged that the Arabs intended to seize the city and impose military rule. [Author's note: Keep in mind that Jerusalem had a separate status under the partition resolution, it was not to be part of the proposed Jewish or Arab state]

President Truman called for an immediate Arab-Jewish truce with the US sharing responsibility for a temporary trusteeship. Although "Trusteeship is not proposed as a substitute for the partition plan".[24]

March 26

A variety of scattered incidents took place throughout Palestine resulting in six Jews and four Arabs officially reported as killed.

Yosef Weitz, director of the Land Dept under the Jewish Agency, called for the expulsion of the villagers from Qumya on the Baysan-Haifa road because they were "not taking upon themselves the responsibility of preventing the infiltration of irregulars" . . . "They must be forced to leave their village until peace comes". According to Israeli historian, Benny Morris, most left on the same day, by coincidence. They were not according to Morris, ordered to leave by their Jewish and Zionist neighbours, but there may have been "friendly advice" to this affect.[25]

A citrus train was blown up by a mine at Ras el Ain near Tel-Aviv. The driver and the fireman, both Royal Engineers were injured.

The Haganah reported a five hour battle on the Haifa-Jordan Valley road when a convoy was attacked. Ten Arab deaths were reported. The settlement of Neve Yaacov was under attack again. However a minefield apparently brought about a retreat by the attackers.

Jewish police foiled a robbery attempt on a newly opened branch of Barclays Bank in Jaffa Road, Jerusalem, by up to 50 men. Arrests were reported.

A tacit truce was arranged between Arab and Jew in Jerusalem where Good Friday was observed by "Western Christians". Arab National Guards, armed with tommy guns, escorted a procession into the Old City past hundreds of armed men observing on the ground and from their sand-bagged positions on the City walls.

March 27

The village of Bayt Daras, north east of Gaza, suffered a mortar bombardment which left nine villagers dead, all non-combatants. Crops and livestock were burned. Two days later the village received another visitation from the Zionists.

"The Arabs feels as strongly about the freedom of his country as any American would if a Jewish State was proclaimed in New York, and is completely intransigent and wooden in the face of any argument or persuasion to recognise the hard facts.......Such is the conflict between Arab and Zionist.....the Arab knows the Zionist Jew a good deal better than most people. He has had the opportunity to see through all the propaganda and all the smokescreen, at the naked spectacle of Zionist aggression on his country as it really is. And it is this aggression that, in his view, the British have been helping and encouraging since the Balfour Declaration of 1917."

Sir Henry Gurney,Chief Secretary, Palestine 1946-48 Diary 27March 1948[26]

March 28

The carnage continued over Easter with the Zionist forces taking relatively heavy casualties - 58 killed and 44 wounded.

Two ambushes of convoys took place. The first began on the Saturday morning when a convoy of 40 trucks with a heavy Haganah escort made a surprise dash from Jerusalem to the isolated colony of Kfar Etzion, situated in the hills eight miles to the north of Hebron. The cargo of goods and munitions was delivered but ran into trouble on the return journey. Arab forces had piled the road rocks interspersed with mines at short intervals with hundreds of men waiting on the boulder strewn hillside a mile or so from Bethlehem near Solomon's Pools. Half the convoy returned to the settlement with the remainder besieged in a large stone house.

Throughout the day and night a Haganah relief force from Jerusalem tried to break through. A Zionist plane went into action dropping supplies to the defenders and bombs on top of the Arab guerrillas. A British task force was forced, initially, to turn back due to the blocked and mined roads.

Eventually armoured cars of the Light Guards and troops of the Suffolk Regiment arrived with two-pounder guns and took up positions but did not intervene.

Meanwhile, British HQ in Jerusalem had arranged a truce with Arab leaders. Under the protection of British troops and observed by hundreds of armed guerrilllas, 100 Haganah men and 10 women appeared from the house and, eventually, as part of the truce, handed their weapons to the British.

The second ambush took place at Kabri, seven miles north of Acre. Forty two bodies were found near five burnt out lorries. It was reported that a force of 250 Arab guerrillas armed with rifles, light machine guns and two-inch mortars carried out a sunset attack on six lorries and an armoured car escort. A British force sent to relieve the Zionists failed to reach them. British artillery then opened up with 12lb and 25lb high explosive shells to force an Arab withdrawal.

A reported 30 hour battle at Nebi Daniyal ended at 5o'clock in the morning. Zionist sources indicated 13 of their force dead with 50 wounded. A British report indicated Arabs dead with Bethlehem hospital full with Arab casualties.

In Jerusalem, during an exchange of fire between British forces and Zionist assailants, three Zionists, including a woman, were killed and two seriously injured. The British suffered one NCO dead, seven others wounded.

Mildred Marston, secretary of the Jerusalem Girls' College was shot dead by a sniper while on her way to attend Easter service in the City. An Arab sniper was responsible and the shooting stopped when a policeman arrived on the scene shouting that the victim was English. Apparently she had been thought to be Jewish and was shot at in retalation for the severe mortar bombardment the previous night.

A Jewish immigrant ship, *Yechiam*, with 800 illegal immigrants was intercepted by a British warship and escorted to Haifa.

Thirteen half-tracks (out of a consignment of 50) reached the Haganah from the US.

The Jewish response was given to proposals made by Richard Graves, chairman of the Jerusalem Municipal Council. The proposals were reported to have provided for a volunteer force from the countries having a direct religious interest in the Holy City - France, Italy, Greece and Britain. The response indicated opposition to the creation of zones under various religious leaders which may not be readily accessible to all those who wish to enter.

The Arab League stated that US President Truman's statements on temporary trusteeship instead of partition had altered nothing. The only difference was that Truman " now has two eyes instead of one."

March 29

The civil war in Palestine had become a "battle of the roads" with Arab guerrilla fighters trying to cut off the lines of communication linking Jerusalem and outlying colonies to the coastal plain around Tel-Aviv. The Arabs had clearly established themselves as effective in this respect.

Shortage of food and supplies was very much evident in the settler colonies.The 100 000 Jewish population of Jerusalem was reported to be suffering from a shortage of food, particularly meat. The Arabs held the view that by holding on to so many outlying colonies, the Zionists were exposing themselves to a war of attrition of the type Lawerence of Arabia taught them to use against the Turks. The Zionists, on the other hand, held the view that "The settlements are our Maltas in a sea of lawlessness, and the convoys will get through whatever our losses." [27]

The Palestine Government warned the Zionists that British security forces will no longer come to the aid of their convoys if they ignore British instructions and are attacked by Arab guerrillas. Apparently the convoy rescued from outside Bethlehem had failed to notify the authorities of its arrangements and, when they were advised of the heavily blocked road, had ignored the advice.

The Stern Gang claimed responsibility for the murder of a Czech woman who, they alleged, had been spying for British intelligence. Vera Ducas, aged 36, wife of a Jew, had been kidnapped from a cafe in the Jewish part of Jerusalem, tried by a "military tribunal", and found guilty. She was found dead on a piece of waste ground, shot through the head.

In Jerusalem, British troops and Palestine police acted as armed escorts for the various religious dignitaries processing to the Church of the Holy Sepulchre. The setting was incongruous. Mediaeval robed priests escorted by tommy gun wielding Scottish soldiers of the Highland Light Infantry and police. As the sparse congregation of about 200 knelt in prayer, the thud of mortar fire and crack of rifle fire could be heard in close proximity.

Clare Hollingworth, The Scotsman Correspondent, reported on a memorable scene:

"In the courtyard of the Church of the Holy Sepulchre I saw a small undecided crowd of young Christian Arabs. They were obviously debating an important decision. As I drew near I heard one young man say, as he pushed a prayer book into his pocket 'Well, we toss up, heads we go to church, tails we go to Bethlehem to watch the battle.'

Tails it was, and they streamed off to join the long procession of cars taking the flower-bordered road to Christ's birthplace, there to watch from the safety of the rooftops some 500 jubilant Arabs attacking a Haganah party which had been besieged in a little stone house in the valley a mile or so away for nearly 24 hours."

Two British officers were released after being held captive by Zionist forces for nearly 24 hours. Their army scout car was stolen. A British police sergeant was killed and three soldiers seriously wounded by Arab snipers in Haifa. Seven Zionists were killed when their armoured car was blown up during an attack on the Arab village of al Maghar, near Lydda. The military blew up a house in Haifa alleged to have been used as a sniper post. Mortar duels between Tel-Aviv and Jaffa were renewed during the night. On the Haifa Tel-Aviv road an armed party of 20 Zionists seized two army lorries containing flour. The uniforms, weapons and equipment of the five escorting soldiers were taken. Four more Zionist bodies were recovered from Kabri, bringing the death toll to 46. Mortar bombs fell near the Freres school and the Greek Orthodox School in Jaffa. There were no reported casualties.

A group of 737 illegal Jewish immigrants left Haifa for Cyprus after their schooner had been intercepted by a British destroyer.

March 30

Zionist gunmen shot dead British social worker, Mrs Thompson, a well known resident of Jerusalem. According to one observer, when her car was forced to stop by a group of men she shouted in loud voice that she was British. This was followed by a burst of fire which riddled the car. She had been visiting the Arab hospital in Beit Safafa and had being saying farewells before departing the country.

Four British and one German prisoner escaped from Acre prison. The British were three British police constables and a civilian. The latter was believed to be Henry Dickson who was serving a sentence for trying to induce British soldiers to sell their arms to the Palestinians.

The diary of Palestinian teacher and writer, Khalil Sakakini, provided an insight to the fear experienced by the residents in the Jerusalem suburb of Qatamon. The entry, for this day, in his diary read

"The Jews launched a heavy attack on our neighbourhood . . . last night . . There were explosions the likes of which were never seen. [Lord] Kitchener, in all of his battles, did not hear what we heard tonight . . . The constant whistle of bullets and thunder of shells. . . What was most distressing and nerve-wracking was the anxiety which has overcome the women and children. . . Many residents of our neighbourhood have left for the Old City or Beit Jala, Amman and Egypt."[28]

During the search of Athlit detention camp near Haifa, a large amount of police clothing, badges, pistols and ammunition was found .Three detainees were found to be missing.

Reports indicated that the "battle of the convoys" was having deepening effect on the food situation in the Jewish areas of Jerusalem. For five days not one convoy had reached the City. It was reported that the Zionists had suffered far heavier casualties in men and vehicles than they were ready, publicly, to admit. There was a wave of dissatisfaction washing over the Jewish community.

The possibility of a truce was mooted with a senior member of the Jewish Agency who commented "Of course we are ready to negotiate a truce. We don't want the war to continue and we don't want to see the country laid to waste - whether it is ours or the Arabs."[29]

The “intransigence” of the Palestine Arab leaders and the Arab Higher Committee over the matter of a truce was compared with the favourable stance of the Arab League, with the latter having any final say. Apparently the American Diplomatic Corp in the Middle East , having discussed the possibility with Arab and Zionist leaders, was the prime mover in this attempt at halting hostilities.

The US delegate to the Security Council presented a resolution calling for a truce to be arranged between the Jewish Agency and the Arab Higher Committee. The Russians rejected the recent U.S. call for temporary trusteeship of Palestine, stating that with the partition of the country, independent Jewish and Arab States was a just solution.

March 31

The Cairo-Haifa train was mined in the vicinity of the Jewish colony of Benyamina, near Caesarea, by terrorists who detonated the mine from the vicinity of a nearby orange grove. Forty persons were killed, and 60 injured - mainly Arabs - when the engine and the first four carriages were blasted off the line. The injured were taken in a military convoy to hospital. More than 30 soldiers on board escaped injury.

Zionist sources claimed that the Stern Gang was responsible, with many of those killed alleged to be members of the Arab Liberation Army.

The railway company announced that the service on the line would be cut to three time weekly in each direction. The military authorities imposed a road curfew on all Jewish vehicles in the area between Lydda and Haifa. Meanwhile Arab sources reported a heavy Arab attack on the large Jewish settlement of Hadera, about eight miles from the scene of the wrecked train.

Palestinian guerrillas ambushed a Haganah food convoy at the village of Hulda (other reports said Hartuv), near Ramleh. An Arab source claimed “many Jews have been killed and wounded.” It was the first attempt to run the Arab blockade for about a week.

The Haganah completed the demolition of Abu Kebir village, near Jaffa.

Liason officials from the Jewish Agency held talks with the Palestine Government to agree to terms for the protection by British troops of food convoys from Tel-Aviv to Jerusalem. The Zionists were told that they must accept certain conditions including obedience to Government orders on movements, limitation on numbers of vehicles in each convoy and agreement that armed Haganah units should not travel with the convoys.

The Government also renewed its request that armed Haganah units be withdrawn from the Jewish quarter of the Old City. The Jewish Agency was also asked to remove Irgun terrorist squads from the Old City. It was felt that the presence of these elements made it harder to arrange a truce in the Old City.

It was reported that the American move for a truce in Palestine was the last hope that order in the country would be maintained once the British left. The worst was apparently accepted and efforts were now to be concentrated on the problem as to whether Jerusalem could be preserved. The Jews were largely in the north and the west of the City, the newer part, while the Arabs remained in possession of the south. The two communities meet on the way to Mount Scopus leading to the Mount of Olives, or in the west, in upper Katamon - a no-mans land ruled by snipers.

There were pockets of the Jewish community in Mekor Haim - essentially a Haganah outpost - and in Yemin Moshe south of the King David Hotel.

There were reports from New York that about 2 500 men had been recruited by the American League for Free Palestine to fight for a "Jewish State". Recruitment was organised by a Major Weiser of the Hebrew Legion of England. State Department officials said that passports would not be issued to Americans seeking to fight in Palestine.

During March it was reported that 271 Jews, 256 Arabs, 14 British soldiers and four British constables were killed with 352 serious injuries.

It was reported that Palestinian passport holders - both Arab and Jew - were being refused visas to enter Cyprus unless it was a return visa. This arose from the uncertainty of the precise status of Palestinians after Britain abandoned the mandate on 15 May and would not be responsible for issuing passports after that date. Cyprus was, apparently, a favourite holiday destination was Palestinian families. The tourist industry in Cyprus was expected to be badly affected.

Notes

1 Michael Palumbo, *The Palestinian Catastrophe*, p.127
2 Norman Finkelstein, *Myths, Old and New*, (Journal of Pal. Studies, Autumn 1991), p.77
3 Walid Khalidi, *Plan Dalet*, (JoPS 1987) p.20-21
4 Nur Masalha, (JoPS Autumn 1988) p.177
5 Khalidi, p.16
6 Finkelstein, p.70

7 Khalidi, p.25
8 Khalidi, p.14
9 AJ Sherman, *Mandate Days*, p.219
10 Benny Morris, *The birth of the Palestinian refugee problem, 1947-1949*, p.44
11 The Scotsman 1/3/48
12 Henry Cattan, *Palestine, the Arabs and Israel*, p.224
13 The Times 2/3/48
14 The Scotsman 2/3/48
15 The Times 3/3/48
16 The Scotsman 4/3/48
17 The Times 13/3/48
18 Walid Khalidi, *All that Remains*, p.565
19 Sherman, p.220
20 Khalidi, p.566
21 The Scotsman 20/3/48
22 *ibid*, 22/3/48
23 Khalidi, p.268
24 Cattan, p.227
25 Khalidi, p.57
26 Sherman, p.224
27 The Scotsman 30/3/48
28 Morris, p.51
29 The Scotsman 31/3/48

April

There were twenty five people, twenty four were killed and only one could escape through a window. . . In another house they captured a boy who was holding the knee of his mother. They slaughtered her in front of him.

Mohammed Aref Sammour, witness of massacre at Deir Yassin

For those who long believed that Zionism was an ideology and practice worthy of admiration this was the month that doubts should have emerged. For the readers of the odd comment or two made by Zionists with a conscience, this was the month that flesh was put on these comments.

> "But while local Arab leaders 'want peace . . . and showed great maturity . . . the people responsible [Haganah commanders] do not understand the seriousness of the situation . . I fear that it will be Jews who will cause the outbreak in Tiberias'
>
> 'The aggressive spirit among Tiberias's Jews will bring about disaster . . Our people continue irresponsible actions..' The Sephardi Jews, in particular, with their 'boastful' talk, badly hurt the Arabs, who 'only want peace'."
>
> 'Heading the security [forces, that is, the Haganah in Eastern Galilee] were young men who had contempt for death and had in their heads only military thoughts and plans . . .They laugh at the need to maintain [good] relations with Arab neighbours . . . They believe simply that there is a need to win using all means then matters will sort themselves out . . .'
>
> *Diary of Yosef Nahmani, Director of JNF office in Eastern Galilee*[1]

One observer, Ya'ari, lamented

> "..the youth we nurtured in the Palmah [elite strike force], including kibbutz members have [occasionally] turned Arabs into slaves; they shoot defenceless Arab men and women, not in battle . . Is it permissible to kill prisoners of war? I hoped that there would be some who would rebel and disobey [orders] to kill and would stand trial - and not one appeared . . . They are not against transfer. What does it mean . . . to empty all the villages? . . What did we labour for . . ?[2]

> "If Rabbi Kaplan really wanted to know what happened, we old Jewish settlers in Palestine who witnessed the fight could tell him how and in what manner we, Jews, forced the Arabs to leave cities and villages . . some of them were driven out by force of arms; others were made to leave

by deceit, lying and false promises. It is enough to cite the cities of Jaffa, Lydda, Ramleh, Beersheba, Acre from among numberless others."

Nathan Chofshi *(Jewish Newsletter, New York, 9/2/59)*
in a rebuttal of charges that Palestinians were ordered to leave by their own leadership[3]

"We came and turned the native Arab into tragic refugees. And still we dare to slander and malign them, to besmirch their name. Instead of being deeply ashamed of what we did and trying to undo some of the evil we committed . . we justify our terrible acts and even attempt to glorify them."

Nathan Chofshi [4]

For those readers of accounts of Zionist arrogance and disregard for the lives and sufferings of others, this was the month that shocked. For those Palestinians who hoped that their land would not be turned over to strangers, this was the month of reckoning.

This was the month that demonstrated, and continues to demonstrate, that terrorism does pay dividends. It was the month that the tactic of targeting the civilian population in their villages started to produce results.

" . . . .but the Jews were at the same time developing another tactic which, as we now know, made a far greater impact on the Arab population of Palestine. Small groups of the Palmach, ten or fifteen strong, were repeating the tactics which General Orde Wingate had taught them ten years earlier during the Arab rebellion.

Marching at night, they penetrated to Arab villages far in the heart of Arab-held territory. Occasionally they blew up a house occupied by an active Arab nationalist or by foreign Arab volunteers; in other villages they confiscated arms or plastered the village with warning notices. The effects of such nightly visitations soon made themselves felt throughout the Arab hinterland. They caused great disturbances and started an exodus from the areas lying near to Jewish districts. The Arabs began to feel unsafe, and as the Liberation forces added to their quota of failure, the Arab flight from the coastal areas began to assume a general character."[5]

It was the month that was to put the words "Deir Yassin" on the lips of every Palestinian.

The massacre at Deir Yassin had a traumatic effect on the Palestinian Arabs who, increasingly, felt insecure in their own homes, on their own land. It was an insecurity which the Zionists were only too ready to exploit.

> "Lately, ever since the massacre at Dayr Yassin, we have been thinking seriously of leaving Jerusalem. The most terrible stories have been reached from eyewitnesses who have escaped from this unbelievable massacre . . . One day, perhaps very soon, we may be forced to leave our house.
>
> Nathan Krystall, *The De-Arabisation of West Jerusalem 1947-50* (JoPS, Winter 1998) p.10

For the survivors of the Deir Yassin atrocity the trauma of that day still lives with them. Radio 4's series "Your land is my land", broadcast during February 1998, interviewed survivors who remembered the massacre as if it were yesterday. In one case 30 members of an extended family were wiped out by bloodthirsty Zionist terrorists.

By the middle of April the use of mortars and barrel bombs to terrorise and convince the civilian population that they should flee and hence avoid their own "Deir Yassin" came to the fore.

There was the Davidka, a drainpipe mortar which made a lot of noise and propelled 60lbs of TNT about 300 yards. The fact that it was not particularly accurate was of little consequence. Aimed in the general direction of densely populated Arab areas, the desired effect was usually achieved.

The barrel bomb consisted of a barrel, cask or metal drum, filled with a mixture of explosive and petrol, and fitted with two old tyres containing a detonating fuse. It was ideal for rolling down the sharply sloping alleys and stepped lanes of Arab urban areas until it crashed into walls and doorways making "an inferno of raging flames and endless explosions." [6]

In addition to the above, Zionist forces resorted to the "ruthless dynamiting of block after block of bazaars and blind alleys until the panic had reached sufficient dimensions to end all resistance." One Haifa policeman recalled the effect of such attacks on Arab civilians. He remembered seeing "people running through the streets unconsciously . . . . People could not bear this shelling for more than three continuous days."[7]

At this juncture, the looting of abandoned Palestinian homes became a fine art. Practised by not a few Haganah regular troops and Irgun terrorists. It was a practice which was soon to be legitimised by Israel's Law of Absentee Property *et al.*

> "The Irgun activities in Jaffa also extended to yet another field. For the first time in the still undeclared war a Jewish force commenced to loot in a wholesale fashion. At first the young Irgunists pillaged only dresses, blouses and ornaments for their girl friends. But this discrimination was soon abandoned. Everthing that was movable was carried from Jaffa -

furniture, carpets, pictures, crockery, pottery, jewellery and cutlery. The occupied parts of Jaffa were stripped, and yet another tradional military characteristic raised its ugly head. What could not be taken away was smashed. Windows, pianos, fittings and lamps went in an orgy of destruction.

It was perhaps natural, though it was certainly detestable, that before long the rest of the Jewish soldiers of the Haganah and the Palmach should join in the orgy of looting and wanton destruction which hangs like a black pall over almost all Jewish military successes. It could have been stopped by firm action at the outset. But it soon became a practice for which there was always a material incentive, a sophisticated justification, and an excuse."[8]

Yosef Nahmani director of the Jewish National Fund in Eastern Galilee from 1935 until his death 30 years later recorded his view of events following the occupation of Tiberias. Within hours of the Arabs' departure "the Jewish mob descended upon [the evacuated Arab area] and began to pillage the shops . ." The looting continued with Haganah contingents taking the lead, followed by the townspeople "old people and women, regardless of age." "Shame covers my face and [I] would like to spit on the city and leave it."[9]

April 1

Shortly after midnight two platoons of the Giv'ati Brigade's 2nd Battalion entered the village of Abu Shusha [pop. 870] south of Ramleh after a guard at the nearby settlement of Gezer had been shot dead while tresspassing on village fields. One house and the village well were blown up. Nearby Arab forces converged on the village, with one Zionist being killed. The Haganah described the attack as "the model of a studied retaliatory operation."

As this attack was being carried out, Ben Gurion and the Haganah General Staff decided to launch Operation Nachshon. The aim was to overrun villages on both sides of the road from Tel-Aviv to Jerusalem. A combined force of 1 500 Haganah and Palmach troops was mobilized for this purpose.

Israeli historian, Benny Morris, described the Operation as "a watershed, characterised by an intention and effort to clear a whole area permanently, of Arab villages and hostile or potentially hostile villagers". He commented that most villagers fled for safety either before or during the offensives on their village. "Expulsion orders" were not necessary. All villages were demolished and levelled shortly after their occupation.[10]

Zionist sources reported that 17 of their fighters were killed along with five Arabs when a food convoy, trying to relieve Jews and Zionists blockaded in Jerusalem, failed in a second attempt to burst through Arab road blocks and mines south of Lydda. The 60 vehicle convoy, which had already lost a number of vehicles, was stuck in "ambush alley" between Khulda and Latrun.

Five armoured vehicles were captured, others destroyed. The loss of the vehicles and the failure of the convoy to get through put the Zionists in a serious situation. At least 50 lorry loads per week were needed to keep the Jewish population of Jerusalem in supplies.

The village of Jaramla, whose residents began to leave during February, finally abandoned their village out of "general fear."

The Montefiore quarter of Jerusalem witnessed its heaviest fighting yet with machine-guns, grenades and artillery fire in action under flare-lit skies. The British fired at least a dozen artillery shells into the battle zone in an effort to break up the fight.

Britain's High Commissioner visited the heart of the "Arab Triangle" - Nablus, Tulkarm and Jenin - which, together with a strong concentration of Arab forces, was virtually under Arab control. Reduction in army personnel gave the British administration a nominal role.

The Security Council voted to call a special session of the General Assembly. It agreed to the US truce proposal of 30 March.

Two consignments of arms arrived in Palestine for use by Zionist forces. These were the first instalment of a Czech Arms Deal.The *Nora*, carrying 4 500 rifles and 5 million rounds of ammunition arrived in Haifa from Split, Yugoslavia. At the same time 200 rifles, 40 machine guns and more ammunition arrived by plane at a Haganah airfield.

The official casualty list for March was announced. There were 566 dead and 1038 injured - the highest total for one month since November.

April 2

In an interesting article on the position of Jewish citizens in neighbouring Arab states, The Scotsman's special correspondent, Clare Hollingworth, reported on the considerable body of anti-Zionism which had emerged in these communities.

"To a large proportion of Middle Eastern Jews the advance made by Zionism, the decision to partition Palestine, and the steps Zionists have made to build up a Jewish State have meant only that their own position, secure for tens if not hundreds of years, have been imperilled. There may be a minority who would like to move into a Jewish State; the majority were perfectly content in the countries of their adoption."

A warning was given to those Britons, whose presence was non-essential, to leave Jerusalem before 15 May since the Government expected "serious trouble" in the city. About 120 British civilians expressed a wish to remain in the city.

The decision by the UN Security Council to call for a truce and hold a special meeting of the General Assembly produced no change in the situation in Palestine. Guns were still firing throughout the country. Decisions in New York were seen to be out of touch with reality and far removed from grim reality.

The Arab reaction was that there could be no cease fire unless the partition scheme was dropped. In direct opposition, the Zionists argued that there could be no truce if the scheme was abandoned. The question of the day was how the Security Council could impose heavy penalties on those who ignored any cease fire order. With the reduction of British strength, there was no international force to enforce compliance.

An Arab spokesman, in Damascus, said that Jerusalem would not be attacked but would be "strangled" by a blockade, "the city itself will not be occupied."

Further fighting was reported as the 60 vehicle convoy trapped at Bab el Wad tried, again, to break out. Haganah sources reported 70 Arab deaths for 20 of their own men killed.

In Jerusalem, armed Zionists held up two Army lorries carrying 300 sacks of flour. They stole two Sten guns and two rifles before making off in the lorry. It was reported that the city's 100 000 Jews were facing slow starvation, with the few lorries reaching the city being unloaded to supply hospitals and nursing homes. The view was that the crisis was not between Jew and Arab, but Jew and Jew. The Jewish Agency was berated for not anticipating that the city - in the heart of Arab-held territory - could be blockaded by an enemy whom, they had been told, was "unorganised, ill-equipped and savage". The Agency's position on the truce was attacked time and time again. The talk in Jerusalem was about the truce, prayers for a truce were said and if the Jewish Agency still resisted negotiations, there was talk of a rebellion by the Jewish community in the city.[11]

April 3

The Haganah captured the village of Castel and nearby quarries, four miles west of Jerusalem. The residents of Castel were expelled. This took place after a dawn attack by Palmach commandoes followed by the main force which fought off counter-attacks.Fifty defenders were forced to withdraw when their ammunition ran out.

It was thought that this might be the first in a series of operations by the Zionists to establish bases linking the coastal area to Jerusalem and hence break the Arab blockade.

The village of Suba, west of Jerusalem, was attacked by the Haganah. Despite aerial support they failed to capture the village (which resisted occupation until 12 July). The villagers of Ijlil, to the north of Jaffa, fled in fear of Zionist attacks. Arab fighters were alleged to have urged them to flee, perhaps for their own safety, since by this time the area between Tel-Aviv and Hertzeliyya had been "cleansed" of its Palestinian inhabitants.

April 4

Plan Dalet was initiated.

The High Commissioner, Sir Alan Cunningham, broadcast an appeal to both sides to honour the truce called for by the Security Council. However the stance of the protagonists remained unaltered. It was quite clear that the address was merely a polite appeal to the combatants. The power of enforcement lay outwith the scope of the British, no retribution could be threatened. And, the sound of gunfire throughout Jerusalem, after the appeal, gave clear indication that the odds were against a ceasefire.

The Arab Liberation Army using armoured vehicles and artillery, attacked the Zionist settlement of Mishmar Haemeq, southeast of Haifa in what was described as the "greatest pitched battle yet fought in four and a half months of fighting in Palestine." They, however, failed in their objective. Three settlers were killed and nine injured.

The Stern Gang announced responsibility for blowing up, systematically, 30 houses in the village of Biyar 'Adas [pop 300], north east of Jaffa. The presence of sandbags round the houses gave the terrorists the pretext for blowing up the entire village, claiming that they were military objectives. The New York Times, however, reported that the Haganah had concluded a truce agreement in the area and that the attackers met no resistance as the villagers had fled.

Haim Bar-Lev, company commander in the northern Negev reported on an efficient method of dealing with the Bedouin. This resulted from retaliatory action following a mine attack on a Zionist patrol in the Shahut area. Two Palmach armoured cars destroyed nine Bedouin "lay-bys" and one mud hut " . . by a blow from an armoured car going backwards . ."

Arab forces looted a cement factory close to the settlement of Artue. Damage at an estimated £150 000 was reported.

Following the appearance of Zionist aircraft, an order was issued prohibiting civil aircraft from flying within 5 miles of Haifa aiport, unless landing. It followed similar restrictions over Jerusalem and other towns.

A group of Irgun, mounted on horses and donkeys, stole 1 000 head of cattle from the village of Samaria. Haganah units later recovered about 100 and returned them to the village.

Hundreds of Palestinian children, Muslim and Christian, from Haifa - under the age of 12 years - were to be evacuated to the safety of Syria and Lebanon.

Jamal Husseini, President of the Arab Higher Committee, was refused entry to Britain when he landed at London Airport on his way to New York. He had no visa. However his stop was unscheduled. He had received late instructions from the Grand Mufti to protest to the British Cabinet over the sale of air strips and military camps in Palestine, which were Arab property.

April 5

The villages of Bayt Lid [pop. 720] and Ghabat Kafr Sur [pop. 740], both near Tulkarm, were evacuated by their residents "out of fear and alarm", being situated to the east of the Zionist colony of Netanya between Tel Aviv and Zikhron Ya'aqor. The villages had already been targeted by Plan Dalet for occupation by the Alexandroni Brigade. The Haganah General Staff had decided to "clear" the area of Arabs before 15 May.

April 6

The Haganah captured the villages of Khulda and Deir Muheisin, near Ramleh, twenty miles west of Jerusalem. This was carried out under the first phase of Plan Dalet, Operation Nachshon. The Palestinian counter-attack failed to recover the village.

Meanwhile Arab forces counter-attacked the village of Castel and the quarries, captured by Zionist forces days earlier. The area echoed to mortar and machine gun fire as the Zionist convoy of 42 heavy lorries, 19 armoured cars and steel plate tenders manoeuvred past on their way to relieve the Jewish area of Jerusalem. The first food convoy in two weeks.The British also brought "4 long trains" of supplies into the city, including oil and petrol.

An attack, carried out by the Irgun according to Zionist sources, on the army camp of Pardres Hana between Tel Aviv and Haifa resulted in the death of the Commanding Officer and six soldiers of other ranks in the Anti-Tank Regiment and Royal Artillery.

The Zionists dressed as British police and driving two armoured cars and a saloon car, burst into the camp as they were packing, prior to loading evacuation lorries. They raced round the camp blazing at the soldiers with machine guns. A sentry was forced into a guardroom, lined up against a wall with three other soldiers and shot dead in the back, according to the official report. A signals clerk was held up and the radio mast blown up.

This followed a "ceasefire" agreement between the Irgun and the Haganah whereby they agreed to stop attacks on the British.

The terrorists escaped with a quantity of arms - 62 rifles, 8 Sten guns, 18 Bren guns and 4 anti-tank missiles. They fled in the direction of Pardes Hana settlement. Four armed Zionists were later arrested in the area, but there was nothing to implicate them in the attack.

To the north of this area, three night attacks were made on the railway. A goods train was derailed, along with the breakdown engine. It was felt that the attack was an attempt to disrupt Army communications as it withdrew northwards.

Arab forces attacked the village of Lahavot and Habashan while a number of clashes occurred on the western edge of Jerusalem. Arab forces agreed to a British brokered 24 hour cease fire at Mishmar Haemek, at the request of the colony's residents. The Haganah broke the ceasefire and counter-attacked extensively, occupying and destroying surrounding villages.

The village of 'Awlaam [pop 740], south of Tiberius, was claimed to be "emptied" of its residents because, according to Israeli military intelligence, the Arab Higher Committee ordered them to go. The fear that they would collaborate with the Zionists was cited as the reason. This version was contradicted by the History of the Haganah. It was claimed that the villagers "fled in fear of the Jews" when units of the Golani Brigade entered on 12 May.[12]

The village of Hadatha [pop 520], southwest of Tiberius, and three others suffered the same contradictory fate as 'Awlaam. With this attack "the Lower Galilee was empty of Arabs".

The villagers of Saydon [pop 210], south of Ramleh, lay to the western entrance to the Jerusalem corridor. It, together with two other villages, was captured with the residents fleeing for safety.

A house in Amman, occupied by the commander of the Arab Legion, Glubb Pasha, was damaged during a botched attempt to blow it up.

April 7

The Zionists used training planes to drop bombs on the Palestinian forces surrounding the village of Castel. The Haganah announced that 20 Arabs had been killed in an "engagement" near Mount Canaan outside Safad.

The Jewish Agency claimed that the truce appeals were "phoney". The Agency alleged that there was a conspiracy of silence over the armed intervention from bordering Arab states which had been "carefully and deliberately" glossed over by the US and the High Commissioner for Palestine.

Britain informed the Palestine Commission that she would be unable to supply food after 15 May, the end of the Mandate. The Commission decided to present a special report on the food situation to the Security Council.

April 8

Four thousand Arab fighters stormed, and recaptured, Castel village on the slopes of Mount Castel, held by the Haganah for five days. During the assault, the guerrilla leader (described in one report as the Chief of the Palestinian National Guard and Commander of the Jerusalem district) Abdul Kader Husseini, was killed. Husseini, cousin of the Mufti of Jerusalem was reported to have been blown up when he entered a booby-trapped house. Other reports said that he had been killed while storming a house and the retreating Zionists had decapitated him.

When Zionist planes failed to break the onslaught, British forces turned up to evacuate the Haganah men who were pursued by the Arab guerrillas to the village of Motza where further heavy fighting took place.

However, at night, Palmach forces re-occupied the village of Castel when they found that it had been deserted. Most of the men were at the funeral of their commander, taking place the next day at the Haram al Sharif in Jerusalem.

All houses including the mosque were demolished.

The Haganah started an offensive against Tiberias. Troops, reported to be Syrian, attacked Lahavot Habashan.

The Zionists besieged in the settlement of Mishmar Haemek, which had suffered sporadic shelling for the past three days, rejected surrender terms from the Arabs. Fawzi Kauwkji, the commander, ordered his field artillery to renew the bombardment.

The Scotsman's special correspondent, Clare Hollingworth, met with Kauwkji during this period. She came across two groups of men. One group consisted of five Jewish prisoners, destined for certain death. They had been accused of spying for the Haganah.

The other group was composed of eight British deserters, serving with Fawzi's army. When asked why they had joined. The reply from one was interesting "Why I joined goes for all of us. We like the adventurous life; we like the Arabs; and we dislike the Jews. We got tired of being shot in the back and of having our friends murdered. I was in a Haifa cafe when the Irgun gang threw a bomb and killed four of my mates. That is why I joined."

Following the engagement at Mishmar Haemek, units of the Haganah and the Palmach attacked a further three villages in the locality Abu Shusha, Abu Zurayq and al Naghnaghiyya [total pop 2 400]. A spokes man for the Jewish National Fund stated that their army was steadily conquering Arab villages with the inhabitants "afraid and fleeing like mice." [13]

The Haganah, mainly Palmach units, started to blow up and level to the ground villages in the vicinity of Mishmar Ha'emek. In this task they were assisted by local settlers. The first to be blown up was Ghubaiya al Tahta, then its sister village Ghubaiya al Fauqa. These were followed by Khirbet Beit Ras and Abu Shusha.

In Jerusalem, the Jewish community took steps to lay in reserves of water following a broadcast that fuel shortages could interrupt supplies. With Solomon's Pool, Jerusalem's main water reserve in normal summer droughts, being in the hands of the Arab community and outlying villages having their own centuries old wells, it was the Jews who would suffer the most.

The Palestine Commission announced that unless the UN or some other agency comes to the rescue, there will be no shipments of food to Palestine after 15 May. Britain said she would be prepared to act as purchaser up to 30 June if funds were provided, since Palestine would be bankrupt.

April 9

In what was reported as a "new phase" in Palestine's civil war, the Irgun and Stern Gang carried out "their first military operation" and "seized" the village of Deir Yassin, two miles to the west of Jerusalem.[14] A small village, situated close to a predominantly Jewish area, with no military significance. However its occupation came within the general framework of Operation Nachshon.

In what was to prove a mastery of understatement, The Times prefaced its small account of the event with "The Jews had an active night, for they took an Arab village, Deir Yassin." But pointed out that, undoubtedly, the Zionists were taking advantage of the disarray following the mourning for the Palestinian leader, Abdul Khader Husseini. His funeral took place the same day in Jerusalem.

Initial reports indicated that the attack was carried out independently of the Haganah. The high number of deaths initially reported, 200 admitted deaths with half being women and children, was blamed on the need to fight from house to house with hand-to-hand fighting dominating.

As subsequent investigation revealed, these initial reports disguised the horror of what had taken place at a very quiet and passive village. A village where there had been a tacit agreement between the *mukhtar* and the Haganah that the latter would be informed if "strangers" appeared in the area. Far from being a "military operation" it was an act of terror and slaughter which had a major impact on how Palestinian Arabs throughout Palestine perceived their future, and that of their families, at the hands of the Zionist forces.

The Irgun version of events stated that the surprise dawn attack against this peaceful village had been preceded by a loudspeaker van urging the residents to surrender. (Later accounts said the loudspeaker vans had broken down and so the population could not be warned.) Apparently 300 people surrendered themselves with the men being taken to Jerusalem and handed over to the police, the women and children being eventually delivered to a Red Cross representative.

The New York Times reported "25 men of the (Jewish) Agency's Haganah militia reinforced 55 Irgunists and 45 Sternists who seized the village." The History of the Haganah conceded that a massacre had been carried out

"without discriminating among women and children and old people. They finished their work by loading some of the 'prisoners' who had fallen into their hands onto cars and parading them into the streets of Jerusalem in a 'victory convoy', amidst the cheers of the Jewish masses. After that these 'prisoners' were returned to the village and killed. The victims included men, women and children; a total of 254 people."[15]

This figure was disputed with allegations that it had been inflated for propaganda purposes, to help further terrorise the Palestinian population. A 1987 report by Birzeit University's Research and Documentation Centre concluded that "the number of those killed does not exceed 120."

Eyewitness account:

"At 2 o'clock this afternoon I saw three trucks driving slowly up and down King George Avenue bearing men, women and children, their hands above their heads, guarded by Jews armed with Sten guns and rifles. The mukhtar of Deir Yassin, his womenfolk and children were in the truck. In front was a young boy, a look of anguished horror bitten into his face, his arms frozen upright. The mukhtar stared blindly ahead."[16]

Michael Palumbo, in his book, *The Palestinian Catastrophe*, detailed the events of the 9 April which eventually emerged.

The initial advice given to the Irgun and Stern Gang was not to attack this "friendly" village. There was a "mutual agreement of non-aggression" between the villagers and the Jews.This was ignored. At a pre-attack meeting "the majority was for liquidation of all the men in the village and any others found that opposed us, whether it be old people, women and children." Rifles and hand grenades were provided by the Haganah. The assault on the village was called Operation Unity "because its goal was to demonstrate cooperation between the Haganah and the terrorist groups."[17]

The terrorists were not able to penetrate the village following their attack at 4.30am Friday 9 April. A platoon of Palmach regulars came to their assistance and, within a short while, the village was occupied. Not wanting to be associated with the terrorists, and having recently been active in attacking another Arab village, the platoon withdrew.

What followed has been described as revenge for the casualties inflicted on the terrorists by the few village defenders.

Mohammed Aref Sammour witnessed the slaughter.

"There were twenty five people, twenty four were killed and only one could escape through a window. . . In another house they captured a boy who was holding the knee of his mother. They slaughtered her in front of him."

Mohammed saw a family of eleven people attempt to surrender but the Zionist terrorists gunned them down, including a woman of eighty and a boy three or four years old.

"They ripped open the bellies of all the women they found straight away with bayonets . . .they would cut off the arm to take the bracelet or cut the finger to get the ring."
Old people reciting the Koran were chased and slaughtered.[18]

In contravention of British policy that British troops should now only intervene in Arab-Zionist conflict if it was in Britain's interests, the High Commissioner, Sir Alan Cunningham ordered that troops should be sent to Deir Yassin. The order was immediately countermanded.

At the time, the only outsider allowed in to witness the aftermath was Dr Jacques de Reynier, Swiss doctor working for the Red Cross. His entry to the village was impeded by two men armed with cutlasses and machine guns. However an Irgun member, who had been rescued three times from German concentration camps by the Red Cross, took him under his wing.

"The first thing I saw were people running everywhere, rushing in and out of houses carrying Sten guns, rifles, pistols and large ornate Arab knives. They seemed half mad."

"We're still mopping up." was the comment. The doctor was particularly horrified by one of the terrorists carrying a knife "A beautiful young girl with criminal eyes, showed me hers still dripping with blood, she displayed it like a trophy."

"All I could think of was the SS troops I had seen in Athens." The slaughter continued in front of the doctor " . . a young woman stab an elderly man and woman cowering on the doostep of their hut." [19]

Another witness, Meir Pa'il, a Haganah regular sent to assesss the combat abilities of the terrorists recorded that the slaughter only stopped when

Jews from nearby Givat Shaul arrived to protest. However prisoners "were loaded into freight trucks and led in a victory parade like a Roman triumph through . . . Jerusalem." They were later executed. The photographs taken, like the official report, remain a secret still kept by the Israeli government.

British investigators concluded that "There is no doubt that many sexual atrocities were committed by the attacking Jews. Many young girls were raped and later slaughtered. Old women were also molested." "Many infants were also butchered and killed. . . . Women had bracelets torn from their arms and rings from their fingers and parts of some of the women's ears were severed in order to remove earrings."[20]

Menachem Begin, a terrorist leader on Britain's "wanted" list, and Israeli prime minister-to-be sent an order of the day to the perpetrators of the atrocity "Accept congratulations on this splendid act of conquest. Tell the soldiers you have made history in Israel."[20]

The Irgun spokesman said that eight Iraqis had been "executed" after the capture of the village. A number of houses were blown up after the village had been thoroughly searched and pillaged. Arms, flour and sugar were sent to Jerusalem. Several thousands pounds in cash, hidden by the residents in their houses, were taken by the terrorists.

The onslaught reportedly lasted only about two hours with subsequent fighting on the outskirts lasting a farther 14 hours. Four Zionists were killed, with 40 wounded.

The joint commander of the terrorists, while banning British correspondents and accusing them of being "untrustworthy", summoned American and Jewish corrrespondents to a press conference.

"This is the first step. We intend to attack, conquer, and hold Arab territory as much as we can. That includes all of Palestine and Transjordan if possible."

Three other Zionist successes were reported for the day.

The village of Castel was retaken by a Zionist force, reported to be 500 strong, following a heavy mortar bombardment. Arab forces, under command of Fawzi Kauwkji of the Arab Liberation Army, later shelled the village in an attempt to dislodge the occupiers. Zionist planes were reported to have dropped bombs on the nearby village of Abu Ghoush, damaging an aerial mast at a police station.

Earlier in the day, an Iraqi encampment at Wadi Sarar was claimed to have been captured with 50 Arabs killed. The capture of Ein Karim four miles to the west of Jerusalem, with an Arab population of about 10 000, was reported later in the day.

In Jerusalem, water supplies were partly restored following landmine damage to the pipeline. The food situation in the Jewish areas continued to deteriorate as only one food convoy had come through in 10 days.

A military convoy en route from Haifa to Port Said was attacked by Arab forces near Barbara, ten miles north of Gaza.

A dawn to dusk curfew, using emergency powers, over a large part of Palestine was ordered by the GOC Palestine. It was thought that the main purpose was to facilitate the withdrawal of British troops during a series of night movements. To a certain extent it could hamper the movement of "illegal armed forces and terrorists." The districts named were Galilee, Haifa, Samaris, Lydda, Jerusalem, Bethlehem and Jericho.

April 10

Deir Yassin described as being "wiped out" was reported to be under fire by both Arab and Zionists. Dr Khalidi, secretary of the Arab Higher Committee said that 50 bodies of men, women and children still strewn around the village were being dumped in a disused well where 150 other bodies were to be found.

Dr Khalidi berated the Zionists for the atrocity carried out at the village. He accused the Jewish Agency of delaying the entry of Dr Renyier of the Red Cross into the village because the Zionists "did not want him to see the mutilated bodies and wanted time to clean up the mess." He bitterly gave details of the victims, including 25 pregnant women, 52 mothers with babies aged between a few months and a few years, and some 60 girls of varying ages.

All efforts to get the British authorities - civil, police and military - to visit the village after the massacre were rejected, according to Dr Khalidi. This, he said, would be brought to the attention of the United Nations.

The Jewish Agency expressed "horrror and disgust" at the massacre in Deir Yassin and appealed to all parties in Palestine to "conduct the present conflict" in accordance with the rules of civilised warfare.

April 11

It was reported that the Jewish Agency had accepted the 'ceasefire' called for by the High Commissioner of Palestine eight days previously. The Arab Higher Committee was still considering the appeal, according to Arab sources.

Meanwhile Zionist terrorists shot and killed a British soldier while he was sitting at a coffee house in Rehovoth, to the south of Tel Aviv. Two other soldiers escaped injury. Their three Sten guns were stolen.

In Jerusalem, Jewish suburbs of Montefiore, Givat Shaul and Beit Hakerem came under Arab shelling, using French 105 and 75mm artillery, in which three Jews were killed. The Arab blockade of the roads to the city was tightened. However concern was expressed over the ability of the Arabs to keep their forces in Jerusalem supplied with ammunition, in addition to the leadership problems following the death of Abdul Kader Husseini.

Several thousand Iraqi fighters of the Arab Liberation Army attacked the settlement of Mishmar Haemek, following an artillery barrage. Fighting continued in the area around Castel village when the Haganah raided the nearby village of Qalunia and blew up some houses.

Newspaper accounts of the fate of a small village, particularly accounts of events taking place at a distance, tend to be prosaic. The reality is rarely depicted. The wider military master plan is never concerned with its results on humanity.

Qalunia, or Qalunya, was one such village. About three miles to the west of Jerusalem, it was identified as the Canaanite town of Mozah (Joshua 18:26) Under the Emperor Vespasian it became Colonia Amosa around 71AD. The Crusaders called it Qalonie and in 1859 it became the first location in Palestine where Jewish immigrants acquired land for cultivation.

For the Palestinian Arab villagers, about 1 260 in number (with a further 350 who were Jewish), it was their tragedy that their village was a main target of Operation Nachson, with the Palmach leading the attack. Two days were spent systematically razing the village to the ground. The New York Times reported that the Haganah "blew up a score of houses and left the entire village ablaze" with the Irgun claiming that the villagers had fled as a result of Deir Yassin.

A more graphic and poignant account was given by one of the observers, an Anglo-Jewish resident of Jerusalem, Harry Levin, who accompanied the Palmach:

"Suddenly the village seemed to erupt. Our mortars started it, and at once became a bedlam of answering fire . . .They fired wildly to all points of the compass . . suddenly an explosion that seemed to rip open the hillside; shrieks of terror. Our shock troops and sappers had reached the houses . . . more explosions . . . in half an hour it was over."

Levin counted fourteen dead "but there were more". As he left the village

"sappers were blowing up houses. One after another, the solid stone buildings, some built in the elaborate city style, exploded and crashed . . ."

"Within sight of Jerusalem I still heard the explosions rolling through the hills; and in between somewhere in the lonely distance, still rose the half-hearted barking of the village dog."[21]

On the night of the 11th, another historic village, Ein Hawd, [pop 650] to the south of Haifa, together with the neighbouring village of Ein Ghazal were attacked by Zionist forces. On this occasion the attack was repulsed.

Three British soldiers were killed and six wounded when two military trucks ran into an Arab mortar barrage in the same area.

As a prelude to attacking and capturing Tiberias the Haganah deployed a tactic which was to be used to good effect elsewhere. This was to capture a nearby village, make an example of it, induce fear amongst the city's residents and stimulate an outflow of refugees.

The village of Nasir al Din [pop 90] was chosen on this day. Two platoons of the Golani Brigade, stationed in the Jewish Quarter of Tiberias, descended upon the village. Some non-combatants were apparently killed and some houses destroyed. Most of the population fled to Lubiya or to Tiberias, from where British troops evacuated them to Lubiya. Eyewitnesses detailed the killing of eight men, one woman and an unspecified number of children. The mud houses were burned, the stone houses blown up and the remaining villagers expelled.[22]

The arrival of the terrorised villagers undermined morale in Tiberias which was effectively isolated from the nearby large village of Lubiya. The city's vulnerablity was thereby enhanced.

A police report detailed an attack on Kfar Darom, the only Zionist settlement on the coastal plain south of Gaza. Eleven Egyptians were reported dead or wounded before a ceasefire, brokered by a British officer commanding troops in the area, took effect.

At a meeting of the Arab League in Cairo it was stated that even the most militant Zionists must realise that they cannot themselves establish a state by force, that a Jewish state established by international arms would have to be sustained by international arms in the face of perpetual Arab hostility, and that there could be no peace in such an entity.[23]

April 12

The sacking of Deir Yassin, the savage and inhumane dumping of 150 corpses, almost all women and children, into the "musty depths of an unused water cistern" was reported to have both inflamed and horrified Arabs throughout the Middle East. A full scale Arab-Jewish war was predicted before 15 May.

Feelings were further aroused by the abject failure of the British authorities to take any action against the terrorists responsible. This despite the fact that a few days earlier the House of Commons had stated that the security forces were searching for the very same terrorists. The message was clear. Whatever happened in Palestine, the British would look the other way.

Reports indicated that with the outrage being considered so deliberately provocative, repercussions were inevitable. Perhaps not by replying in kind, by slaughtering Jewish women and children, but the isolated Zionist colonies must be on their guard.

The Red Cross began the burials of the victims of the Deir Yassin massacre.

An Arab Legion convoy was fired upon by Zionist fighters based in the settlement of Kfar Etzion (although the Zionists claimed the opposite had happened) in the Hebron area. Haganah troops and ten armoured cars descended upon the convoy. Help, in the form of a "flying column" of Life Guards arrived from Jerusalem, and engaged in battle with the Haganah. A Zionist two seater Austin plane arrived and machine gunned the British and Arab Legion troops. It was shot down by the Light Guards, killing the pilot.

Fighting continued around Castel with contradictory reports on who occupied the village. A similar situation prevailed around the settlement of Mishnar Haemek. Several Arab villages in the Jaffa and Ramleh areas were reported to be under attack. The large village of Al Kafrin was attacked and partly destroyed. At night the Palmach attacked the village of al Mansi [pop 1 200] to the south east of Haifa. It was occupied along with the neighbouring village of al Naghnaghhiyya [pop 1 320]. The houses of both villages were subsequently blown up.

During the same operation the Palmach gained control of Abu Zurayq [pop 720]. Thirty houses were blown up in the process, five of them were occupied. Fifteen adult males were taken captive (fate unknown). Some 200 women and children were expelled towards Jenin.

The Palestinian newspaper, *Filastin*, reported that the next day a Haganah unit came across a number of villagers lying face down on their fields - old men, women and children. The troops opened fire killing two women and four children. Forty were taken captive. An Arab force later counter attacked, liberating the captives and taking them to Jenin.[24]

The Tiberias-Nazareth road was rendered impassable by Zionist demolition squads. In Haifa, three Arabs were shot dead by snipers. To the east of the town, Arab forces attacked the Zionist colonies of Yohanan and Kefrata, near the Christian village of Shefar Amr. Haganah radio claimed that the village of Abu Shusha, south east of Haifa, alleged to have been used by Iraqi forces as a base, had been destroyed. The New York Times reported that the villagers had been "evacuated" and the Haganah blew up "many houses" as a "punitive measure."

Fighting for the Jaffa road seemed to have ceased. Reports that emerged indicated that because of differences in command, Arab forces from the north had departed, taking their artillery with them. The sentiment was expressed in one report that many Arab supporters hoped that an outsider would take over the Jerusalem area, sort out some of the factions, and institute some type of training for the many bands of "impromptu" soldiers waiting on the sidelines.

A British troop and ammunition train was attacked by Zionists in the orange grove belt near Rehovoth. Large quantities of arms were looted.

The south-west corner of Jerusalem, which housed the British residential security zone and various foreign consulates, was reported to be under threat. The Palestinian forces had taken up positions in Katamon, with the Zionists entrenching themselves on along ridge 200 yards away.

The eldest son of Viscount Samuel and director of the Palestine broadcasting service, Edwin Samuel, narrowly escaped being abducted by two Arab gunmen in Jerusalem and dragged in to the Arab quarter. He managed to break free and escape into a nearby British security zone.

The Zionist General Council, meeting in Tel-Aviv, ratified a resolution to bring Zionist "dissident" groups - the Irgun and Stern Gang terrorists -

under "Jewish national discipline." It was agreed to proclaim the independence of a Jewish State on 16 May, immediately upon the end of the British mandate.

The process of removing the British presence from Palestine moved up a gear. Camps were disappearing overnight. Where previously there were rows of tents and Bren guns covering barbed wire entrances, there was left a few rusting tins and shallow brick surrounds. The road to Haifa could be seen filled with lorries filled with furniture from military messes and offices.

The High Commissioner of Palestine, Sir Alan Cunningham, signed an order banning British troops and police from marrying Palestinian girls - Arab or Jewish - without prior consent. A British source alleged that some Jewish girls were offering between £400 and £500 to British troops and policemen as marriage dowries. As British subjects they would then be evacuated from Palestine along with their husbands.

April 13

One of Jerusalem's 'hottest' battles raged for six hours during the day, resulting in the deaths of two British soldiers and a senior police officer who, as part of a Highland Light Infantry squad, arrived in time to save a ten vehicle Zionist convoy from being annihilated on Mount Scopus. At least ten Arabs were killed following the arrival of the British forces.

The convoy had been trying to reach Hebrew University and Hadassah Hospital when it was hit by two inch and three inch mortars. The area was covered with piles of burned corpes of at least 35 Zionist fighters by the time the British brokered a truce was implemented. The Arabs collected their own casualties while the British soldiers carried the wounded Zionists to Hadassah Hospital.

Two convoys totalling about 200 lorries arrived in the Jewish area of Jerusalem with food from Tel-Aviv.

This was the day that the family of Palestinian writer and teacher, Khalil Sakakini, decided to flee their home:

"Day and night,the heavy artillery shelling and firing of machine guns has been continuous, as if we were on a battlefield . . . Night falls and we cannot get any sleep, and we say that when the morning comes we shall leave our neighbourhood of Qatamon for somewhere else, or leave the country altogether."[25]

A force of 500 Haganah troops attacked the village of Saris [pop560] to the west of Jerusalem. In this early morning attack mortars and small arms were used. Seven villagers were killed, including some women. Up to 35 houses were destroyed in addition to the village mosque and school.

Later the Haganah chief, Israel Galili, wrote to the JNF official, Yosef Weitz, urging that a settlement be established on Saris "as soon as possible." It was deemed that a settlement at this and seven other sites was "important for security."[26] These sites were Beit Mashir, Saris, Ghuweir, Abu Shusha, Kafr Misr, Khirbet Manshiya, Tantura and Bureir. Most of the village sites had yet to be abandoned at this point.[27]

With the ending of Operation Nachshon, the Haganah launched Operation Harel. Along with Saris, the villages of Biddu, Beit Surik, and Suba (Jerusalem district) were attacked and destroyed.

Twelve Palestinians were killed and fifteen wounded when Zionist forces attacked the village of Lajjun near Jenin.

Zionist self-government plans started to be implemented in advance of the proclaimed commencement date of 16 May. Palestine Government ID cards and Press credentials would no longer be adequate for passing through Jewish quarters. All Jewish publications printed in Palestine together with photographs made in Jewish areas were to be censored. No attempt was made, at this stage, to censor outgoing news stories. The Hebrew Civil Service Commission filled key posts.

An army of approximately 5 000 uniformed Syrians, Iraqis, Lebanese, Egyptians,Trans-Jordanians and Palestinians left, in small groups, from Syrian training camps. It was described in reports as "the second Arab army for the Liberation of Palestine" and was expected to establish itself to the south of Fawzi Kauwkji's army. A third force was expected to move into Southern Palestine from Egypt.

April 14

A procession of several thousand Orthodox Jews marched through the streets of the Jewish quarter of Jerusalem with banners demanding peace and a ceasefire. According to a statement issued by the Orthodox Jews, the Haganah arrived, tore down the banners and assaulted the demonstrators with their rifle butts.

Later, a larger Haganah force was bussed in to the city. They fired in the air to disperse the demonstrators and "also beat the demonstrators without mercy, using their rifle butts."The comment was also made that the Zionist leadership was trying to hush up the matter.[28]

It was reported that 12 Arabs were killed and 15 injured following further clashes at Mishmar Haemek settlement halfway between Haifa and Jenin bringing Arab casualties, according to Zionist sources, to 46 in number. No Zionist casualty figures were released.

The Haganah attacked the Palestinian Druze villages of Hosha and Khirbet Qasir, near Haifa.

A British soldier was shot and injured by Arabs near Tiberias. Another soldier was injured in Safad when a Jewish house was blown up. An aeroplane was used to bomb the village of Deir Tarif. Five villagers were wounded including a two year old child. The village of Daliyat al Rawha [pop 600 inc 320 Jews] was occupied by the Haganah.

Yosef Weitz, the JNF official recorded in his diary:

"Is it not now time to be rid of them? Why continue to keep in our midst these thorns at a time when they pose a danger to us ? Our people are weighing up (solutions)."[29]

By this date, ten villages in the Mount Castel area were in Palmach hands. Each had been systematically destroyed on the night it was occupied.

All Arab workers walked out of the Consolidated Refineries plant in Haifa. They demanded that the Iraq Petrol Company accept responsibility for the injuries and deaths of workers on the roads. The company ceased operations.

A meeting of Arab leaders took place in Cairo, with the shortcomings of the Arab resistance movement against partition very much on the agenda. In particular, lack of arms and reserves of war materials and trained men, all shortages suffered by both Palestinian Arab fighters and members of the "Liberation armies." The question of general leadership and the possible establishment of an Arab Government for Palestine was crying out for an answer. The latter was answered by the continuation the status quo of having a "military regime"in the Arab areas, including the fighting zones.

Inevitably political interests, of the various parties involved, impinged themselves on the deliberations. However the Secretary-General of the Arab League had striven for months to maintain a balance, to preserve unity among the various Arab states and parties, and find an acceptable solution to halt Zionist expansionism. The consensus seemed to be that he had been successful, so far.

The British Government rejected criticism levelled at it by the UN Palestine Comission.
"The fact that political developments outside the jurisdiction of the Palestine Government made it almost impossible for them to operate is surely a poor foundation upon which to blame the Palestine Government for the situation now facing the country."[30]

The Commission decided to proceed immediately with the creation of a nucleus of a UN police force for Jerusalem. Apparently 200 British members of the present force said they would be willing to serve.

The Security Council completed drafting the resolution on a truce in Palestine. It called upon the representatives of the opposing factions to cease a number of actions viz. military actions, sabotage and violence; the bringing of armed bands and war materials into Palestine; political activity prejudicial to the rights of Arab and Jew. It was assumed that with no military force to impose the terms of the truce, it would be rejected.

April 15

Following an all night battle, the Haganah claimed to have inflicted a heavy defeat on the Arab forces in the Megiddo area of the strategic Emek Valley, with the Arab Liberation Army in full retreat. More than 100 Arabs were reported dead.

It followed two weeks of military action around the colony of Mishmar Haemek. This culminated in the night attack by well armed Haganah units. Armed with machine guns and mortars, they advanced from a number of settlements in the area, supported by some small aircraft. They succeeded in isolating the Arab forces, occupying four villages in the process. Their advance stopped near Jenin at the apex of the Arab triangle - Nablus-Tulkarm- Jenin.

With the evacuation of army camps by the British, struggles took place for their possession. Twenty one Arabs were killed in the resulting conflicts.

A few hours after troops moved out of Tel Litvinsky camp, Arab and Zionist forces moved in, with the former being forced to withdraw. It was of strategic importance, standing on the border between Jewish and Arab areas with a position of dominance over the road to Lydda Airport.

There was a repeat performance at Sadi Surar, 15 miles to the south east of Tel Aviv, on the supply route to Jerusalem. Iraqi troops took first possession, followed by the Zionists who attacked and blew up several buildings.

After receiving "friendly advice" from the Haganah, the village of al Tirah with a mixed population of about 150 Arabs and 50 Jews was "emptied" of its Arab residents.[31] Zionists forces attacked Lajjun

The town of Salama [pop 6 730], to the east of Jaffa, was subjected to a mortar bombardment of 3 inch shells. By the end of the month the defenders had run out of ammunition and were forced to leave.

The Haganah ordered the villagers of Miska [pop 1 060] to leave, but the order was ignored.

A Haganah squad carried out a raid on the village of Sarafand al Amar [pop 1 950] and demolished a three storey building. It was alleged that it was used by militia forces led by the Palestinian guerilla commander Sheikh Hasan Salam. There were varying accounts of the casualties, with the British stating 16 dead and 12 wounded in the ruins of the building.

The village of al Manshiyya, identified by Haganah chief, Israel Galili, as being "important to security" and an important site for a settlement, was evacuated. Apparently an agreement had been reached with the Haganah that local settlements would safeguard their property until they could return at the end of the war. By the end of the month the Haganah were systematically destroying the houses with the assistance of local settlers.

The bodies of three British soldiers were found stripped of their uniforms after mines exploded under their railway inspection trolleys near the Jewish area of Rehovoth.

The Colonial Secretary, Arthur Creech Jones, commented in New York "I hope British troops will be out of Palestine before August 1. Make it quite clear that we are not staying on. We've had enough." [32]

Proposals for a truce in Palestine was formally submitted to the Security Council without eliciting any comment from either party to the conflict.

There was wide speculation that armed Arab intervention from neighbouring states would take place if open warfare developed in a month's time, when the Mandate ends.

April 16

It was reported that the Zionist forces, estimated at 10 000 frontline troops, had carried out a a major offensive to break the Arab stranglehold of the roads throughout Central and Northern Palestine. In the first phase, the Zionist forces achieved a considerable measure of success in driving the Arab forces from their positions of dominance on the main Tel-Aviv Jerusalem road. In their drive westwards, to attack and hold the supply route to Jerusalem blockaded by the Arabs, several villages were occupied by the Zionists.

They then occupied the hills around the village of Saris, eight miles west of Jerusalem, below Castel. During a dawn attack on the village the 500 attackers destroyed the village mosque, the school and 25 houses with mortar fire. Three women were reported killed.

On the Plain of Armageddon a battle took place for the possession of seven Arab villages. Aircraft and artillery were in action with over 200 casualties reported.

The guns of the Arab Liberation Army shelled some settlements and some Jewish suburbs of Jerusalem before withdrawing to the north to renew attacks on the colony of Mishmar Haemek.

This was an attack carried out by Druze forces who had established themselves in the villages of Hawsha and Khirbat al Kasayir for the purpose of sniping at local settlements to relieve the pressure on the Arab forces at Mishmar Haemek. A unit from the Haganah Carmeli Brigade had engaged the Druze in hand to hand combat but were forced to retire. A decision was then made to occupy the villages with a dawn attack carried out by two Haganah companies. With only a few village guards present, it was easily accomplished. A counter attack was launched, lasting all day, with the Haganah conceding that "the enemy soldiers displayed extreme courage in this battle." It was claimed that 130 Arab Druze were killed following nine successive attacks launched during the day. However it was the Haganah heavy machine gun that won the day for the Zionist forces.

It is believed that the attacks on the two villages may have facilitated the fall of Haifa.

The New York Times quoted British authorities as saying that Haganah demolition squads had blown up the remaining houses in the village Abu Zurayq, south east of Haifa. The paper also reported on the capture of al Lajjun, to the northwest of Jenin. "Lajjun is the most important place taken by the Jews, whose offensive has carried them through ten villages south and east of Mishmar Ha'emak." Women and children were, according to the report, "removed" from the village. Twenty seven houses were blown up by the Haganah. The mosque was eventually converted into a carpentry workshop.

April 17

Three American soldiers were reported killed and five wounded following a Zionist attack on an ammunition train at Binyamina, 20 miles south of Haifa. Four Britons were reported missing, with three Zionists killed and ten wounded. It took place north of Hadera with uninjured guards being forced to load the ammunition into lorries.Three of the Zionists were killed when a relief train arrived, but 20 tons of arms and mortar ammunition was successfully looted. It was reported that Jews took the wounded British to hospital.

The timely arrival of British armoured car at the Waldheim, established in 1902 by German "Templar" colonists and described in one report as a "German village"- an enemy aliens internment camp since 1939, saved the lives of three British guards. The camp had been taken over by Zionists and the guards were in the process of being strung up when the troops arrived. Further troops were sent to rescue 80 Germans in the camp by which time two Germans had been killed.

The historic village of Abil al Qamh (with traces of habitation as far back as 2900BC) [pop 428] to the north of Safad was seized by the Palmach. It became a base for launching attacks into Syria under the name of Operation Yiftach, commanded by Yigal Allon.

The Palestinian Arab villagers of Wadi Hunayn [pop 3 380 including 1 760 Jews] fled after being targeted or threatened in the course of the Haganah's coastal "clearing" operation. The nearby Zionist settlement of Nes Tziyyona was built on land purchased from the village in 1883 and one of the few settlements that employed non-Jewish labour. It was described as "the only genuinely 'mixed' locality in Palestine where Zionist immigrants and Palestinians actually lived in close proximity."[33]

Druze Arab forces were reported to have suffered heavy losses when they launched an attack on Ramat Johanan.

April 18

Reports abounded of imminent arrival of King Abdullah's troops from Transjordan, in particular, the Arab Legion. There were denials from Fawzi Kaukji, commander of Arab forces in Palestine, that a large force had started to move over the border from Syria.

There were numerous reports of foreign troops serving on both sides of the conflict. Kaukji was convinced that Russian troops were serving with the Zionist forces - as demonstrated by the physical appearance of Russian speaking troops together with their different methods of action. Further allegations were made of Russian commanders leading the Zionist forces at Mishmar Haemek. They had arrived disguised as civilians in a boat load of illegal immigrants. Fifty Russian officers, up to the rank of colonel, were alleged to be active in Northern Palestine.

These reports were flatly denied by Zionist sources. But they did give rise to reports that King Abdullah of Transjordan was considering the early intervention of his forces in the wake of Russian involvement.

The largest convoy since the Arab blockade started - 300 lorries with 1 000 tons of supplies - reached Jerusalem. Apparently the convoys were being organised by a former British colonel.

It was reported that a "strong sense of disbandment and disorganisation" had descended on Palestine. Means of communication or supervision had failed. "Hearsay" prevailed in the already semi-independent Jewish and Arab areas.

A battle was reported around the settlement of Nevi Yacouv which sat astride the main road from Jerusalem to the Arab triangle. It was reported that the Arab Judean Army had entered the settlement and destroyed some houses. The Haganah, while admitting that a "terrific fight" was in progress, denied the settlement had been evacuated. The Highland Light Infantry reported that the Arabs "won a victory and captured 20 Jewish armoured cars."

In Jerusalem a heavy explosion and a few lighter ones were heard in the Jewish quarter following bomb warnings to the foreign press HQ. A house on the fringe of the Yemen Moshe quarter was blown up.

[One source stated that the village of Khirbat Nasir al-Din was attacked by the Haganah on this day, resulting in a massacre. However the 11 April is the accepted date for this particular atrocity.]

The fall of Tiberias, on the shores of the Sea of Galilee, merited little attention in the press. With nearly 50% of the community Jewish, and resident on the hillside overlooking the old town, the Palestinian Arab population were at a disadvantage. Prior to being attacked by the Haganah, the latter had been well warned not to cooperate with outsiders and not to resist partition. However, with the imminent departure of the British, the Palmach had been sent to bolster the Jewish militia in the town.

Under cover of darkness, a coordinated effort was made to cut the Arab part of the town in two. The civilian population was terrified by a night assault using barrel bombs, dynamite, loudspeakers constantly broadcasting "horror sounds". So much so that by dawn the population, with Deir Yassin very much on their collective mind, only wanted a safe refuge. An appeal was made to the British to help them. It was agreed that they would stay on for a few days. A request was made to King Abdullah of Transjordan for help. In the only action of its type, lorries were sent by the King to take the women and children to safety. The British, who did not want to be involved in any fighting, persuaded the reluctant men to go.

By 19:00 the town was in Zionist hands. During and after the battle in the town looting was reported, with churches being targets for desecration. UN investigator, Captain F. Marchal, commented

"In spite of the guarantee given several times by the Jewish authorities to respect churches, convents, schools and other buildings belonging to the religious community, those places have been submitted to depredations committed at Tiberias undoubtedly by the Jews, although these places were private property. They have been occupied by troops without any notice and sometimes without any necessity."[34]

On this day, the parents of young Palestinian Arab, Anis Sayigh, arrived in Sidon in the Lebanon. With his father a clergyman in the Christian church with responsibility for his parishioners, a British officer had gave Father Abdallah, Protestant pastor in Tiberias, and his wife Afifa, instructions to leave their peaceful town. The town was apparently due to fall to Zionist forces in a few hours and the pastor was advised that "It is the will of God to bring the children of Israel back to their country after 2 000 years of exile so that they may establish their state . . . . this is their land and now they are returning."

Anis Sayigh, *A Personal Testimony*, (Cornerstone, Autumn 1998 p.6)

In preparation for another evacuation, this time from Haifa, General Stockwell gave advance notice of the intention to quit to the leaders of the town's Jewish community. He failed to give the Arabs the same warning. This was to give the Zionist forces plenty of time to plan the take over strategic points within the town and ensure the subsequent flight of its Palestinian Arab residents.[35]

A record of the occupation of Khirbat al Wa'ra, northwest of Tiberias has yet to be published. It probably happened on the 18th, following the fall of Tiberias.

April 19

On a daily basis, the disintegration of organisation and authority accelerated. There were reports of increasingly precarious essential services with communications, food, water and power supplies at times non-existent.

Crime was reported to be on the increase with "patriotism" whether it be of Jewish or Arab flavour being used as an excuse for acts ranging from petty theft to murder. The theft of government vehicles had reached such proportions that a warning was given that private vehicles may need to be requisitioned. The departure of British officials was seen to add very much to the disintegration - a total of 2 000 personnel were due to leave during March, with a further 2 900 (mostly police) due to evacuate in May.

The presence of a "Jewish navy" was reported to be operating along the shores of Palestine. Although the Haganah tried to suppress news of its existence it was believed to consist of a number of small armed vessels with, perhaps a couple of corvettes. Larger ships had been bought abroad but were waiting the end of the mandate. They were manned mostly by ex-Royal Navy personnel.

During the day two schooners, one Egyptian and the other Palestinian, were stopped and searched. There was talk of harassing Arab shipping in the Mediterranean, assisting the arrival of immigrants and blockading Jaffa.

With the blowing up of three trains in recent days, with heavy loss of life, the 125 mile stretch of railway between Gaza and Haifa, along the coastal plain, was declared a "closed area" by the Palestine Government. This was to facilitate the evacuation of British troops, police and Government officials.

The HQ of the Arab Liberation Army (the Yarmuk) at Samaria was bombed with one villager killed. Zionist sources denied knowledge of the attack.

The Haganah commander in Tiberias proclaimed "Jewish independent rule"[36] in the city following an official announcement that the entire Arab population had been "evacuated under military supervision". Law and order was now being maintained by Jewish military police.

The villages, or in the "military speak" of the Haganah, the "enemy bases" of Al Mazar, Zir'in and Nuris, to the north of Jenin, which had repelled the Haganah on 18 March, inflicting heavy losses were once again targeted by the Haganah. The Palmach HQ issued an order which read, in part "..with the capture of Zir'n, most of the village's houses must be destroyed while some should be left intact for accommodation and defense."[37]

Following the rejection of a ceasefire by the Haganah and the Jewish Agency during the fighting around Mishmar Haemek, the decision was taken to attack and destroy about ten villages near the settlement. Al Kafrayn [pop 1 420] was the largest. Its final destruction was postponed until the 19th, allowing it to be used to train Zionist units to fight in built-up areas. The Haganah General Staff was then informed "At the end of the exercises, the village of el Kafrin was blown up completely."[38]

April 20

Two British soldiers were killed and another seriously wounded as they went about their task of announcing over a loudspeaker the nightly border area curfew along the Jaffa Tel-Aviv road. They were fired upon by a large party of Zionists.

Arab sources claimed that a Haganah arms factory in Haifa had been torched with the deaths of five Haganah men. It was also claimed that part of the Palestine mills at Haifa had been destroyed. Twenty five of the Haganah guards were reported killed in the action.

A post-office van was held up by Arabs in Jerusalem. Seventy six bags of mail were looted.

A convoy of 300 trucks with a Haganah and Irgun escort of 2 000 men was engaged in battle for most of the day in the valley of Bab el Wad, 12 miles to the west of Jerusalem. Twenty lorries were destroyed by Arab forces firing from the hillside with machine guns, mortars and grenades. Zionist losses were put at 10 with 30 wounded. Arab casualties unknown. The remaining trucks eventually reached Jerusalem.

Zionist forces occupied the villages of Beir Surik and Biddu, five miles northwest of Jerusalem. It was reported that the villagers had fled following loudspeaker warnings from the advancing force. Explosives and 6 inch mortar fire demolished many houses in the village.

Units of the Alexandroni Brigade attacked the village of Miska and forcibly expelled its inhabitants.

Reports indicated that the villagers of Sarafand al Kharab [pop 1040] fled, fearing an attack. A week earlier, twelve houses had been blown up up in nearby al Ramla. The situation was repeated in ‘Arab al Zubayd [pop 890] where the villagers fled fearing a Zionist attack.

The American cargo ship, *Exford*, was held by Beirut port authorities when it was found to contain explosives and automatic weapons believed to be destined for Palestine. The 600 ton cargo was unloaded.

April 21

A battle for the control of the Haifa, from which an estimated 25 000 Palestinian residents had already fled, was reported. Most of the city had been vacated by the British earlier in the day, with the exception of the port, its oil installations and a strip of land connecting it to the British HQ at the top of Mount Carmel. Britain intended to hold on to the port area until withdrawal was complete by 1 August.

Gunfire was heard along the slopes of Mount Carmel, with firing between the all-Jewish Hadar Carmel and the mixed Jewish-Arab areas lower down. Sniping soon took over once the British had withdrawn. British casualties during the withdrawal was one police sergeant killed and two constables wounded. One Arab was reported killed and 11 injured. Jewish casualties were one dead and one wounded.

The Sisters of Saint Ann, a convent in Haifa, were expelled by Zionist forces. This followed an assault on their house where bullets and grenades were directed at the main door.[39]

Two British soldiers were found with serious bullet wounds on the Haifa Tel-Aviv road. It was believed they had been fired upon by a passing Jewish lorry while repairing their jeep.

Fighting was reported along the coastal plain of Sharon. Arab forces blew up two bridges west of Bab al Wad, making the Jerusalem Tel-Aviv road impassable.

An eight hour battle near the Lebanese border was reported in a Haganah radio broadcast, with 20 Arabs and 21 Zionists reported dead. The Haganah also claimed that they had a “secret weapon” a type of rocket projectile with considerable destructive power. Unconfirmed reports said the prototype had been smuggled in from Czechoslovakia and was in large scale production in Jewish factories.

In an announcement designed to instil fear into the Palestinian civilian population, the Haganah announced to the Palestinians that unless they sent away "infiltrated dissidents" they would be advised to evacuate all women and children, because they would be strongly attacked from now on.[40]

A communique from Damascus observed that it had been definitely established that Russian forces were fighting with the Haganah.

April 22

The assault on Haifa by Zionist forces (in accordance with Plan Dalet), which had started the previous evening, continued throughout the day, the eve of the Jewish feast of the Passover. In so doing, they "jumped the gun", starting hostilities in order to gain strategic positions within this main seaport before the withdrawal of British security forces.

The attacking forces made liberal use of psychological and terror tactics. Jeeps with loudspeakers broadcast "horror sounds" - shrieks, wails, anguished moans of Arab women, wails of sirens and alarm bells. One Haganah officer commented on a sepulchral voice calling out in Arabic 'Save your souls, all ye faithful! Flee for your lives!' accompanied by threats to use poison gas and atomic weapons.

The Carmeli Brigade was ordered to "kill every [adult] male encountered" and to attack with firebombs "all objectives that can be set alight".[41] The Brigade commander, Moshe Carmel, feared that many Arabs would remain in the city and ordered the shelling of Arab crowds on the market square with three inch mortars. The terrorised crowd broke into the port area, stormed the boats and fled. The mortar fire lasted all day, even although no resistance was shown by the civilian population.[42]

A British observer noted that during the morning the Haganah was "continually shooting down on all Arabs who moved in Wadi Nisnas and the Old City." This included completely indiscriminate and wanton machinegun fire and sniping on women and children "... attempting to get out of Haifa through the gates in the dock ... There was considerable congestion outside the East gate of hysterical and terrified Arab women and children and old people on who the Jews opened up mercilessly with fire."[42]

The "efficacy" of these "indirect methods" was singled out by an IDF intelligence report of June 1948 in its recommendations for precipitating the exodus of Palestinian Arabs from their land.[41]

There were those who reported on the carnage in approving, sanitised tones "The planning and execution by our fledgling army was, by all accounts, perfect: a three pronged attack from Mount Carmel and a series of concerted pincer movements in the Arab sectors lower down. In the level stretches, units of our men sprung up like clockwork and battered their way into key points . . ."[43]

Heavy casualties were reported with hundreds of Palestinian women and children being evacuated to the western part of the town or Acre. By the end of the day hospitals were filled with the wounded, with the Haganah claiming to have killed 400 Arabs, undoubtedly the majority being civilians. The port area continued to be held by British troops, as was the connecting road to the military HQ on Mount Carmel.

The Haganah offered a five day truce with conditions. However, on the Arab side it was said that they could not guarantee that all Arabs would accept the conditions. They apparently preferred to evacuate the city, leaving a few to maintain property and the religious places. Britain's Major-General Stockwell promised assistance with the evacuation. The Haganah commander issued a radio proclamation to Haifa Jews. Arab property and religious places had to be respected. Nothing belonging to the Arabs had to be stolen. Those guilty of such theft would be severely punished.

Immediate eyewitnss reports spoke of the"instantaneous" reaction of Zionists when the British evacuated buildings. As each building was occupied, the Zionist flag went up.An observer described the "pitiful remnants" of the inhabitants of the "bazaar area" as they straggled out with their belongings. British troops helped ferry some across the bay to safety in Acre.

It was commented that the battle for Haifa was but a prelude and a spur for the Zionist forces to attack other towns within Palestine. Hints were given that Jaffa, Lydda (with its international airport) and neighbouring Ramleh on the Jerusalem Tel-Aviv road were next in line. The intention seemed to be to present the UN General Assembly with a *fait accompli* by 14 May, with forceful possession of the land allocated to a Jewish state under the partition resolution - with Jerusalem as an added bonus, if possible.

King Abdullah of Transjordan called on "Arab kings and rulers" to send their armies along with his own Arab Legion into Palestine after the British mandate ends on 15 May. He said the Arab world "must take action against Zionism. Our peace and liberty are at stake."[44] He called on all Arab countries to help "retain the Arab character of that country when the British end their mandatory rule."But they must not take part in the battle for Palestine until the end of the Mandate.

The opposing forces were reported to be lined up to fight for control of the two British security zones where evacuation was proceeeding, with indications that the Arab Legion was preparing to take over control of Arab areas.

In Jerusalem it was reported that a "wave of panic and depression is sweeping over Palestine". Communications were breaking down with reports of fighting in Haifa taking more than 12 hours to reach the city. It was feared that nothing could prevent open warfare in the city, with the destruction of holy places a clear possibility. One resident observed:

"I was sickened by the sight. There before me lay the results of those incessant conflicts near our school. The new part of Jerusalem [the Sheikh Jarrah Quarter] was reduced to a ghostly shambles: not a building was unmarred; most were roofless, gutted frames of what had been homes and shops."[45]

In the city itself, armed Arab raiders held up the staff of Barclays Bank in Allenby Square and fled with £18 000.

The consensus was that the entry of the Arab Legion into the conflict would bring much fighting to an end. They were regarded as the only match for the Zionists. It was felt that "moderate Jews" in Jerusalem would welcome their arrival in the city since with the destruction in Haifa, supplies would be scarce. The small poorly trained detachements of Iraqis, Syrians and others, including half-trained bands of Palestinian Arabs, were discounted.

The Scotsman correspondent spent two days "illegally" with the Arab Northern Army, having crossed into Palestine from the Lebanon through frontier posts from which all British personnel had withdrawn.She watched the recruits train and concluded that with weapons no heavier than rifles, no real battle experience, little transport (they had no petrol) they had, all the same, managed an effective siege of Zionist colonies along Palestine's northern frontiers.

Zionist forces were reported to have "carried their aggression" to the west of Nablus and, according to reports, losing 20 men in the process. The Arabs claimed to have lost three men and captured some arms.

It was reported that the villagers of Kafr Sabt, southwest of Tiberias and dating back to Roman times, fled their homes following an attack by the Haganah four days earlier. Another historic village, al Majdal, identified as the home of Mary Magdalene, was "emptied" of its inhabitants - fearful for the safety following the fall of Tiberias.

Words such as "emptied" never convey the harsh reality of being forced to leave your home. Close to Tiberias was also the village of Ghuweir which was approached, on this day, by Jews from a neighbouring settlement. The Jews and the villagers were well known to each other with the latter being advised to flee their village because the Palmach intended to secure the road to Safed. This way heavy Arab casualties would be avoided.

When, eventually, the Palmach arrived, the poorly armed defenders were forced to flee to neighbouring al Rama. This village, in turn was occupied by the Palmach. The villagers were assembled and the Druse members given the privilege of returning to their homes. The remainder, Christian Arabs, were ordered to head to Lebanon. "Anyone who dares to take any belongings will be shot." About 40 young men were not allowed to go with their families. They were taken as "prisoners of war". This action coincided with the presence of a UN observer team in the area. It was noted that "The acts of looting in the village are similar to those in all of the villages evacuated by the inhabitants."[46]

Three naval ratings were found guilty of desertion at a naval court in Gibraltar. They had jumped ship in Beirut and admitted to attempting to join the Arab forces in Palestine.

April 23

The Haganah reported that most of the Arab population of Haifa had been "evacuated", with nearly 40 000 having left by sea and road. It was reported that the Zionist forces, including the Irgun, had agreed to permit the evacuation providing arms and ammunition were left behind. Arab leaders had rejected the conditions of a Zionist truce which included the withdrawal of "foreign fighting forces" - an apparent reference to the Arab Legion and groups of fighters from neighbouring Arab states.British military personnel assisted in transporting the refugees or, as reported, the "evacuees".

The Arab residents of Jaffa, the port next to Tel Aviv, were increasingly on the edge, fearing a Zionist onslaught. There were reports that some Palestinian Jerusalemites, fearing the worst, had sought refuge in outlying areas.

Meanwhile, Sir Alan Cunningham, High Commissioner for Palestine, was blaming the Arabs for the previous days fighting in Haifa. He alleged that "The battle was the direct consequence of continuous Arab attacks during the past four days." He said that the attack had been carried out by the Haganah and was "no massacre." "The Arabs themselves were responsible for the outbreak, despite repeated warnings. As always, the Army was completely impartial, and any suggestion that they are taking sides is not only untrue but deeply resented."[47]

Three British officers were wounded helping the Palestinians. Casualties were given as 100 Arabs and 15 Jews killed not counting the "probable casualties" amongst the fleeing women and children.

In much the same tenor of blaming the victims for their own plight, The Jewish Agency asserted that they had not wanted such an "evacuation" and denied that a policy of "extermination" was being carried out against Arabs in Jewish dominated areas. The "unnecessary" evacuation from Tiberias was recalled and allegations were made that Arab leaders were ordering such moves in order to "besmirch the Jews", to arouse feelings in adjoining Arab states and so bring about armed intervention.

In further action to secure control of the approaches to Jerusalem, Zionist forces attacked three villages. Shufat, on the main Nablus road, was raided and some houses destroyed. The deserted village of Beit Iksa, two miles northwest of Jerusalem, was occupied. Alleging that it had been used by Arab troops and that arms had been found, the village was razed to the ground.

The neighbouring village of Nabi Samwil was attacked. Arab sources indicated that counter attacks were taking place.

The Security Council appointed a three-power commission - French, Belgian and U.S. consuls - to assist in bringing about the observance of its Palestine truce resolution. The vote was eight in favour, none against, with the Ukraine, Russia and Colombia abstaining.

Ben Gurion, in an eve of Passover message, spoke in terms of "liberating Tiberias and Haifa" a choice of language which has echoed throughout the land of Palestine ever since. "Tiberias was again Jewish after hundreds of years."[48]

April 24

In the early hours of the morning, the Irgun (with their reputation well earned at Deir Yassin and other attacks) moved across the battle scarred no-man's land between Tel-Aviv and Jaffa. The entry of up to 3 000 terrorists drawn from all over Palestine for this particular operation, into Jaffa which, according to the partition plan was outwith the area allotted to a Jewish State, had been preceded by a barrage of mortar shells. This was followed by an infantry and armour thrust, then the Irgun advanced from house to house using handgrenades and anti-tank bazookas - much of the armour and some of the arms having been captured from the British army and police.

It followed months of daily exchanges of fire, with the Irgun using the pretext of Jaffa being used as a base for attacking Jews in Tel-Aviv. Early in the day Arab sources confirmed that the Masnsheih quarter had been penetrated and the police station taken. The Zionist refused to allow foreign correspondents into the "combat zone". However it was evident that well equipped Irgun members, both male and female, were taking part.The Irgun's chief and future Israeli prime minister, Menachem Begin, was reported to be directing the attack which came to a halt when the Irgun eventually faced British troops backed by mechanised equipment.

There was no confirmation that it had been communicated to the Haganah that if the Irgun did not fall back to the original position along no-man's land then the British would counter attack and shell Tel-Aviv. The Irgun withdrew from Jaffa and by late afternoon only the odd burst of gunfire could be heard, with no smoke or sign of flames to be seen. The Haganah estimated that 10 Arabs had been killed and 50 wounded. Foreigners in Jaffa, mostly French religious workers, were believed to be safe. The Haganah claimed that they had been a restraining influence, advising against the attack.

However one objective had been achieved. Many of Jaffa's 60 000 residents, fearing such an attack, had fled a few days earlier - by road and sea. Fleets of small crafts, some packed to the gunwhales with desperate refugees, could be seen pulling out into the Mediterranean.

The former RAF station at Ein Shemmer, 20 miles to the south of Haifa, was occupied by Zionist forces following the departure of the British.

A battle raged around Lydda Airport vacated during the day but reported to be still in the possession of a company of Argyll and Sutherland Highlanders. The Arab Legion had taken control of that part devoid of the British, with Zionist forces reported to be on the attack. A British Overseas Airways official said that before leaving, staff from the Jewish Airlines had sabotaged communications equipment assisted by the airport's hotel waiters. With the exception of Egyptian Airways, all international services were suspended, including the BOAC service from London, due to "operational difficulties at Lydda."

The village of Ghwway Abu Shusha, near Tiberias, which was first attacked in January was re-visited. On this occasion, the village was taken over by Zionist forces. The village of Balad al Shaykh, near Haifa was likewise re-visited and taken over by the Zionists after British troops evacuated the remaining residents. Apparently 22 old rifles, presumably used for defence purposes, were handed over. The neighbouring village of Yajur was also emptied of its inhabitants.

In the case of Ghwway Abu Shusha, it was visited by the Palmach at dawn. With few arms at the villagers' disposal, the women and children had already been evacuated to the nearby al Rama. The 48 remaining defenders had only 35 to 40 rifles between them. With "no-one in the village to protect" they withdrew to al Rama.

A meeting took place in Amman of various Arab leaders and their military personnel. Intervention in Palestine by regular troops was discussed, in the light of the inability of the Arab Liberation Army and Palestinian Arabs to cope with Zionist threat.

Palestine Arab leaders warned on the Arab Liberation Radio "Certain elements and Jewish agents are spreading defeatist news to create chaos and panic among the peaceful population. Some cowards are deserting their houses, villages or cities . . Zionist agents and corrupt cowards will be severely punished."[49]

April 25

The mortaring of Jaffa continued, causing heavy casualties and accelerating the exodus from the town. The Irgun claimed to have come face to face with British troops, anti-tank guns being used by both sides. Haganah radio dismissed Irgun claims to have penetrated into Jaffa as "fictitious."

The Damiani family, who left Jaffa for Beirut by sea :

"My father originally refused to leave Jaffa. But the rest of the family insisted because we did not want him to be endangered. We were peaceful people. We did not care much for politics. . . . We carried only suitcases and clothes and we had a case with our jewellery and the registry deeds to our land inside. We never thought that we would not be able to go back. If we had thought that, we would never have left. We took our front door keys with us . . . When we pulled out of Jaffa. I stood on the stern and looked out over the old city. I could see our soap factory in the *serail* on top of the hill and St Peter's church next to it. . . . .I said to myself 'If this ship could turn round now, would return to Jaffa.' We were foolish. It was too late."[50]

It soon became clear that a three pronged attack had been carried out on Haifa, led by the Irgun. The Haganah joined later, with an attack being carried out on Tireh village to prevent Arab reinforcements arriving.

To stop "further looting" a curfew was imposed on the Arab section of Haifa. Haganah guards, some only armed with rubber "koshes" were rounding up Arabs and issuing them with ID cards, valid for a short duration. The stated purpose was to ensure that there were no "foreign Arabs" in the town. Although it was also the start of reinforcing the status for Palestinian residents of Haifa of being strangers in their own town and land.

Talks took place between Arab and Jewish leaders concerning food supplies, with the latter wanting the Arabs to settle down to a normal routine [Author's note: It later became evident that there was a fear that the mass exodus of Palestinians could bring about a labour shortage in the town.] It was reported that most Arabs felt there was nothing for which to remain.

The Arab League stated its grievance over the British responsibility for events in Haifa. With the British initially agreeing not to withdraw from Haifa until the final stage of withdrawal, the Arabs were taken completely by surprise. It resented the High Commissioner's version of events, pointing out that Haifa Arabs were less than half the population, they were weakly armed, cut off by Zionists from the rest of the country, on the defensive. To accuse them of aggression was unfair considering the restraint exercised following DeirYassin and Tiberias.

With the commencement of Operation Jevussi for the conquest of the whole of Jerusalem, Zionist forces attacked Jerusalem at two points.In the north where Nablus Road enters the city and Katamon in the south, where they penetrated the Sheikh Jarrah quarter. At this juncture the British intervened attracting complaints from the Zionists that some of their men had been surrounded, this action being dubbed "unwarranted interference."

Arab resistance was reported. Roads were blocked and Zionist armoured cars were mined. The village of Shufat continued to resist occupation. Haganah attempts to cut off Jerusalem from Jericho failed.

The Jerusalem fire brigade which had been partitioned between the opposing sides lost its Arab section. The engines were held up at Jaffa Gate and stolen.

Three Britons were killed when a troop train was derailed. A section of the track had been removed. Another was shot dead by Arab assailants in the middle of Jerusalem.

The last houses in the village of al Ghubayya al Tahta, near Haifa, were demolished. It had been the scene of pitched battles with the Arab Liberation Army.

On this date Operation Chametz (the "Passover cleaning") commenced with the purpose, by the end of the month, of seizing all the villages connecting Jaffa to the hinterland. One of the first to go was Beit Daja which was occupied by the Alexandroni Brigade. The Haganah assisted by local settlers destroyed the houses of Wadi al Hawarith, near Tulkarm, and other neighbouring villages ensuring the return of the villagers to be "all but impossible."

Khirbat al Mansura, near Haifa, was attacked by the Haganah. No traces remain of the village.

A small vessel was intercepted by the Royal Navy. Its 785 illegal Jewish immigrants were off-loaded at Haifa and, within an hour, were being shipped to Cyprus.

April 26

It was reported that the Transjordan government had declared war on "Zionism". The armies of Syria, the Lebanon, Transjordan and Iraq signed an agreement to join a three-front campaign to open before 1 May.

In an interview with King Abdullah the view was expressed that military measures were the only options open to decide the situation in Palestine "since the Jews had started warfare without waiting for May 15." The Jews, he said, had already attacked peaceful Arab villages, Haifa, Jaffa and a great part of Jerusalem. He had sent a message to the Jews urging them "to accept to live as citizens in a Palestinian Arab State." He pointed out that he did not accept a state of war in Palestine, only "inhuman attacks by Jews". Arabs, he felt, had waited in vain for justice from the UN and now must safeguard their rights themselves. He was prepared to try to implement any truce on "condition that the status quo is restored in Tiberias and Haifa." In view of recent events, the protection of Jerusalem, Bethlehem and Nazareth must be placed in the hands of the Arabs. Referring to Russia and her satellites he concluded "Arab people understand the truth, and will not be slaves to these States or their decisions." [51]

A unit from the Transjordan army occupied Jericho - five miles from the Palestine-Transjordan border.

The Irgun renewed their attack on Jaffa, the only remaining Arab port, "according to plan". An Irgun spokes man said it was intended to capture the whole of Jaffa and incorporate it within the Jewish State. By the end of the day, much of Jaffa was still in Arab hands. Civilians were still fleeing, mostly to the countryside to the southeast of the city. Parts of Tel-Aviv, controlled by the Irgun, were shelled by mortars and light artillery. Unconfirmed Zionist sources accused British troops in Jaffa of contributing to this attack.

Zionist attacks on Acre, on the northern coast of Palestine, were reported. Schooners, armed with mortars, took part with shelling by Haganah forces lasting five hours. Residents in the suburbs fled to the safety of the walls of the old town.The attackers were driven of by the town's defenders. Later 140 Arab prisoners from Acre prison escaped when mortar shells fell on the roof.

Arabs attacked Atarot and Lahavot and blocked off the road at Bab al Wad.

British light tanks intervened when Zionist forces, using mortars and heavy machine guns, tried to capture the Arab village of Tira (famed for its olive oil production), less than ten miles from Haifa. British troops helped evacuate the women and children. In Haifa itself, bread was distributed to the "needy and dispossessed" Arabs through a committee of leading local Arabs. Jewish bakeries made the bread which was distributed free, according to reports, through the Haganah.

In Jerusalem, a Haganah brigade under the command of Yitzhak Rabin, captured the Sheikh Jarrah area. The Zionist forces were then forced out by British troops because the area lay alongside British evacuation routes. However an agreement was reached with the British commander that Sheikh Jarrah would be returned once the British had departed. This agreement was eventually honoured.

Yosef Weitz, of the Jewish National Fund and who sat on the Transfer Committee which deliberated the fate of the Palestinian Arabs, recorded in his diary that the northern part of Zevulun Valley was completely clear of Bedouin, their shacks destroyed and their fields ploughed over. His published diary omitted the comment recorded in his notebook at that time "We must be rid of these blackmailers and parasites." The following day Weitz "ordered" kibbutzim representatives "to finish the job within five days." A month later he was able to record "and there is almost no trace of those who had trespassed on our lands."[52]

A Jewish illegal immigrant ship with a cargo of 600 Jews was intercepted by the Royal Navy off Haifa. Egypt warned all shipping to stay out of territorial waters along the 20 mile coastal strip of southern Palestine from 1 May.

When troops from the Suffolk Regiment pulled out of the Alemein Camp, near Jerusalem the area was immediately occupied by Arab forces. This was regarded as the largest British installation yet to fall into Arab hands.

Jamal Husseini, spokesman for the Arab Higher Committee, commented that it was common knowledge that the Jewish Agency was buying huge quantities of arms from the United States with a "certain South American republic" as an intermediary. He also alleged that Zionist supporters were amassing in certain Balkan ports ready for trans-shipment to Palestine for 16 May. "It is also common knowledge that Jews and non-Jews have and are being trained in the fine art of terrorism and sabotage in Poland and Russia for exhibition in Palestine . ."[51]

Fawzi Kaukji alleged that three "Russian Battalions" had opposed his forces at Mishmar Haemek. One Russian lieutenant-colonel had been killed in battle. Another had been hanged by Arab fighters. Their ID papers had been sent to the United Nations.

April 27

The British authorities gave instructions to the army to oppose the occupation of Jaffa by the Zionists. The message from the District Governor of Lydda, Mr W Fuller, was sent to the Mayor of Tel-Aviv, Israel Rokach. This coincided with an Irgun report claiming progress in the continuing conflict in Jaffa.

Sir Alec Kirkbride, the British Minister in Amman, denied recent reports that Transjordan forces had entered Jericho. Doubts about any Egyptian Army support in Palestine continued with a Cairo newspaper reporting that the Defence Ministry would "allow Army officers, NCOs and men to volunteer for service in Palestine."

It was reported that Iraq has agreed full military cooperation. Up to 10 000 troops and 25 planes were said to be moving into Transjordan. Troops of King Abdullah's Transjordan army were reported to have taken up position on both sides of the Allenby Bridge over the Jordan river - the main link between Transjordan and Palestine. A company of the Arab

Legion, under British orders, took up position in the Jericho area to ensure the road to Transjordan was kept open. The Legion was active along the frontier following reports that the Zionists were mobilizing about 1 000 men in the area. A Palestine Government spokesman confirmed that the Arab Legion was under control of GOC British Troops, and their conduct was not in question.

The Haganah, the Jewish "Defence Force" and the Irgun terrorist organisation signed an agreement in Tel-Aviv for full cooperation in military operations throughout Palestine. This ended a period of bitterness between the two organisations.

It was reported that the Administration in Palestine was one of "disintegration and indifference" with 24 hours to go until its virtual extinction. By then 100 officials from Jerusalem will have left, leaving only 20 together with fast disappearing clerks and employees from all offices. In the past 24 hours two Britons were killed, believed to be the victims of Arab attacks, with robbery the motive. Today was the day that heads of government departments were drawing cash for final payments from Barclays bank.

It was reported that all airline employees were preparing to quit Lydda Airport, with British troops occupying all the buildings. Five looters were shot, one dead, after troops followed orders to shoot at anyone touching equipment. The Customs building was said to be on fire. Air France employees had left before noon with KLM hoping to follow.

Zionist terrorists were in action with the manager and other officials from Barclays Bank in Tel-Aviv being taken from their homes in the early hours and forced to open the bank's vaults. It is believed that 100 terrorists were involved in an operation which netted about £250,000. [Later reports placed the responsibility on the Stern Gang who first "dealt with" the Haganah guard on duty at the bank].

A large Jewish shop close to Allenby Square was wrecked by three explosions. The previous day it had been occupied by armed Jews, with its Arab employees vacating the premises.

Outside Jerusalem armed Zionists held up an armoured car. The attack was foiled when a second armoured car arrived on the scene. One Zionist was killed.

The military correspondent for The Scotsman gave an overview of the situation from the military perspective:

The Haganah and the Irgun together command about 100 000 in arms compared with the Arab opposition of about 20 000. The Zionists intend to hold the three Palestinian seaports and thereby ensure a flow of munitions and recruits from overseas - while blockading the Arabs. The first reinforcements would come from some 30 000 illegal immigrants, young and able bodied, drilling and training in internment camps in Cyprus.

Thereafter the the intention would be to seize control and fortify the main road-centres such as Lydda-Ramleh, Jerusalem, Tulkarm, perhaps Nablus and Jenin in the heart of the Arab hills. This would give themselves, and deny to the Arabs, freedom of movement.

Arab strength lay outside Palestine with the armies and gendarmeries of Egypt (latest reports indicated that mechanised units were on their way to the border with two trains laden with soldiers departing to an "unknown destination"), Iraq and the Lebanon - perhaps 120 000 men and 200 aircraft - with a safe bet that not all of this number would be put into battle in view of the difficulties of maintenance. A common plan of action by this mixed contingent was deemed unlikely, with guerrilla warfare deemed the likely option.

By this point the British had withdrawn from the Negev in the south and Galilee in the north with evacuation proceeding from Lydda and Sarafand. The keypoints along the two main routes of Jerusalem-Nablus-Jenin- Haifa and Tulkarm-Haifa would be held to the last in order to effect evacuation to Haifa. A small perimeter will be held around Haifa harbour for final departure on 1 August.

April 28

With the assault on Jaffa by the Irgun into its fourth day, British forces went into action. Tanks, artillery, mortars and cannon firing Spitfires tried to break up the attack.

Reports indicated that the Arabs were weakening, with the Irgun occupying Manshieh quarter and other parts of Jaffa to the north and west, in their drive to the port area. Meanwhile the Haganah attacked from the south into Jaffa's suburbs, capturing four villages en route.

The Spitfires directed their attention on the Irgun HQ from where artillery fire had been directed against Jaffa. The troops concentrated their efforts on key points within the city and the Tel Aviv boundary. The Jewish Agency said that Jews do not wish to stay in Jaffa nor to disrupt the normal life of its people.

During the evening, the Irgun launched a second assault using explosives. Row by row, blocks of houses were blown up creating panic among Arab civilians. Within 24 hours they had reached the sea. Such terrorist actions led to observations such as that of General Murray:

"I saw a scene which I never thought to see in my life. It was the sight of the whole population of Jaffa pouring out on to the road carrying in their hands whatever they could pick up. . . . . as fast as their legs could carry them. It was a case of sheer terror."[53]

And even when it was apparent that the "cleansing" of Jaffa was being successful, the ordeal was not over. As in Haifa, the terror stricken people were targets for Zionist gunmen and snipers. "Those bullets went through the bodies of people standing by the seashore" recalled 12 year old Iris Shammout. As they filed into small boats in an effort to reach a Greek steamship which they hoped would take them to safety, many people were drowned. Babies fell overboard with mothers struggling to save them.[54]

It would have been around this time that the family of 11 year old Sabri al-Banna fled their home town of Jaffa. The young boy would have experienced the terror and trauma of Jaffa being "liberated" - to borrow a phrase much used by the ardent Zionist of the day. He would not have known that the citrus plantations and the citrus export business to Europe, owned by his father, were to be lost to his family. That the family property was to be confiscated by the Israeli government.

He also did not know that, one day, under the *nom de guerre* of Abu Nidal, his name would be known world-wide as he translated the terrorist tactics, witnessed during the cleansing of Jaffa, into a weapon against those he perceived to be his enemy.

British troops re-occupied Lydda Airport. One British and three Arab constables were killed by Zionists at their colony of Nahariya, north of Haifa.

Zionist sources claimed that the Arab Legion had been in action in the Katamon area of Jerusalem.

The Haganah launched Operation Matate and Operation Yiftach to expel Palestinians from eastern and central Galilee and to capture Safed. This was followed by an attack on the town of Samakh, south of Tiberias. The residents fled for safety. North of Safed, the Haganah attacked and occupied Biriya.

It was reported that hopes had risen for a truce over Jerusalem [when the UN Trusteeship Council obtained Jewish and Arab agreement for a truce covering the Old City], with the Jews, more than the Arabs, aware of the realities of their situation. The former were fearful of the Arab Legion. Haganah units were poised to take over key points in the city - the railway station, police HQ, post office etc - once they were vacated by the British. In certain areas of Jerusalem dwindling numbers of troops and police were trying to maintain a semblance of order, if only to keep open the "evacuation routes." Elsewhere the Zionists were almost completely in command.

Jerusalem was a city of desolation with no way of estimating how many of its 165 000 inhabitants had fled. Large areas were dead and deserted, with the tons of accumulated litter blowing about in the strong winds. Life returned at night in the form of snipers operating from demolished buildings. There was a feeling that the Battle of Jerusalem would not be long, with the Zionists coming up trumps in so many of the recent engagements.The remnants of the British community had started to move into the sanctuary (and hoped for safety) of St George's Anglican Cathedral.

With the Katamon area of the city subject to weeks of heavy artillery shelling, the Arab National Committee of Jerusalem ordered its local branches to relocate women, children and elderly people from the area.

The Palestinian Arabs were reported to be leaderless - mainly due to the tendency of the members of the Arab Higher Committee to fight the battle for Palestine from Cairo, Damascus or Beirut. Little faith was put on Jamil Husseini's statement that an Arab State would be declared on 16 May. King Abdullah of Transjordan was seen to be the mainstay behind any possible effective action.

Police and FBI raided a New York house and seized rifles, pistols, machine guns, grenades, ammunition, knives and bayonets concealed in bags of clothing and food destined for Palestine. Members of a young Zionist movement were taken into custody.

April 29

The Zionist forces besieging and attacking Jaffa agreed to a ceasefire following an ultimatum to the Jewish Agency. To reinforce their determination to strike at Zionist targets if the Irgun and Haganah continued with their assault, a formation of Spitfires flew overhead as truce negotiations proceeded. Although the Irgun did not confirm the truce, their mortars fell silent at 4pm. It was later agreed that the ceasefire would become operative as long as the Zionists did not extend beyond the areas they had already captured in the northern part of the city. On the south side of Jaffa, Arab forces recaptured two positions held by the Zionists in Tel el Rish area. During the fighting with British troops when the Irgun were forced back by tanks and infantry, 11 Zionists were known to have been killed with 30 seriously wounded. Thirty Arabs were reported killed with about 100 wounded.

The Irgun eventually broke the truce, shelling the city centre with heavy mortar fire. British artillery returned the fire and broke through the Zionist land blockade of Jaffa. Arab reports stated that Arab reinforcements had reached Jaffa, including Iraqis with artillery. The Irgun claimed to be within 700 yards of the port and to have taken 1 000 Arab prisoners.

During the previous evening 100 Arab prisoners escaped from Latrun detention camp, assisted by the absence of most Arab warders from their post. In Jerusalem there were only 20 senior officials, aided by a handful of local employees, primarily concerned with winding up the affairs of the Administration. Arabs and Jews were reported to be watching the thinning down of of British military forces "counting their ammunition and sharpening their knives" for the battle to come.

It was reported that the Jewish Agency had established a number of air-strips for use by Zionist leaders and a mail service. They would facilitate communication between Tel Aviv and Jerusalem.

Anti-British feeling was reported to be rapidly increasing throughout the "Arab areas" of Palestine. A convoy which was to have taken 1 000 British police, the few remaining wives and their possessions to Haifa had to be postponed to await a strong military escort. Fawzi Kauwkji, who had returned as Arab commander of the Arab volunteers in Palestine sent a threat to police HQ saying that "the convoy will be attacked as a reprisal for help given by the British to Jewish forces in Haifa."[55]

Following King Abdullah's recent promise "to rescue the Palestine Arabs", the Arab Legion clashed with units of the Haganah which had attacked the Jisr Majawi police-post, south of Tiberias. The Haganah were shelled by the Legion when they fired at a patrol on the Transjordan side of the border. Arab sources said some 150 Zionists had been killed.

Sources in Amman said that 30 000 regular troops from Arab States under the titular command of King Abdullah "will rescue Palestine before May 15."

In Haifa a few Palestinians started to return to their homes. However many were still waiting on the coast for fishing boats to take them to Acre and the Lebanon.

No politician, Arab or Jew was willing to comment on the truce agreement for the Old City of Jerusalem. Within the Old City, two British constables were attacked and beaten in an attempt to seize their rifles. One escaped and the other was rescued by the Arab National Guard.

April 30

A Haganah force of about 200 men launched an attack on the Katamon district of Jerusalem. They failed in their initial objective and ended up lodged on two sides the Greek monastery of St Simeon's on top of a wooded hill used by Arab forces as a military HQ. The offensive was preceded by a mortar barrage and heavy machine gun fire. Thirty Arabs were reported killed with at least 34 wounded. Zionist sources admitted 15 dead and 20 wounded. Late in the evening two heavy explosions rocked Katamon district. They were attributed to Haganah demolition squads.

The attack on Katamon coincided with military action in the Yemin Moshe Jewish quarter of the city. Arabs in a stolen Jewish bus, drove past, firing into the area.This was accompanied by a mortar bombardment into the same area by Arab forces positioned on the Old City's walls. In an effort to stop the fighting, British troops fired two pounders into Yemin Moshe and laid a smoke screen between the combatants. Earlier a police armoured car had directed its fire at a Jewish house from which shots had been fired at a military post overlooking Katamon.

Earlier the UN Truce Commisssion had refused to attempt to negotiate a truce in Katamon, stating that their concern was to obtain a truce for the whole country. However, as in Jaffa, the British authorities in Jerusalem decided to intervene. District Commisssioner, J H Pollock threatened "powerful military intervention" if Zionist operations continued.The threat of using the RAF was reported to have taken aback the Zionist authorities.

With over an estimated 20 000 Palestinian refugees fleeing to the Lebanon and Syria in recent days, it was reported that truce talks continued between the British military authorities and the Jews and Arabs in Jaffa. British troops were ready to position themselves between opposing sides in Jaffa with the cease fire terms stating that there should be no aggressive action from either side. Unarmed Palestinians should be allowed to return to the area they had left. Infringements would be dealt with, without prior warning, by the army.

In Haifa, it was reported that British troops were, once again, patrolling the Arab areas.

Ben Gurion visiting Salama [pop. 6 730], near Jaffa, to inspect this recent conquest, commented in his diary that he had found "only one old blind woman."[56] Two weeks earlier Zionist forces had blitzed Salama with mortar fire.

The United States delegation at the UN proposed that a temporary trusteeship for Jerusalem as a whole should be arranged. It found favour with the Jewish Agency because, as proposed, it would save the Haganah the effort of keeping the road from Jerusalem to the coast open. The Arab representative, in a comment from The Times, "did not trouble to be polite about it."

The president of the Security Council read a telegram to the political committee from the Palestine truce commission. It reported that the general situation was deteriorating rapidly. The Jewish Agency was trying to provide services to Jewish areas. The Palestinian Arabs relied upon municipal authorities within the towns. Villages had no central authority. Camps and other important areas vacated by the British became immediate battle grounds.

The Egyptian government reported to Arab newspapers that the United States had begun to exercise some pressure on the Arab Governments and disapproved of their determination to resort to armed intervention in Palestine.[57]

Notes

1 Benny Morris, *Falsifying the Record,*(Journal of Palestine Studies, Spring 1995) p.54
2 Norman Finkelstein, *Myths, Old and New*, (JoPS, Autumn 1991) p.88
3 Walter Laqueur, *The Israel-Arab Reader, Israel and the Arab World 1948-67*, p.185
4 Laqueur, p.188
5 Jon Kimche, *Seven Fallen Pillars*, p.216
6 David Hirst, *The Gun and the Olive Branch*, p.140
7 Michael Palumbo,*The Palestinian Catastrophe*, p.64-65
8 Kimche, p.224
9 Morris, p.55
10 Walid Khalidi, *All that Remains*, p.278
11 The Scotsman 3/4/48
12 Khalidi p.514
13 *ibid* p.142
14 The Scotsman 10/4/48
15 Khalidi, p.289

16 H Levin, *Jerusalem Embattled*, p.57
17 Palumbo, p.48
18 *ibid* p.50
19 *ibid* p.54
20 *ibid* p.55
21 Levin, p.66
22 Khalidi, p.534
23 The Times 12/4/48
24 Khalidi, p.143
25 Benny Morris, *The birth of the Palestinian refugee problem, 1947-49*, p.51
26 Khalidi, p.315
27 Finkelstein, p.78
28 The Scotsman 16/4/48
29 Khalidi, p.158
30 The Scotsman 16/4/48
31 Khalidi, p.63
32 The Scotsman 16/4/48
33 Khalidi, p.419
34 Palumbo, p.107-108
35 *ibid* p.63
36 The Scotsman 20/4/48
37 Khalidi, p.169
38 *ibid* p.169
39 Palumbo, p.65
40 The Times 22/4/48
41 Finkelstein, p.72
42 *ibid* p.87
43 Levin, p.87
44 The Scotsman 23/4/48
45 John C Trever, *The untold story of Qumran* p.100
46 Palumbo, p.109-110
47 The Scotsman 24/4/48
48 The Times 24/4/48
49 Laqueur, p.183
50 R Fisk, *Pity the Nation*, p.26
51 The Scotsman 27/4/48
52 Benny Morris, *Falsifying the Record*, (JoPS, Spring 1995) p.55
53 Palumbo, p.87
54 *ibid* p.90
55 The Scotsman 30/4/48
56 Khalidi, p.257
57 The Times 1/5/48

May

The destruction of the villages became a major political enterprise.
Benny Morris, Israeli historian

"By May 1948, the Palestinian fighting force consisted of four thousand soldiers. These were joined during the first few months of 1948 by eight thousand volunteers, mostly irregular Arab soldiers. . . .Palestinians made up even less than one-tenth of the overall number of volunteers. . . . this indicates that the Palestinian political leadership in fact governed no military power of its own and that without outside Arab assistance in the form of regular armies the Arabs of Palestine had absolutely no hope of achieving any significant military gain against the Jews. Even with the volunteers, the Palestinian fighting force numbered only 12 000, facing a Jewish force of 22 425 active military personnel."[1]

For those regular armies of some of the Arab states, there was still no comparison with the Zionist war machine:

"We entered the war with so little preparation that there was no time to carry out a general mobilisation. I had to hire twenty-one trucks from Palestinian Arabs in order to haul my troops from Rafah up to Gaza, and I had to leave some of my six-pounders behind for lack of tractors. The terrain was too difficult to haul them behind our trucks. The officer in charge of the abandoned six-pounders cried for shame, and there were tears in my eyes as well."[2]

With the media concentrating on events in Jerusalem, Jaffa, the United Nations and the capitals of various Arab states it was left to researchers, historians and diarists of the future to record events which happened elsewhere in Palestine.

The Chief Secretary of the Palestine Government, Sir Henry Gurney, was one person who seemed to be unaware of the terror experienced by those Palestinian civilians facing the Zionist onslaught when he compared the search for safety and security with fleeing "rabbits." And cynically alleged that many of the better-off Palestinians had "discovered urgent business in Beirut or Cairo."

In the time honoured fashion, certainly as far as the Palestinian experience is concerned, of blaming the victims, he castigated assistance from the Arab states as "ill-organised and stupid intervention." As if Zionist aggression and expansionism, the variety of well planned military operations which were soon to be come apparent, would never have materialised in the absence of resistance.[3]

The coming weeks were to show how well the Zionists had planned for a state "cleansed" of its indigenous population. They were to show how effective the creation of terror and fear in a civilian population, firmly rooted in its history, culture and land, was in dispossessing them of their birthright.

In the words of Israeli historian, Benny Morris:

> "In conformity with Tochnit Dalet (Plan D), the Haganah's master plan . . . The Haganah cleared various areas completely of Arab villages - the Jerusalem corridor, the area round Mishmar Haemek, and the coastal plain. But in most cases expulsion orders were unnecessary; the inhabitants had already fled, out of fear or as a result of Jewish attack. In several areas Israeli commanders successfully used psychological warfare ploys to obtain Arab evacuation (as in the Hula Valley, in Upper Galilee, in May).[4]

Outside major urban centres "it was standard Haganah and IDF policy to round up and expel the remaining villagers (usually old people, widows, cripples) from sites already evacuated by most of their inhabitants."[5]

May was the month that the Zionist forces revisited many Palestinian villages - perhaps attacked months or weeks earlier - to ensure that the local population did not stay around.

As the fourteenth of May approached, and with the majority of the Arabs who eventually became refugees still *in situ*, the full fury of the Zionist military machine was unleashed. Palestinians who fled the field of attack, even if lingering right outside their villages or towns until the terror abated, were blocked from returning. Palestinians who lagged behind or failed to "get the message" were generally expelled outright. The villages that were home to these Palestinians were systematically destroyed.

Many Palestinian villages, deeply rooted in time and history, were razed to the ground, part of the eventual Zionist propaganda onslaught to try and convince the world that there was no such a place as Palestine, no such a people as Palestinians. However, there was always the occasional Zionist with a conscience who was prepared to put his thoughts into print. In early May, Aharon Cohen, director of Mapam's [an early Zionist political party with a Marxist outlook] Arab Department wrote that "A deliberate eviction [of the Arabs] is taking place . . . Others may rejoice - I, as a socialist am ashamed and afraid." A few days later he observed that " 'transfer' of the Arabs from the area of the Jewish state" was being executed "out of certain political goals and not only out of military necessity."[6] He further added that the complete destruction of villages was not always done because there were "no sufficient forces to maintain a garrison."[7]

According to the analysis of Israeli historian, Benny Morris, it was in early May that the destruction of Palestinian villages changed from being primarily a military objective, to a political one. While he concedes that in some areas other reasons for the destruction may have dominated (eg revenge), it was during this month that the idea of permanently removing the Palestinians took root. "The destruction of the villages became a major political enterprise."[8]

The end of the British mandate over Palestine took place on Friday 14th. During the weekend that followed there were claims from all sides with regards to military conquests. It was only in the light of day that legitimate claims as distinct from propaganda, could be discerned.

However, as was subsequently revealed, by mid-May there was no doubt in some minds that the Palestinian refugees would not be returning. Yosef Weitz of the Jewish National Fund, for one, was concerned over the fate of the "abandoned" Palestinian land. which at that point amounted to some 75 000 acres.

His concern was two-fold. First of all there was some opposition within the JNF directorate to any expropriation of Arab land. Secondly, any expropriation, under whatever legal gloss, might not give custody of the land to the JNF. Months later the government eventually agreed to give control of this purloined land to the Fund. It gave the JNF the right to lease the land to settlements or, at the very least, control over the Ministry of Agriculture's leasing policy.

May 1

As part of Operation Yiftach the Palmach attacked and occupied the village of Ein Zeitun [pop 820] to the north of Safad in Eastern Galilee. This was a village with a long history of animosity towards the Zionist colonisers. It had strategic value, in that any invader wanting to control Safad and the surrounding area had to control Ein Zeitun.

The attack began at 3am with the usual mortar attack followed by a ground assault with hand grenades. The Palmach rounded the villagers up and threatened them with mass execution.Thirty seven teenage boys were selected at random and taken captive. They were never seen again.The rest were humiliated, stripped of their possessions and, with gun fire directed over their heads, forced from their village into the surrounding area where their distressed presence would be guaranteed to terrorise others.

Israeli historian, Benny Morris, reckoned that the captives were part of a group later slaughtered two or three days later by order of Moshe Kelman, the commander of the Palmach's Third Battalion. In anticipation of Red Cross visit, he ordered the hands of the victims to be untied to conceal that the killing had been done in cold blood.[9]

The Qatamon neighbourhood of Jerusalem finally fell under sustained Zionist attack. Looting of the affluent Palestinian homes immediately commenced.

In the words of one eye-witness, Hagit Shlonsky, a Jewish nurse stationed in Katamon:

" . . . I was stunned by the beauty of the houses . . . a piano, and carpets and wonderful chandeliers . . For days you could see people walking by carrying looted goods . . . I saw them walking by for days. Not only soldiers, civilians as well. They were looting like mad. They were even carrying dining tables. And it was in broad daylight, so everyone could see . . ."[10]

It was reported that the Lebanon and Syria intended to send troops to Palestine on 15 May, at the end of the Mandate.

Ben Gurion paid a visit to Haifa. On watching the scenes of Palestinian Arabs leaving the city he exclaimed "What a beautiful sight." Soon after, while speaking to a group of Jewish dignitaries he said "It is not our duty to see to it that the Arab returns." He later rebuked a city official who had been trying to persuade the Arabs of Haifa to remain "Doesn't he have anything better to do?" This attitude soon rubbed off on any Zionist with a consience or concern and attempts to halt the flow of Palestinians seeking refuge elsewhere came to an end.[11]

May 2

Following the assault on, and occupation of, Arab strong points in the Katamon district of Jerusalem over the past couple of days, Arab guns bombarded the area during the night. Several deaths, including that of children were reported in this Haganah controlled area. By the end of the night a 48 hour truce had been agreed or, some might say, imposed, with the British warning retaliation against those who tried to advance on any area already occupied. During daylight, apart from the occasional sniper and mortar fire, peace prevailed in Jerusalem. Troops from the Highland Light Infantry moved into Katamon to enforce the truce.

It was reported that the truce in Jaffa was broken by Arabs attacking the Zionist lines. This provoked a limited response from British tanks and artillery.

The roads between Hebron and Bersheeba, Gaza and Bersheeba were reported to be impassable following Zionist actions in blowing up bridges and culverts. British troops cleared mines on the Jerusalem-Jericho road.

The Haganah were reported to have used heavy aircraft for the first time. Two engined planes bombed Arab forces attacking Zionist settlements in Upper Galilee.

The evacuation of Safad started today, following the capture of several nearby villages by the Haganah.These villages included: Ein Zeitun, occupied the day previously. The village houses were either blown up or burned, partly to terrify the residents of Safad who could view the destruction from nearby hills. The sight of this act had a demoralising effect in Safad and other villages in Eastern Galilee.

The village of al Ja'una was partially evacuated. The villages of Mughr al Khayt and Qabba'a and Fir'im were mortared during the night "in order that in the end the Arabs would flee from them" according a military report on the operation.[12]

Yosef Weitz, of the Jewish National Fund, recorded in his diary after observing, at first hand, the results of the Haganah's actions in the Jezreel Valley

". . .the Arab villages [are] in ruins . . . the houses and huts are completely destroyed ." The Arabs left "in a psychosis of fear."

Rather incredulously he added

"Village after village was abandoned in a panic *that cannot be explained.*"[13]

Meanwhile, in Amman, a meeting of officials and notables from Haifa agreed that their people should return to Haifa. In the following days, coordination with the British to achieve this objective looked possible when the British army removed Haganah road-blocks and moved into empty Arab neighbourhoods.[14]

Britain announced that she was sending considerable military reinforcements to Palestine because of the deterioration in the situation. This was seen as affirmation that Britain intended to take stringent measures to combat violence during the last 13 days of the Mandate.

The announcement stated:

"Owing to the unwarranted aggression on the part of the Irgun Zvai Leumi in Jaffa, the situation has seriously deteriorated during the past week. This theatre has now assumed operational priority over some other commitments in the Middle East. As a consequence, considerable reinforcements of infantry, tanks, guns and Marine Commandos have had to be dispatched to Palestine in the cause of general security."[15]

With the "get-tough" policy being directed mainly at the Zionists, a government spokesman said there would be no hesitation in taking action against the Arab forces should the need arise. Reports indicated that two companies of British troops had landed at Jaffa, possibly the second such landing in 24 hours.

The Jewish Agency was not slow in protesting the slur directed at the Irgun. Allegations were made of Arab aggression against Zionist positions in the past few days, of Syrian and Lebanese army units active in attacking border settlements in North Palestine. This was dismissed as "Jewish propaganda" after the RAF had flown over the area and found no sign of fighting.

The Liverpool Regiment arrived from its previous duty of guarding illegal Zionist immigrants in detention camps in Cyprus to the more arduous task of keeping Lydda Airport open. They joined the Argyll and Sutherland Highlanders already in position. It was regarded as imperative to keep the airport open and give security to the Arab employees following the walk out of Jewish members of staff and their sabotaging of communications equipment.

There were a variety of reports concerning Arab mobilisation in preparation for an outright war after 15 May. At the forefront was King Abdullah and the Arab Legion. Iraq dispatched troops to Transjordan, en route to Palestine.

Three plane loads of arms from France arrived for the Haganah.

The position of oil supplies in the Meditarranean area was the subject of speculation and reporting. With the refinery in Haifa having closed down on 13 April following hostilities and the cessation of oils supplies from Iraq, it looked as if the supply of refined oil would be a major determining factor as regards the outcome of any war in Palestine.

Efforts to bring about a truce throughout Palestine continued. This would have given the UN a start once the British mandate came to an end. The British were concentrating their efforts on the Arab leadership.The result was that the Arab states felt that their intervention would come to late to save the "Arab cause."

The Americans concentrated on the Zionists. The latter, flushed with their successes, were reported not to be amenable to any approach.

May 3

Paradoxically, as preparation for war in Jerusalem was reported to be near its final stages, the city had its most peaceful 24 hours for months. The city was reported to resemble two fortified armed camps, with heavy barriers thrown up, gun emplacements and road blocks guarding the entrances to the various quarters. Both "camps" were filled with troops with reinforcements of various Arab nationalities arriving daily.

Lieutenant-General Gordon MacMillan was reported in the New York Post as saying that Britain would resist "with full force" any attempt by Arab states to invade Palestine while the Mandate was still in force. All convicted prisoners in Palestine, Arab and Jew, were at liberty following the withdrawal of British prison personnel. HMS Newcastle was reported to be "demonstrating off Jaffa". Two hundred lorries with British troops arrived in Southern Palestine from the Suez Canal area.

Palestinian refugees continued to stream out of their homeland in search of safety. At the Allenby Bridge over the River Jordan, the flow was temporarily halted as Iraqi volunteers crossed over the bridge from Transjordan into Palestine.

British troops patrolled Jaffa as the mass exodus continued. With only a few thousand Arabs left, both Zionist and Arab combatants were warned of British retaliatory shelling if hostilities were renewed.

Zionist colonists from Gush Etzion, south of Jerusalem, ambushed traffic on the way to the city.

Arab forces carried out a mortar attack on the Zionist colony of Neve Yaacov.

Yosef Weitz of the Jewish National Fund was lobbied by local Jewish representatives from the Jordan Valley who, now that their area had been "emptied" of Arabs were keen that settlements should be established. They demanded that settlements be established at Khirbet ad Duweir and As Samra on the southern shore of the Sea of Galilee.

A Mr Rex Farran was killed when he opened a parcel, addressed to his brother, Capt Roy Farran. The parcel bomb coincided with the anniversary date of the disappearance of member of the terrorist Stern Gang, Alex Rubowitz. Captain Farran had been charged with his murder, but acquitted. Since then the Stern Gang had threatened to follow him "to the end of the world."

May 4

The cease fire in Katamon was still holding while talks, hopefully leading to a truce, progressed. Fresh British troops arrived in Jerusalem to assist the Highland Light Infantry who have been responsible for security in two of the "hottest" areas in Jerusalem - the walled Old City with its warren of narrow passages and caves and "no-mans land", Sheikh Jarrah quarter, with its nightly fights to obtain possession.

The job of the HLI, since November, was seen to be one of preventing some 25 000 Arabs from massacring 1 500 Jews.

Within Jerusalem life in the Jewish part was reported to be "fairly steady". Men were to be seen in uniform and those without were questioned to account for themselves. The Arab areas tend to be deserted but with no large scale exodus evident.

Only a few thousand Palestinians remained in Jaffa, uncertain what to do, in the full knowledge that the British would soon depart.

Heavy fighting was reported between Arab assailants and the Zionist defenders of a Russian Orthodox monastery five miles south of Bethlehem. The Haganah claimed to have killed 50 Arabs, knocked out 20 armoured cars, with eight of their defenders killed.

The Irgun reported that Arab forces, allegedly the Arab Legion, had launched a strong counter attack against Yehudia village, seized earlier by the Irgun. It was suggested that this was part of a strategy to open up a route to Lydda Airport.

The village of 'Aqir to the south west of al Ramla was surrounded by an estimated force of 400 Haganah troops of the Giv'ati Brigade. A demand was made that all guns should be handed over with eight villagers taken hostage. Following British intervention, the Brigade withdrew. However the incident prompted the flow of 3 000 people from the village. Within weeks, the remaining 30 or so villagers were expelled.

The Irgun occupied the village of Abbasiyah, near Jaffa. The Arab Legion, operating under British command, shelled Gush Etzion in retaliation for the previous day's ambush.

As part of Operation Matate (Broom), designed to "sweep" Palestinians out of the area east of Safad and the Jordan River, the village of al Qudayriyya was attacked by the Haganah and the residents expelled. The village probably suffered immediated demolition. According to military sources, this Operation had "tremendous psychological impact."

The village of al Zanghariyya and two others suffered the same fate. With orders that they should be attacked and "their inhabitants expelled and their houses blown up" the Palmach had an easy job. When they appeared, the villagers fled towards Syria, such was the fear. The following day, sappers methodically blew up fifty houses.[16]

The historical village of al Tabigha was occupied and partially destroyed by the Haganah. A few villagers tried to return but, within a week, the activities of the Haganah made it impossible. A neighbouring historical village, al Samakiyya (close the site of Capernaum) was occupied and destroyed. Following a shell and mortar attack by the Palmach, the village of 'Arab al-Shamalina [pop 650] suffered a similar fate. The Operation Commander, Yigal Allon, commented "We regarded it as imperative to cleanse the interior of the Galilee and create Jewish territorial continuity in the whole of Upper Galilee."[17]

Operation Yiftah continued on its way, characterised by demolition of conquered Arab villages as the entry in the Operations log book outlined ". . . at 9.00 o'clock the units reached their objectives as, on the way, they blow up all the houses and burn all the bedouin tents."[16]

Yosef Weitz of the Jewish National Fund recorded in his notes, but omitted from his published diary, his thoughts on the land owned by a mix of Jewish and Palestinian Arab owners in Bet She'an (Baysan) Valley. The land was coveted by the JNF. Weitz complained to the local Jewish leaders that "the valley was still seething with enemies. I said. - the eviction [of the Arabs] from the valley is the order of the day."[18]

King Abdullah of Transjordan called on "every man of strength and wisdom, every young person of power and faith [from Palestine], who has left the country, let him return to the dear spot." He thanked those who had remained "in spite of the tyranny prevailing."[14]

May 5

The terrorist Stern Gang, which recently merged with the Haganah, was responsible for carrying out an attack on a British military breakdown lorry two miles south of the Jewish town of Nathanya. Forced to stop when its path was blocked by a stolen armoured lorry, members of the Gang opened fire from an adjacent orange grove. Six British soldiers, all members of the Royal Electrical Mechanical Engineers, were found dead. Each had been shot through the head.

A spokesman said that they were "redeclaring war on the British" in retaliation for new troops being sent to Palestine.

Despite optimistic truce talks, violence flared up again in Jerusalem, centred on the Sheikh Jarrah area. The Arabs mortared St Simeon's Monastery, captured the previous week by the Haganah. It commanded the south west suburbs of Jerusalem.

About 600 villagers from al Tira, which had been attacked the previous month (it had also been attacked by the Irgun on 12 December 1947 when 13 villagers, including women and children, had been massacred), were evacuated to Jenin and Nablus by the British. The Arab Liberation Army, under the command of Michael Issa, withdrew from Jaffa. This marked the end of the city's resistance.

The Golani Brigade began a siege of the town of Beisan from which the wealthy families had already fled. Informed opinion sympathised with those who had already left since, it was the rich who had been politically active and financed the purchase of arms to fight the Zionists. They would have been the first victims of any reprisals under Zionist occupation.

The Mandate government announced, in an indirect attempt to encourage Arabs to return to Haifa, "In the view of the Government the Arabs can feel completely safe in Haifa."[14]

The UN Truce Commission returned empty handed after meeting Arab League delegates in Jericho.The British High Commissioner was asked by the UN Security Council to try and arrange terms between Arab and Jew in Jerusalem for the implementation of the truce agreement.

The large movement of Palestinian refugees was reported to be causing problems. In Gaza there was reported to be a lack of food. Some refugees returned to Haifa following the reclamation of parts of the Arab areas, by British troops, from the Zionists. It was felt that since Haifa would remain under the British for some time to come, there was sufficient security to encourage this inflow of exiles.

It was reported that, with the Zionist successes in Palestine, an overbearing note had crept into Zionist pronouncements on the issue. Prolonged discussion on the subject, as reported in The Times, was treated with scorn, with many Jews obviously feeling that their destiny, and, perhaps, the final answer for Palestine, lay in their hands alone.[19]

In the House of Commons, the Parliamentary Secretary for the Colonies gave approximate numbers for those killed or wounded in Palestine between 1 May, 1947 and 24 April, 1948

Arabs : 1 300 killed and 2 500 wounded
Jews : 1 000 killed and 2 000 wounded

British subjects killed:	Armed Forces	137
	police	53
	civilians	11

May 6

Safad, the main town in Upper Galilee was attacked by the Haganah. Almost 11 000 Arab residents had fled. It was reported that the leaders of the 3 000 strong Jewish community in the town had urged them to stay. This was the culmination of Zionist attacks on neighbouring villages during the previous ten days.

In general, the Zionists were steadily increasing their hold on southern and eastern Galilee following the British evacuation to Haifa.

The British Army was reported to be in full control of all entrances to Haifa. Areas had been delineated within the town into which armed Zionists were denied access. In the Zionist controlled areas there was "orderly control" with the "disarming of terrorists" being carried out. There were moves afoot to encourage Palestinian refugees to return to the town.

Units of the Giv'ati Brigade surrounded the historical village of Qatra, demanding that the villagers hand over their weapons. The troops then moved into the village and began looting. One was shot dead by a villager. Within a few days, the villagers had either been ordered or intimidated into leaving.

Units of the Golani Brigade attacked the village of al Shajara at dawn. When the village was overrun, twenty bodies of the defenders were found. A counter-attack was launched, but the village remained in the hands of the Zionists. [Author's note: al Shajara was the home village of Naji al-Ali, the political cartoonist assassinated in London in 1987.]

Zionist sources stated that forces from Syria and Lebanon shelled the settlement of Ramot Naftali during the night. There was a report that Arab forces had renewed their attack on the settlement of Mishmar Haemek.

The Stern Gang carried out another attack on an army convoy on the Jerusalem Jaffa road. There were no casualties. Meanwhile the Haganah accused British gunners of directing artillery fire against the industrial suburb of Givat Shaul in reprisal.

Five artillery pieces from France reached the Haganah.

Golda Myerson, following a visit to Haifa a few days after its conquest, revealed a few of her feelings in a report to the Jewish Agency Executive[20]. She found it

". . a dreadful thing to see the dead city. . . . there were houses where the coffee and the *pitot* were left on the table, and I could not avoid [thinking] that this, indeed, had been the picture in many Jewish towns."

The report illustrated Myerson's inner conflict with regard to the return of Palestinians to their land. There was no enthusiasm for encouraging the fleeing Arabs to return. Neither was there support for treating the remaining Arab population in Haifa badly so as to discourage others from returning. She commented "I am not among those extremists - and there are such, and I applaud them - who want to do everything that can be done in order to bring back the Arabs."

She had no problem with those who were deemed to be hostile to Zionist ambition. It was those "friendly" villagers who had fled the fighting which caused some soul-searching with regard to their intention to return to their deserted villages.

In the end her call for the Mapai party to hold comprehensive discussions on the "Arab problem" was ignored.

May 7

Arab leaders agreed to a truce for Jerusalem, to commence the next day, "if the Jews also cease fire." Later the Haganah agreed its adherence to the cease fire. While no one was over-optimistic at the news, there was a tangible sense of relief in the city. The main stumbling block was the road to Tel-Aviv. The Zionists wanted it opened with the Arabs not inclined to agree to this stipulation.

This was followed by a brief bout of fighting between the two side in the Yemen Moshe section of the city. British troops and artillery opened up fire with a six-pounder, two- pounders, machine guns and mortars in heart of the city, to stop the fighting.

Reports made it clear that the Zionists had the apparatus of government already functioning, or ready to function in eight days time. A Department of Justice was opened in Tel-Aviv, with courts ready to operate under the control of the Jewish National Administration. An Economic Department and Import and Export Licensing Office had been established.

All in sharp contrast to Arab dominated areas. There was no political unity nor central leadership. Local communities ran their own affairs, not made any easier by the movement of about 200 000 Palestinian Arabs, one fifth of the Palestinian nation, reckoned to be roaming about in the search of a safe haven, whether this be in Palestine, the Lebanon, Syria or Transjordan.

A typhoid epidemic was reported in Acre, with outlying villages being infected, possibly by fleeing refugees.

May 8

Firing ceased in Jerusalem as truce negotiations continued. Zionists took control of the railway from Samakh to Haifa.

Operation Maccabi was launched for the conquest of the villages remaining between Ramleh and Latrun. The village of Beit Mahsir was attacked.

May 9

In Jerusalem the cease fire which had been in place since the previous day was reported to be holding. The Palestine Government said that it would agree to the placing of Jerusalem under the protection of the Red Cross if both Arabs and Jews made a formal request to the Red Cross. Effectively this would make Jerusalem and "open city." It was reported that the Jewish Agency felt "piqued" at the imposition of the ceasefire without prior consultation. Some commentators felt that this was due to a feeling of "national pride", with the mandate due to end in one week.

The Arabs were prepared to allow convoys into Jerusalem under the supervision of a third party. For their part, the Zionists demanded right of access along the whole road from Tel-Aviv to the Wailing Wall and the expulsion of all those armed Arabs who came from outside Palestine, from the city. At this point an inconsistency entered the arena. The Zionists would not agree that their armed personnel should also leave the city, arguing that they would simply go underground. Apparently this reasoning was not to be applied to the Arab forces.

According to Zionist sources, the Palmach launched an attack on the Arab held heights which dominate the Jerusalem Tel-Aviv highway near Bab el Wad, 14 miles from the city.

The picture painted of Jaffa, until a few days previously the largest Arab city in Palestine with a population of 90 000, was a sorry one. Under the UN partition plan Jaffa was designated an Arab enclave in a Jewish state. However with Arab gun posts deserted, a few score refugees boarding small coastal vessels ready to take them to a destination unknown, only a few hundred Palestinians could be seen wandering about their city, dazed, confused and impoverished. It was estimated that only up to 3 000 Palestinians remained, all on the verge of starvation.

At the French Hospital on Jaffa Hill, Catholic nuns cared for the sick, wounded and orphans. British tanks and artillery were in place in the city. Without them the Zionist forces could have walked in. However they were in no rush. The British were due to leave in a few days. They concentrated their efforts in neutralising any resistance on the Jaffa Jerusalem road.

With Jaffa in Zionist hands, this left Gaza as the only Palestinian sea port of any stature. Meanwhile 16 large ocean going freighters had anchored off Tel-Aviv ready to discharge thousands of tons of supplies to the emerging Zionist state.

Under Operation Yiftach, the village of 'Akbara [pop 390] to the south of Safad, was chosen by the Haganah as a target which was intended to help "soften-up" the residents of Safad. Units of the Palmach's first Battalion attacked in order to "create among the Arabs of Safad a feeling that they were about to be surrounded and would be unable to flee . ."[21] There were accusations that the village housed "Syrian spies".

The village militia of 15-20 men put up resistance, but were forced to retreat to the village outskirts. A few houses were destroyed, the mosque partially demolished and the village livestock looted, before the Palmach withdrew.

For those who travelled across Arab populated Palestine from Jaffa to the River Jordan, there was little sign of meaningful military activity. A few unguarded Arab roadblocks, unhappy arms bearing Palestinians looking like members of a home defence unit. With at least 150,000 townspeople on the move, seeking refuge, life in this area seemed to be as normal - threshing the grain, tending orchards and flocks of sheep.

There was official confirmation that the greater part of the Palestine police headquarters in Jerusalem was now in Haifa, having moved in a 25 vehicle convoy.

A British Army sergeant was killed and two soldiers wounded in Acre. They were spraying the area with DDT to help combat an outbreak of typhoid.

King Ibn Saud of Saudi Arabia promised Sausi Arabian troops for the "fight against Zionism" in Palestine (although only the elements of a small regular army existed, together with a few aeroplanes - with training organised by a British military mission for just over a year). Egyptian forces were reported to be inside Palestine to a depth of 55 miles with equipment including artillery and tanks.

May 10

According to Haganah sources, they were in virtual control of the Arab heights next to the Bab el Wad road block on the Jerusalem Tel-Aviv road. "Pioneers" were reported to be forcing a passage through the 200 yard barrier which had been holding up a convoy for 20 days.

On this day Yigal Allon ordered the main attack against Safad. There was heavy use of mortars against Arab strongpoints. However, one of the most effective weapons was the use of loudspeakers which threatened the use of an atomic bomb. Captured prisoners spoke of the belief in a Zionist 'secret weapon' which made fire spout out of the earth and houses collapse. The behaviour of the town's defenders greatly assisted the exodus from Safad.The commander of the Transjordanian troops left the village on the orders of King Abdullah who, apparently, preferred to see the Zionists in control of Safad, rather than his rival, the Grand Mufti. Other Arab commanders were absent from the village when the Palmach attacked. Rumours then spread that the Arab Liberation Army had withdrawn; all this precipitated panic.

Great brutality was directed against the towns people. During 1929, at the time of the Arab Revolt, the town's Jewish community had been attacked with a number killed. Revenge was now on the agenda.

One Palmach recruit wrote honestly of the slaughter of several groups of captive Arabs, resulting from the attack on Safad, by interrogators of the intelligence service. Netiva Ben Yehuda spoke of the scene in one interrogation room where ten prisoners were tortured to death. The interrogator refused to allow the accumulated tortured corpes to be carried out. The hope was that the sight of the bodies, blood, teeth and brains splattered about the room would induce the condemned to talk.[22]

Between the 10th and 15th May, as part of Operation Yiftach, a "whispering campaign" designed to stimulate the flow of refugees from Eastern Galilee was instituted. Those who had not fled despite attacks or intimidation were expelled as soon as their villages were occupied.

Yigal Allon, commander of the Operation, wrote "We regard it as imperative to cleanse the interior of the Galilee and create Jewish territorial continuity in the whole of upper Galilee. . . . Clearing the area (Eastern Galilee) completely of all Arab forces and inhabitants was the simplest and the best way of securing the frontier."[23] The tactic of using a "whispering campaign" was outlined by Allon:

"We saw a need to clean out the inner Galilee and to create a Jewish territorial continuity in the entire area of the upper Galilee. The long battles had weakened our forces . . . . We therefore looked for means which did not force us into employing force, in order to cause the tens of thousands of sulky Arabs who remained in Galilee to flee . . . . I gathered all the Jewish Mukhtars, who have contact with Arabs in different villages, and asked them to whisper in the ears of some Arabs, that a great Jewish reinforcement has arrived in Galilee. . . . They should suggest to these Arabs *as their friends* , to escape while there is still time. . . . The flight numbered myriads. The tactic reached its goal completely."[24]

Following a mortar bombardment and ground assault the village of Beit Daras, north east of Gaza, was occupied by the Giv'ati Brigade. Over 2 750 villagers fled from the attack, the start of Operation Barak. Their houses were blown up as part of "clearing" the Giv'ati southern front. The same brigade attacked and occupied the village of Barqa situated in the same vicinity.

Al Tira, to the north east of al Ramla, was attacked. Its fate at this point was unknown. However the ALA defenders reported that they had insufficient ammunition to "wage battle."

During the night units of the Golani Brigade attacked al Ashrafiya [pop 230], part of Operation Gideon. The villagers fled to the safety of Transjordan. The Haganah were reported as wasting no time before they started to blow up the village houses. Likewise the neighbouring village of Farwana was captured and completely destroyed.

Kfar Darom colony in the Negev was attacked by Egyptian irregulars.

Despite earlier reports that both sides to the undeclared war had agreed in principle to a Red Cross plan to de-militarise Jerusalem and place the whole city under its flag, the Jewish Agency issued a denial.

Perhaps it was happy with events as they were. On the same day the Agency informed the British that in Katamon district the "listing, collection and removal of household goods is being done in an organised manner . ." The British, however, noted that former Arab residents saw their property being looted "Jewish trucks driving up, being loaded with property being brought out of the houses and being driven off to an unknown destination."

The Jewish Agency refused the British request that some residents be allowed to return to reclaim their property, one of the excuses being that "the removal of goods whose ownership is in doubt has not been completed . ."[25]

It was not long before these residents, from their refugee camps in East Jerusalem, were able to observe Zionist immigrants moving into their homes.

The claim by former residents of Katamon that civilians had been killed by the occupation forces was verified by the Red Cross. By using his nose (the Haganah refused to give any assistance) a Red Cross doctor was led to a cave where the stench of decaying flesh was so powerful that one medical orderly collapsed. The sight was as bad as the smell with "A group of bodies . . piled in a heap, including soldiers, women and even a mule." With the eventual assistance of an American volunteer who was able to withstand the horror of the massacre, two lorries were filled with decaying bodies.

The news travelled fast throughout the city. One YMCA official in Jerusalem, A L Miller, observed that Arab morale was affected by this atrocity and, with regard to the ongoing Palestinian exodus, noted "In my opinion the atrocities were committed with this in view."[25]

It was agreed that a special mixed board of one Briton, one Arab and three Jews would run Haifa after the mandate ended. At least three British port officials stayed on.

Aharon Cohen of the Mapam Party completed a memo "Our Arab Policy in the Midst of War", for the consideration of the Mapam Political Committee, attacking the policy of "transfer" of the Palestinian Arab. "The complete destruction of captured villages is not always carried out only because of 'lack of sufficient forces to maintain a garrison' or only so 'the gangs [ie irregulars] will not be able to return there so long as the war continues.'"[8]

Golda Meir was dispatched to Transjordan to explore, with King Abdullah, "desirable arrangements" for the latter to control that part of Palestine outlined for Arab state-hood in the Partition Resolution. The King was reported to have affirmed that he would not attack those parts of Palestine allocated to the Jewish state. A peace agreement would be reached once the "dust had settled."[26]

Sources in the UN leaked details of Britain's financial intentions in Palestine, come the end of the mandate. To protect her own and other foreign economic interests in Palestine (the Iraq pipeline, Haifa oil refinery installations, civil aviation rights, potash plant on the Dead Sea) Britain will not release certain assets of the Palestine Government, believed to total £50,000,000, until she obtains assurances that the interests will be respected.

May 11

The battle at the 200 yard road block at Bab el Wad on the road from Tel-Aviv to Jerusalem continued. The Zionists were reported to have broken through and had cleared the area of Arab units in the triangle formed by Deir Aiyub, Latrun and Imwas. Arab forces were reported to be closing in for a decisive battle.

Meanwhile the ceasefire in Jerusalem was broken with heavy firing and mortar bombardment from both sectors of the city. The breaking of the four days of quiet was, in the view of Zionist sources, the result of an Arab initiated attack.

British troops officially quit the dock area of Jaffa.

The village of Beit Mahsir, west of Jerusalem, was the target of the Palmach for three consecutive nights. A reported 400 to 500 strong Palmach force returned on the 11th for the start of 36 hour battle. They succeeded in penetrating the village which was then systematically demolished. There is no record of the fate of the villagers.

The Golani Brigade began to shell the town of Beisan. Once the high ground was captured, morale in the town plummeted. The townspeople fled to escape the shelling. The following day the mayor and the local priest surrendered the town.

According to Zionist sources, the strategically important town of Safad was finally in Zionist hands. The knock-on effect of this was felt in surrounding villages.

The villagers of al Buwaayziyya fled after hearing about events in Safad. A request for an "agreement" with the Haganah was turned down. A similar request from the villagers of al Khalisa was turned down. The village militia remained until they were shelled from a nearby settlement as an armoured Zionist column approached.

Weeks later returning villagers reported that their houses had been burned and destroyed [Author's note: Two years later the settlement of Qityat Shemona was built on the site. The now modern town includes a factory that makes Uzi machine guns.]

The coastal village of al Bassa [pop 2 950, including 1 590 Christians] was attacked by naval forces. Although most of the women and children had fled, in anticipation of an attack, some remained. The village militia were taken by surprise and retreated. Those remaining, mostly the elderly, were ordered to gather outside the church. The Zionists took a few of the younger ones, including at least one woman, and shot them dead. Thus suitably terrorised, the remainder were ordered northwards. A few were later killed in a vain attempt to salvage some of their belongings.

The Egyptian Senate approved a motion authorising the Egyptian army to join forces with other Arab armies and enter Palestine "to restore stability and prevent massacres."An allocation of £4 000 000 was made for this purpose. The Egyptian contingent earmarked for service in Palestine was estimated at 15 000 men. Three airforce squadrons were stationed at the frontier.

King Abdullah of Transjordan gave a press conference where he said that "War is not being declared, relieving Palestine from the grip of Zionists is not war against the Jews. The Jews have gained their strength because during 30 years of British administration they have been arming. If the British did not assist them they at least closed one eye. . . . . The Arabs did not arm in an organised manner, therefore the Jews became stronger."

The schisms and enmity within the Arab alliance were revealed. He accused the Arab Higher Committee of bringing "misery" to Palestine. Also accused was the Syrian prime minister and his "Arab League collaborators" of compelling the Palestinian Arabs to cooperate with the League.[27] The Arab "Liberation Army" was dissolved as was the Arab Higher Committee, a move regarded as opening the way for Abdullah to don the mantle of saviour of Arab Palestine.

It was reported that the Arab leaders feared that the Irgun may have success in forcing on Jewish opinion their plan to expand a Jewish state to include not just the whole of Palestine, but also Transjordan. This fear reflected the ideals and aims of the right wing Zionism tendency.

This coincided with the arrival in Amman, the capital of Transjordan, of streams of Palestinian refugees reported to be openly bitter at the failure of their leaders, regarding themselves as the victims of political intrigues.

Another parcel bomb featured in the UK domestic news. It arrived at the home of General Sir Evelyn Barker, former GOC of British troops in Palestine. It was the second one to arrive at the home of the General in recent months. This one, which had been posted in London, was successfully defused.

May 12

According to the Palestine Arab HQ in Damascus, the Arabs won the battle for Bab el Wad, with the Zionists retreating and leaving their dead on the field. Some 8 000 men were reported to be massing in the area to consolidate the victory.

On the minus side, Arabs at Beisan surrendered to the Haganah after a bombardment which started the previous night. Situated to the south east of Haifa, only a quarter of its population of 6 000 remained when the Zionist forces entered. The latter reported that Iraqi soldiers were amongst those captured.

Arab-Jewish negotiations for the surrender of the port of Jaffa were reported to be in progress. It was stated that the Haganah were still waiting for an Arab reply to the surrender terms.

The proposed terms of a truce for Jerusalem were made public, with a reply awaited from both sides. These were: cessation of hostilities, entry of supplies under impartial control, free access for Jews to the Old City and the Wailing Wall, the evacuation of the Katamon district by the Jews. One Jewish commentator summed up the situation in Palestine with the comment that until the Zionists succeed in securing the goodwill of the Arabs a dark and foreboding shadow will hang over their "National Home"[28]

Four Zionist settlements south of Beersheba were attacked, allegedly by Egyptian forces. The attack started the previous day with artillery and light tanks being used. The Haganah arrived at the scene when the hard pressed colonists signalled for reinforcements. Zionist forces claimed 40 Egyptians were killed with scores wounded.

The Irgun claimed to have captured five Palestinian villages in the Tulkarm area.

The Zionists revisited the village of 'Awlaam, south of Tiberias, this time in the form of the Golani Brigade. It was reported that the villagers "fled in fear of the Jews". During this same action, part of Operation Gideon, the Haganah occupied three other villages, Ulam, Hadatha and Ma'dhar, and thus "the Lower Galilee was emptied of its Arab inhabitants."

Operation Barak was launched to "open the way" to the Negev. The villages of Bureir,Huleikat and Kawkabah were occupied as well as neighbouring villages in Gaza district.

Burayr, to the east of Gaza, was occupied by the Haganah. Bashshit, described as a "strong Arab centre" was also occupied by the Haganah. The village of al Hamidiyya was deserted by its residents "under the influence of the exodus from the town of Beisan and under pressure from the Haganah." It was later demolished following pressure from neighbouring Zionist settlements. During Operation Gideon, when the Golani Brigade swept through the entire Baysan valley, the village of al Sakhina was taken. No physical evidence remains of the village with the entire area now agricultural land.

Sirin, to the north of Beisan, was occupied. The History of the Haganah states that "the inhabitants fled in fear of the Jews. And Jewish Lower Galilee became empty of Arabs."Likewise the villagers of Ma'dhar, southeast of Haifa, "fled in fear of the Jews" when it was overrun by the Golani Brigade. In the same area, the village of Khubbayza was occupied by the Irgun. Many of the residents were incarcerated behind barbed wire for days, before being forcibly expelled. It is unclear when it was demolished however, some villages in the vicinity were razed following occupation, others by the Jewish National Fund in 1948.

Troops from the Arab Legion were reported to have attacked the cluster of settlements at Kfar Etzion, five miles south east of Bethlehem. Armoured cars and light artillery were used.

One Zionist was killed and several wounded following a clash with a British armoured car on the Haifa Tel-Aviv road. The Irgun warned that retaliation would be taken immediately if British troops "interfere or attack our soldiers during the British evacuation."

The Zionist mobilisation authorities in Palestine broadcast an urgent appeal to all ex-Servicmen hitherto exempt from military service to report immediately for duty. A state of emergency was declared in the Arab countries with all able-bodied Palestinian males refused entry.

Airlifts of arms arrived in Palestine, from Czechoslovakia, destined for the Haganah. There were 5 000 rifles, 1 200 machine guns and 6 million rounds of ammunition.

In Damascus, Arab League officials declared that the League would establish an Arab civil administration in Palestine after 15 May. The League's secretary-general, Azzam Pasha, said the decision was reached after the League's political committee and the Arab war council defeated a proposal to establish a Palestine Arab State similar to the one the Zionists were expected to launch at the end of the mandate.

The Scotsman's special correspondent reported on the role of the Arab Legion in Palestine. There would be no "D-Day" when they would be expected to march in to the country. Those already there would stay at the request of local Palestinians who were afraid of further massacres. Reinforcements of the Legion were expected over the next few days and would be based in Jericho where a Transjordan flag was already flying over the police station and post office.

An interview with an officer of the Legion gave an insight into the thinking and strategies to come. They were anxious not to attack Jewish towns and settlements nor any part of the intended Jewish State."I hope we learned something from the sad mistakes of the Liberation Army. We Arabs are good at fighting in open country but have no experience of street fighting, and our enthusiastic young soldiers must be taught not to try and attack heavily fortified Jewish positions, with rifles as their sole weapons.

The Arab Legion's morale was high with the greatest concern of the senior officers being to protect Arab towns such as Hebron and Nablus which had specifically appealed to King Abdullah for help. Stress was laid in maintaining lines of communication "That is why we will not rush to the coast." Any operations would not be aimed at the Jewish State. But, should the Haganah try to carry out any of the recent wild threats, attack or bomb Transjordan, then the situation would change. Transjordan would invoke her treaty with Britain, which obliged the latter to come to her assistance.

May 13

With one report that the Haganah had obtained 600 "bombing planes" stationed in Italy, many of the Arab capitals took precautions. Egypt proclaimed a state of siege, anti-aircraft guns were at the ready and "suspects" put into a former British internment camp. Troops were ready to enter Palestine one minute after midnight on the 14th. In Syria the expectation was that a new 12-member coalition would be formed to give unaniminity to future actions. Air raid precaution drill were carried out in Damascus. Tanks and armoured vehicles were observed moving south. Likewise in Iraq and Transjordan troops were on the move with Arab Legion mechanised units heading towards the Allenby Bridge across the River Jordan.

The Colonial Office and Foreign Office issued the following statement:

"Eighty-four thousand troops, who received no cooperation from the Jewish community, proved insufficient to maintain law and order in the face of a campaign of terrorism waged by highly organised Jewish forces equipped with all the weapons of the modern infantryman. Since the war 338 British subjects have been killed in Palestine, while the military forces there have cost the British tax-payer £100 million. Although British responsibility for Palestine has ceased, it is the earnest hope of His Majesty's Government that, as both sides come to realise the tragic consequences of trying to conquer Palestine by force, some compromise may yet be possible which will prevent the destruction of all that has been achieved during the last 30 years and which will enable the people of Palestine to live at peace and govern themselves. To that end the Government are still prepared to give every assistance in their power, short of imposing by force a solution not acceptable to both peoples."[29]

The Haganah announced that the Arab Legion, with heavy artillery and armoured vehicles, had penetrated the Kfar Etzion group of settlements near Hebron. One of the four settlements was captured.

The Arab Liberation Army reported the death or injury of 800 Zionists at Bab el Wad. Their commander-in-chief had been killed, three armoured squadrons destroyed.

Al Batani al Sharqi, northeast of Gaza, was occupied by the Gi'vati Brigade. The village houses were eventually demolished. The villagers of nearby Najd were expelled by the Palmach's Negev Brigade.

In December 1947, the villagers of Kafr Saba, identified as the Roman Caphar Saba, met with Jewish community leaders when a joint pledge to keep the peace was made. However the Haganah decided that it should be "emptied" of its Arab population. The attack on 13 May was the second in three days, with resistance being met on both occasions. It is likely that the villagers fled or were expelled shortly after.

Another historical village, al Zib, north of Acre, with roots back to the 18th century BC and mentioned in chronicles stretching over 2 000 years, was one of the main villages targeted by the Haganah as part of Operation Ben Ami. Most villagers fled during a mortar barrage. Moshe Carmel, the commander of the operation, ordered that the village be razed to the ground to "punish" the villagers and to ensure "they could never return."

The Haganah attacked and occupied the villages of Aqir, Katra, Bashit, Beit Daras and Barqah in Ramleh district. They attacked the hamlets on the slopes of Mount Carmel and occupied the village of Kafr Saba. The village of Tireh, near Qalqilyah, repulsed an attack. The latter also repulsed a later attack. The Haganah were ordered to occupy all the Palestinian villages on the coastal plain near Tulkarm.

With the signing of an Arab-Jewish agreement, imposed by the victor, Jaffa became a Jewish controlled port. All Arab arms and ammunition had to be handed over to the Haganah. There was an estimated 4 000 Palestinians left in the city.The Zionists now controlled all important coastal points except Haifa and Gaza.

Jerusalem was reported to have been without water for three days. Supplies were unlikely to be re-connected until the fighting ended. Apparently the Zionists blew up a section of the pipeline, by accident, at Bab el Wad.

It was announced in the House of Commons that the Political Committee of the Arab League accepted the truce proposals for Jerusalem. A reply was still awaited from the Jewish Agency. An American Quaker, Mr Harold Evans, was chosen by the UN as municipal commissioner in Jerusalem. Count Folke Bernadotte was appointed by the UN as mediator in Palestine.

An Irgun-Haganah agreement was signed for the conquest of the whole of Palestine. Fifty artillery pieces and 24 heavy mortars arrived at Haifa destined for the Haganah.

The British notified the Jewish Agency that the Arab Legion of Transjordan was no longer under British command.

May 14

Operation "Pitchfork" (described variously as Klashon, Kilshon and Schfifon) was launched to occupy Jerusalem's strategic areas, those evacuated by the British and Palestinian residential quarters outside the Old City. In coordination with the Haganah, the British handed over the huge central compound containing the city's vital installations.

With the departure of the British from Jerusalem steady firing could be heard. However the Zionists now controlled the central area including the police station, leaving the city cut in two, from Damascus Gate to Princess Mary Avenue.

Fifty two years were to pass before the Palestinian oral tradition of a little known massacre at the village of al Tantura, near Haifa, was confirmed by a young Israeli historian, Teddy Katz. Other sources put the date of the massacre as 22-23 May, perhaps a reflection of the Zionist practice of attacking on one date and "finishing off" at a later date.
[See 22 May for details]

The villages of Kafr Qar' (Haifa), Qubab (Lydda) and Abu Shusha (Jaffa) were captured by the Haganah.

The three remaining colonies in Gush Etzion surrendered to the Arab Legion. Unconfirmed reports gave the figure of 195 Zionists dead. The battle gave rise to reports of an incident which Ben Gurion believed "will stand out forever in the annals of Jewish military history." Local Palestinian Arabs had joined the Arab Legion for the final assault on the colonies. When called upon to surreneder, 15 Zionist defenders came out and gave up their weapons. Whereupon, despite the protests of an officer, a "local Arab" stepped forward and mowed down the line of Zionists with a machine-gun.[30]

The village of al Manshiyya, to the east of Acre, was revisited and occupied by Zionist forces. It is probable that the village had been "emptied" by this date. Likewise the village of Abu Shusha was revisited following an assault using artillery. Once the villagers had fled, some of the houses were dynamited. This action was carried out under Operation Barak.

The village of al Na'ani was surrounded by the Haganah's Gi'vati Brigade, hostages were taken, and the villagers ordered to hand over their weapons. It was then occupied. Many villagers stayed put until 10 June when they were probably compelled or ordered to leave.

The village of al Sumayriyya, north of Acre, perhaps named after the Jewish sect, the Samaritans, was attacked by an armoured unit of the Carmeli Brigade. An attempt was made to repel this surprise attack, which left behind many dead and injured village defenders. Photographs in the New York Times, about two weeks later, showed a village in ruins caused by the actions of "Jewish demolition squads."

Haganah forces started to encircle Acre in preparation for an attack which met little resistance.

While the forces of Zionism relentlessy picked away at the Palestinian Arab presence in the land of Palestine, the attention of the world was focused on the ending mandate and the preparations for the "new dawn".

The Jewish state of Israel was proclaimed at an evening meeting of the Jewish National Council. It was immediately recognised by President Truman of the U.S.,followed closely by Guatemala. This act by the U.S. took everbody by surprise, including the U.S. delegation at the UN General Assembly where voting was taking place on the implementation of a trusteeship for Palestine. That morning the U.S. delegation had voted against a resolution which implied recognition of a Jewish governmental authority in Palestine. By late afternoon this position had been undermined by their President. The Arab states and Cuba complained of U.S. duplicity and double dealing.

David Ben-Gurion, a Polish immigrant, was the state's first premier. Moshe Shertok, a Russian immigrant, was foreign minister. One of the first acts of the provisional government was the revocation of the British White Paper of 1939, which limited immigration to Palestine, and legislation limiting land sales.

The newly opened Voice of Israel broadcast the Council's proclamation. It stated that the Jewish National Council was the representative of "the Jewish people in Palestine and the Zionist movement of the world." It further claimed that "The State will be open to all Jewish immigrants, will promote the development of the country and all its inhabitants, will be based on the precepts of liberty, justice and peace taught by the Hebrew prophets, will uphold full social and political equality for all its citizens without distinction of race, creed or sex, and will guarantee full freedom of education and culture." A pledge was made to safeguard all shrines and religious places. Membership of the United Nations was sought.

The Arab Office in London issued a statement accusing the British Government of indulging in "cant" with regard to her position as having held the UN mandate on Palestine.

"The general theme of the obituary chorus is that the execution of this Mandate conferred benefits on everybody in Palestine and only failed in its ultimate object because of the irreconcilability of Arab and Jews. The truth of the matter, however, is that the entire Palestine tragedy was created by the Mandate and by Britain's obstinate attempt to carry out for thirty years the disastrous policy laid down in it. It was precisely the Mandate that created the situation in which a mortal conflict between Arab and Jew became inevitable. The Mandate provided for the establishment of a national home for one people in the country of another. The Zionists had been enabled to establish for themselves a position in Palestine, economic, political, and military, which threatened with a deadly menace the very existence of the Arabs. When Britain came to Palestine the country belonged to its people and there was peace in it. She left it poisoned by hatred and rent by a fearful war."[31]

Within the new state, a partial black-out of the cities was imposed. Rural settlements were told to dig trenches. This activity was mirrored in the various Arab capitals.

Iraq proclaimed martial law, by Royal decree. Four military commanders were appointed. The Lebanese government promulgated an emergency law enabling special security measures to be taken. King Abdullah of Transjordan proclaimed that with the ending of the mandate "the Balfour Declaration has disappeared." Partition and trusteeship had been rejected by the Arabs, there was therefore no basis "for the claim to independence by the Jewish community in Palestine." In Egypt 10 000 troops were ready to cross into Southern Palestine and put "an end to massacres perpetrated by terrorist Zionist gangs against humanity."

At midnight, amid some pomp and ceremony lasting 10 minutes - including a few farewell word to the Jewish mayor and Arab deputy mayor of Haifa- the High Commissioner, General Sir Alan Cunningham, sailed for Britain. There were no reported demonstrations.

The withdrawal of Britain from Palestine was compared, by some, with "abandonment":

"Withdrawing without a successor, the British had not so much transferred power as abandoned it. The United Nations, caught up in red tape and politics, had intended to send out a secretariat to take over essential services, but only a handful of officials were actually on the ground, and it was finally armed Arabs and Jews who stepped into the vacuum, grimly battling for strategic advantage even as the last British troops departed."[32]

Dr Lester, Director of Medical Services, observed "When the end came on 14 May one felt a feeling of relief at leaving Palestine with a whole skin, a feeling of disappointment at the collapse of a fine service, and a feeling of shame at leaving the Arab hospital staff in Jerusalem to wave their Red Cross flags at the lines of armed Jews drawn up to take the zone. So the British left Palestine."[33]

Despite the fact that the new state owed so much to Britain, there was no hint of thanks from foreign minister, Moshe Shertok.

With Haifa, its chief port and source of revenue, still in British hands. With a group of Zionist colonies being occupied, the previous day, by the Arab Legion under nominal British command, he was in a bitter mood. He asked the British to explain their involvement in the latter event. The US came in for criticism because they had tried to find a way out of forming the new state. He said that the Jews would not compromise even to suit the United States. "One does not commit suicide to gain a friend." he commented.[31]

May 15/16

At midnight on Friday, troops of the Arab Legion and the Iraqi Army crossed the Palestine frontier. The former crossed by the Allenby Bridge, the Iraqis at a point further north, Jisr el Majami, using a pontoon bridge to replace the existing one blown up by the Zionists. At the same time the forces from Egypt, Lebanon and Syria entered Palestine at predetermined points.

Reports indicated that the Egyptians had engaged the Israeli forces 40 miles from Tel-Aviv, the newly proclaimed Israeli capital, and were moving along the coast road under artillery and mortar fire, with the fortified Zionist colonies en route providing resistance. Spitfires of the Egyptian Royal Air Force dive-bombed Tel-Aviv's harbour. A total of eight such attacks since Friday were recorded, with the Haganah claiming to have shot down two planes.

Communiques from the warring parties made various claims. Iraqi forces captured Rutherberga power installations, some ten miles south of the Sea of Galilee. Israeli sources acknowledged that they had been capt-ured by the Arab Legion on the 15th. Iraqi forces occupied the village of Kawkab al Hawa. They held it for three days with the loss of 23 men. The village was subsequently destroyed, but the local Crusader castle, Bevoir castle, was retained (and developed into a tourist attraction).

The Arab Legion reported that Kfar Etzion along with four other colonies near Jerusalem had surrendered. Three hundred prisoners were taken, including 86 women and children. The latter were sent to the Red Cross in Jerusalem, the rest were interned in PoW camps. Transjordan troops were reported to have occupied Jericho.

Lydda airfield and the adjoining Kalandiya Colony were reported to be in the hands of the "Liberation Army." Syrian troops claimed to have occupied a former British army camp near Samakh, settlers had been driven from three settlements. Nuqeib on the Sea of Galilee was encircled, and the Syrian airforce had raided several others in support of the advancing Lebanese army.

The Lebanese army recaptured the two Lebanese villages, Malkiya and Qadas, captured earlier by the Haganah. In the case of the former, Zionist paratroopers were reported to have engaged the Lebanese who, according to Haganah sources, suffered 200 fatalities.

The Haganah, as part of Operation Ben Ami, besieged the Arab seaport of Acre, north of Haifa. Under the partition plan, Acre was apportioned to the intended Arab state.They claimed to have captured the strategic village of Deir Ayoub on the Tel-Aviv Jerusalem road together with the Christian village of Latrun, a former detention camp for Zionists. The Giv'ati Brigade captured the village of al Maghar.

Haganah units received orders to strike at villages inland from Haifa in order to "clear" the area of its residents and establish an alternative route for Haganah convoys going south. Villages such as Umm al Zinat and Khirbat Qumbaza (an ancient Cannanite village, Karitah - Joshua 21:34) stood in their way.The Haganah also claimed that the Egyptians bombed an RAF temporary aifield wounding eight Britons. They also machine gunned a British armoured unit on the Hebron- Rafah road.

Heavy fighting was reported in Jerusalem with Arab forces shelling the Jewish quarters of the Old City. The Israelis launched an attack on Arab positions, particularly in the area of Jaffa Gate. The Zionists resorted to their loud speaker vans, urging the Arabs to surrender, and claiming that they had surrounded the Old City.

In West Jerusalem, the district of Baq'a fell under Israeli control

"There was no resistance of any sort; they just walked in . . . Nearly every house was empty: set tables with plates of unfinished food indicated that the occupants had fled in disarray, haste, and fear."[34]

With the Haganah and the Irgun now united as one army, Jaffa - earmarked as an Arab enclave under the partition resolution - was under

Israeli military command.Menachen Begin, Commander of the terrorist Irgun, made his first public appearance. In a "fiery speech" he said that the Irgun accepted the state of Israel within its present frontiers. However there was every indication that the terrorists would continue their activities outside the yet-to-be-defined frontiers of the Jewish state.

Moshe Shertok, took issue with Britain, claiming that her rule was still effective in the Middle East. The Arab Legion, was officered and led by Britons, with finance coming from Britain, he alleged. The promise that the Legion would leave Palestine before the end of the Mandate had not been kept. His fire was also directed at the Arab League which, he claimed, was an instrument of British influence in the Middle East.

His one consolation was that the U.S. "after many hesitations, fears, and suspicions" had recognised the state of Israel. This recognition (foll-owed by Guatemala then Sweden) was enthusiastically welcomed as giving a strong bargaining point when it came to eventual talks with the Arab states.

In Italy, among thousands of Jews in special camps, letters were received from the Haganah appealing for volunteers to enrol in "defence of the new State". The Irgun asked for gifts of gold to help finance arms purchases.

Dr Chaim Weizmann, one of those responsible for the securing of the Balfour Declaration in 1917, and former president of the World Zionist Organisation, was elected president of the provisional council of the State of Israel.

May 17

Tel -Aviv continued to be subject to bombing and strafing raids by Spitfires. Some small calibre bombs hit the city, with direct hits recorded on oil facilities, others landed in the sea as the merchant ships moored in the vicinity moved out to sea to escape the bombardment. About a dozen Jews were killed in the raids with a number wounded. Despite a Red Cross on the roof, it was reported that a hospital was repeatedly strafed with some fatalities. This was denied by Egyptian sources. Six aircraft were destroyed on Tel-Aviv airfield.

The Shemen settlement was bombed with fuel tanks, ammunition dumps and military supplies destroyed.

Israeli planes dropped incendiary bombs on the police station in the village of al Nabi Yusha, while ground forces blasted their way through the vill-age's defences. The defenders withdrew and it is probable that the villag-ers fled or were expelled at this time.

Forces from the various Arab states continued to attack Zionist positions, concentrating on mainly Arab areas.In the south of the country, five colonies were were shelled and besieged by two Egyptian divisions driving up from the Negev. These attacks were repeated in the north by Syrian and Lebanese forces. In the west the Transjordan Frontier Force, reported to be flush with fresh supplies and ammunition to last them to the end of the year, was approaching the Jordan Valley with Jerusalem in its sights. The Red Cross had evacuated some 150 women and children from Kfar Etzion.

Heavy fighting was reported at the Jaffa and Damascus Gates of Jerusalem, with the Jewish Quarter of the city still being heavily shelled. The Haganah reported that their position in the Old City and the German colony, Baka, and Mousrara, had improved.

The settlers of Neve Jaacov were forced to evacuate the colony following an assault by the Arab Legion. All were brought out safely, but had heavily mined the houses and roads. A bomb disposal unit composed of British volunteers spear-headed the entry and made harmless mines manufactured from biscuit tins, milk churns and pipes. One member of the squad was killed and one wounded while disarming the mines. Once the settlement was accessible, about 100 neighbouring Arab villagers poured in, looting everything which could be moved - including doors, window frames and roof timbers. Reports indicated that loot was not the only motive. Neve Jaacov and the adjacent settlement of Ataroth were symbolic, the first Zionist colonies in Palestine to fall into the hands of the irregulars

With the abandonment of Neve Jaacov and the flight of the settlers from Ataroth colony, near Kalandia Airport, the Arabs were in complete control of the main road to the north of Jerusalem.

There were reports, from the Soviet news agency Tass, of Arab armies joining forces in various parts of Palestine. Russia recognised the state of Israel.

In the first few days the military strategy of the Zionist state became apparent to observers. This was to concentrate their efforts in seizing the ports. Most had already been seized with Acre about to fall. They were in the position to control Haifa once the British left.The success of this strategy would ensure that the supporters of the Zionist state would be able to provide supplies, breaching the Egyptian blockade if necessary.

By concentrating on building up their existing areas of control, they could defer any offensive action, and invite the Arabs to attack them.

Military action so far supported this hypothesis. There had been only two areas of serious fighting. The first in the north where the road from the Litani River, and the Lebanon, to Acre had been cut. The second in the central plain where the strategically important road junction at Lydda-Ramleh was the scene of fierce fighting.

May 18

Arab Legion troops occupied the walled Old City of Jerusalem in the early evening following a barrage, using field guns and mortars, on the Jewish quarter inside the walls. Despite heavy automatic machine gun and mortar fire from the Zionist forces few casualties were inflicted.The Legion was now in a position to shell the Jewish held areas of the city defended by the combined forces of the Haganah and the terrorist Irgun and Stern Gang, forces amounting to a few thousand. This body had been cut off from the main Zionist forces - estimated at about 50 000 in the coastal plain. Zionist sources claimed that "Jewish forces in Jerusalem to-day captured Mount Zion as well as other important objectives near the Old City. Seventy enemy soldiers were taken prisoners, with their arms. Heavy battles are going on in the Old City."[35]

Various expatriates still functioning in Jerusalem were reported to be under fire. The French Consul, who was a member of the UN Truce Commission, was besieged in the French Consulate.

Tel-Aviv was subject to more air raids. In the fifth raid Zionist sources reported the deaths of 41 people, with more than 60 wounded, when a bomb scored a direct hit on a bus station. This incident was described as a "terror raid." One plane was reported to be shot down with the pilot taken captive.

Syrian sources reported Syrian aircraft attacks on settlements with Arab ground troops "wiping out" a Zionist ambush near the Lebanese border. Thirty two Zionist deaths were reported. The Syrian communique reported the shooting down of an Israeli plane and added that "the enemy is resisting strongly." Syrian troops recaptured Samakh following a four hour battle, and occupied the Zionist colonies of Shaar Hagolan and Masada. The Zionists revisited Samakh during the night, inflicted heavy losses on the Syrian defenders, but failed to capture the village.

Iraqi troops were reported to have crossed the River Jordan and captured the Zionist colony of Geshar, south of the Sea of Galilee. In the north, the ancient crusader port of Acre finally succumbed to the Zionist onslaught.

Surrender terms included the handing over of all arms and about 4 000 foreign Arab troops to the Haganah.The latter claimed to have drowned up to 500 Iraqi soldiers, south of Lake Tiberias, when they bogged down tanks and other equipment by opening a dam near Daganya.

The village of al Batani al Gharbi, north of Gaza, and three others were occupied as part of Operation Barak. It was reckoned that most of the inhabitants had fled before or during the attack. Some were possibly expelled, according to Israeli historian, Benny Morris.

Members of the Sde Nechemya kibbutz wrote to the Agricultural Centre asking for over 400 acres of land belonging to the neighbouring village of al 'Abisiya [pop 1 510 including 290 Jews]. The village was not occupied until 25 May.[36]

Acre was captured by the Haganah. While the newspapers barely commented on this conquest of an Arab port that was intended, under the partition plan, to be given to the Palestinian Arabs, detail which subsequently emerged deserve a mention.

Its Arab population of 25 000 had almost been doubled by refugees from outlying areas seeking safety. These people were then subjected to a mortar bombardment which wreaked havoc amongst the refugees who lacked shelter. The water supply was cut off, coinciding with an outbreak of typhoid. Psychological warfare in various forms including the inevitable loudspeaker vans with their messages of death and destruction were used.

So successful were these methods that by the time the Zionists entered Acre, there were only about 4 000 left out of the initial 50 000. Those remaining were then subjected to a reign of terror.

Several months later a UN observer, Lieutenant Petite, arrived in Acre to investigate reports of maltreatment. His report confirmed this. Looting was being conducted in a systematic manner by the Haganah - furniture, clothes and any other item that could be used by the incoming Zionist colonisers. He observed that the looting was similar to that taking place all over the new state, all part of "a Jewish plan to prevent the return of refugees."

At least 100 Arab civilians had been murdered. Particularly those residents of the new part of the city who refused to leave their homes and be "ghettoised" in the old city. The new part of the city was to be off-limits to Arabs in the new Jewish state.

While the UN observer felt that the Zionist troops who were murdering civilians were not doing this in obedience to orders, he felt it showed the total contempt for Arabs which prevailed within the new

Israeli army. He cited the example Mohammed Fayez Soufi.

Mohammed and four of his friends who had been "relocated" into the old part of the city went back to their former homes to try and get food. They were apprehended by a gang of soldiers. At gun point they were forced to drink cyanide. While Mohammed was able to fake his drinking, his friends could not. Their bodies were later washed up on the shore. These and many other atrocities were verified from other sources.[37]

Egyptian artillery attacked targets in the Imara region, southeast of Gaza, a Zionist repair and supply base. Several explosions and fires were reported. The settlements of Deir Sied and Nagaba were strafed with the loss of one plane.

The Polish and Czech states recognised the state of Israel.

The Times printed an article outlining the British involvement in the Arab Legion. Some 40 British officers served with the Legion operating, as far as was known, on the front line. Of these, 30 were seconded from the British army in accordance with treaty obligations. These obligations obliged Britain to provide, on request, British service men to ensure the efficiency of the Transjordan forces. They were under the orders of King Abdullah.

Provided that the Arab Legion did not act illegally, and was not found to do so by the UN, there was no reason for Britain to depart from her treaty obligations. Pending a ruling by the UN, Britain was likely to continue payment of the subsidy called for in the treaty with Transjordan and to supply arms to the Arab States.

Ezra Danin, one of the powerful members of the new state's executive, wrote to Yosef Weitz of the Jewish National Fund appealing for an institution " whose role will be . . . to seek ways to carry out the transfer of the Arab population at this opportunity when it has left its normal place of residence."[38]

In outlining his idea of trying to find Christian groups prepared to work in assisting refugees find a permanent home in Arab countries, Danin made it quite clear that if the state did not want to encourage the Palestinian Arab to return home, then they must be presented with *fait accomplis* including, the destruction of their houses.

May 19

The Scotsman correspondent, Lovett Edward, toured Acre and the villages in Western Upper Galilee. Until the fall of Acre the villages and the resort of Nahariya had been almost completely cut-off, relying on their own resources or the occasional drop of petrol or oil delivered by air.

Along the main road to Lebanon and then parallel to the Lebanese border, within sniping distance, there was not one Lebanese soldier to be seen or heard. Local settlers claimed that the Lebanese had retreated behind the hills. Nahariya was described as "spick and span" and un-damaged.

The villages most damaged, following intense fighting, were Ass-umeria and Zib. The residents had either fled for safety or remained, where they were given identity cards by the Zionist occupiers. Colonies within a mile of the Lebanese border were being turned into strongholds in anticip-ation of further hostilities.

In Acre, prisoners were being sorted out - local Palestinian Arabs from foreign ones. The correspondent reported the distinct impression that not only were the Zionists more technically advanced but "the more sincere, determined fighters."

In Jerusalem and its environs, the Arab Legion was reported to be advancing with heavy guns and armoured cars into northern districts of the city, according to government sources in Amman. The Sheikh Jarrah quarter was reported to be clear of Zionist forces with "the Jews flying in panic, with heavy losses, outside the Old City." The Zionists sustained heavy losses following Legion attacks on Kufr Saba and Abugosh. Artouf settlement was evacuated by its residents.

It was estimated that some 8 000 Haganah, Irgun and Stern Gang members faced the Arab Legion, possibly holding out hope to the besieged Zionist forces in the Old City who, on several occasions, turned down the opportunity to surrender.With the loss of Sheikh Jarrah to the Arab Leg-ion, the Jewish university and Hadassah hospital were isolated, with Ramallah road once again being open to the Arab population.

Haganah communiques earlier reported that Zionist forces had fought their way into the Old City to link up with the besieged 1 300 Jews. Two British officers, it was claimed, were captured, together with their arms, by the Haganah when they captured Zion Hill. The Zionists claimed to have captured the huge former army base at Sarafand between Lydda and Tel-Aviv. According to the Haganah "The outpost fell into our hands without any casualties." The local villagers probably fled or were evicted at the same time. The Zionists had agreed to pay Britain $2.5 million for the base. By capturing it, this sum of money was saved.

The fortified Arab village of al Kubeiba, between Rehovoth and Yavneh, also fell to the Zionists.

In southern Palestine, Egyptian artillery were said to be shelling various Zionist colonies at the rate of one shell per minute. The main objective being Deir Seneid. Beit Hanoun, north of Gaza, was said to have been occupied by the Egyptians "after heavy sacrifices." Tel-Aviv continued to be attacked by bombers with the repaired runway hit again, and hangars destroyed. The quayside and warehouses were also hit.

Abdel Rahman Azzam Pasha, secretary-general of the Arab League declared that the Arab forces were not just fighting to protect the Palestinian Arabs, but were fighting Zionism. The Arab attitude to the Jews in Palestine had not changed. The Zionists were trying to create a purely Jewish State. The Arabs were fighting for a Palestinian State in which Jews would have full and equal citizenship. There would be no differences and no discrimination between Arab and Jewish citizen.[39]

The Sunday Times correspondent, Major Richard Wyndham, was killed by Zionist machine gun fire while in a forward Arab Legion post in Sheikh Jarrah quarter of Jerusalem.

At a meeting of the Security Council, the US put forward a resolution ordering the cessation of hostilities in Palestine. While Britain was sympathetic she could not agree to the invocation of Article 39 which would have given the UN authority to impose a cease fire by military means or be economic sanctions. There were no means in place to carry out the enforcement.

In addition, Britain argued, the juridical status of the geographical entity known as Palestine was obscure. Some maintained that Palestine had achieved independence. Others maintained she had been divided into two states. The proclamation of the Jewish State was a unilateral act not based strictly on acts of the United Nations Commisssion - quite apart from the fact that the proclamation was made before the end of the mandate.[39]

Yugoslavia announced its recognition of the Israeli state. Britain countered a request from Israel for recognition by awaiting the conditions necessary for recognition, including known frontiers.

May 20

Arab shells were reported to be "screaming across the skies" in Jerusalem, escaping the Holy Places. The few Haganah defenders left were threatened with "annihilation", unless they surrendered, by the Arab commanders. On Mount Scopus one wing of the Hadassah hospital had been destroyed by shellfire. Likewise the National Library and the Hebrew University Library were under shell fire.

In the "new city" in West Jerusalem, mostly occupied by Jews, debris from the shelling littered the streets. With the exception of a limited telephone service, municipal services had ground to a halt. A Transjordan communique said that Arab guns landed a direct hit on an ammunition dump in the "new city", at the former Palestine police depot. The Zionist forces in the Sanhedria quarter, adjacent to Sheikh Jarrah, were shelled as they prepared to counter- attack. Heavy losses were inflicted with the Zionists being dispersed.

The Arab Legion suffered a reverse when four of its armoured cars were knocked out by a single two-pounder gun, from a Haganah armoured car, as they made a first attempt to advance to the west off the Nablus road. The Legion conducted mopping-up operations at Samakh and then pushed their way to the colonies of Dakonia and Bikania. Heavy resistance was met, and heavy casualties inflicted upon the enemy.

Al Kabri, to the north of Acre, was occupied by Zionist forces. An unknown number of villagers were taken captive, some were killed. Others were killed during their dispersal throughout Galilee when their killers found that they originated from al Kabri [See: March 28].Moshe Carmel (Zalizky), commander of the Carmeli Brigade had previously issued an order to his battalion "To attack in order to conquer, to kill among the men, to destroy and burn the villages of al Kabri, Umm al Faraj and An Nahr."[40]

Michael Palumbo, in his book *The Palestinian Catastrophe* gives an account of one villager from al Kabri. Amina Moussa and her husband fled the village as the Zionists approached. Shortly after they were captured by the Haganah. Amina's jewellery was stolen by one soldier who taunted her that the necklace would be given to the soldier's girlfriend. With the help of a collaborator, the Zionists identified Amina's husband and five other captives as being from Kabri. The next time she saw her husband he was lying dead with a bullet in the back of his head.[41]

Umm Faraj and al Nahr were captured in accordance with the orders. There is no record of the villagers' fate however, the villages were demolished by the Haganah "both to punish the villagers . . . and to make sure villagers could and would never return."[42]

Arab al Safa and al Ghazzawiyya were taken by the Golani Brigade who, it was stated in the History of the Haganah, "cleansed the entire Beisan valley of bedouins."[43]

The Egyptians reported on a two pronged attack from their base in Beit

Hanoun with one prong occupying the mainly Arab town of Beersheba and the other following a ten hour battle at Beit Seneid to the north of Gaza. The latter was used by the Zionists as a main supply and dispersal centre for men, arms and munitions in southern Palestine.

In the Galilee, three Zionist colonies were attacked by cannon-firing Spitfires while in the Negeb desert area, a waterworks was heavily shelled, according to the Haganah. Pushing forward from Sarafand, the Zionists occupied a Palestinian village and raided and destroyed a Syrian supply camp housing heavy artillery. This action was too late to save two colonies from falling into the hands of the Syrians, to the south of the Sea of Galilee. Other settlements - Maishmar Hayarden, Kinnereth and Yavnil, together with a convoy - were all hit. Arab Legion armoured units and Iraqi artillery, concentrated in the Samakh area, were the targets of the first raid by the Israeli airforce.

Tel-Aviv announced a new Arab attack on the colony of Yad Mordechai, north of Gaza, by tanks, artillery and infantry. The report also claimed that the Arab Legion in the Jerusalem area had been reinforced. In the Jordan Valley the colony of Deganya was heavily attacked by tanks, armoured cars and bombed by planes.

In the Tel-Aviv area Egyptian planes bombed for the sixth day, using a heavier calibre of bomb. A power station, oil tanks, workshops, chemical and oxygen factories were the target. Followed by the Negeva settlement and a convoy near Rehovoth which was strafed.

The American ship, *Marine Carp*, called in at Beirut where 69 American Zionists, on their way to Palestine, were taken off the ship. Those capable of bearing arms were sent to a concentration camp.

Moshe Shertok, Israel's foreign minister, announced that the citizens of Israel will be called Israelis, not Israelites commenting "Israelites was the Bible time's name. This is a modern nation."

The Times reported on the reaction of the president of the American University in Beirut to President Truman's immediate recognition of the State of Israel. In a letter to the *New York Times* he said that the Arabs "had for weeks negotiated in good faith of the American delegation which was trying desperately to arrange a truce in Palestine. In the very midst of these negotiations word arrived of the President's action. Our own delegation was shocked and embarrassed."

Count Folke Bernadotte of Sweden was chosen as the United Nations mediator for Palestine (on a salary of £6 500 per year, not including expenses). His function, as established by the General Assembly, was to act in a mediatory capacity for the whole of Palestine and carry out those administrative functions entrusted to him by both sides.

May 21

The battle for the Old City of Jerusalem was reported to be near its end.

Arab irregulars stormed past the Haganah defences, taking the Western or Wailing Wall. The Old City shook to the vibrations of demolition charges as the Arab forces dynamited into the Jewish quarter of the Old City in order to seal the entrances of the underground tunnels from which the Haganah and Irgun made their last stand.

The Jewish quarter was reported to be turning into a mass of rubble. Zionist positions in and around the great central Tifret Synagogue, a few hundred yards from the Wailing wall were also demolished. Despite frantic resistance from the Zionist defenders, based in the rabbit-warren of tunnels under the Old City, Arab irregulars with the help of covering fire from the Arab Legion fought their way into the domed synagogue. Arab artillery and bombing squads began to demolish the building, shrouding it in thick clouds of smoke and dust.

When the Arab Legion artillery began to shell the Hadassah hospital and Hebrew University on Mount Scopus, the American Consul was reported to have asked the Legion to stop this action. The Legion commander declined, pointing out that some 400 Zionists fighters were entrenched in the buildings from where, despite repeated requests for them to stop, they continuously mortared and machine gunned the Sheikh Jarrah quarter. The Consul was handed surrender terms to convey to the Zionists.

At this juncture the Arab position, as articulated by the commander of the irregulars, was "We gave the Jews many chances to surrender but they have refused and now it is a fight to the finish." The Zionist position was given by a senior Haganah officer "The Arab aim in the Jerusalem battle is not merely to clear the roads for strategic purposes. It is the capture of the whole city. We shall fight it out."[44]

Jewish prisoners were reported as saying that many Jews trapped in the Old City want to surrender but the "Irgun have taken over command and the quarter will be destroyed."It was reported that the terrorist groups, the Irgun and Stern Gang still maintain their independence. Irgun members held up the Jewish owned Eden Hotel, and took blankets and sheets.

During the night a 1 000 strong Zionist force tried to penetrate Zion Gate to relieve the Jewish quarter but were beaten back. Unidentified aircraft flew over north Jerusalem during the night and dropped six bombs.

Reports indicated that the Arab Legion was attacking Jerusalem on three fronts, north, south and east with Zionist troops on the western side fighting fiercely to prevent encirclement. While Arab morale was reported to be high, that of the Jews in the "new city" was believed to be at breaking point according to Arab sources. With shells crashing into buildings and streets, the 100 000 Jews concentrated in the area were desperately looking for food and water from which they were cut off.

The Jewish agency claimed that its aircraft bombed artillery emplacements of the Arab Legion at Shufat, north of Jerusalem. Chief Rabbi Herzog addressed an appeal to the world community concerning the number of dead lying in Jerusalem unburied.

Egyptian forces were reported to have advanced 40 miles from Beersheba and were close to Bethlehem. Their bombers had attacked a steel works in Tel-Aviv and oxygen factories east of Jaffa. Other targets included Ramle airfield, munitions trucks, the settlements of Negeva and Shdernot and a goods train.

Israeli sources indicated that Zionist forces had captured large quantities of arms and artillery at Samakh, a village on Lake Tiberias with strategic value because of its proximity to the railway line. This followed two days of attacks by Israeli aircraft and shelling from four heavy artillery guns that had been unloaded at Tel -Aviv days before (the village site is now a public park).They repulsed a Syrian attack on Degania

Al Lazzaza, north of Safad was captured by the Zionists as was al Ghabisiyya, north east of Acre. In the case of the latter, the village militia decided not to confront the attackers because they were poorly armed and few in number. Many villagers were killed and injured by shelling while they were fleeing.

Heavy fighting continued in the Lydda-Ramleh area and around Latrun. The Arab Legion occupied the area under control of the Palestine Potash company near the Dead Sea. This followed traces of fire at the potash works and a nearby settlement following a request that they should surrender.

The U.S. government announced a Congressional enquiry into whether or not US financial aid was being used by Britain to help the Arab armies in Palestine. This followed allegations by Senator Brewster that British officers plus £8 000 000 yearly was supplied by Britain to the Transjordan frontier force "out of American taxpayers' pockets." The importance of this announcement lay in the fact that the Senate Appropriations Committee had yet to vote on the £1 325 million for the first year's European recovery programme. The Committee had the power to limit the amount going to Britain.

The Security Council received a cable from its commisssion in Jerusalem making the point that if the intention was to stop the fighting then it could not content itself with resolutions exhorting or ordering the belligerents to cease fire. Only a neutral force sufficiently large and powerful to force its will on both parties would have any chance of success.

May 22

The US Consul in Jerusalem,Thomas Wasson, was shot dead by a sniper's bullet as he was returning from a Truce Commission meeting. Both sides blamed each other for the murder.

A cease fire ultimatum was issued by the Security Council, as a result of a British proposal. It was stated that the Zionist forces were prepared to honour this if the Arab forces did likewise. The Zionist enthusiasm for the cease-fire was put down to two reasons. They were in virtual control of all the area allotted to them under the partition resolution. A cease-fire would bring military and political activities to a standstill. It was felt this would be to the advantage of the Zionists. In addition, compliance would be viewed favourably by the U.S. This, together with an Arab refusal, would make it easier for the U.S. to lift its arms embargo on the Middle East.

Meanwhile Egyptian and Transjordan forces were said to have linked up two miles to the south of Jerusalem.

The fishing village of al Tantura (built on the ruins of a Canaanite town, Dur, mentioned as far back as 13th century BC) to the south of Haifa, was attacked and captured by the Alexandroni Brigade. Israeli historian, Benny Morris, makes it clear that the aim was to empty the village of its residents, with some clearly being expelled.

This "some" amounted to 1 200, expelled to nearby al Furaydis. By summer most had been expelled from Israeli held territory, apart from 200, mostly women and children with relatives in Israeli detention. Some Israeli officials apparently expressed concern at these 200 Palestinian civilians, forced to sleep in the open and short of clothes.[45] Their fate was never recorded. [The site of the village is now an Israeli recreational area].

Fifty two years were to pass before the full details of what transpired at al Tantura was revealed. Despite the testimony of Palestinian oral tradition, which had always been ignored, the world had to wait for Israeli historian, Teddy Katz, to publish his dissertation for the University of Haifa.

Evidence was uncovered of the slaughter of as many as 200 Palestinians, about one eighth of the village population. It followed the killing of 14 soldiers of the Third Battalion of the Haganah's Alexandroni Brigade by village defenders. In what was described by eyewitnesses as "summary execution", successive groups of village men were lined up against the cemetery wall and shot. The slaughter only ceased when a settler from the nearby settlement of Zichron Ya'akov arrived and threatened to shoot himself if it did not stop.

Other accounts talk of an attack from the sea, on three sides of the village, with dawn revealing corpses of the village defenders lying about the village streets. The bodies were then dumped in the one spot with the women and children of the village forced to view the dead bodies of their husbands, fathers and brothers. These accounts confirm the shooting of selected groups of men in revenge for the deaths of some of the Zionist attackers.

Nearby is the Israeli resort of Dur. One of the parking areas used by visitors to the resort is the site of three mass graves, the last resting place of scores of victims.Village survivors, who were children at the time, still remember the names of butchered family members, can recite street names, point out where the boys and girls schools used to be and the glass factory where 52 men were massacred

Part of the village was subsequently bulldozed with Kibbutz Nachsholim established on village land[46].

As from this date, the British refused all Transjordan pleas for ammunition with which to supply an increasingly desperate Arab Legion.

May 23

The Old City of Jerusalem continued to be shelled by Arab forces. The 1 000 or so Jews rejected yet another demand for unconditional surrender, vowing to make a last stand in the catacombs. In the New City, in the western part of Jerusalem, 100 000 Jews were running out of food and water. Arab guns concentrated on the Tel-Aviv road repelled any attempts at relief. A Jewish Agency spokesman said "We are not over-optimistic, but we are confident, confident that if our imports of arms by sea continue we shall be able to win."

The Arab Legion was reported to have entered the Zionist colony of Ramat Rachel in Jerusalem's suburbs. They claimed that Zionist forces in the south of the city were completely encircled.

The Egyptian airforce bombed petrol depots and industrial targets in the south east of Tel-Aviv. Direct hits were recorded on ammunition lorries at Ramleh airfield. A train was destroyed north of Nathanya.

A communique from Cairo described an Egyptian attack on a British airfield within the security zone in Haifa as a "mistake." The attack on Ramat David airfield claimed the lives of four RAF men, with six wounded. Five Egyptian Spitfires were lost following British retaliatory action.

Arab forces claimed to have repulsed an attack on Samakh. The Zionists issued a counter-claim saying they had repulsed an attack. It was reported that the Lebanese forces had withdrawn from the conflict. Apparently they only intended to carry out defensive operations in the event of a Zionist advance into Lebanon.

The Times had very little to say concerning events, on the ground, in Palestine. It was more concerned with the deliberations of various Zionists and their perceptions of British aid to the Arab Legion.

The chief Rabbi of Palestine, Isaac Herzog, accused Britain of financing assaults on civilian populations, of financing the destruction of various historical and holy places. In America, Zionist rabbis in their sermons in the synagogue, were openly political. They exhorted the U.S. to lift its arms embargo. In newspaper adverts they urged the U.S. to cease giving economic aid to Britain until she stopped sending "arms to Arabs."

The Board of Deputies of British Jews in a resolution which expressed its appreciation of the part played by the British people in establishing a "Jewish national home" and bringing to an end the alleged "2 000 years of wandering and homelessness" made no mention of this apect of British involvement that vexed so many supporters of Zionism elsewhere.

The Arab League pointed out that the Zionists had refused earlier truce proposals because they wanted to seize all Jerusalem after the British left. The recognition of Israel by "certain Powers" had made the situation worse, the Zionists had become less compromising and the Arabs were determined to fight on.

The Times made an interesting comment on the position of the U.S., stating that although it was difficult to find any official prepared to defend the White House policy on Palestine, the President's reliance on "extremist advisers" would seem bound to lead him and the world into further trouble.

This comment was illustrated by the American letter of protest to the Lebanon regarding the Lebanese holding of American citizens, of arms bearing age, on their way to Palestine. The note of protest introduced anti-Semitism into the incident when it said "The Governments of other countries do not discriminate against the bearers of American passports on the grounds of race, colour or creed."

May 24

With the Arab League and its forces feeling that thing were going "smoothly", with any cease-fire adversely affecting their organisation and pursuit of objectives, the decision was taken to ignore the cease-fire. An Arab condition for any cease-fire was stated to be that all Haganah personnel without Palestinian nationality should be expelled from Palestine.

An Egyptian army communique stated that Egyptian forces had stormed the "Zionist fortress" of Deir Suneid, eight miles from Gaza. This followed a nine hour battle where the enemy "suffered a great number of dead, wounded, and captured" with insignificant losses to themselves. The Zionist casualties were estimated at 500 with an Israeli plane shot down in an attempt to parachute supplies into the settlement.

In and around Jerusalem, a bitter war of attrition was reported, with destruction threatening a large part of the Holy City. The area under Notre Dame convent was a scene of much fighting. While high explosive shells from the Arab Legion and the Arab Liberation Army crashed into Irgun and Haganah positions, Arab Legion troops and armoured cars with the support of a few thousand "irregulars" fought bitterly from houses to house through sandbagged and barbed wire streets of "Jewish new Jerusalem."

There were reports of the starvation and thirst facing up to 100 000 Jews. Many wanted a face-saving truce rather than a surrender. It was reckoned that about 400 fighters and 200 non-combatants were still holding out in the Old City.

A Haganah spokesman said that an aircraft bombed bombed Zionist occupied Jaffa for the first time. A few casualties were reported. Jewish areas shelled included Mekor Haim, Lifta, Lydda railway.

Unreported in the media was the ongoing Zionist onslaught, under the guise of various operations, on Palestinian rural areas.

The village of Indur [pop 620], southeast of Nazareth, was occupied by the Golani Brigade as part of its "cleansing and defending" of the Baysan Valley.The village of 'Ammuqa [pop 140] southeast of Safad, was shelled and captured by the Palmach as part of Operation Yiftach. Jahula and al Zawiya, both to the north of Safad, were "emptied" of their residents as part of Operation Yiftach.

South Africa became the first Commonwealth country to recognise Israel.

A "Boycott Britain" campaign was launched in the U.S. urging Americans not to buy British goods until she changed her Palestine policy.

In the reply to the American note of protest over the detention of some U.S. citizens, the Lebanese government pointed out "it was manifest that the able bodied among these illegal immigrants were going, as some thousands of others who have preceded them, to join elements of trouble and anarchy in Palestine . . . I should moreover point out that certain of the illegal Jewish immigrants disembarked, and the bearers of American passports, far from claiming American citizenship and protection, gloried in obedience to the State of Israel."

May 25

A number of statements emanated from Zionist sources. The President of Israel, Dr Weizmann, was over in the U.S. pleading for a loan of up to £25 000 000. He seemed to think that his appeal, together with that for a lifting of the arms embargo on Israel, was not in vain.The money was wanted for arms, reconstruction work, and to finance the entry of 15 000 displaced persons per month into Palestine.

He castigated the British for "undoing the work of Richard Coeur de Lion" by "leading" Arab armies into Jerusalem. He said that Israeli forces were prepared to leave Jaffa and Acre as soon as hostilities ceased. Jerusalem was different, although not allotted to Jews under the partition resolution, they felt the city was theirs.

With the cease-fire being postponed for 48 hours, Zionist sources expressed their astonishment. The Arab League's support for a cease-fire was reported to contain three conditions: Dissolution of all Zionist groups in Palestine; complete ending of immigration; non-recognition by Arabs of the Jewish State.

The Zionist pocket in the Old City was reported to have been split in two by the Arab Legion. The majority of the Haganah-Irgun had retreated in and around the ruins of the great "Hurva"Synagogue. The Jewish Agency were informed by the Red Cross that the synagogue would be demolished unless the Zionist forces withdrew.

Operation Ben-Nun was launched to gain control of the road to Jerusalem. The newly formed Sheva' Brigade and the Alexandroni Brigade were repulsed at al Latrun after a 24 hour battle with the Arab Legion. An official Arab communique said the Zionists had been "exterminated" with 600 fatal casualties. Large quantities of arms were captured.

An official Egyptian communique claimed that the strategic village of Irak Soueidan, a key communication centre for settlements in southern Palestine, had been captured. Army patrols attacked Zionist convoys and armour heading south, forcing them to retire.

The villages of al Dawwara (the site of one of the most copious spring wells in all of Palestine), al Abisiyya and Mallaha, all in the vicinity of Safad, were evacuated either as a direct result of military assault or psychological warfare in the closing stages of Operation Yiftach. [The area was converted into a fish hatchery.][47]

The Haganah claimed that the entire Jordan Valley had been cleansed of "enemy forces."

The Scotsman included a report on Jaffa.While observing that Tel-Aviv is bulging with a new "intense generation of khaki-clad youngsters" just across the road there is a five minute walk from "life into death." Of Jaffa's once bustling 70 000 there remain about 4 000. Once again, in the mould of blaming the victim, there is the comment that the rich fled first followed by the poorer as they supposedly "packed up" and fled in panic.

Now there is a Jewish District Commissioner and military commander. Streets are empty. Houses shuttered and decayed. Shops gutted and smashed. Barbed wire cuts off whole areas. Mines lie about in overgrown gardens. House fronts are pock-marked, the pavements bear star-shaped scars where the many mortar bombs fell.

The paternalistic DC alleged little looting had taken place (Author's note: eyewitness accounts tell otherwise). He had no idea when the refugees would return. There is the occasional sound of a small explosion, described as "casual fire" by the Zionists. In an Irgun controlled area, the terrorists were loading "chintzes" on to a truck. Palestinians can be seen walking home with small packets. The overall impression is a vast, empty, snail-shell of a city.

The Austrian office of the Jewish Agency called upon all able bodied Jewish men and women in the displaced persons' camp of the U.S zone of Austria to volunteer for the Israeli armed forces. The response was reported to be strong. In Germany, all Jews between the ages of 17 and 35 were being registered for service in the Israeli army, according to a Haganah representative in Berlin.

May 26

Concern was expressed by Arab representatives at the UN that the campaign aimed at lifting the US arms embargo was a mere smokescreen. In private, well informed Zionists concurred. Israel was already receiving 'planes, tanks, anti-tank guns, large calibre field artillery. These were arriving in increasing numbers with Soviet bloc countries thought to be responsible for some of the imports.

The Arab League, while expressing concern that it would be viewed as being the aggressor for rejecting the Security Council's cease-fire order, pointed out "It was not the Arabs who built pill-boxes and fortified 'settlements', who smuggled arms and built up a Hagana. But they are now being made the defendants."

The U.S State Department, through Mr Marshall, made it clear that American recognition of the new state was confined to the boundaries set by the UN partition plan. He refused to answer a question as to the difference, in the State Depts' view, between the presence of Jewish troops in Jaffa and Arab troops in Jerusalem.

The bombardment of Notre Dame and surrounding buildings in Jerusalem was said to be under the control of a British major and other British officers. Within the Jewish part of the city queues formed at water points. Bread rationing was also introduced to ensure that the fighters had enough to eat. In an air-drop, food containers targeted for Jews fell into the hands of the Arab residents of the Old City.

In line with the Jewish Agency accusations, the suffering non-combatants blamed the British for all their woes. Typified by a comment from the Palestine Post "The Arab attackers are fighting wildly at the the whim of Bevin and his Transjordan ally" However it was reported that regardless of the fact that Jerusalem is outwith their boundaries, a city with international status, the Zionists regarded the battle for Jerusalem as the battle for their new state. With the Egyptians expected to join up with the Arab Legion, one last push by the Haganah to raise the siege was expected.

Reuters reported that fresh Zionist forces had arrived in Jerusalem from Tel-Aviv. Both sides were using 'planes with the Arabs bombing Zionist strongholds in the city and the Haganah bombing the Hebron area and capturing Ramat Bridge. The battle for Latrun was renewed with the Arab Legion claiming many Zionists dead. Zionist sources described this battle as "the heaviest in Palestine." The Transjordan Defence Ministry announced that the Latrun casualty figure was close to 800 Zionists killed. A Zionist stronghold near Abu Ghosh, a former radar station, had been captured.

Fir'in [pop 740] east of Safad was evacuated following an Israeli military attack.

May 27

While gunners and demolition squads of the Arab Legion pressed hard on the dwindling perimeter of the ruins of the Hurva Synagogue which sheltered the remnants of the Zionist defenders, King Abdullah of Trans-jordan, commander in chief of the Arab armies in Palestine, drove through the walled ramparts of Jerusalem. He visited and prayed at the Omar mosque, visited the Church of the Holy Sepulchre and the grave of his father, King Hussein.

By noon the Arab flag was flying over the Hurva Synagogue with the Legion commander saying that it would be spared further destruction because it contained no more Zionist gun-posts.

A Haganah broadcast said that the battle for Latrun and Bab el Wad was fiercer than previously. A major Haganah attack was carried out on the large Arab town of Majdal, north of Gaza, where buildings housing Egyptian forces were destroyed. Reports said that the Zionist forces went into attack with ropes attached - to make recovery easier in the event of death or injury.

Once again, out of the media spotlight, the Zionist forces were entrenching themselves.

Al Samiriyya, southwest of Baysan, was evacuated following an assault by the Golani Brigade's 4th Battalion

The strategic village of Julis, northeast of Gaza, was attacked by the Giv'ati Brigade, gaining partial control, as part of Operation Barak.

Also under the auspices of Operation Barak, al Qubayba, west of al Ramla, was occupied by the Giv'ati Brigade whose commander, Shimon Avidan, "wanted only empty villages." This was repeated at Zarnuqa, southwest of al Ramla. This particular military action on the village gained a certain amount of prominence when one of the members of Haganah who took party related an account of the events to a member of the Mapam party. A few days later, the party daily *Al Hamishmar* printed the account:

"The soldier told me how one of the soldiers opened a door and fired a Sten at an old man, an old woman and a child in one burst, how they took the Arabs . . . out of all the houses and stood [them] in the sun all day - in thirst and hunger until they surrendered 40 rifles . . The Arabs claimed that they hadn't [weapons, and] in the end they were expelled from the village towards Yibna . . screaming and crying they left the village."[48]

Reports from outwith the Jerusalem area indicated that apart from the Negev, the Zionists suffered no major setbacks with the Arab's advances being repulsed. At one point in the Jordan valley, south of Lake Galilee,

Syrian, Transjordan and Iraqi troops operated together. The Iraqi commander and the forces under his contol had now retreated across the frontier into the hills. The Zionists claimed to be the masters of the frontier and of the deep wide valley. Some had followed the retreating Arab forces into Syria.

On the diplomatic front, efforts continued try and bring about a four week cease-fire with various conditions attached. The UK representative on the Security Council, Sir Alexander Cadogan, announced immediate arrangements to ensure that the 21 seconded British officers with the Arab Legion should not serve in Palestine (the remaining 16 were not subject to British orders). The financial obligations to Transjordan and supply of military material to other Arab states would be reviewed in the light of any decision taken by the UN with regard to supply of arms to both sides.

He argued that the responsibility for the continuing conflict in Palestine could not be allocated on the basis of the Arab states' response to the Security Council's latest resolution. Earlier resolutions of the Council, he recalled, envisaged a truce that would be political as well as military in nature. This basis was removed by the proclamation of a "Jewish State" on 14 May. Cadogan argued that the tacit abandonment by the Security Council of political terms which the Arabs consider just and reasonable had to be taken into account if the Arabs' present attitude was to be fairly appraised.[49]

The Syrian delegate pointed out that it was easy for the Zionists to accept an unconditional cease-fire, they had already carved out their state. At the same meeting, hints of Zionist involvement in germ warfare was revealed. Two Zionist prisoners admitted that they carried out orders to poison wells used by the Egyptian army with typhoid and dysentry germs. The Jewish Agency representative found it convenient to dismiss this allegation as "An anti-Semitic libel."[49]

May 28

The news was dominated by the surrender of the Zionist forces who had been holding out in the Jewish Quarter of the Old City of Jerusalem. Between 1 500 and 1 600 Jews including members of the Irgun and Stern Gang surrendered to the Arab Legion after an onslaught lasting 12 days. About 300 (other reports said 2 000) women, children and old men were turned over to the International Red Cross. Younger men were to be placed in an internment camp "outside Palestine."

With the exception of Sheikh Jarrah, which was quickly encircled by the Arab Legion, the New City was under control of the Zionists.

The village of Zir'in (identified with the Canaanite town of Yizre'el, Joshua 17:16) was occupied by the 4th Battalion of the Golani brigade. The Brigade's orders, issued on 19 April read "With the capture of Zir'in, most of the village's houses must be destroyed while [some houses] should be left intact for accomodation and defence."

Beit Jiz, southeast of al Ramla, was occupied by the Sheva' Brigade during Operation Ben-Nun. This enabled the Israeli forces to establish an alternative supply route to Jerusalem, bypassing al Latrun.

The New York Times reported that Associated Press correspondents who toured the north and east with Israeli forces observed an area "swept almost virtually clear" of its Palestinian Arab population by an operation called "The Broom."

Claims and counter-claims emanated from both sides with regard to the ongoing battle at Latrun, on the road to Tel-Aviv. It was stated that the Zionists were of the opinion that not only was this battle crucial for the immediate future of Jerusalem but could determine the future role of the Arab Legion in Palestine. Iraqi bombers were shot down over Latrun and over the Jordan Valley.

The proposal was made to Foreign Minister Shertok that a Transfer Committee be appointed. It was reported that Shertok agreed that the "momentum of [Arab flight] must be exploited and turned into an accomplished fact."[50]

May 29

A new cease-fire order calling for a four week truce while the UN further discussed events in Palestine was passed by the Security Council. Its provisions included: No arms to be taken into Palestine or the Arab States within the next month; cessation of entry of fighting men into Palestine and Arab League States; Jews of military age introduced to Palestine during the month not to receive military training.

Al Muharraqa, east of Gaza, was captured by the Palmach's Negev Brigade. At Nuris, northeast of Jenin, the village was captured and the villagers expelled by the Golani Brigade. On the Lebanese border the village of al Malikiyya, to the north of Safad, fell to Haganah troops disguised as Lebanese reinforcements "with the exception of the enemy dead, a large quantity of ammunition, and a number of French mortars, nothing remained in place."[50]

May 30

The Irgun officially broadcasted an appeal to Russia asking for help to "liquidate Arab-British aggression." Britain, in collusion with the US State Department, was accused of pushing through the Security Council a resolution which, in the eyes of the Irgun, prevented Zionist reinforcements from reaching Palestine while opening avenues favourable to Arab reinforcements. This was reference to the new cease-fire order.

In Jerusalem about 1 000 Jewish non-combatants were taken to empty hotels in the Katamon district, captured by Zionists two weeks previously. About 350 prisoners were taken to Transjordan with a further 150 wounded being treated in the Old City. An estimated 200 Zionist were unaccounted for, presumed dead.

Zionist resistance appeared stiffen over the weekend. Success was claimed in capturing Jerusalem's water supply station at Ras el Ein from an Iraqi force. On the Lebanese border the Israeli army captured an army camp at Malakieh village together with the neighbouring village of Kadis, following the destruction of Lebanese armoured cars and trucks.

The village of Kawfakha, to the east of Gaza was captured by the Negev Brigade. Although the villagers "earlier repeatedly asked to surrender, accept Jewish rule and be allowed to stay . ." they were driven out of their village, their request was denied. The official reason given was that such requests were always "either insincere or unreliable."[52]

Al Mazar, northeast of Jenin was captured by the Fourth Battalion of the Golani Brigade. The Zionists then went on to attack Jenin itself, with no success.

The Israeli governement claimed to have a copy of Arab Legion orders outlining the bombing, shelling and use of gas on the New City of Jerusalem. Meanwhile it was reported that all officers seconded from the British army to the Arab Legion were to be withdrawn from Palestine by midnight. Transjordan forces were reported to have reached Lydda-Ramleh , 13 miles from Tel-Aviv. The Egyptians captured Isdud, 28 miles south of Tel-Aviv. Extensive air operations were reported with raids on settlements and Tel-Aviv's coastal defences.

The Scotsman's correspondent in Amman gave a resume of the Arab position on the four week cease-fire proposals. Egypt and Iraq suspected the proposals while the other states tended towards a qualified acceptance. All Arab states supported the belief that the Zionist intention was to gain all of Palestine and Transjordan, citing the assault on Jerusalem, Acre and Jaffa, even before the end of the mandate.

Some Arab states felt that acceptance of the cease-fire, as Britain (as their sole friend amongst the major powers) had appealed for them to do, would be proof of their "good intentions" and would help negate Zionist propaganda. The general tendency was to regard the U.S. as the Arab's bitterest enemy. Zionist violence was attributed to American "encouragement and intervention."

May 31

The Arab League met in Amman to discuss the British proposals for a truce in Palestine. It was considered that the Arabs faced a dilemna. Domestic public opinion, bolstered by over-optimistic and exaggerated reporting felt that victory was round the corner, wanted the conflict to continue. The reality was that if the Arab side rejected the truce prposals, the arms embargo on the Zionists would be cancelled and one would be imposed on the Arab states.

In Cairo, the Egyptian prime minister was optimistic about the cease fire being accepted. He considered that events had changed in favour of the Arabs.

Count Folke Bernadotte, the UN appointed mediator left Cairo for Tel Aviv, for his first contact with the Zionists.

Officials of the Christian Union of Palestine issued a draft document accusing the Zionist armed forces in the Holy City of violating churches, convents and religious institutions by using them as bases for military operations. Eight religious buildings had been occupied, 14 churches, convents and other property, including the Church of the Holy Sepulchre had been damaged. Three priests had been killed, two wounded and hundreds of children, women and combatants killed "since the Jews began the attack".

Zionist attacks continued between Haifa and Jenin with latter regarded as the target, in view of the fact that the British withdrawal could be completed during June. Zionist fighter planes were active in northern Palestine and in the Ramleh area, attacking Arab communications. Air and artillery operations were carried out against Arab-held Lydda, near the large airport. Arab attempts to recapture Lajjun village were repulsed.

In the Latrun area, an attack by Zionist forces was halted by the Arab Legion. Reports indicated that the attackers left 114 dead with much military equipment, arms and ammunition captured or destroyed. Egyptian land forces were reported to be "mopping up" to the south of Tel-Aviv with bombers and fighter planes raiding the fortified Rehovcth, dropping high explosives and incendiary bombs.

The village of Huj [pop 1 040 including 230 Jews] to the east of Gaza was occupied by the Golani Brigade who then ordered the villagers to leave their homes. Many Zionist officials considered the village to be "friendly" but was officially viewed as "unreliable", being near the front-line with the Egyptian army. Once the villagers were expelled, to the west, their homes were looted and blown up.

Israeli historian, Benny Morris, regarded the debate which subsequently centred on the refugees created by these expulsions as a clear statement of Israeli determination not to allow Palestinian refugees to return to their homeland.[53]

Notes

1 Ilan Pappe, *The Making of the Arab-Israeli Conflict 1947-51*, p.65
2 Mohammed Neigub, *Egypt's Destiny*, p.20
3 AJ Sherman, *Mandate Days*, p.238
4 Nur Masalha,*A Critique of Benny Morris*, p.95 (Journal of Palestine Studies, Autumn 1991)
5 Norman Finkelstein, *Myths, Old and New*, p.71 (JoPS, Autumn 1991)
6 *ibid* p.80
7 Masalha, p.181
8 Benny Morris, *The birth of the Palestinian refugee problem, 1947-49*, p.160
9 Walid Khalidi, *All that Remains*, p.437
10 Nathan Krystall,*The De-Arabisation of West Jerusalem 1947-50*,(JoPS, Winter 1998) p.11
11 Michael Palumbo, *The Palestinian Catastrophe*, p.76
12 Khalidi, p.450
13 Finkelstein, p.79
14 Morris, p.134
15 The Scotsman 2/5/48
16 Khalidi, p.507
17 *ibid* p.455
18 Benny Morris, *Falsifying the Record*, (JoPS, Spring 1995) p.47
19 The Times 6/5/48
20 Benny Morris, *The birth of the Palestinian refugee problem, 1947-49*, p.132
21 Khalidi, p.429
22 Palumbo, p.113-114
23 Khalidi, p.429
24 Walid Khalidi, *Plan Dalet,Journal of Palestine Studies, 1987* , p.18 (JoPS, Autumn 1988)
25 Palumbo, p. 100
26 Benny Morris, *Refabricating 1948*, (JoPS, Winter 1998) p.88
27 The Scotsman 12/5/48
28 The Times 13/5/48
29 The Scotsman 14/5/48
30 Sydney D Bailey, *Four Arab-Israeli wars and the peace process*, p.16
31 The Scotsman 14/5/48
32 Sherman, p.243

33 *ibid* p.242
34 Krystall, p.12
35 The Scotsman 19/5/48
36 Walid Khalidi, *All that Remains*, p.430
37 Palumbo, p.119
38 Benny Morris, *The birth of the Palestinian refugee problem, 1947-49*, p.135
39 The Times 20/5/48
40 Khalidi, p.28
41 Palumbo, p.106
42 Khalidi, p.32
43 *ibid* p.49
44 The Scotsman 22/5/48
45 Khalidi, p.193
46 *Middle East International* 28 January 2000
Return Review February 2000
The Jerusalem Times 11 February 2000
47 Khalidi, p.445/472
48 *ibid* p.425
49 The Times 28/5/48
50 Morris, p.135
51 Khalidi, p.471
52 *ibid* p.120
53 Morris, p.152

June

By their past encouragement of the terrorists, whom they secretly supported whilst publicly denouncing them, the Jewish leaders have created a Frankenstein which will eventually cause them far more trouble than it ever caused the British.

Clare Hollingworth, Special Correspondent, The Scotsman

The Israeli Defence Forces intelligence service produced a report entitled "The Emigration of the Arabs of Palestine 1/12/47 to 1/6/48"[1]. This was the period of time by which about half of the eventual Palestinian refugees had fled their homeland. Three main reasons were given as to why about 391 000 Palestinian had departed in such haste.

1] Direct hostile Haganah/Israeli army operations against Palestinian population centres.

2] The knock-on effect of the Zionist military actions against Palestinian population centres. In particular, the fall of large towns or villages.

3] The operations of the terrorist (euphemistically referred to as "dissident") groups.

Mentioned were the results of psychological warfare, "whispering campaigns" etc. Given a low profile were direct orders for expulsion, a fact which Israeli historian, Benny Morris, found "somewhat low" resulting, perhaps, from an "understandable tendency - - - to minimise the role of direct expulsions orders played in bringing about part of the Palestinian exodus."

Interestingly, the report confirmed what Palestinian and other sources have said for long enough, and yet was long denied by Israeli propaganda. Namely, Arab institutions fought hard against the phenomenon of Palestinian flight and exodus. They tried to curb emigration to the extent that "the Arab Higher Committee decided to impose restrictions, and issued threats, punishments and propaganda in the radio and press to curb emigration." In the report the myth of radio broadcasts fared worse than that of alleged Arab orders to flee Palestine. There is no mention of any blanket order issued over Arab radio stations or through other means to Palestinians to evacuate their homeland[1].

Yet, at the start of June, Yosef Weitz of the Jewish National Fund and founder member of the Transfer Committee could cynically comment, with regard to the fleeing Palestinians, with words such as "miracle", "unexpected phenomenom"[2]. Earlier, on 2 May, Weitz was exclaiming "Village after village was abandoned in a panic *that cannot be explained.*"[3]

Israeli kibbutznik, Yosef Argaman, gave an account of the methods used to strike fear into the villagers on the coastal plain, in the process of emptying the villages along the Haifa Tel-Aviv highway. He and his fellow settlers would shoot into the villages at night and, as in the case of Caesarea, the crescent at the top of the village mosque would be stolen. They would enter the village coffee shop with full display of weapons, engage the locals in conversation and emphasise that for every Jew killed, 1 000 Palestinians would be slaughtered. The Haganah, he related, would enter a town and start to tear the tiles of the roofs. Slowly but surely the villages emptied.[4]
During the month of June a number of colonial settlements were established, mostly on Jewish-owned land but with their fields taken from "abandoned" Palestinian Arab owned land. These were Hahotrim (south of Haifa), Reshafim and Sheluhot (on the lands of Al Ashrafiya, Beit Shean Valley), Nahsholim (on the lands of Tantura), Ein Dor (on the lands of Kafr Misr, Galilee), Netzer-Sereni (at Bir Salim, Ramleh), Timurim (on the lands of Ma'lul, Galilee) and Kfar Yavetz on the Coastal Plain).

For the month of June, scrutiny of Ben Gurion's diary gives no indication of who or what was responsible for the moves to "ethnically cleanse" occupied areas of their Palestinian Arab inhabitants. No mention, not even as an aside, of the existence of the Transfer Committee, never mind its function - destruction of the villages, prevention of Arab cultivation and harvesting, purchase of Arab land to encourage emigration.[5] Yet it is on record that the great majority of Zionist settlements, including the *kibbutzim*, and officials supported these policies.[6]

For 16 June, for example, there was no mention in his diary of his sources of information, who was responsible and the reason for the destruction of the villages.[5] On the same date the cabinet of Israel's provisional government and, with no formal recorded vote, agreed the fate of the eventual 750 000 or so Palestinian refugees. They were not to be allowed to return to their homes.A decision which, for many, meant being exiled from the land of their birth.

Despite the importance of such a decision, it was never published. In the words of Israeli historian, Benny Morris "The decision carried moral undertones and political meanings that could be construed as embarrassing . the statements made at the meeting . . . were to undergo successive rewritings to conform to accepted international political norms of behavior and speech." For example, four years later, in a published collection of speeches Ben Gurion severely criticised the extensive looting of Arab property as the only "moral shortcoming". There was no mention of massacres, individual killings, rapes and expulsions.[7]

Throughout the month, the prevention of Palestinians from harvesting their crops evolved into a set policy to demoralise villagers, adversely affect them economically and perhaps induce the villagers to leave their land. Previously, the destruction of fields and crops had been a Haganah strategy for retaliation and collective punishment following Arab attacks. It was now used as a tactic for separating the Palestinian peasant, both physically and psychologically, from his land.

The various brigades were constantly reminded to use small arms to prevent Palestinians from reaping their crops. In inaccesible areas it was the practice to burn the crops in order to prevent harvesting.

And the flow of refugees continued. During the First Truce, which commenced 10 June, the Greek vice consul in Jerusalem, C X Mavrides, recorded the images in his diary of the "chain" of refugees from the Old City seeking refuge in surrounding towns and villages.

The streets were filled with porters, pack-animals, women, children and the elderly, all of them carrying something under the burning June sun. As the four week truce drew to a close the chain of people and animals grew denser by the day.

June 1

Both parties to the conflict cabled the Security Council indicating their willingness to comply with the Council's request for a four week truce in Palestine.

Various claims were made by the parties to the conflict.

The Iraqis claimed to be within nine miles of Tel Aviv, Kalkilieh had been taken by their forces, as had the settlement of Kfar qa Sim. In cooperation with Arab irregulars, they recaptured the main water pumping station of Ras el Ein which supplied Jerusalem

The Egyptians attacked all Zionist colonies on the coast between Tel-Aviv and Isdud. Syrian planes attacked Naharia, sinking two anchored ships.

The Israeli army claimed to have penetrated the flank of an Egyptian army column up to 5 000 strong, near Yibna. The previous day's bombing of Amman killed at least 12 Arabs, with King Abdullaḥ's palace being a target.

Records show that, as part of Operation Barak, the 1 420 villagers of al Nabi Rubin, west of al Ramla were expelled.[8]

An Israeli spokesman issued a statement confirming the Zionist military position over the past two weeks. It claimed that in addition to the whole of the territory of Israel which was free of "invaders", 400 square miles outside this territory had been seized in "operations of active defence". The whole of the Galilee was controlled by Israeli forces as was the coastal plain from the Lebanese border to south of Isdud.

In Jerusalem, the bombardment of the "new city" continued, with the occasional lull. The Arab Legion informed the Red Cross of its intention to shell the Hebrew University area in response to mortar fire from the University which had hit its forward positions in Sheikh Jarrah. No supply column had reached the city for seven weeks, causing severe shortages. It was reckoned that the gunners of the Arab Legion were becoming more accurate and deadly through experience. Since the start of the bombardment, 1 400 people had been killed or injured.

The last Jew to be evacuated from the Old City was reported, in The Scotsman, to have been surprised by the "agreeably fair treatment" that he and other evacuees had received at ther hands of their captors, the Arab Legion.The newspaper's correspondent in Jerusalem gave a revealing assessment of the conduct of the Zionists in the Jewish controlled "new city."

Comparing it with a cleaner Berlin in August 1939, she pondered as to why the Jewish administration copied Germany in its method of government. There was suppression of freedom of speech and action, curtailing of civil liberties. In a comment reminiscent of current practices in the occupied West Bank and Gaza Strip, "security"is given as the usual excuse. All unpleasant orders are accompanied by the "security" catch-all.

The dominant force in the country, the Haganah, remained almost underground with no badges indicating rank on their uniforms. The Haganah's commanding officer in the city was nameless, as were all senior officers. The terrorist groups were increasingly regarded as "good Jewish organisations" with many Jewish police and government officials now coming out of the closet and proudly proclaiming their membership of the terrorist gangs.

However as it became increasingly harder to impose law and order in the "new city" the tone changed. The Jewish Agency and the Haganah blamed "dissident groups" who had "let down" the fighting forces. The Irgun, now popularly called the "Etzel" began to throw its weight around. The correspondent pointed out that the Jewish Agency knew exactly the composition of the terrorists and could have apprehended them if they had so wished.

The fruits of this policy of ignoring and effectively supporting the terrorists started to show. "Appalling lawlessness in Jerusalem and other

Jewish towns" was reported. The "Jewish Frankenstein" contributed to weaknesses in Jewish morale, it was claimed.This morale was particularly high amongst the richer classes. However it was this group that was targeted by the Irgun and the Stern Gang with no protection offered from the official bodies.

The report concluded "Irgun is in fact becoming the 'SS' of the new State. There is also a strong 'Gestapo' - but no one knows who is in it."[9]

At a meeting of Israeli Cabinet Ministers, including Ben Gurion, the question of the return of Palestinian refugees was raised. This was the first in a series of such meetings. Ben Gurion made it clear that the military were to be used to prevent Palestinians returning to their land, their homes and their businesses. "Commanders are to be issued orders in this matter."

This would have been music to the ears of the 1 700 Jewish community of Safad (the 10 000 Arab community had fled in May). It was around this time that the community leaders appealed, up to Cabinet level, for a ban on the return of Arabs to their homes. They further appealed for a ring of new colonial settlements around the town together with the settlement of Jews in the abandoned Arab houses. Their reasoning was quite clear. If the Palestinians returned to their homes they, the Jews, would leave since "The Jewish community would not be able to withstand the pressure of the returning Arabs, especially in view that most of the Arab property in Safad has been stolen and plundered since the Arabs left."[10]

Around about this time a self-appointed Transfer Committee was formed to look at the question of the return of refugees.[11] As in many affairs to do with the Palestinian Arab, the hand of Yosef Weitz of the Jewish National Fund was involved. He was also busy elsewhere, being involved in the destruction of the villages of Al Mughar (near Gedera), Fajja (near Petah), Tikva, Biyar Adas (near Magdiel), Beit Dajan (east of Tel Aviv), Miska (near Ramat Hakovesh), As Sumeiriya (near Acre), Al Buteimat and Sabarin (near Haifa). Weitz was on the look out for villages that should be destroyed and those suitable for Zionist settlement.[12]

June 2

There were conflicting reports of breaches of the cease fire order with the Zionists reserving the right to "resume major operations" if violations did not cease. Despite reports that the Zionists had adhered to the cease fire order on all fronts, the Arab Legion reported four attacks on the Old City of Jerusalem during the night. It was claimed that 80 attackers were killed, while Legion combat troops and irregulars crouched in firing position with Zionist mortars sailing over the walls and exploding near their positions.

An Israeli communique reported that Egyptian forces - tanks, artillery and infantry - attacked the colony of Neba, in the southern Negeb. Their Spitfires bombed the village of Hulda in the Latrun area. Israeli forces penetrated eight miles into Transjordan, killing eight policemen at a rural garrison.

June 3

Britain issued an Order, which essentially extended an existing Order, revoking all licenses for the export of war materials to Egypt, Iraq, Palestine, Transjordan, Syria, Lebanon, Saudi Arabia and Yemen. In response to a US Congressional committee set up to establish if Britain was using aid from the Marshall Aid plan to assist Arab armies, Britain responded that she had yet to receive any such aid.

The UN mediator, Count Bernadotte, was given the freedom by the Security Council to interpret the Palestine truce terms, the setting up of controls, as he saw fit. This was in response to disputes which had arisen between the warring sides. Britain regarded the cease fire order for Palestine as giving justification to her continuing policy of not allowing Zionist male immigrants of military age to leave the detention camps in Cyprus (where many received military or para-military training).

This issue of Zionist immigration resulted in the quick termination of a debate in the Security Council. Jamal Bey Husseini, for the Arab Higher Committee said that if the truce terms meant continued Jewish immigration, the truce would not be maintained. Arabs would be unable to bear the sight of young militant Jews pouring into the country. For Israel, Mr Eban said that men of military age "can and will enter."

During the short debate, Husseini pointed out that if the Jews wanted the Arabs to withdraw from Jerusalem they themselves could withdraw from the Arab cities they occupied. If they wanted something done for the Jews in Jerusalem, they on their side should do something about the Arabs, 300 000 of them, who had been driven from their homes.

Following a day of many air raids, two Egyptian planes were shot down near Tel-Aviv.The Israelis also reported that, as part of Operation Barak, an Egyptian army column near Isdud, north of Gaza, had been surrounded. The Egyptians reported 400 attackers dead at Isdud during counter-attacks. However thousands of the local population fled for safety from the historical area. Its name derived from the ancient town of Ashdod, one of the five major cities of the Philistines. Excavations showed that it had been occupied almost continuously from the 17th century BC until 1948.

Egyptian naval forces launched an attack on the port of Caesarea.

June 4

The Scotsman's special correspondent, Clare Hollingworth, spent two weeks involuntarily besieged inside Jerusalem. She reported a steady and insidious destruction and disintegration, a city of empty buildings and accumulated rubbish, adorned with rusting tangles of barbed wire. She was surprised to find how little damage individual shells had done to the stone buildings.

As regards the Zionist occupied "new" or modern city of Jerusalem, the destruction appeared to be widespread and extensive. Not that she, nor the civilian Jew, was allowed any access. This area was dominated by the Haganah and their terrorist comrades in arms, the Irgun and Stern Gang.

Jerusalem increasingly became less attractive. Although ground within the modern city had been consecrated for Jewish burials, little effort was made to retrieve the many corpses in the city outskirts. There, they were lying rotting in the hot sunshine, along with foetid odours from accumulated garbage.

In "Jewish Jerusalem" very few shops were opened with fewer customers. Initially shelling and sniper fire was the excuse for staying off the streets. This, according to Hollingworth, was no longer the case. The fear was the actions of the "young toughs" from the Irgun and Stern outfits. Soon to be revered as heroes and subsumed within the mythology of the "purity of Hebrew arms", the terrorists had turned their tactics on their own people - so much so that they "- - who are beyond whatever law there is have cleaned out most private houses of the richer classes and started to prey upon the shopkeepers." Steel shutter still afforded some protection against the depredations of the Irgun and Stern members, hence the shops stayed shut.

Hollingworth's observations on the situation facing the Jews of Jerusalem are worth recording in full:

"By their past encouragement of the terrorists, whom they secretly supported whilst publicly denouncing them, the Jewish leaders have created a Frankenstein which will eventually cause them far more trouble than it ever caused the British. It is obviously due to the presence of the Jewish 'Gestapo', which taps telephones and has its spies and informers everywhere, that everyone pretends to be in excellent spirits.The Jews must not be cast down by the siege or by the prospect of a 'new Stalingrad' which some of the more fanatical military leaders actually appear still to want. Nor is it advisable in Jerusalem to question the policy of the Jewish authorities or to hope that the war and the siege will soon end. Women who break down under the strain and weep in public make haste to explain that they are bewailing the loss of a relative. No amount of control, no threat or penalties can hide the fact that the ordinary people of the new Jewish State hate the war and long for peace.. They are, however, quite powerless to make their desires felt against the burning fanaticism of the small group of people who now rule Jewish destinies."[13]

Zionist forces were reported to have penetrated Jenin at the apex of the "Arab triangle" formed with Nablus and Tulkarm. Iraq claimed that 5 000 Zionists had eventually fled Jenin, leaving 580 dead littering the battle area. The nascent Israeli navy engaged Egyptian forces off Tel-Aviv in a three hour battle. Their bombers were also in action, with one failing to return. The four Egyptian ships were driven off.

The ancient village of Yibna (probably the site of the Philistine town of Jabneel) was hammered with mortars as part of Operation Barak. It was found to be deserted except for some old men and women who were "sent packing." At sunrise it was possible to see streams of villagers fleeing towards the coast for safety, according to the History of the Haganah.

A night attack on the village of Qaqun, with artillery and heavy mortar fire, was met by stiff resistance from the Iraqi defenders. It ended with hand-to-hand combat with knives, grenades and rifle butts. The Israeli version gave 450 Iraqi dead for 12 of their own men reported dead. [Zionist forces re-visited the village of al Ja'una one year later to the day. At midnight Israeli army trucks surrounded the village and forced the villagers into the trucks "with brutality . . . with kicks, curses and mal-treatment." Isreali Knesset member Eli'ezer Prai protested. He was told by prime minister Ben Gurion that military reasons were "sufficient."[14]]

Within Jerusalem, two mortar shells crashed into two Greek Catholic churches less than 24 hours after church leaders had telegraphed the UN protesting against the violation of churches and convents in the Holy Land. The Arab Legion immediately responded with a volley of artillery shells aimed at "Jewish Jerusalem."

Three members of the self-appointed Transfer Committee discussed ways by which the Palestinian Arab "exodus" could be made permanent. Destr-uction of their villages and the settling of Zionist settlers in others was the answer. This would prevent Arab return. Yosef Weitz allocated Jewish National Fund money to start demolition activities in the Beit Shean Valley and on the Coastal Plain.[15]

Count Bernadotte reported that he did not know when the truce would begin. The two sides had many reservations and would not meet together. In particular, from the Arab perspective, to admit convoys into Jerusalem would completely nullify their advantageous position gained by the blockade of the Tel-Aviv Jerusalem road. With the Jews in Jerusalem short of rations and ammunition they did not want them to restock in order to prolong the struggle in Jerusalem should any truce fail to produce a peaceful settlement.

The real fear was that they would be offered terms which appeared reasonable, and so hard to refuse unless they wanted to look like the obstacle to peace, but which would weaken the Arab position.

June 5

A meeting took place in Tel-Aviv between Yosef Weitz and David Ben Gurion where the former presented a memo "Retroactive Transfer: A scheme for the Solution of the Arab Question in the State of Israel". In this document the Transfer Committee proposed measures to block the return of Palestinian refugees, to facilitate their resettlement elsewhere and to encourage emigration by those Palestinian Arabs still in the country. These measures included the destruction of Arab villages; the prevention of cultivation and harvesting of crops; the renovation of specified villages and their resettlement by Zionist colonists; the settlement of colonists in "abandoned" Arab neighbourhoods; the use of propaganda to prevent refugee return.[16]

Weitz reported that the committee had already begun "here and there destroying villages." In his published diary, this comment was altered to read "here and there 'improving' villages." He further commented that Ben Gurion gave his approval.[15]

June 6

Following a failed attempt by Zionist infantry to storm the Old City's Zion Gate, the Arab Legion shelled the Haganah-held districts of Jerusalem, the heaviest shelling since 28 May.

The Syrians claimed that a combined Syrian and Lebanese assault on the northern villages of Malikiyya and Qadas reulted in their recapture and occupation and the death or injury of 250 Zionists. Iraqi and Egyptian sources reported minor advances while the Arab League announced that Saudi- Arabian troops had entered Palestine.

Yosef Weitz sent Ben Gurion a list of abandoned villages and towns, stating that in accordance with their previous meeting, orders had been given to start "operations" in different parts of Galilee - Beit Shean Valley, the Hills of Ephraim and Samaria (ie east of Hadera).

The evacuation of Haifa was reported to be almost at an end with British controlled areas contracting in size, daily - much to the dismay of the remaining Palestinians who faced an uncertain future. War material which could not be removed was destroyed or dumped into the sea - much to the chagrin of protesting Israeli officials who were prepared to pay almost any amount for the ammunition and tanks which suffered the latter fate. Acres of rusting, ruined vehicles were sold to the Israelis along with a large number of serviceable three-ton lorries.

June 7

Count Bernadotte finalised his proposals for a four week cease fire, with the Israelis quick to point out that it did not preclude the entry of men of military age into the country, but did place a ban on their mobilisation and training during the cease fire.The Arab response was to the effect that this would happen over their dead bodies.

The Old City of Jerusalem continued to suffer from occasional three-inch mortar fire which caused some damage but no casualties. The usual response was for the Arab forces to hurl back 20 for every one they received. With Zionist artillery fire continuing to come from the vicinity of Hadassah Hospital on Mount Scopus, the Arab Legion waited for orders before returning fire.

Egyptian forces occupied the Zionist coastal settlement of Beit Sanim, near Isdud. They also claimed to have bombarded Zionist armour concentrations inflicting heavy losses. A patrol ambushed an armoured column, killing 66 and wounding many more, it was claimed.

Zionist reinforcements attacked Arab positions in the strategic Latrun area.

June 8

Count Folke Bernadotte proposed that the four week cease fire should commence on Friday 11 June at 7am (BST). Tel Aviv sources indicated that the Zionist military leaders were not keen on a cease fire since they believed they could lose military advantages.The Irgun and Stern indicate dissent. They did not recognise the authority of the provisional government outwith the "boundaries" of the state of Israel.

Over the previous three weeks the Zionists had managed to retain possession of the southern gateway to the modern town of Ramat Rahael where the road from Bethlehem, Hebron and Egypt entered Jerusalem. In addition the major former British army camps were under their control. To the west of the city they had an unbroken line from Mekor Haim through the Arab suburb of Katamon to Romema, close to the main Jewish districts on the Tel-Aviv road.

The northern section was in the hands of the Arab Legion, as was the important Nablus road. The eastern sector was entirely in Arab hands with traffic along the Jericho road described as "normal." Between the road and the walls of the Old City the Palestinian villagers on the valley slopes were reaping their crops and tending their flocks as though there was no war.

It was reported that Britain was to release, prior to the final departure of British troops, 12 Zionist Jews, including Stern Gang members and others detained after the hanging of two British sergeants the previous July. In Cyprus, about 24 000 Jewish interns decided to extend their 24 hour hunger strike in protest at Britain's ban on able-bodied men going to Palestine.

During the night Tel-Aviv suffered bombing by individual, high altitude planes - the first day of obvious indiscriminate Arab bombing. By mid-day there were about twenty deaths with an estimated 20 small calibre bombs being dropped over the city.

In Jerusalem, the main dome of the Church of the Holy Sepulchre was penetrated by a mortar shell fired from a Zionist position.

Zionist sources reported the strategic Arab town of Jenin to be deserted.

June 9

Both sides accepted, unconditionally, the Security Council's four week truce order. Operation Yoram was launched with the Har'el and Yiftach Brigades making a fourth attempt to occupy the Latrun area. They were repulsed by the Arab Legion.

The village of Hittin, to the west of Tiberias, was attacked by an armoured unit and infantry from the nearby settlement of Mitzpa. This followed an attack by the villagers on a retreating Zionist armoured unit following a failed attack on the village of Lubya. After a four hour battle, the Zionist forces retreated.

June 10

The first threat to the truce in Palestine emerged 24 hours before it was due to come into force. The so-called "dissident groups", the Irgun and the Stern Gang declared bitter dissatisfaction with the provisional Zionist government in terms only slightly less immoderate than those reserved for "Nazi Britain." They reserved the right to act "where necessary" and regarded Count Bernadotte, as "an emissary of Britain" and UN observers as "enemies of Israel." They claimed that since Jerusalem was not under Zionist control, they had freedom of action in the city.

The two terrorist groups denied that they no longer existed and were entering the "Hebrew Army" as Battalions, not as private individuals. Both reserved small groups which would operate outwith Government control. Fighting for the "natural frontiers" of Israel, including Transjordan, and continuing the war against Britain. Effectively there were two private armies within the State.

Reporting from Amman, The Scotsman's correspondent stated that in general the Arabs felt that the Zionists would not obey the truce order. The view was that the Zionists could not be trusted and would try to use the truce for advantages not intended by the sponsors. There was resentment and apprehension that Americans were amongst the UN observers.

The report commented that there was no conception of how small the scale of the fighting, and the number of troops involved, had been so far. It ended:

"The Jews, even before the Mandate ended, had protested so vigorously that they were being attacked by massed forces of the Arab Legion, and have repeated this at intervals ever since, that the world at large began to believe that there has,in fact, been a full-scale Arab invasion of the Jewish parts of Palestine. In fact the Jewish propaganda machine has so thoroughly misinterpreted the entire situation that it will take long and laborious work to arrive at the true facts."[17]

As for the Zionist view, The Times quoted foreign minister Shertok as claiming that acceptance of the truce was not a military necessity. Israel had "burst its bounds". Nearly 200 Arab villages were in Zionist hands, while Jaffa, Haifa, Tiberias, Safad and Jenin were all euphemistically declared "deserted." In four weeks of fighting the Zionists, apart from some parts of the Negev had not lost any of the land apportioned to them under partition. They had gained 1 200 square miles of Western Galilee approtioned to the projected Arab state. A large part of the new city of Jerusalem was in their hands.

Yosef Weitz sent two officials to tour the Coastal Plain in order to identify empty villages suitable either for demolition or for Zionist settlement. The village of al Maghar, previously home to about 1 750 Palestinians, was selected for destruction. Around this time Ben Gurion noted in his diary that the village of Daliyat al Rawha', home to 600 Palestinians, had been completely demolished.

The Voice of Israel radio reported that groups of Arabs had asked to return to their homes now situated within Israel. They had been told that the government "can never reconsider the return of refugees as long as a state of war still exists." Israeli broadcasts made it clear that refugees were not welcome to return. And for those who refused to heed the message, there were other means to reinforce that they were not welcome - land mines, barbed wire around their land, booby traps and police dogs.

Many were to be killed in the attempt to repossess their birthright and heritage.

Cairo sources said that at least 300 Zionist troops had been trapped and killed at Isdud. The Italian government announced a ban, for the period of the truce, on Jewish combatants and supplies passing through the country.

With one night to go until the truce was implemented, the History of the Haganah recorded that many operations were planned and carried out that night.

Yasur, north east of Gaza, with it population of 1 070 Palestinain villagers was targeted. The nearby village of al Batani al Sharqi was occupied by the Eighth Battalion of the Giv'ati Brigade. The village of Julis, adjacent to a former British army camp was likewise occupied by the Giv'ati Brigade. Egyptian sources claimed that this happened just after the truce took effect. The remaining villagers of al Na'ani to the south of Ramleh, which had been occupied about a month earlier, were according to Israeli historian, Benny Morris, "probably ordered to leave or intimidated into leaving." [18]

June 11

A host of complaints with regard to Zionist violations of the truce were made.

Cairo radio announced that "gangs of the so-called Zionist State" had violated the cease fire in Beersheba, the Syrian and Jordan fronts. One hour after the cease fire, an Arab Legionnaire climbed out of his trench to be met by fatal machine gun fire. A Zionist attack was reported on the international airport at Lydda. David Marcus, former New York City Commissioner of Correction and supreme commander of Israeli forces on the Jerusalem front was "killed in action" according to an Israeli spokesman.

With the announcement of the truce, further looting of the palatial, Palestinian residences in West Jerusalem commenced. According to John Rose, one of the few remaining non-Jews left in West Jerusalem:

"During this time looting of Arab houses started on a fantastic scale, accompanied by wholesale vindictive destruction of property . . .
From our veranda we saw horse-drawn carts as well as pick-up trucks laden with pianos, refrigerators, radios, paintings, ornaments and furniture, some wrapped in valuable Persian carpets . . .
Safes with money and jewellery were prised open and emptied . . .
[it] continued for months. Latecomers made do with what remained to be pillaged. They prised off ceramic tiles . . . removed all electric switches and wiring, kitchen gadgets, water pipes and fittings.
Nothing escaped . . ."[19]

The Scotsman correspondent reported on a visit to the Palestinian hill town of Quagun, a few miles from the main Tel-Aviv Haifa road. Three days earlier, during a night attack, the villagers were driven out by the attackers. The orange groves and wheat fields were filled with the "foul sweet smell of death" from corpes of Iraqi soldiers waiting to be buried by Arab prisoners. Tulkarm rose in the distance, the next target of the Zionists should the truce fail. Arab gunners, positioned about a mile away, shelled the area - with little worthwhile result.

Further north, at the village of Kuwaykat, a few miles outside Acre, the Zionist forces were giving it a further visitation. It had first been attacked during January. Now the local militia of around 60 men armed with up to 50 assorted firearms and one Bren gun repulsed a "large attack."[20]

East of Acre, the village of al Birwa, with its population of 1 460, was probably occupied by the Carmeli Brigade in the aftermath of Operation Ben-Ami.

North east of Gaza, the village of Beit Daras was occupied shortly after the start of the truce. Its residents had already fled following an attack on 10 May. Similarly the nearby village of Iblis was attacked, with Egyptian forces repelling the Zionist attackers.

June 13

After two days of cease fire the Israeli government stated that its army had been"compelled to renew its activities in self-defence, following violation of the truce by the enemy" in the area near Lake Tiberias. A report from two American UN truce observers found that all fighting had ceased. In turn the Arabs threatened "a general attack on all fronts" if the Zionists did not strictly keep the peace.

Count Folke Bernadotte sent the Security Council a "coded" report on the situation. It was believed that the findings favoured the Arabs, with Zionist forces being blamed for breaches of the cease fire.

Despite the fact that a number of countries had recognised the state of Israel, at the outset, the question was raised within the columns of The Scotsman as to the legitimacy of the new state. Israeli censorship prevented the dissemination of information and essential detail of the state.It was not known if the Provisional Government conformed to the demands of international law for recognition. Were there clearly defined boundaries ? Established authority, acting with at least the positive consent of the populace ?

While the former point was never answered, the latter raised further questions. An Israeli Army Ordinance of 26 May founded a Defence Army of land, sea and air components as the single legitimate defence force apart from the police. It terminology implied that attempts to overthrow the established authority was not considered impossible. Then, Irgun and Stern Gang stepped into the limelight.

Yet again there was mention of them dissolving and being absorbed into the Israeli army so that their continued existence would be illegal. Yet the Palcor Agency bulletin of 7 June, distributed in Britain by the Jewish Agency, reported that the groups were still recruiting and fund raising. This official government agency then went on to contradict the substance of earlier reports of the dissolution of the terrorist groups.

In the bulletin the Irgun announced that they had not dissolved but promised not to continue as an "underground army" in Jewish controlled areas. Here it would be a political movement. In Jerusalem it would continue as an armed organisation until the city was ruled by Jews. Its members must collect funds because they did not receive any government assistance.

June 14

Yosef Weitz of the Jewish National Fund visited the the site of the village of al Maghar which had been captured by Zionists about a month earlier. The destruction and demolition of the village had started some three days earlier. Commenting on the process of erasing the village, the birth place of the noted eighth century Islamic jurist Abu al-Hasan Muhammad al-Maghari, he observed "Three tractors are completing its destruction. I was surprised that nothing moved me at the sight. No regret and not hatred, as this is the way of the world . The dwellers of these mud-houses did not want us to exist here."[21]

On the same day, Ezra Danin a senior Haganah intelligence officer and official of the JNF reported to Weitz on the progress of the destruction of the houses in the village of Fajja, east of Jaffa, former homes to about 1 600 Palestinians. The Gazan village of Kawkaba was occupied by Zionist forces, in violation of the newly agreed truce. The 700 or so villagers were expelled.

The Red Cross were informed by the Arab authorities that a large group of the elderly, women and children from villages on the coastal plain were being "detained by the Israeli military authorities" [At this stage it was common practice for the Zionists to seize all able-bodied Palestinian men, even if they were unarmed, and send them to concentration camps or use them for forced labour]. Red Cross assistance with their evacuation was requested.[22]

Meanwhile, all fronts were reported to be quiet for the first time since hostilities began. Count Bernadotte was stationed on the Greek island of Rhodes planning for a lasting peace in Palestine. An immigrant ship arrived from Marseilles with 420 passengers. Of those, it was reported that 128 men of military age were taken to a detention camp in compliance with the truce conditions.

At the United Nations it was reported that the Arab states were faced with the inevitability of accepting some kind of "Jewish State" if the truce was to continue beyond 9 July. Optimists felt that territorial "adjustments" could be made. The pessimists felt that further conflict was waiting round the corner. The "pessoptimists", to borrow a phrase from the lexicon of Palestinian phraseology which has sprung up over the intervening decades, felt that close consultation with Washington would have a better chance than usual of helping President Truman to resist Zionist pressure, since Congress would by then have dispersed and American attention would have been diverted for a moment to the Party Convention in Philadelphia.

June 15

UN planes began to patrol Palestine to prevent the entry of arms and fighting personnel. Observers were already at the ports of embarkation for many Zionist emigrants to Palestine. At the Security Council the feeling was that, in the long run, the cease fire would not continue unless one side or the other retreated from their claims. The "betting" was that the odds were against the Arabs.

The Scotsman related an account of Zionist violation of the Benedictine Abbey on Mount Zion. On 18 May the Haganah fought their way into the building with hand grenades and machine guns in order to use the belfry as an observation and sniping point. During this period the Abbot together with 12 priests and 11 brothers were forced into the cellar with no light nor sanitation. The pretext that they were German and helped the Arabs was given.

The Abbot's gold crucifix and ring were stolen. Many sacred pictures, objects and furniture were destroyed.[23]

The Arab League protested to the UN mediator over Zionist actions on 11 June after the cease fire commenced. Zionist forces attacked several Arab villages, evicting the residents. In each case, the letter of protest claimed, the Zionists attacked the civilian population, destroyed their homes, kidnapped women and children.

A letter from Moshe Sharett said "The most spectacular event in the contemporary history of Palestine . . . is the wholesale evacuation of its Arab population. . . . The reversion to status quo ante is unthinkable."[6]

The return of Palestinian refugees was out of the question.

Two thousand British troops departed from Haifa.

June 16

Arab leaders informed Count Bernadotte that the Arab basic conditions for peace in Palestine were "no partition" and "no Jewish state". It was announced that the Haifa enclave was to be passed into the hands of the UN mediator for the remainder of the truce period. The US reminded Syria and Egypt that it did not recognise the blockade imposed by the two countries along the Palestine coast.

In Haifa, the UN mediator claimed that a British-Zionist clash had been averted following the seizure, by the latter, of a camp evacuated by the British. A clear breach of the truce.

Israel's agricultural minister, Zisling, spoke at length on the destruction of Palestinian villages during a cabinet meeting "This course [of destroying villages] will not reduce the number of Arabs who will return. It will [only] increase the number of [our] enemies." Responsibility was placed on Ben Gurion's shoulders.[24]

Ben Gurion's diary entry for this day recorded the destruction of a number of villages:

For the village al Manshiyya, occupied by Zionists about 4 weeks earlier, he reported that the destruction of the village was already underway. The village site is now part of Acre. Likewise the destruction of Fajja, near Jaffa, was noted by Ben Gurion. This village had been repeatedly attacked by both Irgun and the Haganah. The same comment was made with regard to Beit Daja. This village was one which linked Jaffa to the hinterland. The fate of the village of Biyar 'Adas, one with which the Haganah had declared a truce but which had suffered attack and partial demolition at the hands of the Irgun was similarly recorded.

The village of Miska, where the residents had refused to leave until two months earlier when they were forcibly expelled by the Haganah, suffered the same fate. This was one, amongst a few near Tulkarm, where the Israeli left wing, Mapam, party opposed the destruction carried out on the orders of the Jewish National Fund.

Other villages whose demolition was recorded were al Mughar, Beit Dajan, Hawassa, As Sumeiriya, Ja'tun, Daliyat [or Ruha]. The demolition of Buteimat and Sabbarin was about to begin. The combined population total for these villages was over 13 000.[25]

Yet, at this point, although Weitz had often pressed Ben Gurion for official sanction of his Transfer Committee's demolition work, none had been forthcoming. Although happy that the work was being done, he could not openly endorse it for a variety of reasons.

On this day the 13 ministers of the provisional government of Israel, without a formal vote, agreed to prevent a refugee return.[7] Ben Gurion spoke out against the return of the Palestinian refugees. ". . we should prevent their return . . . We must settle Jaffa, Jaffa will become a Jewish city . . ." And with regard to refugees in general "I will be for them not returning after the war."

Sharett agreed "They will not return. This is our policy, they shall not return." Compensation should be paid for "abandoned" land but "they will not return. [That] is our policy. They are not returning."

This stance was complicated by the position of the left wing Mapam party which "opposed the destruction of Arab settled areas which is not dictated by immediate military necessity." and which, the day previously, had agreed to support the return of "peace minded" refugees at the end of the war.[26]

June 17

Zionist forces broke the cease fire when, according to Damascus, they attacked and set fire to the village of Zingaria, to the north of Capernaum, on the shores of the Sea of Galilee. Fifty UN guards were dispatched to supervise truce negotiations along the supply route from Tel-Aviv to Jerusalem.

In one report, Jerusalem was described "like a barren island quite forgotten by the rest of the world . . . rigidly cut into two as if a great river flowed in between." In the Zionist controlled "New City" an odd rifle shot could sometimes be heard. This apart, all was quiet and peaceful. A half hearted attempt had been made a tidying up this "seedy suburb." Barclay's Bank, formerly a symbol of wealth and the colonial presence was a "shabby shell" (the Stern Gang had fought the Arabs in hand to hand combat, from room to room).

The short road to Damascus Gate was scarcely passable. On either side lay the dynamited facades of the Hospice of Our Lady and the Convent of Perpetual Adoration. The sun hardened skeletons of two Arab soldiers lay in the gutter. Everywhere there was shell scars, deterioration,shabbiness and exhaustion. The people were hungrier than ever, water was half a bucket per day. Rations were likened to those available in Germany with cigarettes, as in Germany, common currency.

Count Bernadotte asked Moshe Sharett "What would be the policy of the Israeli government with respect to the 300 000 Arabs who had left the Jewish areas; would they be allowed to return after the war and would their property rights be respected." The reply was that "The question could not be discussed while the war was going on" but "property rights would be respected." This despite the the fact that Sharett was one of the many encouraging the Israeli policy of destroying Arab homes and businesses.[6]

18 June

Newspapers speculated on the nature of a settlement, in the hands of Count Bernadotte, which might just be acceptable to both Arab and Zionist. One such idea was a "Palestine Union" with undivided sovereignty with the Zionists having increased autonomy than that originally envisaged in the Arab scheme of things. The pros and cons were discussed with the idea of sanctions mooted. This would present no problem in Zionist controlled parts of Palestine. There were practical and "delicate" interests to be taken into account in the Arab sector of the equation - not least of all, British and American oil interests.

The Times printed a letter from Edward Atiyah of The Arab Office in London questioning the assumption that recognition of the Zionist state was the only basis of a possible settlement in Palestine. He raised the question as to whether the Zionist state had become a sacrosanct reality merely because the Zionists chose to proclaim it by a unilateral declaration, which had no basis in law or morality, and because certain Powers, for reasons of their own, had chosen to recognise it.[27]

Concern was known to be expressed by Bernadotte over the extent to which the terrorist Irgun and Stern gangs were controlling the Jewish population in Palestine. It made truce maintenance difficult. It also acted as a control on the expression of majority and possibly moderate opinion by Palestine's Jews. Particularly those who would welcome a settlement.

During a visit to Tel-Aviv he made urgent representation to the Zionist authorities to do everything possible to bring the terrorists under control.

A Zionist attack on Ein Ghazal, south of Haifa, was repulsed. It was not until July when mass killings took place that the village was occupied. The Red Cross, responding to an appeal from the Arab authorities, organised the evacuation of about 1 000, elderly, women and children who had fled or been expelled from villages in the Coastal Plain. One Red Cross official noted "It was a moving scene with women carrying enormous bundles on their heads while in their arms were two or three small children."[28]

For some reason the destruction of the town of Beisan apparently worried Ben Gurion. He cabled the Golani Brigade's HQ to find out if the town had been burnt down in whole or in part, and on whose authority.

The Irgun blasted part of the al Latrun monastery, claiming that it was stronghold for the Arab Legion. However an Associated Press correspondent visited the monastery and reported:

" . . in the face of repeated shelling by Israeli guns, the venerable Trappist monks still cling to their famous Latrun monastery . . Neutral foreign reporters accredited to the Trans-Jordan Arab Legion have visited Latrun continually during the Palestine hostilities and have never detected the slightest violation by the Arabs of the monastery's sanctity."[29]

June 20

Two bomb explosions in Cairo's Jewish Quarter killed 25 people, injuring 54. The explosion came from inside, not outside, the Quarter thereby lessening the consequences. A search of the area revealed two wheel barrows loaded with gelignite.

It subsequently emerged that the police had, earlier, arrested seven Jewish boys with a barrow containing a time fuse and explosives. It was claimed that they were of the same type found at the scene of the explosions.

The Board of Deputies of British Jews passed a resolution urging the British government to recognise the State of Israel "thereby laying the foundation of lasting friendship."

The provisional government's Minority Affairs Minister, Bechor Shitrit, raised the question of the "destruction of al Qubeiba and Zarnuga." Yitzhak Gvirtz, Director of Absentee Property, wrote to Shitrit "[I am] ready to accept the premise that we do not want the return of the Arabs to these villages. But why the wanton destruction? Why not first extract some benefit (doors, frames, tiles &c)?[29]

June 21

The Israeli army clashed with the Irgun when the latter tried to beach and unload a European ship laden with hundreds of tons of military equipment. With acknowledged casualties, deaths and injuries, the Israeli provisional government called for national unity. The Irgun, in characteristic style, threatened "a blood battle between Jews" if the Irgun continued to be attacked while defending the ship.

Four Arab and four Israeli "technical" experts met Bernadotte to advise on technical points only, they had no power to negotiate at a political level. The Commissioner for Jerusalem resigned stating that it was best that the mediator be given a free hand to deal with Jerusalem as part of the general Palestine settlement.

More British troops and police left Haifa.

It was obvious that the reality and the mechanics of establishing a new state was of more interest to the media than reporting the ongoing ethnic cleansing essential, despite the truce, to the Zionist perception of a viable state.

Reporting from Tel-Aviv indicated a rapid build up of government structure after a month of existence and one week of truce. Apart from the strengthening of defences and the rush to get supplies to Jerusalem, the framework of a permanent state was, inexorably, being established.

All the laws of the British Mandate, except those related to land transfer and immigration resulting from the White Paper of 1939, were adopted - for the time being. Various committees had set to work - drafting election laws, writing a constitution, preparing a new code of law combining British Statute and Common Law, old Ottoman land law, Jewish ritual law and various minority religious laws.

Most judges who worked under the Mandate were retained. There was even a report of appointing an Arab judge for Haifa "and possibly Jaffa should it remain within the State."

June 22

The media was dominated by the potential for civil war within the nascent Israeli state. The fate of the Palestinian people, as far as the written word was concerned, had already been consigned to history for the time being. The focus was on the fighting between the Israeli army and the terrorist Irgun - still being referred to as "dissidents" under the new name of "Etzel".

While the Jewish Agency had tolerated and had given tacit agreement to the activities of the two Zionist terrorist groups when it came to terrorising and dispossessing the Palestinians, there was obvious disagreement when it came to the same groups defying the authority of the 5 week old state.

This was made clear on when the Panama registered *Atalena*, with a cargo of arms and illegal immigrants (from the perspective of the truce), Irgun recruits, arrived from the United States. A landing craft was used to bring the new Zionist recruits ashore, under fire directed at them from the Haganah army of the new state. Many of the recruits were seen to be hit. Mortars were later used to deter further incoming landing craft. Tension in Tel-Aviv was reported to be high, with armed Irgun members establishing a beach-head in defiance of the steel helmeted Haganah.

Talks then took place but when it became apparent that the terrorists were not prepared to obey government orders not to land the illegal immigrants, further force was used. This resulted in the *Atalena* being shelled, catching fire with explosions amongst it cargo of munitions. The ship had to be abandoned with many casualties.

President Truman announced that the United States and the provisional government of Israel had agreed to exchange envoys.

A rare event took place at the village of al Birwa, to the east of Acre, when it was recaptured by the villagers. Now wanting to harvest their crops, over 96 armed men and an equal number of unarmed men and women took part. They remained for two days, harvesting their crops, before the village was retaken.

June 23

It was reported that Count Bernadotte did not regard the previous day's incident at Tel-Aviv as coming within the scope of the mediator. He did ask the truce chief in Palestine, Colonel Bonde, to investigate the number of Irgun recruits which had landed - estimated at 200 - and the quantities of ammunition in Tel-Aviv. Concern was expressed at the trouble experienced in controlling the Irgun and Stern groups who were opposed to the truce. The conviction was also expressed that they were receiving arms from the Soviet bloc countries in Eastern Europe.

Reports from new York indicated that the Haganah blew up the *Atalena* with mortar fire. The decision had been taken that the sovereignty and authority of the state was paramount. To allow the Irgun to unload the ship was to allow political and military anarchy. Apparently the Irgun had intended to share the cargo - ranging from ammunition for small arms to tanks - with Irgun units within the regular army and the remainder of the army.

Although it was believed that the ship was loaded at Marseilles, it was understood that the finance came from an extremist Zionist group in the United States.

June 24

A curfew was imposed in Tel Aviv, with restrictions on the movement of the population. This was followed by mass arrests of Irgun leaders. Severe clashes were reported in the streets with 15 killed and scores injured as the Haganah carried out its task.

June 25

Palmach troops drove Irgun units out of the southern part of Tel-Aviv during the night. Irgun terrorist leader and Israeli prime minister-to-be , Menachem Begin,escaped from the HQ building by the back door. A manhunt followed. Former Irgun members were arrested in towns throughout the state. Two members who left the Israeli Cabinet, following the *Atalena* incident, withdrew their resignation, bringing to an end a crisis in government.

The arrangement by which the Irgun and Stern terrorists could serve in the army, under their own commander, was ended. Such people were given an amnesty and could re-enlist. The Irgun advised its members not to re-enlist but to re-group at Jerusalem and elsewhere outside the state in order to carry on the fight against the Arabs.

The UN formally charged the Egyptian forces with breaking the truce on the southern front.The passage of UN food convoys to the Negev was prevented, a UN aircraft was attacked as were Zionist positions to the south of Tel-Aviv.

A hint of the ongoing intrigue over Palestine was given in a report from Rhodes, where the UN mediator, Count Bernadotte was based. Kings Abdullah and Farouk were willing to recognise some form of Jewish enclave or state on the coastal plain. Both monarchs stood to increase the size of their respective kingdoms by such a tacit recognition of partition.

Syria and Lebanon, for their own reasons, were keen on the reinstatement of the Mufti of Jerusalem, whose standing and that of his followers in the Palestinian community had never been lower.

It was reported that Russia and Israel were to exchange envoys.

The Israeli army announced that it had inflicted 100 casualties, while recapturing the village of al Birwa, in clashes with Arab units.

There were indications that Yosef Weitz of the Jewish National Fund was "frustrated and wary" about the progress of his Transfer Committee. There were no tools or materials. Growing opposition from the left wing Mapam political party about the "destruction of Arab villages" was also reported. With nothing in writing nor any political leadership to endorse his actions in destroying Arab villages, he gave instructions for all activities to cease.

June 26

Correspondents were keen to point out the perils facing the Zionist state which, for once, could not be explained away by an "eloquent communique". There was talk of a state within a state, despite a solemn treaty being signed by the Irgun, undertaking to dissolve its structure and place its members and arms at the disposal of the state. This second "state" was aptly described as one which "bargains, makes and breaks treaties, and blackmails" - a description which is still not far off the mark when it comes to the current Israeli treatment of the Palestinian people and the world at large. However 50 years ago, the mind-set of the terrorists was a threat to Israel itself. This was highlighted by the desertion of former Irgun members from frontline posts facing the Arab enemy to give their support to their colleagues under fire from the Haganah during the *Atalena* debacle.

The Irgun still reserved the right to act at will outside the state, including Jerusalem. This view was supported by many who, because so much blood had been shed over the city, felt that Jerusalem was naturally theirs - not to forget that by choosing the appropriate period in history for Biblical Israel, Zionist claims extended to all of Transjordan and beyond.

The leaders of the remaining Palestinian Arab population of Jaffa presented a petition asking that the exiled relatives of those Arabs still in Jaffa be allowed to return. The appeal was based on the surrender agreement of 13 May where it stated that every Arab who left Jaffa and wanted to come back, could do so by submitting a request, as long as their presence did not constitute a threat to peace and security.

It was an appeal which stimulated debate in the upper reaches of government, particularly since a similar request had been submitted from Haifa. It was an appeal which ultimately failed.[30]

June 27

While the members of the former Haganah were manning "dull front-line positions" facing the Arab forces, the Palmach, which previously had been under threat of dissolution (it apparently had a separate General Staff and its units had strong left-wing affiliations), gave ample demonstration of loyalty to the new government.

During the previous two days, its soldiers had roared through the streets of Tel-Aviv in scout cars and armoured lorries questioning young men and bundling them away if there were suspicions of Irgun membership. There were occasional bursts of fire. By the end of this period about 360 arrests had been made.

Meanwhile the last few thousand of British troops were ready to leave Haifa, with troopships standing by.

Count Folke Bernadotte demanded that Israel recognise "the right of the residents of Palestine who, because of conditions created by the conflict there, have left their normal places of abode, to return to their homes without restriction and to regain possession of their property."[31]

The World Jewish Congress met at Montreux, the first time since 1939. At the top of the 10 day agenda was a motion to mobilise world Jewry to contribute money, men and materials to the state of Israel.

The truce continued but with reports of Arab irregulars attacking Zionist settlements and traffic near Affula.

June 28

Count Bernadotte sent his secret proposals for a "Holy Land settlement" to both Zionist and Arab leaders. It was requested that the proposals be kept secret until he received notification of their first reactions.

The last 12 Zionist prisoners held by the British military authorities were released at Haifa. They included five youths suspected of hanging the two British sergeants the previous year and five Stern Gang members.

June 29

Lt-General A Macmillan announced that British forces would cease to occupy any area of Palestine from July 1st. Three tanks were stolen from Haifa Airport in the early hours of the morning, believed to be the work of British deserters and a Jewish technician. One was recovered.

It was reported that a considerable number of British deserters, many of them Jewish, were left behind. In addition there were technical personnel who could earn as much as £150 per month, paid by the Israeli forces.

Arab League sources repeated that no settlement would be possible if the mediator called for recognition of a "Jewish State."

June 30

On Wednesday, 30 June, the last of the British presence departed from Palestine after 31 years of increasingly discredited rule. General Macmillan was the last to leave following on the heels of 3 000 men and their equipment. As the troops embarked - with fixed bayonets and loaded rifles - they were reported to be "singing and laughing like children released from a difficult term at school." In their wake, 140 specially picked Jewish policemen took over the empty camps and harbour installations.

A working port was handed over to the Zionists. Nothing was demolished. The furniture was as the soldiers left it. A menu was flapping on the cookhouse wall.

The Scotsman's reporter, Patrick O'Donovan, commented that "No Jews went into the street to wish them God-speed". Only a dozen disconsolate dogs mooned around the quays. "In all Haifa they alone showed any sign of regret."[32]

As if in preparation for the next half century, of the Palestinian people there was not one mention.

On this day the Israelis issued their first "Abandoned Areas Ordinance".

Once this thin veneer of legality was in place, the theft, looting and seizure of thousands of Palestinian homes and businesses was given it first coating of legal gloss.

The lands and property of Arab refugees were considered abandoned, even for those who fled only a few miles from their homes. They all found that under Israeli law they had no right to reclaim their property - even for those who returned a few weeks later.

Essentially the Emergency Regulations (Cultivation of Abandoned Lands) empowered the provisional government to declare depopulated, conquered areas as "abandoned". "Existing laws" could then be imposed upon the area, or existing regulations could be varied, as appropriate. This included confiscation of property. Leasing of land was dealt with at a later date.[33]

As from the end of June, with Britain refusing all requests for supplies for the Arab Legion (See May 22), the Legion was effectively *hors de combat.* [34]

Notes

1 David Gilmour, *Debunking the myths of the '48 Exodus* (Middle East International, Issue 286, 24/10/86)
2 Norman Finkelstein, *Myths, Old and New* (Journal of Palestine Studies, Autumn 1991) p.88
3 *ibid* p.78
4 Michael Palumbo, *The Palestinian Catastrophe*, p.141
5 Benny Morris, *Falsifying the Record* (JoPS, Spring 1995) p.49
6 Palumbo, p.145
7 Morris, p.56
8 Walid Khalidi, *All that Remains*, p.403
9 The Scotsman 2/6/48
10 Benny Morris, *The birth of the Palestinian refugee problem, 1947-49*, p.138
11 Palumbo, p.144
12 Morris, p.137
13 The Scotsman 5/6/48
14 Khalidi, p.459
15 Morris, p.161
16 *ibid* p.136
17 The Scotsman 12/6/48
18 Khalidi, p.400
19 Nathan Krystall, *The De-Arabisation of West Jerusalem 1947-50*,(JoPS, Winter 1998) p.13
20 Khalidi, p.22
21 *ibid* p.395
22 Palumbo, p.142
23 The Scotsman 16/6/48
24 Morris, p.163
25 Khalidi, population figures from 1944/45 census

26 Morris, p.141 [Also, See Note 6]
27 The Times 19/6/48
28 Palumbo, p.143
29 Khalidi, p.393
30 Morris, p.144
31 *ibid* P.142
32 The Scotsman 1/7/48
33 Morris, p.174
34 Benny Morris, *Refabricating 1948*, (JoPS, Winter 1998) p.93

July

Children were dying, as were the sick and the elderly. The dead were covered with stones, branches and a quick prayer. Children, abandoned, were wandering about crying.

Lydda-Ramleh Death March, *"The Palestinian Catastrophe"*

At the start of July,Yosef Weitz of the Jewish National Fund was reported to have suspended his campaign of destruction of Palestinian villages. This resulted from opposition in the Israeli Cabinet from members of Mapam, and others, which effectively terminated the activities of this first, unofficial and "self-appointed", Transfer Committee.

It was the month when the contradiction between destroying Arab villages and the need to preserve them in order to accommodate incoming Zionist settlers started to make itself evident. In Haifa and Jaffa, with the remaining Arab residents concentrated into ghetto areas, the largest concentrations of empty Arab houses were to be found. It was proposed that 2 000 new immigrant families would go to Haifa, with 1 000 families going to Jaffa.

Further contradictions and ironies arose when it came to the looting of the harvest of abandoned Palestinian fields. Some settlements avoided payment to the government for the produce they were stealing from the fields. Kibbutz Ma'ayan Zvi received a letter from the Committee for Abandoned Property "I heard with bewilderment and sorrow that [your] members . . are stealing vegetables in the eastern fields of Tantura. Don't your members have a more honourable way to spend their time these days?"[1]

During this month, outright expulsion of the Palestinian people from their land and villages moved up a gear despite, as Israeli historian, Benny Morris, insisted "there was no Cabinet or IDF [Israeli Defence Force] General Staff-level decision to expel" the Arab population. It became clear that "from July onward, there was a growing readiness in the IDF units to do just that"[2].

Operation Dekel, during which most of Lower Galilee, including Nazareth, was occupied commenced during this period. It led to the widening of the coastal strip occupied by the Zionist forces in Acre district. One feature of the military assaults during this Operation (and others) in the north of Palestine was the discriminatory treatment afforded to Christian and Druze, compared with the Muslim.

Often it was the Muslim who feared most the approaching troops since they were the ones who tended to be involved in resisting the Zionist forces. The Christian and Druze communities tended to be passive and cooperated with the occupier. The Druze villagers, according to Israeli sources, often collaborated and provided intelligence to the advancing Israelis. The latter were met, on occasion, by dancing and cheering Druze villagers [Author's note: Members of Israel's Druze community are the only non-Jewish soldiers who serve in Israel's military establishment].

July was the month that the full horror of Zionist aggression was invited upon the heads of the civilian population of the towns of Lydda and Ramleh.

> "This is our country and these are our homes; get out!"[3]
>
> *directed at residents of Lydda-Ramleh*

It was only as time passed that the full horror of the Zionist actions at Lydda-Ramleh became apparent. Actions which ensured the expulsion of the Palestinian residents of the two towns from their homeland.

On 2 August, the UN mediator Count Folke Bernadotte, visited their refugee camps near Ramallah. His car was stormed by thousands of desperate people. He wrote "I have made the acquaintance of a great many refugee camps but never have I seen a more ghastly sight than that which met my eyes here at Ramallah." The refugees shouted that they wanted to return to their homes. It was apparent that they had been through a horrific ordeal.

This from a man who had done much valued humanitarian work at the end of the Second World War to assist Jewish and other European refugees who had survived Nazi concentration camps[4].

First there was the slaughter of civilians - men, women and children. Then there was the terror created by the events which the residents of Lydda and Ramleh were witnessing round about them. This was reinforced by the inevitable loudspeaker trucks warning the people to leave if they wanted to avoid the fate of those whose corpses were still lying, decomposing, at the nearby Dahmash Mosque. It was a very potent warning.

Before they were force marched to the east with the injunction "Go to King Abdullah" ringing in their ears, the Arab refugees were stripped of their possessions. Eye witness accounts and reporting testified to this. *The Economist* reported "The Arab refugees were systematically stripped of all their belongings before they were sent on their trek to the frontier. Household belongings, stores, clothing, all had to be left behind." Those who showed any resistance were shot in cold blood. Accounts of rape were eventually forthcoming.

Then the "Death March" to the Arab Legion's lines began.

While Israeli prime minister-to-be, Lt Colonel Yitzhak Rabin commented that there was no way of avoiding firing warning shots in the air to get people to undertake the 10 hour walk, bullets found the way to the air inside people's lungs (to coin a phrase from Afif Safieh, a prominent Palestinian representative). Many were shot dead.

July 1

The Arab League continued to study the peace proposals of Count Bernadotte with the need to recognise "the existence of a Jewish State" promising to be a major stumbling block for any acceptance of the proposals. Of the Zionist reaction, there was no sign.

The Count indicated that if either side should turn the plan down he would consider that his mission had ended and return the mandate to the United Nations.

At a press conference King Abdullah indicated that the seriousness of the situation to the Arab States was not merely due to Jewish pressure but also to the "world wide supporters of the Jews."[5]

July 2

Both the Arab League and the Provisional Government of the State of Israel announced their rejection of Bernadotte's proposals for Palestine. In the case of Israel, the main stumbling blocks were immigration and Jerusalem. The mediator was informed, at this juncture, that there was a six month limit from 21 May on his efforts at mediation.

Meanwhile there was the odd comment or two, in the media, with regard to events within Palestine. Outside Haifa, Balfour Forest (named after Lord Balfour, whose name was firmly attached to events leading to the dispossession of the Palestinian people) on the slopes of the Nazareth hills was set ablaze by soldiers of the Arab Liberation Army. Roads in the Jezreel Valley were raked by mortar bombs.

In an effort to restrict the movement of Zionist "dissidents", particularly those of the Irgun, it was reported that Israeli representatives in several European capitals had been told to use discretion in issuing entry permits.

With 93 military observers in Palestine, 31 each from the US, France and Belgium, disquiet was expressed by the Arabs at the manner in which they, and the Americans in particular, were carrying out their duties at Bab al Wad and at other points in Palestine. This, together with the earlier theft of two tanks and the illegal landing of nearly 1 000 Irgun terrorists made the extension of the truce very unlikely.

July 4

It was reported that the Irgun was massing its forces in Jerusalem, allegedly avoiding detection by arriving in small groups. They were operating openly without fear of arrest. Only a few ring-leaders remained detained, with many previously arrested being released.With negotiations being conducted to allow the re-entry of the terrorists into the army, it was clear that the government was trying to avoid opening a further breach between them.

There were Zionist complaints that the Arab forces in Jerusalem had breached the truce. This was countered by a communique from the Transjordan Defence Ministry accusing the Zionist forces of several breaches. An advance on an Arab Legion sentry post had been forced to retreat under heavy covering fire from Hadassah Hospital. It resulted in a number of exchanges between the opposing forces until midnight.

Details of Bernadotte's plan emerged. Suggested was a union between Israel and an enlarged Transjordan. Emphasis was given to the reallocation of the Palestine territories allotted to Arab and Zionist Jew. This would remove some of the "jig-saw" aspects of the original partition plan, by creating two homogenous blocks. The current status quo with the Zionists in control of Western Galilee (and Jaffa) and the Arabs holding the Negev would prevail. Equal rights would be given in Haifa. It was argued that with the truce being of great benefit to the Zionists, and Bernadotte's proposals offering them all they had demanded in the past, there was no valid need for the Zionists to demur.

It was confirmed that the proposals would not, unlike the original partition plan, be imposed upon the parties. There would have to be mutual acceptance.

Out of the lime-light, the process of ensuring that any returning Palestinian family would have no home to which they could return, continued apace. Within the Cabinet of the provisional government of Israel, agricultural minister Zisling raised the issue of the destruction of villages in the Jezreel Valley, on the orders of the army.

Meanwhile, seemingly light years away and giving no hint of being aware of the inhumanity being perpetrated against the Palestinian people, the World Jewish Congress, meeting at Montreux, expressed the sentiment that the State of Israel "might occupy a position in the Middle East analagous to that of Switzerland in Europe."

July 5

An extension to the 4 week truce was proposed by Count Bernadotte. He also suggested that Jerusalem, Haifa, its port, refineries and terminals should be demilitarised, with armed guards from those countries already providing observers being stationed in the demilitarised areas.

An Israeli communique accused the Egyptians of violating the truce by sniping and shelling the isolated Zionist colony of Kfar Darom in southern Palestine.

Jewish leaders of the 1 700 strong Jewish community in the town of Safad - from which the 10 000 Palestinian Arab residents had fled in May - re-iterated an earlier plea. If Jewish Zionist settlers were not brought to Safad, then it were best that "the Arab houses . . . be destroyed and blown up lest the Arabs have somewhere to return to."[6]

The provisional government of Israel replied to Count Bernadotte's letter of 27 June demanding that Israel recognise the rights of Palestinians to return to their homes and regain possession of their property. The reply was in the negative, dismissing a number of the mediator's suggestions and suggesting that he reconsider his "whole approach to the problem."[7]

Even when promises had been given that refugees could return, these were eventually ignored. One such case was in the surrender agreement with Jaffa where it was agreed that those who wanted to come back could do so - as long as their presence did not present a security risk. A letter written on behalf of Ben Gurion said ". . the prime minister is opposed to the return of the Arab inhabitants to their places so long as the war continues . ."[8]

July 6

With two days remaining of the truce, Count Bernadotte began 48 hours of intensified effort to bring Arab and Zionist Jew together, with some form of limited agreement. The Israeli provisional government published its rejection of the Count's proposals stating that they would resist with all force "imposition of Arab rule over Jerusalem."

The UN Palestine Truce Commission suffered its first casualty. A French officer was killed and another injured when their jeep hit a land mine near Nazareth.

The IDF General-Staff issued an order that outwith the actual time of combat, it was forbidden to destroy, burn or demolish Arab towns and villages and expel their inhabitants unless permission or explicit instruction was given.

It was a humane looking instruction on paper and brought about a suspension of the activities of Yosef Weitz and his Transfer Committee. The reality was to prove to be different in that the Israeli army continued to demolish villages, apparently with Ben Gurion's tacit approval.

July 7

It was reported that Arab leaders were convinced that Count Bernadotte's advisers were all partisans of partition and the Zionist state. They would therefore resist diplomatic efforts to persuade them to accept a further cease fire.

Five Britons, officials of the British-owned Jerusalem Electric Corporation, were kidnapped by armed Zionists in Jerusalem. They were taken to an internment camp "somewhere in the city."

The Times' correspondent filed a report which included an item on the "Jewish defence army" parading in Jerusalem with its armour and other artifacts of war on full display. Members of the truce commission and the consular corps attended a ceremony where the "flag of Jerusalem" was handed over to the "Jerusalem district commander".

A reader could be excused for wondering if The Times had lost its objectivity or sense of reality. After all, it was only "modern" or West Jerusalem that was under Zionist occupation. A glance at the end of the article explained this rewriting of reality. It included the one word *Censored*. Already the outside world was being presented with a sanitised, Zionist view of events.

The Givati Brigade were issued with their operational orders The 1st Battalion was to take Tall as Safi area, in the south of Palestine, and "to expel the refugees encamped in the area" with the excuse added "to prevent enemy infiltration from the east."[9]

July 8

It was announced by Azzam Pasha, Secretary-General of the Arab League, that the Arabs would begin fighting the next day at 7am (BST). All appeals for an extension of the truce were rejected. The exception was the Old City of Jerusalem. The cease-fire would be observed in the Old City, it would not be used as a base for military attacks on the outskirts "so long as the other side does not launch any attacks against this holy old city."

An Arab League statement accused the Zionist forces of "many atrocities against the civilian population, plundering their homes, and pillaging their property and forcing them to work in the erection of fortifications, digging trenches, and other hard labour. These flagrant violations of the truce constituted in themselves sufficient justification for the immediate resumption of fighting by the Arab States. Zionists continued their aggression against Arabs in areas under their occupation and steadily persisted throughout the truce in pursuing their policy of smuggling immigrants, arms and ammunition into the country, as had been witnessed by United Nations observers. They have also occupied a number of villages and positions which had not been in their possession at the time of the cease-fire."[10]

The village of Hulayqat, north east of Gaza, was recaptured by Egyptian forces in a surprise attack. In the same area the Third Battalion of the Giv'ati Brigade attacked the village of 'Ibdis, defended by two companies of the Egyptian army, capturing the village after a "long battle."

During the next few days, up to the 11th, the area comprising the northern Negev and and the western Hebron district foothills, was overrun by the Giv'ati Brigade. Over 20 000 people were estimated to have fled the approaching troops.

During the next few days, under the aegis of Operation An-Far, the area comprising the northern Negev and the western Hebron district foothills, was also overrun by the Giv'ati Brigade. The village of al Tina was captured at this time.

This Operation involved a major push from south of Ramleh to the Negev in the course of which some 20 000 Palestinian Arab residents from 16 villages were driven out. It was believed that the fall of Tell as Safi undermind the morale of surrounding villages.

In the western hills of Galilee a number of villages were captured between the 8th and 14th. Amqa (Druze), Kuweikat (Muslim), Kafr Yasif (Muslim and Christian), Abu Sinan (Druze and Christian), Julis (Druze), Al Makr (Christian and Muslim), I'billin (Christian and Muslim) and Shafa 'Amr (Muslim, Christian and Druze)

Reports indicated that the five Britons kidnapped by the Irgun terrorists were being interrogated on suspicion of espionage, possible radio contact with Arab forces concerning shell hits and other information from their vantage point inside the Zionist lines.

July 9

The chairman of the consular truce commission in Jerusalem reported that the Haganah had taken over the King David Hotel while it was still under

UN protection. It was decided that, as a symbolic gesture, a guard of three French and three American citizens would move into the hotel. The Zionist authorities said that they would be forcibly ejected.

Reports of Egyptian truce violations were unconfirmed.

Hostilities started with an Egyptian Spitfire bombing Tel-Aviv, Three people were killed, including two children. Iraqi guns shelled the town and settlement of Petah Tikva near Tel-Aviv. In the upper Negev, two villages had been occupied by Egyptian forces the previous evening - before the truce ended. Zionist forces captured a cluster of four villages near Majdal

Israeli forces, including war planes, began operations against several thousand Palestinian villagers in Western Galilee and in Lower Galilee. South of Haifa, they began hostilities with the aim of "clearing" the road to Tel-Aviv.

Arab aircraft bombed Zionist positions north of Jenin, with Iraqi forces following up with a ground attack.

In Jerusalem there were echoes of stray shots from rifles, the occasional sound of mortar bombs. Some shots were fired from Zionist positions in Mount Zion. Thick clouds of smoke from Zionist held areas were believed to indicate that demolition was in progress.

Just before the truce ended, a local truce was organised for the city which lasted a couple of hours. This was at the request of a Dr Weingarten. Together with his daughters and accompanied by two others described as mayors of Jerusalem districts, discussions were held. These were confined to the future of the Jewish Quarter in the Old City.

The village of al 'Abbasiyya, east of Jaffa, which was first visited by the Irgun in December 1947, was occupied "practically without any fighting."

As part of Operation Dekel the attack on the village of Kuweikat, which had refused to surrender, was preceded by a heavy artillery barrage with the predictable result as outlined by the army commander, Dov Yirmiya

"I don't know whether the artillery softening up of the village caused casualties but the psychological effect was achieved and the village's non-combatants inhabitants fled before we began the assault"

The concept of "artillery softening up" is, of course, a euphemism for striking terror into the hearts of the villagers. One villager later recalled:

"We were awakened by the loudest noise we had ever heard, shells exploding . . the whole village was in panic . . women were screaming, children were crying . . . Most of the villagers began to flee with their pyjamas on. The wife of Qassim Ahmad Sa'id fled carrying a pillow in her arms instead of her child."[11]

The retreating village defenders fled to neighbouring Amqa which was captured soon after (the only Druze village in Western Galilee to be evacuated). The few, mostly elderly, remaining in Kuweikat were expelled to adjacent Abu Sinan. Most were refused shelter and fled to Upper Galilee or the Lebanon.

Deir Tarif, attacked as part of Operation Dani, successfully opposed the attackers.

Situated to the north east of Gaza, the hamlet of Bi'lin was occupied by the 1st Battalion Giv'ati Brigade. Its population of about 180 and others were expelled in accordance with the orders from Brigade Commander Shim'on Avidan ". . expel the refugees encamped in the area, in order to prevent enemy infiltration from the east to this important position."[12]

On this day, Operation An Far "cleared" a number of villages of their inhabitants. The Operation was carried out ". . to eliminate the threat and danger posed by the presence of Arab civilian concentrations at the rear of the front." The villages "cleared" were

> al Jaladiyya, north east of Gaza [pop 360]
> al Masmiyya al Saghira, north east of Gaza [pop 530]
> Qastima, north east of Gaza [pop 890]
> Summil, north east of Gaza [pop 950]
> Sajad, south of Ramleh [pop 370]
> Tal al Turmus, north east of Gaza [pop760]
> Barqusya, north west of Hebron [pop 330]
> Ibnibba, south of Ramleh [pop 490]
> Jilya, south of Ramleh [pop 330]
> al Khayma, south west of Ramleh [pop 190]
> Qazaza, south of Ramleh [pop 940][12]

The Scotsman gave an overview of the strength of the opposing military forces.

On the Arab side, the small motorised division of 10 000 troops, with sixteen 25 pounder guns, of the Arab Legion was considered, by far, the most reliable component. From Transjordan there was about 20 000 men including police, with about half in Palestine. Iraq contributed about 2 000 men, Egypt 8 000. Saudi Arabia had a token force.

The Syrians and the Lebanese appeared to have faded away, with recent hostilities indicating a Sudanese presence. Finally there were the irregulars, the Arab Liberation Army under the control of Fawzi el Kaukji. This was composed of mainly Palestinian Arabs and former members of the disbanded Transjordan frontier force. In all they were about 15 000 strong. This made a total of about 40 000 with 200 armoured cars and light tanks. Between Iraq and Egypt there were 200 planes. Ammunition was considered to be in short supply.

On the Israeli side there was a fully trained army of 42 000 backed by a part-time militia of 50 000. Light and heavy machine guns, mortars, anti-tank guns, home made armoured cars - they were in plentiful supply. They were believed to have B2 bombers, fighters and plenty of ammunition.

July 10

As part of Operation Dani, the village of Deir Tarif, near Ramleh, was captured despite putting up stiff resistance.

This particular Operation saw one of the most brutal expulsions of the conflict, with the towns of Lydda and Ramleh as the target. "Softening up" of the population took the form of air attacks. By mid-day the General Staff was informed "There was a considerable [civilian] flight from Ramle. There is great value in continued bombing." Renewed bombing was requested and one of the brigades was informed "Flight from the town of Ramle of women, the old and the children is to be facilitated. The [military age] males are to be detained."[13]

The village of Khirbat Jiddin and site of a Crusader castle was captured. The ruined fortress had been used by the 'Arab al Suwaytat bedouin. The village of Beit 'Affa was taken, briefly, by the Israelis during the night but was recaptured by the Egyptian army.Israeli sources spoke of 300 Egyptian and Sudanese soldiers killed and 200 captured.

To the north west of Hebron, the villages of Mughallis and Tall al Safi (identified as the Philistine city of Gath and appeared on the 6th century BC Madaba map) were captured and "ethnically cleansed" as part of Operation An Far. The capture of the latter was reported to have undermined the morale of the surrounding villages. The villages of al Barriyya and Daniyal, both a couple of miles outside Ramleh and Lydda were captured. Both were used as a base for launching the attack on Lydda and

Ramleh.

The Egyptian 6th Battalion was ordered to recapture the village of Julis, near Gaza. The lack of preparation of the Egyptian forces for a battle was underlined by staff officer Gammal Abd al Nasir "Once again we were facing a battle for which we had made no preparation. We had no information about the enemy at Julis." The attack was called off with considerable loss of life. "None of the defenders were injured."[14]

With most of the villagers evacuated following an attack a couple of days earlier, only 200 man remained within Innaba, to the east of Ramleh. The village was attacked from three sides with the defenders fleeing when they ran out of ammunition. Of the village's 300 buildings, only nine were left standing to house a small garrison. The rest were dynamited.

Jimzu and Kharruba, villages to the east of Ramleh, were occupied by the Yiftach Brigade. The latter village was immediately demolished, as ordered. The village of Qula, an important crossroads to the north of Lydda was subject to a tug-of-war between the Arab Legion and the Israeli Armoured units of the Alexandroni Brigade. The latter eventually gained control following Israeli "heavy losses". Likewise, al Tira was occupied and destroyed. Lydda was now cut off from the north.

The four week truce came to an end with artillery duels between the opposing sides within the Old City of Jerusalem. Damage was reported to be extensive but casualties low. By this point in time, out of an estimated population of 67 000 (including refugees from outlying areas), only about 6 000 remained. These were reckoned to be too poor to afford to move to safety.

Israeli historian, Benny Morris, observed that Operation Dani units were ordered to blow up whole or parts of villages on conquest during the period 10 - 13 July.

July 11

Azzam Pasha of the Arab League proposed that the world consider setting up a symbolic State, like the Vatican City, to represent its 12 000 000 Jews.

While in Rome, Count Bernadotte was reported as commenting that while he was dissappointed at the attitude of the Arab States, he could sympathise with their view that the truce "was onerous to them."

The provisional government of Israel accepted the proposal to demilitarise

Jerusalem if an international force was placed in the city to guarantee security. This was reported to have been rejected by the Irgun leaders. Armed resistance to the occupation of the city by troops of any nationality was threatened.

In Jerusalem the Irgun announced that the five kidnapped Britons would face "serious charges" at a "trial".

Hostilities were reported throughout the land of Palestine.

The large village of Ein Karim which had been partially abandoned following the massacre in Deir Yassin, two kilometres to the north, was completely abandoned. This followed the capture of two nearby hilltops which were then used as vantage points to shell the village.

The Iraqi Army and Palestinian Arab irregulars were in battle 10 miles from their Jenin bases. The Iraqi's reported capturing seven Zionist occupied villages on the outskirts of Jenin. Light aeroplanes joined the advancing heavy artillery aimed at the large Zionist road and rail terminal at Affula. The Iraqis reported more than 200 Zionist casualties out of 3 000 troops used in an effort to stem the Arab advance. This was followed by an assault on Zirin, the last Zionist stronghold before the strategically important Affula.

Capture of Affula would complete a front from Lebanon to Egypt and cut the only Zionist supply route from Haifa to Tel Aviv.

Clouds of smoke hung over the mountains to the east and west of Nazareth. The Arab Liberation army was reported to be attacking Jewish villages overlooking the fertile plain of Esdraelon. Zionist sources said that their forces had entered the foothills of Western Galilee, capturing four Arab villages. The Arab advance north of Jenin was reported to have been halted. Jenin was bombed by Israeli planes.

From Acre, the Haganah was reported to be pushing towards the Lebanese frontier and Nazareth - all territories outwith Israel's boundaries. An operation was started to re-capture the village of Mishmar Hay Yarden. Bombing of the Syrian village of Kuneitra was reported. The Zionists abandoned the isolated settlement of Kfar Darom and conceded heavy Egyptian pressure at Majdal.

The village of Beit Nabala, an Arab base to the north east of Lydda, was captured. This action suggested that an attempt was being made to encircle the towns of Lydda and Ramleh.

Operation Dani HQ ordered the Yiftach Brigade units "to dig in every place captured and to destroy every house not intended for occupation [by IDF troops]"[15] The Brigades's intelligence officer reported "The bombing from the air and the artillery[shelling] of Lydda and Ramleh caused flight and panic amongst the civilians [and] a readiness to surrender. The HQ repeatedly asked for further bombings including use of incendiaries.[16] The *New York Times* reported that the residents of Lydda and Ramleh were fleeing on "camel trails" towards Ramallah. The main road was blocked elsewhere. What the paper neglected to add was the reason for the people fleeing.

In the early evening, at the head of the 89th Commando Battalion, Major Moshe Dayan "blitzed" and terrorised the civilians of both towns for less than one hour. His personally recruited troops contained a contingent of Stern Gang terrorists. The *Chicago Sun Times*, in describing this "ruthlessly brilliant charge" reported that "practically everything in their way died. Riddled corpses lay by the roadside" including men, women "and even children".

With the invaders not keen to take prisoners, a loudspeaker exhorted those who wanted to be safe to go inside a local mosque. Hundreds of Arabs sheltered within the precincts of the Dahmash Mosque, hands on head in surrender. A female member of the Palmach, Netiva Ben Yehuda, recalled what happened. In retaliation for a previous incident, over 80 Palestinians were machine-gunned to death. The bodies eventually lay decomposing for ten days in the hot sun. This was to be the start of terrorising the people of Lydda.[17]

At Ramleh, town notables were detained by the Israelis and eventually signed a surrender document which came into effect the following morning

The Druze village, 'Amqa, in Western Galilee was shelled and "cleansed" following an attack and artillery shelling by the Sheva Brigade and the Carmeli Brigade. It was reportedly the only Druze village to suffer this fate.

Al Masmiyya al-Kabira, to the north of Gaza, was occupied by 11 July. Al Jura, overlooking what is now Mount Herzl to the west of Jerusalem, was probably captured on this day.

The Zionist settlement of Ben Shemen, east of Lydda, was reported to have been "freed". The media reported semi-official sources which indicated that Zionist forces had entered Lydda and Ramleh, taking large numbers of prisoners.

Egyptian planes bombed the western suburbs of Jerusalem. Arab Legion artillery opened up in retaliation to heavy Zionist mortaring of the

Old City. Notre Dame Hospital, from which the Zionists poured their fire onto the Old City, was set on fire. Zionist artillery continued to bombard Arab gun emplacements around Jerusalem and in the vicinity of Damascus Gate in the Old City.

July 12

The village of Suba was bombarded by the Palmach with artillery and mortar fire. The defenders were eventually driven off.

As part of Operation Dani, the following villages were cleansed: Abu al Fadi and al Haditha, both north west of Ramleh. Majdal Yaba and al Muzayria, both to the north of Ramleh. In all, a combined population of about 4 000 people plus any refugees who may have been sheltering in the villages.[15]

The Times reported the battle for Lydda and Ramleh as being "short but bloody". Following an artillery barrage, the towns were surrounded by infantry and at dusk a motorised column drove down the main street "spraying the houses and side-streets with heavy machine gun fire."

The events in Lydda-Ramleh deserve a look in closer detail.

Lydda-Ramleh expulsions[17]

Within Lydda between 300-400 Israeli troops dispersed into isolated pockets in the midst of tens of thousands of hostile residents, some carrying arms, when three Arab Legion armoured cars entered the town. The Israeli troops felt threatened and vulnerable, believing that the town had surrendered. So a certain amount of confusion was evident when the ensuing fight killed, amongst others, two Israeli troops.

The order came to the Israeli troops from OC Moshe Kelman to suppress any sniping with the "utmost severity." Troops were ordered to shoot any "clear target" or, alternatively, at anyone "seen on the street." Dozens of unarmed detainees in the mosque and church compounds in the centre of the town were shot and killed.

In less than three hours, the troops from the Yiftach Brigade caused "some 250 dead . . and many wounded." No more than four Israelis were killed with about a dozen injured. Yet "The inhabitants of the town became panic stricken. They feared that . . the IDF troops would take revenge on them. It was a horrible, ear-splitting scene. Women wailed at the top of their voices and old men said prayers, as if they saw there own deaths before their eyes."[18]

Thus commented Yeruham Cohen, an Israeli intelligence officer.

When it came to deciding the fate of the towns people there was no doubt that expulsion was the order of the day.

Ben Gurion met with a number of generals including prime-minister-to-be Yitzhak Rabin, then a Lt Colonel and Chief of Operations for Operation Dani.One of them proposed expelling the residents of Lydda and Ramleh, but with no reply from Ben Gurion. Together Ben Gurion, Allon and Rabin left the room whereupon Allon posed the question "What shall we do with the Arabs?" Ben Gurion made a dismissive, energetic gesture with his hand and said "Expel them [garesh otam]."

At 13.30 Operation Dani HQ issued the following order to the Yiftach Brigade

1] The inhabitants of Lydda must be expelled quickly without attention to age. They should be directed towards Beit Nabala. Yiftach must determine the methods and inform Dani HQ and 8th Brigade HQ immediately.

2] Implement immediately.
The order was signed by Yitzhak Rabin.

At this point in time the two towns had a combined population of up to 70 000, of whom about 15 000 were refugees from Jaffa. By the end of two days only 1 000 remained

In what became known as the "Death March" - about 335 people died on the long trek east - the exiled gave harrowing accounts of their experience. Some had been stripped of their possessions as they left their town or at check points en route.

Father Audeh Rantisi in *Blessed are the Peacemakers* wrote:

"Without water we stumbled into the hills and continued for three deadly days. Jewish soldiers followed, occasionally shooting over our heads to scare us and keep us moving. Terror filled my 11 year old mind as I wondered what would happen."[19]

The trek of the Lydda refugees was described by one soldier:

"A multitude of inhabitants walked one after another. Women walked burdened with packages and sacks on their heads. Mothers dragged children after them . . Occasionally, warning shots were heard . . Occasionally you encountered a piercing look from one of the youngsters .

[which] said 'We have not yet surrendered. We shall return to fight you.'"

Other soldiers recorded impressions of how "children got lost". How a child fell into a well and drowned, ignored by those clamouring for water. Not only was all hope abandoned but eventually possessions and bodies.

". .to begin with utensils and furniture and in the end, bodies of men, women and children, scattered along the way."

During the march, with no food or water and in 100^0 midsummer heat, some people drank their own urine. A few men attacked nursing mothers in attempt to suck a few drops of moisture from their lactating breasts. Some of the marchers resorted to chewing grass in an attempt to find some moisture. Children were dying, as were the sick and the elderly. The dead were covered with stones, branches and a quick prayer. Children, abandoned, were wandering about crying.

Pregnant women went into premature labour as a result of their ordeal. None of the babies survived. With no opportunity for burial, they were coverd with grass and abandoned. The trauma can only be imagined.

At steep uphill climbs, soldiers continued to shoot in to the air. Low-flying planes buzzed overhead.

Eighteen year old survivor, Ismail Shammout, recalled the moment he discovered some water and rushed to fill a pot. "At that moment a jeep pulled up with three people. One of them, an Israeli officer, got out. He pulled a gun and put it to my head and ordered me to put the water down."

There was another survivor, a 22 year old medical student from the American University in Beirut, paying a visit to his home town of Lydda. He witnessed many scenes of horror. He was called away from a hospital filled with dead and wounded to bury his older sister who had been killed.

Forced out of his home when it was stormed by Zionist fighters, his neighbour's son was shot dead in front of him when the boy refused to let looting soldiers search his person.[20] During the march from his homeland he was forced to drink his own urine. And he vowed vengeance.

As Dr George Habash, his name was to be well known when he later repaid the terrorism suffered by his own people. He was responsible for planning a number of PLO operations, including the hijacking of airliners.

The estimate of the number of deaths resulting from the Lydda-Ramleh expulsions - before, during and after the events - was estimated at 1 000. Eventually the Arab Legion commander, John Glubb Pasha, was to write "nobody will ever know how many children died."[21]

The bombardment of the Jewish held districts of Jerusalem by Arab Legion artillery and mortars continued. Low flying Egyptian fighter-bombers made raids on the western suburbs of the city. Zionist bombardment of the Old City started fires in the area, with large numbers of Palestinian civilians leaving the densely populated quarters. Street fighting took place in Sheikh Jarrah.

The Arabs counter-attacked the Israeli army on the heights overlooking Ein Karim.

On the Syrian border there was heavy fighting around Mishnar Hayarden, with large numbers of prisoners and booty taken, according to Israeli sources. The Lebanese said a Zionist attack in the north-east had been repulsed. Heavy Zionist losses were reported at Tershisha and Mesdel-kroum. Zionist forces evacuated the heights near Jenin.

Israeli sources claimed that the Palestinian towns of Lydda and Ramleh surrendered the previous evening. Those expelled were forced to travel on foot to Beit Nabala where an Arab Legion force of up to 150 soldiers was stationed. The Legion's armoured cars were no match for Israeli tanks, and the village fell.

As part of Operation Dani the following villages were captured:
al Lawz Khirbat, Sara and Sataf, all west of Jerusalem. Deir Abu Salama, north east of Ramleh - with a combined population of about 1 400. Deir Abu Salama is now an Israeli picnic area with the stone from the demolished houses used for construction in the area. A forest dedicated to Moshe Dayan is now on the site of al Lawz Khirbat.

On the night of the 13th a company of the Irgun and two platoons from the Palmach Youth Battallion entered al Maliha, outside Jerusalem, home to the influential Jerusalem family, al Shaykha.

July 13

The Israeli army captured Ras El Ain, the source of Jerusalem's water supply and the position from which Iraqi artillery had bombarded Petah Tikva, the Jewish town and settlement adjoining Tel-Aviv. Military activity moved to the Latrun area where the Arab Legion had a stranglehold on the Jerusalem Tel-Aviv road. Aircraft was used to bomb Beit Nuba in the Latrun area.

Arab forces were reported to be attacking the Musrara quarter of Jerusalem.

The Scotsman correspondent, Patrick O'Donovan, filed a report and analysis on the situation in Palestine. It makes interesting reading:

It observed that the "second half" of the war in Palestine would be much different than the first - if there was to be no external interference in the conflict. A changed Israel would emerge. If Bernadotte's efforts failed then the Zionists would wage a war aimed at acquiring the maximum amount of Arab land much of which would be retained because it had been emptied of its Palestinian Arab inhabitants.

The Arabs had proven to be less effective than expected. They had been denied further supplies of arms from Britain. Zionist propaganda - "700 000 Jews against 30 million Arabs plus the support of Britain" - had been mercilessly conducted against Britain so that the French army had been glad to load up the *Atalena* and every young Zionist Jew must have considered whether it was a duty to fight for Israel. They had been arriving in their hundreds.

The article continued

"Israel is no longer the mild liberal haven that Dr Weizmann and the Zionists envisaged. . . They now have censorship which is ruthless and amoral. In Haifa it is frankly political . . . criticism is not permitted. In Haifa too, they have opened a ghetto for the Arabs. Four of the meaner streets have been wired off and, just like the Jews in medieval Cracow, Christian and Moslem Arabs must sleep and live there under guard. Businessmen can apply for passes if they wish to emerge during the day. . . It would be hard to visualise a more subdued and frightened population than the Arabs left in Israel. In spite of government protestation they are clearly marked down for second class citizenship.

Ben Gurion, the Prime Minister, has adopted ruthlessness in dealing with critics of his policy, denying them the floor of the House and, in fact, ruling untrammelled by effective criticism. Places go to loyal supporters. . .

Just now only a minority of the Jews would choose in cold blood to carry on this war. They are mostly young men from the towns who delight in having a gun on their hip, in the authority that it gives and in the strange freedom that danger somehow brings. . . . If Israel is forced, or permitted, (it depends on your point of view) to carry through the second phase in the war against the Arab states she will emerge the most powerful single state in the Middle East, organised, totalitarian, and devoted, owing no loyalty to any other state, with her favours and small concentrated strength for sale on the open market."

[Author's note: How prophetic much of this last statement has turned out to be.]

At the Security Council the Israeli spokesman asked for unconditional abandonment of Arab "aggression". This drew the comment from The Times that the long-winded reflections on the morality of the Arabs came strangely from the spokesman of an organisation that had shown "no inhibitions in promoting its own political aims."

Faris Bey, of Syria, commented that the United States saw no aggression when Jewish immigrants used force to create a State in Palestine, but it did when the inhabitants resisted. He added that there would be no peace in Palestine until a settlement based on justice had been achieved.[21]

The chairman of the truce commission reported to the Council that "The Jews in Jerusalem . . appeared to be increasingly inclined to ignore the most elementary rules of international war."[22]

July 14

At the UN an American resolution calling upon the protagonists to lay down their arms or face sanctions was supported in principle by the members, with disagreement on detail. An Israeli spokesman said that despite reservations, Israel would accept it if the Arabs did likewise.

Arab spokesmen continued to insist on the unfairness of a policy which threatened Arabs with sanctions for the use of force against "an immigrant State created by force." There was a feeling in the Council that, in light of the military situation in Palestine, it might be in the interests of the Arab states to accept the resolution.

Britain argued that, while supporting the substance of the U.S. proposal, she felt that the Arab position had not been fully appreciated by the United Nations.

The Arab press provided grounds for comment.

A significant change was noted in the Lebanese press - no glowing accounts of Arab victories, but realistic analysis of the implications of the present situation. In Damascus and Baghdad the big drum was still being violently beaten, with much angry comment on Britain's new role. Especially in the preventing of the Arab Legion making a whole-hearted war effort.

The hopes of a truce were reported to be in the ascendancy particularly since the leaders now seemed to realise the seriousness of the situation. A marked increase in anti-British feeling was reported, following on from the imposition of economic sanctions and the refusal to supply arms and ammunition to the Arab countries.

The small hamlet of 'Aqqur was occupied during the second phase of Operation Dani. It is now the site of thick forest, established by the Jewish National Fund in memory of four Zionist Jewish Americans. The village of Ma'lul, west of Nazarreth, was also occupied during this second phase, "cleansed" of its residents and levelled - except for its two churches and a mosque, at times used by a neighbouring kibbutz as cow sheds. In the same area, al Mujaydil, suffered the same fate, as part of Operation Dekel. Apart from a church and monastery, the rest of the village was levelled.

The Muslim area and military positions in the village of Shafa 'Amr sustained a heavy artillery barrage causing the Muslim residents to flee. The previous night the Druze leaders had met with Israeli intelligence officials and arranged a sham Druze resistance to be followed by a Druze surrender.

Within the Israeli Cabinet, questions continued to be raised by Mapam members with regard to the destruction of villages. In reply to assertions that he, Ben Gurion, professed not to know who was destroying several named villages, Ben Gurion retorted that he could not be expected "to send out men to look for destroyed villages."[23]

July 15

By seven votes to one (other reports indicated eight votes to one) with three (or two) abstentions the Security Council adopted a resolution ordering a cessation of hostilities in Jerusalem within 24 hours and three days for the rest of Palestine. Non-compliance could mean "coercive action" being undertaken - the first time in its history that the Security Council threatened sanctions.

The chairman of the consular truce commission reported the commission's opinion that the earlier abduction of the five Britons (by terrorists disguised, it was revealed, as the Israeli army) was part of a Zionist plan to seize Jerusalem's power station.

A young Norwegian serving as a UN guard in Jerusalem was killed in the Mount Scopus area.

In and around Jerusalem, artillery duels were commonplace - but not during daytime when the Arab forces observed Ramadan. Part of the village of Beit Safafa was captured by the Etzioni Brigade. Units of the Irgun and Stern Gang captured the semi-abandoned village of al Maliha.

The Irgun and Stern Gang announced that they would regard foreign troops in Jerusalem as invaders even if they came to the city to enforce the internationalisation of the city, as demanded in the partition resolution of 1947.

In a debate within the left-wing Mapam party, criticism focused on General Allon's use of tens of thousands of refugees as a weapon of strategy.

"Many of us are losing their [human] image . . . How easily they speak of how it is possible and permissible to take women, children and old men and to fill the roads with them because such is the imperative of strategy. And this we ask, the members of Hashomer Hatzair, who remember who used this means against our people during the [Second World] war . . . I am appalled."[23]

It was reported that the Israelis had renewed their assault (their fifth attempt) on the Latrun area, the only major point acting as a blockade on the Tel-Aviv Jerusalem road. Zionist forces also headed towards Nazareth from Shafa Amr, a village which had been attacked and captured the previous day.

Al Damun, to the south of Acre, was a victim of the second phase of Operation Dekel when the Sheva' Brigade moved into Western Galilee. Some villagers fled during the initial bombardment, others were expelled. The village - which is mentioned by the Muslim traveller, Nasir Khusraw, in 1047AD when he paid it a visit - was completely destroyed. Mi'ar, to the east of Acre, suffered a similar fate. It is now the site of a leisure and picnic area.

Ein Hod, south of Haifa,was captured with its residents either expelled or treated as POWs. It was not destroyed and has long been an artists colony, populated by those with a Bohemian tendency. The village mosque was turned into a cafe/restaurant. Ironically, those of the village who did not become refugees remained in the area and founded a Mark II version of their village, also named Ein Hod. It currently forms one of Israel's 100 or so "unrecognised" villages within the Israeli state. Its status is such that, as with all "unrecognised" villages, it receives no municipal services - no school, no roads, no electricity, no water or sewage provision etc.

The village of Kafr Lam, established in the same area in the 8th century, was subject to shelling from two warships and captured. Bir Ma'in, east of Ramleh - appearing in crusader records as Bermenayn - was captured by the Yiftach Brigade. This gave the Israelis control of the road from al Latrun to Ramallah. The Arab Legion suffered heavy casualties in a counter attack the following day. The site of the village was eventually used for target practice and other military purposes.

Saffuriyya, north of Nazareth, a village reputed to be the home of Jesus' grandmother, became a centre for Jewish religious life following the Jewish Revolt in 70 AD. The beginning of its end came shortly after three Israeli planes dropped "barrels filled with explosives, metal fragments, nails and glass" killing and wounding a number of villagers.

The arrival of thousands of refugees from Shafa 'Amr had already undermined local morale. The unexpected air bombardment and that of nearby artillery, the failure of the Arab Liberation Army to respond to a plea for help also took its toll. The local militia proved to be unorganised and ineffective, fighting independent of each other. Within 24 hours a mass exodus began, with shelter sought in nearby gulleys and orchards.

Most of the villagers who remained were expelled in September. The last were removed by trucks in January 1949. The site is now that of a pine forest planted by the Jewish National Fund to commemorate the successes of others eg Guatemala's Independence day.

In the aftermath of the occupation of Lydda and Ramleh, the village of Barfiliya was occupied. Al Burj suffered the same fate - despite a fierce counter attack by the Arab Legion.

From July 15 - 18, during the second phase of Operation Dekel, the 7th Brigade captured Ar Ruweis (Muslim), Ad Damun (mostly Muslim), Kabul (Muslim), Sha'b (Muslim), Tamra (Muslim), Mi'ar (Muslim), Kaukab and Kafr Manda. With assistance from battalions drawn from the Golani and Carmel Brigades, Nazareth was captured along with surrounding villages. These were Al Mujeidil (Muslim), Ma'lul (Christian and Muslim), Yafa (Christian and Muslim), 'Ilut, Saffuriya (Muslim), Ar Reina (Muslim and Christian), Kafr Kanna (Muslim and Christian), Rummana (Muslim), Uzeir, Tur'an (Muslim and Christian) and Bu'eina (mainly Muslim).

As in the first phase of this Operation, it was the Muslim communities which bore the brunt. Christian communities were not expelled.

Iraq announced that Zionist activity in the country was criminal offence with sentences ranging from imprisonment to the death penalty. The latter was reserved for Zionist activities within the armed forces - as in the case of Communism.

For the first time, The Times featured an article attributed to "From a Zionist correspondent".

July 16

The provisional government of Israel accepted the Security Council demand for a second truce, provided the Arab states decided likewise.

The Arab Legion launched an offensive against Zionist held "new Jerusalem" with heavy artillery support. Strategic positions were occupied against strong opposition from Zionist forward positions. Shells pounded the Zionist positions with reports that the Zionist held Notre Dame building was showing the white flag. It was believed that Zionist plans to attack and capture the whole of Jerusalem had been forestalled by the action of the Arab Legion. Observers were of the opinion that an all out battle for the city had commenced on the eve of the second truce being implemented. Arab reinforcements were reported to be on their way from Transjordan.

Elsewhere in Palestine, hostilities continued.

An Israeli communique claimed that Nazareth had been occupied with many prisoners taken. Entry into the town was, according to reports, considerably facilitated by intelligence supplied by the neighbouring Druze. With the Zionist forces entering the town disguised as Arabs, complete with *kaffiyeh* or *iqal,* there was no time to organise any resistance and only one Israeli soldier was killed and one wounded.

There were reports of "an almost helpless mass of refugees" on the road leading north east from Nazareth. But, Nazareth was one of the few towns spared mass expulsion. Eye witness accounts talked of the role of Arab soldiers who "stopped us and forced all the people to return to the city." This turned out to be fortuitous since the Israeli commander, Chaim Laskov, had orders to exercise restraint with specific instructions not to harm anything.

Such was the concern that the birthplace of Jesus should not reach the headlines that Ben Gurion ordered that unauthorised soldiers should not enter Nazareth, looting and desecration was forbidden. He even stipulated that "if there is any attempt at robbing by our soldiers, a machine gun should be used without mercy."[25] Not that this prevented the people of

Nazareth and the large mass of refugees from outlying areas from being treated any differently by the victors.

Passports were confiscated and Israeli I D cards issued. Currency had to be changed into the much devalued Israeli denomination. Military rule was imposed immediately. Arab land was seized and there was no redress to the civil courts. Travel outwith the town was severely restricted, even with the required permit. Travel to see a doctor or to work required a permit, which could only be obtained by standing in long queues, often for more than one day. Like all other Palestinian Arabs under Israeli rule, imprisonment, house arrest, house demolition, loss of employment - all with no recourse to civilian courts - was the order of the day. And all judgements handed down by the military courts were sacrosanct, justified by reference to "security".[26]

The Syrians tried to increase their bridgehead in Eastern Galilee but were apparently repulsed by the Israelis. At Tira, on the Tel-Aviv Haifa road, about 1 000 Arab troops were dispersed by an Israeli assault. In the Latrun area, the Arab Legion held its position, with the Zionist forces, in a flanking movement, capturing several villages north east of the area.

The Egyptian airfield at El Arish was attacked by Israeli aircraft following an attack on Cairo. Tel-Aviv had a number of air raids with some bombs being dropped.

Al Ruways, south east of Acre, is now covered by a eucalyptus forest. Then, it had a population of over 300 who probably fled as the Seventh Brigade approached.

In the Haifa area, al Tira was bombarded by the warship Eilat, then overrun. Most of the vllagers - who had survived a two month siege - were expelled or incarcerated in a POW camp. Accusations were made of a massacre, with charred bodies found at the neighbouring village of Ein Ghazal where some had sought refuge. Subsequent investigation found no bodies though the Israelis conceded that corpses had been found in an advanced state of decomposition and were burned by Israeli troops. How they died was never ascertained.

It was reckoned that al Sarafand fell at the same time as al Tira.

In the Jerusalem area, at Deir 'Amr, the village and farm school were occupied.The Principal and Deputy of the Boys Farm - established for orphans following the 1936-39 rebellion - were forced into exile with shots fired behind them. The farm buildings were transformed into an Israeli mental hospital, Eytanim.

Ishwa was "cleansed" of its residents by the Fourth Battalion of the Har'el Brigade. The villagers who remained were expelled. The nearby village of Kasla suffered the same fate.

In the Tiberias area the village of Hittin was occupied after the fall of Nazareth. It was felt that the capture of Nazareth hastened the flight of the demoralised villagers. However the soldiers of the Arab Liberation Army present were few in number and low in ammunition. They, together with the villagers who had used up all their ammunition, fled to the north. The village of Nimrin probably fell at the same time.

The Irgun were still holding the five British abductees, having yet to decide whether to pass them to the provisional Israeli government. The terrorists view was that since Jerusalem was not part of Israel, they were not subject to the authority of the state.

While The Times printed articles from "a Zionist correspondent", The Scotsman's Michael Davidson hung his credentials like washing out to dry. While regretting the "piles of dead houses climbing the hillside, empty and crumbling" and commenting that in Haifa, of the original 80 000 Arabs, 4 000 remain confined to a ghetto with a further 3 000 "roped off" in Jaffa - he extolled the achievements of Zionism seemingly unaware of the contradictions and ironies abounding in his eulogy.

In referring to a "clash of two just causes" which was to result in the brutal and, in consideration of the methods used, cowardly, dispossession of about 750 000 people he found that "creative valour" was responsible for the founding of a nation state. His reference to "a community dispossessed, striving to regain the homes and land that their ancestors have occupied down the centuries" could have been taken from a primer on Zionism.[27]

However it is a good indication of the way the conflict was starting to be viewed, with Zionism in the ascendancy, and the rights of the Palestinians consigned to near oblivion.

July 17

Zayta, near Hebron, was occupied at the end of Operation An-Far.

West of Tiberius, the village of Lubya fell easy prey to the advancing Israeli armoured unit. The fall of Nazareth had "terrified" the local population which, with the exception of a poorly armed militia and some old people, left towards Lebanon. Some of the elderly took refuge in a cave and eventually escaped. The fate of the others remains unknown. The "Lavi" pine forest was planted on the site by the Jewish National Fund.

At Hatta, north east of Gaza, a platoon from the Givati Brigade stormed the village, with the Egyptian troops retreating. Operational orders required that the villagers be expelled ostensibly "to prevent enemy infiltration." The village houses were demolished.

Jusayr, in the same area, suffered the same fate - probably at the end of Operation An-Far. Egyptian officer ʻAbd al-Nasir observed "there was no indication that our High Command was aware of what was really going on." The site is now a garbage dump[28].

In a fierce battle with Egyptian troops, Karatiyya was captured by the Third Battalion of the Giv'ati Brigade and the Ninth Commando Battalion of the Armoured Brigade. Fifteen Irgun were killed and there were claims of being "let down" by the Haganah. But the Egyptians held on to the road thus preventing a breakthrough into the Negev. Most of the houses, on the southern outskirts of Jerusalem, still stand, occupied by Jewish families[29].

The Irgun captured the strategic village of al-Maliha [pop. 1 940] following several days of fighting.

West of Jerusalem, the village of ʻArtuf was attacked. Most of the villagers had fled with the start of a night time mortar barrage. The few left in the village (and others in the same area) were expelled as part of the second half of Operation Dani. Rafael Eytan, who was to be named as one of those responsible for the slaughter at Sabra and Shatila refugee camps in Beirut (1982), was one of the commanders.

Operation Dani also claimed Deir Rafat. Its buildings survived until September when they were blown up for "military" reasons. ʻIslin, now an industrial site, was also captured, as were Kasla and Ishwa. Most of these villages had been on the front-line since April. Those villagers who withstood the inevitable mortar bombardment which preceded the arrival of the Harel Brigade units, were expelled when the Israelis entered their villages.

July 18

The Arab States accepted the Security Council's demand for a truce throughout Palestine. It was pointed out that although the Arabs had agreed to a cease-fire, the truce could not continue unless three conditions were met

1] Complete cessation of Jewish immigration pending UN attempts to solve the Palestine problem.

2] The 300 000 Palestinian refugees must be allowed to return home. They must be restored to their property.

3] The mediator had admitted that there was an element of advantage to the Zionists inherent in any truce. In fairness to the Arab side, the period of the truce must be fixed, not of indefinite duration as stipulated by the Council.

The Arab League repudiated the suggestion that the Arabs were the aggressors or that their actions constituted a threat to world peace. Arab forces had "entered Palestine to restore order and security in the vacuum created by the withdrawal of the mandatory Power." Exception was taken to the reference of the provisional government of Israel in the preamble to the resolution. It was regarded as a violation of the terms of the first cease-fire which guaranteed respect for the claim of both sides. The UN was warned that an attempt to create a Jewish State would not be calculated to serve the cause of a peaceful solution.

In Amman there were demonstrations against the Arab League and the decision to accept the truce. Damascus was bombed twice over the week-end with few casualties.

A few hours before the cease-fire, Israeli troops adavanced to the north east of Nazareth, opening up the Haifa-Tiberias road. Zionist forces broke the truce within 24 hours when they carried out a dawn attack into the Mea Shearim quarter in Jerusalem. The Arab Legion regrouped and counter-attacked in a successful bid to regain their positions.

The Egyptian army claimed to have captured the town of Aslug "which the enemy occupied during the last truce." It was also claimed that the towns of Bet Tamah and Holiouat were occupied with the Zionists losing 87 dead in a counter- attack.

The sixth and last attempt was made to capture al Latrun with armoured vehicles and two tanks. However the Israelis had to wait until 1967 for success. Then, the villages in the area were razed to the ground with even the stone carted off to leave no trace. It included the biblical village of Amwas or Emmaus. The site is now a picnic area in Canada Park.

East of Ramleh, the hamlet of Shilta was occupied by the First Battalion of the Yiftach Brigade. This victory proved to be short-lived with the lives of 44 Zionist soldiers being claimed. "Thus, in the few hours before the truce took effect, we experienced the most severe blow of Operation Dani, which had been full of triumphs."[30]

It was reported that Nazareth was largely undamaged during the recent battle. Israeli soldiers were forbidden to enter holy places. Sentries had been placed at large places of worship and retreat. " . . benediction was sung in many chapels, and the few Muslim inhabitants were still being called to prayer."

The five kidnapped Britons were handed over to the Haganah, with the Irgun having been given assurances that they would be tried publicly on the suspicion of spying.

A report in The Scotsman shed light on the planes acquired by the Israeli airforce. A war surplus Flying Fortress, detained in Nova Scotia because it was believed destined for Palestine, "escaped" to the Azores overnight.

Three Flying Fortresses, apparently B17s, had "disappeared" on a Transatlantic flight the previous months. The same planes had bombed Cairo and had been observed over Nazareth. Reporters spoke to American pilots claiming to have flown the planes. Unsubstantiated reports said that planes had been flying into Israel from secret bases in Italy and Corsica.

In the "Ten Days" between the two truces, it was estimated that up to 30 000 new refugees had been added to those already crowding Upper Galilee and southern Lebanon.

July 19

Fighting continued, despite the truce, with each side accusing the other of violating the cease- fire order. In particular there was heavy fighting in the north, at Azaziyat, where the Zionists held positions inside Syrian territory. Syrian forces maintained heavy attacks near Mishmar Hayarde and, on the eastern shore of the Sea of Galilee, attempted to recapture Suseita overlooking the settlement of Ein Gev. Suseita had been occupied by Zionist units a few hours before the cease-fire deadline.

On the Haifa Tel-Aviv road the hamlets of Jaba, Ghazal and Izzam had been active, in earlier days of the conflict, in impeding Zionist trucks on their way to Tel-Aviv. They were now home to a substantial number of refugees. The surrender of the villages had been demanded by the Israelis, before the second truce came into effect. The surrender demanded had been rejected by the village elders who wished to wait until the truce commenced.

At 9am the Zionists arrived.

A stiff resistance was put up against tanks and aircraft. The 5pm cease-fire came and went. The onslaught continued and was to continue every day for a week. The air attacks were particularly devastating, with the defenceless villages being strafed on every bombing run. However the villagers refused to surrender or flee despite many deaths.

It should be noted that both Iraq and Syria had rejected the truce while Saudi Arabia, Egypt, Transjordan, Lebanon and Yemen accepted it. The acceptance of the truce conditions by the Political Committee of the Arab League was attributed to the "perilous shortages" of arms, ammunition, transport and petrol. It was recognised that the decision could have adverse consequences for the domestic situation facing the Arab governments. Many of their people had been led to believe that victory over the Zionists was just around the corner and hence could not understand why the truce had been accepted.

The two Cromwell tanks stolen by Zionist forces from Haifa airfield during the previous truce were seen in action trying to break the Arab Legion road block in the Latrun area. Three light tanks and ten armoured carriers took part. Legion sources said the attack had been repulsed with two light tanks destroyed.

Tel Aviv radio announced the execution of Meir Tubiansky, a Jew, found guilty by a Haganah military court of spying for the Arab Legion. He had been an official of the Jerusalem Electric Corporation, the employing company of the five kidnapped Britons who, it was also announced, were to be tried by a civil court.

The King, accompanied by the Queen, inspected 350 officers and men of the Palestine police force when they paraded for the last time. After presenting medals he congratulated them on "a job well done."

July 20

With many of the 300 000 Palestinian refugees coming from territories under Zionist control, political sources spoke of the idea of "population exchanges" between Israel and surrounding Arab states. This was the first reported comment on a racist philosophy which assumed that because the Palestinian people were Arab, they should be prepared to stay in any Arab country rather than the land of their birth.

A large bomb explosion in Cairo's main shopping centre killed four and injured 17. There was an official denial that the "Israelite" airforce dropped a bomb. The statement also spoke on behalf of the terrorist groups, the same groups which the provisional government apparently found hard to control. It claimed that no "Jewish organisation" was responsible.

July 21

The hamlets of Jaba, Ein Ghazal and Izzam were invited, by their local collaborator, to meet with the Zionists and the Red Cross to arrange the collection of bodies. It soon became apparent that this was a ruse to put them off their guard. That night the hamlets were first bombed then subject to a ground attack by infantry and troops. Sound trucks were brought up to Jaba declaring "yield or we will destroy the whole village." Still the villagers continued to resist.

Mirvak, the newspaper of the Stern Gang, declared that "every Briton must be regarded as a secret agent and must be imprisoned or expelled from the country." The threat was extended to Count Bernadotte and his Swedish assistants. It was supported by the Irgun who had kidnapped the five Britons and the main opposition party, the right-wing Revisionist Party. The threat had also the support of some influential American backers of the Irgun and the Revisionists.

The UN mediator was singled out. "Does the fact that Sweden has not recognised our State give her subjects the rights to do spies' work in our country." The statement was a reflection, according to The Scotsman, of the frequent allegations in many Jewish quarters and newspapers that Count Bernadotte was pro-Arab and was working, mainly on British instigation, against the Jews.[31]

Within the Cabinet of Israel's provisional government an attempt was made to silence the voices of those dissidents who disagreed with the razing of the Palestinian villages. Agreement was reached that jurisdiction over the "abandoned" villages should reside with the Ministerial Committee for Abandoned Property. In reality this Committee was to prove of little value in the face of continuing private initiatives and the actions of army units in destroying villages.

Elsewhere, a call was made for the creation of four settlements in the Jerusalem corridor "within one or two days." The haste was explained by the need to create 'facts on the ground' before the arrival of truce observers who might regard the creation of new settlements as a violation of the truce. The chairman of the Jewish National Fund, Granovsky, "doubted the legality of settlement on Arab land."[32]

With the exception of a small area south of Lake Hula held by Syrian forces and small pockets on the Tel Aviv road, the Zionists held all areas ceded to them under the partition resolution.Considerable advance had been made into Arab held territory. Two thirds of "Arab Galilee" particularly to the west and south was under Zionist control, as was the central front of Lydda-Ramleh and a wide corridor to Jerusalem.

The fighting had brought about political changes, with the provisional government of Israel of the opinion that boundaries would have to change to ensure security. Economic union between Jews and Arabs was considered necessary though currently impossible because of the reality of 300 000 refugees and the absence of any central Arab authority.

July 22

Truce observers arrived in Haifa and Tel-Aviv. American destroyers flying the UN flag were presumed to be resuming patrol duties as they did during the first truce. Indications were that the truce was expected to be of a lengthy duration since UN officials negotiated to take over one of Tel-Aviv's large hotels for a "few months."

An "official spokesman" described the situation in Palestine as "generally quiet." A "no-man's land" was demarcated along the Jerusalem front, by mutual consent of the warring parties.

The Times reported that only 90 000 of the 350 000 Palestinian Arab population who lived within that part of Palestine given to the Zionists now remained. Of those left, 60 000 were described as nomads with no political aspirations or consciousness, living in the Negev desert. The remainder were villagers or residents of Haifa.

July 23

It emerged that the 5 men kidnapped by the Irgun were being held under the British Mandate Defence Emergency Regulations, Section 136. It was felt that, in the absence of codified Israeli law, if found guilty of any charge, they would be expelled.

Despite protests from the UK government, oil refining began of the remaining oil stocks at the British owned refinery in Haifa. This action was justified under the emergency powers of the mandate. These powers were regarded to be still in force "in accordance with the decision of the provisional State Council of May 14."[33]

The village of Ajjur, north west of Hebron, was "depopulated" following a miltary assault.

Ben Gurion called for the immediate creation of between 10 and 12 settlements in the Jerusalem Corridor and the Lydda-Ramleh area - all outwith the partition boundaries.

July 24

The villages of Jaba, Ijzim and Ein Ghazal - all to the south of Haifa - were known as the "Little Triangle." Following a day long massive aerial and artillery bombardment, a special force drawn from units of the Golani, Carmeli and Alexandroni brigades attacked. Despite overwhelming odds, the villagers held out for a further two days before fleeing or being forced to flee.

Designated Operation Shoter (police) it was planned as a "police operation against a population in revolt against the State, and which refuses to recognise legitimate sovereign authority." This designation as a "police operation" as distinct from a military operation,was used as spurious justification for carrying out the attack and not regarding it as a breach of the truce. An argument totally rejected by the Truce Commission.

A village elder of Ijzim, Hajid-Had Saleh recalled "during the evacuation women and children were attacked with machine-gun fire from enemy aircraft." Other survivors reported being machine-gunned by ground troops who never failed to neglect the looting of livestock, valuables and money whenever possible. Most of the homes were then destroyed[34].

A UN report put the number of people killed or missing from the three villages at 130, with 8 000 made homeless. The report concluded that the attacks on the villages were unjustified, particularly in view of the villages' willingness to negotiate. It found that the villagers had been "forced to evacuate". Count Bernadotte stated "I am strongly of the opinion that measures taken involving the destruction of the two villages [Jaba and Ein Ghazal] were excessive and constituted a violation of both the spirit and the letter of the terms of the truce."[35]

He demanded that the villagers be allowed to return, with Israel responsible for restoring their damaged or demolished homes.

The provisional government was not happy with the findings of the UN and, in contradiction of all available evidence, denied that the villagers had been expelled. The mediator's demand that they be allowed to return was rejected.

At an internal debate of the Mapai party, at the Mapai Centre, concerns were raised over the events of the previous ten days, with the Lydda-Ramleh expulsions partricularly in mind.

Yosef Sprinzak, secretary general of the Histadrut and critic of the forcible transfer policy, articulated his concerns:

"There is a feeling that *fait accomplis* are being created . . the question is not whether the Arabs will return or not return. The question is whether the Arabs are [being or have been] expelled or not . . This is important to our moral future . . . I want to know who is creating the facts? And the facts are being created on orders . . [There appears to be] a line of action . . . of expropriation and of emptying the lands of Arabs by force"[36]

Others at the debate had a different perception of Israel's "moral future."

Shlomo Lavi, an influential Kibbutz movement leader, stated that "The . . . transfer of Arabs out of the country in my eyes is one of the most just, moral and correct things that can be done. I have thought of this . . . for many years."

This view was backed by Avraham Katznelson, another prominent Mapai leader. There is nothing "more moral, from the viewpoint of universal human ethics, than the emptying of the Jewish State of the Arabs and their transfer elsewhere . . . This requires the use of force."[37]

July 25

It was reported that three British soldiers were being held prisoner by the Israelis, captured while fighting for the Arab side. One was Joseph Simpson of Perth who was wounded, then captured, at the fighting in Lydda-Ramleh.

Thirty-five tons of high explosives, on its way to Palestine, was seized in Genoa. Several members of a "secret organisation" were arrested.

The military governor of Jaffa, Yitzhak Chizik, resigned.This followed weeks of battling with army units, various Zionist bodies, vandals and private looters all with their eyes on the property of Jaffa's refugees. His replacement immediately set about the task of uprooting the remaining Palestinian Arabs of Jaffa and ghettoising them in one area. The orders were "to evict the Arabs where Jews were to be settled."[38]

July 26

The Zionist controlled section of Jerusalem was proclaimed "occupied territory" by the Israeli Government, to be placed under a military governor and administration. This followed a three hour talk between Count Bernadotte and Israel's foreign minister, Moshe Shertok. The mediator's proposal for demilitarisation of the city was opposed, particularly with regard to withdrawal of troops and men of military age.

Apparently the decision took UN observers and officials by surprise. The deciding factor, it was argued, was the alleged lack of control over the terrorist groups ensconced in the city and outwith "the jurisdiction of the provisional Government."

Azzam Pasha of the Arab League said that, in principle, they were prepared to make Jerusalem an open city. However, they were not prepared to assist in the "provisioning" of its 100 000 Jewish population while about 400 000 dispossessed Palestinian refugees were left homeless and without resources. It was pointed out that if Jewish immigration did not stop and the Palestinian regugees were not repatriated the "Arabs would be obliged to renew the struggle."

It later emerged that Bernadotte met with Israel's foreign minister, Sharett (Shertok), in Tel-Aviv and in reply to a question concerning the readmission of Palestinian refugees replied "The Jewish government could under the present conditions, in no circumstances permit the return of Arabs who had fled or been driven from their homes."[39]

In further response to Bernadotte's prodding on the issue of repatriation of refugees, Shertok, replied that there could be no return during hostilities and thereafter the matter could only be considered "in the context of a general peace settlement."[40]

Meanwhile, the Committee for Abandoned Property which was supposed to be in charge of "abandoned" villages admitted that it was not possible for it to function. The army did as it saw fit and representatives of the Committee were "not even allowed to enter occupied territory . ."[41]

The Scotsman's correspondent, on the spot, reported that while there was yet no official comment on the matter, the indications were that the refugees would not be allowed to return.

By their "mass flight" the Palestinians had forfeited the right to return to the land of their birth. This argument was described as a "moral" argument. This Zionist morality then went on to spin the web of disinformation which was to dominate for decades. An argument which, although specious, was to be rarely questioned.

"They were not driven out; most left before they were attacked. Haifa, with 70 000 Arabs, was captured by fewer than 200 armed Jews. Safad in Galilee was abandoned . ." No attempt at investigative journalism here. More a willing acceptance of the Zionist line that the Palestinians merely " . . quit their homes, crops, flocks and and personal belongings and fled . . ."

A hint of justification enters the article. Was there "obedience to the directive of the Mufti . ." ? But no hint of the immorality of the situation. After all, if the Israeli leaders are to be believed, the fighting was only "against invading armies and not against local Arabs, who had no need to go." No mention of the fact that, in war, civilians do flee the conflict zones, never mind the tactics used by the Zionists to stimulate an exodus.

The question is raised of who would pay for the re-settling of any returning refugees. Israel could not afford it, it was stated. What about the Arab League? The possiblity of Britain, given that nearly half of all eventual refugees were under British jurisdiction and protection at their time of flight or expulsion, and the member states of the UN footing the bill is never broached.

However, the article has a prescient observation.

"The wisdom of the present Israeli attitude however, may well be questioned if only from the standpoint of Israel' long-term security. Surely a contented and prosperous Arab minority, enjoying equal status . . . would be more likely to win . . cooperation of her neighbours than an all-Jewish enclave, exclusive and self-conscious, thrusting into Arab hostility."[42]

July 27

The Security Council refused a request from Syria that the opinion of the International Court of Justice be taken on the international status of Palestine arising from the termination of the mandate. Six members, including the UK voted in favour of the request. Five members including the US, the Soviet Union, France and Canada voted against or abstained.

The British government proposed a resolution, in the Security Council, with regard to the five Britons who "at serious personal risk kept an important public service going while the battle was raging in Jerusalem" were abducted by the Irgun. It met with opposition from both the US and the Soviet Union. One of the abductees had, meanwhile, been released on bail.

A member of Kibbutz Beit Zara complained of the demolition of Palestinian villages and the acquisition of the village land in the Jordan Valley by the local Settlements Block Committee.

"Once again proof is given that behind the government's back, action is taken aimed at destroying Arab villages and expropriating their lands."[43]

However by late July it became apparent that Arab land was being coveted by the Zionist settlements on a large scale. The Tel Mond Settlements Block Committee wrote to the Agricultural Centre expressing an interest in "receiving in perpetuity" two tracts of Arab land. Kibbutz Neve-Yam asked for lands belonging to the villagers of As Sarafand. Mishmeret asked for permanent possession of the land of At Tira. Kibbutz Ein Harod wanted the land of Qumiya and Kibbutz Schiller wanted land belonging to Zarnuqa and Al Mughar.

The Mapam- affiliated kibbutz, perhaps as a sop to their socialist ideals, were keen to point out that the land they desired belonged to foreigners, *effendi*, not the peasant *fellahin*. Undoubtedly the truth lay closer to the reason given by the *moshava* Nahalal in the Jezreel Valley when it asked for 175 acres of land belonging to the village of 'Ilut. Stressing that an Arab village could, at some point, be built on the land "It seems to us that the time is now ripe to transfer this land to permanent Jewish possession."[44]

July 28

Iraq al-Manshiyya, a village to the north east of Gaza was attacked by the Giv'ati Brigade.It was successfully repulsed by the Egyptian forces.

Count Bernadotte submitted a 'Note' to Tel-Aviv which suggested that "from among those who may desire to do so, a limited number . . . and especially those formerly living in Jaffa and Haifa, be permitted to return to their homes."[45] He accepted Israel's differentiation, on security grounds, of males of military service age and "others." However he was not successful.

Notwithstanding Israel's arguments for refusing this request, on the 18 July, at the start of the Second Truce, the Israeli army instructed its units to prevent the return of refugees "also with fire."[45]

A plan, calling for the establishment of 21 settlements on mostly Arab owned land in the Jerusalem corridor, Lydda-Ramleh and Western Galilee was presented to Ben Gurion. It forced the socialist Mapam to face the ideological problem of Jewish Zionist settlement on Arab owned land and on land earmarked for Arab sovereignty. No mean problem considering the party supported Jewish-Arab coexistence and the return of refugees.

However the establishment of settlements on both sides of the partition boundary was viewed as essential for strategic and security interests. This circle was squared by the expedient of agreeing that land could be set aside for any returning refugees, compensation could be offered. The concept of "development for two peoples" won the day for those on the left of the political spectrum. Never mind that this involved the theft of the land and property of others.

July 29

The provisional State Council in Tel-Aviv announced the rejection of the UN mediator's proposals for the demilitarisation of Jerusalem. The partition resolution of 29 November 1947 was now regarded as being no longer binding "in view of Arab aggression". Israel would not agree to the repatriation of Palestinian refugees before a final settlement was reached since "humanitarian considerations could not be separated from the political and military issues."

The first UN supervised convoy to Jerusalem was stopped by three Arab Legion armoured cars at the Latrun. It was forced to divert along a roughly constructed miltary road before eventually reaching the city.

July 30

With 12 days of the truce having passed, violations were reported to have increased over the past 48 hours. With the full complement of truce observers yet to arrive, the whole exercise was regarded as ineffectual. So far, truce observers were not acting as a deterrent. In the south, where fighting was reported to be increasing in intensity, observers had to withdraw because their lives were in danger.

Notes

1 Benny Morris, *The birth of the Palestinian refugee problem, 1947-49*, p.172
2 Norman Finkelstein,*Myths, Old and New*, (Journal of Palestine Studies, Autumn 1991) p.81
3 Michael Palumbo, *The Palestinian Catastrophe*, p.132
4 *ibid* p.134
5 The Times 2/7/48
6 Morris, p.138
7 *ibid* p.142
8 *ibid* p.144
9 *ibid* p.212
10 The Scotsman 9/7/48
11 Morris, p.199
12 Walid Khalidi, *All that Remains*, p.91
13 Morris, p.204
14 Khalidi, p.115
15 *ibid* p.356

16 Morris, p.205
17 Palumbo, p.126
18 Morris, p.206
19 The Jerusalem Times 29/6/98
20 "Interview with George Habash" (JoPS, Autumn 1998)
21 Morris, p.210
22 The Times 14/7/48
23 Morris, p.164
24 *ibid* p.211
25 Palumbo, p.123
26 Najwa Kawar Farah, *A Continent called Palestine*, p.45
27 The Scotsman 17/7/48
28 Khalidi, p.118
29 *ibid* p.304 and p.118
30 *ibid* p.415
31 The Scotsman 22/7/48
32 Morris, p.183
33 The Times 24/7/48
34 Palumbo, p.140
35 Khalidi, p.166
36 Nur Masalha, *A Critique of Benny Morris*, p.96 (JoPS, Autumn 1991)
37 *ibid* p.93
38 Morris, p.191
39 Palumbo, p.147
40 Morris, p.143
41 *ibid* p.164
42 The Scotsman 27/7/48
43 Morris, p.168
44 *ibid* p.174
45 *ibid* p.145

August

the right of Arab refugees to return to their homes at the earliest possible moment should be reaffirmed.

a message from UN Mediator, Count Folke Bernadotte, to the UN Security Council

The expropriation of Palestinian land, the destruction of the villages, to ensure that refugees would have no home to which to return, continued apace. These activities were rarely, if ever, reported in the press.

In the north of Palestine the work of Yosef Weitz and his Transfer Committee could be traced by the destruction wrought.The well rehearsed excuse was to prevent the emptied villages being used for military purposes. Occasionally reasons closer to the truth emerged, as when complaints were made by socialist oriented Mapam members:

> "But I spoke to a number of members from [Kibbutz] Ma'ayan Baruch and nearby kibbutzim and I got the impression that there exists the possibility that there is a desire to destroy the villages and [the Arabs'] houses so that it will be impossible for the Arabs to return to them. A week ago a representative of the JNF came to visit. He saw that in the abandoned village of As Sanbariya, which is a kilometre from Ma'ayan Baruch, several houses are still standing, albeit without roofs. He told the secretariat of the kibbutz to destroy the houses immediately and he said openly that this will enable us to take the village's lands, because the Arabs won't be able to return there. I am sorry to say the kibbutz agreed immediately without thinking what they were doing."[1]

In early August, Meir Ya'air, co-leader of the Mapam party lamented

> "the youth we nurtured in the Palmah [elite strike force], including kibbutz members, have [occasionally] turned Arabs into slaves; they shoot defenceless Arab men and women, not in battle .. Is it permissible to kill prisoners of war ? I hoped that there would be some who would rebel and disobey [orders] to kill and would stand trial - and not one appeared. . . They are not against transfer. What does it mean . . . to empty all the villages? . . . What did we labour for?"[2]

Mapam members were also to the fore in the case of 'Arab al Zubayd, a small village to the north of Safad. During August they prevented Golani Brigade units from blowing up the village. Following complaints, Ben Gurion denied responsibility "No permission was given [by me] to any commander to destroy houses." He promised to investigate. In reality the destruction of the village was postponed for a few months. The villagers were never allowed to return. Part of the village land is now a nature reserve.

In late August, the curiosity of a ten year old Palestinian boy got the better of him. Together with his parents, the boy had been spared the Death March from Lydda. A Jewish family had taken over their home and along with other Arab families they had to live on the outskirts of Lydda, forbidden to enter those parts of their town reserved for Jews. Indeed, Israeli reports noted that Lydda residents who had not been expelled were "roaming about without food in the fields" afraid to enter the city.

As a member of a Christian Arab family he experienced "privileges" not accorded to those of the Muslim faith. On a Sunday he could ride on a train to church. An attempt, as his mother explained to him, by the Israelis to drive a wedge between the Palestinian people.

The boy, Fouzi al-Asmar, was not aware of the military regulations in sway over the town of his birth on the day that he and his friends decide to find out what was happening in Lydda. The slightest infraction of these regulations could result in imprisonment or expulsion for the offender.

Lydda had been an affluent town and, shortly after the expulsions, Jewish Zionist families had moved in to the better homes. Once prosperous Palestinians could pass their own homes now occupied by complete strangers. What met Fouzi's eyes shocked him. Israeli soldiers looting houses and shops, merchandise and private property being loaded into trucks. He was "shocked on the visit by the sight of this large city completely deserted, the houses open, the shops broken into and the remaining merchandise rotting."[3]

Throughout this period, the number of Palestinian Arab refugees was underestimated in the reports. The oft quoted number was in the region of 300 000 whereas it was probably closer to 500 000. Figures which came from UN sources would also be obliged to include the 6 000 to 7 000 Jewish refugees which resulted from the conflict.

August 1

Attention, internationally, focused on Jerusalem. The demilitarisation of the city was accepted in principle by both parties. However, with Israel having established a land bridge to the city, with the western part in Jewish Zionist hands, there was a clear possibility that it would be incorporated within the "Jewish State." The international status, bestowed upon the city by the UN, was about to be ignored.

The Irgun, which still operated as a separate entity within the city, was in the vanguard. It was reported to be collecting signatures for a mass lobby in support of the proposal "Jerusalem as capital of the Israeli State."

A convoy travelling to the Jerusalem was forced to divert along the "Burma" road to avoid Arab Legion fire at the Latrun, the first since the truce began. In the city itself, fighting took place at Jaffa and Damascus Gates, Mount Zion and along the line through Mea Shearim and the Musrara quarter.

The UN force of truce observers was reported to be nowhere near its full complement.There was a shortage of personnel, helicopters, light aircraft and vehicles. Hence the investigating of complaints was seriously hampered. The observer force was put on alert along the Palestine coast line when two landing craft with a cargo of arms for the Zionist forces were reported to be arriving from Italy.

The UN mediator set out on a tour of Jewish and Arab "centres" with Israel refusing to give clearance to accompanying correspondents. The situation facing at least a quarter of a million refugees and those Palestinians living in isolated groups in hostile territory gave cause for concern.

Israeli foreign minister Sharett replied to the mediator's request that a limited number of refugees be allowed to return. It contained a refusal to allow small numbers of refugees to return to Haifa and Jaffa. His carefully worded reply pointed out the problems of re-admitting them - problems which were never encountered when it came to Jewish Zionist immigrants arriving in Palestine. He expressed sympathy for the refugees since "our people has suffered too much from similar tribulations for us to be indifferent to their hardship." Later that month, in a private letter, he expressed the determination "to explore all possibilities of getting rid, once and for all, of the huge Arab minority which originally threatened us."[4]

August 2

At the UN, Britain called attention to the problem of 200 000 displaced Jews and the reality of more than 550 000 Palestinian refugees - the result of ". . . United Nations proposals for a Palestine settlement . .". Increasing Jewish pressure on Palestine had intensified Arab fears and the sense of injustice that other Powers had been content to leave the problem of anti-Semitic persecution to be solved almost exclusively by settlement in Palestine.

Britain's offer to contribute an immediate £100 000 achieved nothing, with the Soviet Union and the Ukraine unwilling to cooperate until "voluminous information" about refugees elsewhere - Europe, Arabia, Cyprus - had been obtained by the secretariat.

The Middle East correspondent of The Times sketched the situation in Palestine from the time of the First Truce.

Prior to the truce, the Haganah and the Irgun were regarded as lacking in tenacity, showed clumsiness in attack and disregarded the elementary rules of warfare. This did much to justify the optimistic view of eventual success for the Arab armies. Despite the poor quality of the Zionist forces, they had occupied large chunks of land ordained to be part of an eventual Palestinian State - with an estimated 300 000 terror stricken Palestinian civilians on the move.

In contrast the Arab Legion "had shown tenacity, discipline and chivalry." It had the most to show, as a result of good leadership. Most of its officers, including the commander at Jerusalem, were Arabs - giving lie to the Zionist picture of a British-led Arab Legion.

To the south the Egyptian army had invaded the Negev, occupied Gaza, Bersheeba and Hebron. The few Zionist settlements in their path had been destroyed. They had however, come to grinding halt when they met hard Zionist resistance some 20 miles from Tel Aviv. They had the habit of issuing "communiques that were a joke even in the armies of their allies."

The Iraqi army had been badly directed with little progress being made against the Zionists. Its 500 mile long line of communications over a desert road under a burning sun did not help. As for the Syrian and Lebanese forces "the less said the better." They had been severly rebuffed with Zionist forces eventually raiding deeply into Lebanese territory.

In general, the Arabs had a shortage of transport and ammunition, while the opposite prevailed within the Israeli camp.

The article examined the question of why the Arab Legion sought a solution by force and concluded that it was felt that the outcome had already been pre-judged at the Security Council in favour of the Zionists. It was felt that those who dominated the Council were resolved, regardless of the merits of the case, to force a solution acceptable to Zionism. A view reinforced by the closing of the eyes to truce violations.

By the 15th day of the Second Truce the Arab Legion had refused to allow convoys and water to reach Jerusalem, in violation of the truce terms. However, the Legion argued that this situation would prevail as long as the Zionists refused to conform to the truce provisions with regard to the demilitariastion of the city.

Hostilities were reported to have resumed to the south of Bersheeba with Egyptian troops attacking Zionist positions at Beer Aluj.

August 3

While fighting to the south of Bersheeba halted with the arrival of truce observers from Gaza, it was renewed a few miles further north at Revivim.

Israel accused Britain of being in breach of the truce, of supplying the Egyptian forces with military equipment from British army stores at Rafah. The equipment, it was alleged, was then transported to the Faluja and Iraq Suweidan, two villages occupied by the Egyptians in the south. Israel had alleged that the Egyptians had broken the truce by attacking a convoy at Hatta. A subsequent attack by the Israelis had resulted in the loss and capture of military equipment and transport by the Israelis.

With the demilitarisation of Jerusalem very much on the agenda, Count Bernadotte visited the Zionist occupied section of the city. A main feature appeared to be the removal of all arms from the city, the evacuation of all armed forces with control of the city left in the hands of the truce observers. "Temporary partition" of the city was also mooted.

During his visit to the city he warned the Arab Legion that its "stubborn refusal" to permit the pumping of water through Latrun constituted a severe breach of the truce.Referral to the Security Council was threatened.

August 4

The Scotsman reported on the situation of 250 000 "Palestine Arab refugees" encamped around the "little hill town of Ramallah." Supply of water was a problem, sanitary arrangements scarcely existed and a very real danger existed of typhoid claiming victims in the next few days. Inoculation was underway but supplies of vaccine were inadequate.

Families were living in the dust under olive trees. There were no cooking utensils which, in reality, was not a pressing problem since the only food available was bread rushed from Amman. A warning was given that shelter, food, clothing and medicine must be found before winter set in or there would be a large number of deaths "though many of them are only a few miles from their native towns and villages."

The refugee division of the UN Social Affairs Department acknowledged that all figures for the refugee population, so far, had been "underestimations."

Count Bernadotte cabled the Security Council asking that "the right of

Arab refugees to return to their homes at the earliest possible moment should be reaffirmed." The Israelis raised "technical objections" to this development.

The Israelis informed the mediator that if any of the five British planes at his disposal landed in Israel again, the crew would be detained. This followed from the provisional government's objection to the mediator's use of facilities from any country "whose neutrality had been compromised."

Israel complained to the Security Council over the continuing detention of 11 000 Jews, including 7 500 men, in Cyprus - arguing that their detention was not necessary under the truce resolution. The reality was that the release of several thousand Jewish Zionists of military age would not have encouraged the Arabs to observe the First Truce, never mind agree to the Second. In addition, the mediator's operational instructions of 27 July indicated that male immigrants of military age should only be permitted to enter Palestine in numbers which ensure "that no military advantage accrues to either side."[5]

August 5

The provisional government of Israel invited the Arab governments for peace negotiations following discussions with Count Bernadotte. This was accompanied by the threat that if, in Israel's eyes, the Arab side continued to violate the truce it would feel free to act on any front and would not limit itself to defensive measures. Effectively the provisional government gave itself carte-blanche for continuing its campaign and military operations against the Palestinians, regardless of the truce.

Israel rejected the need for the demilitarisation of Jerusalem although it was conceded that discussions for "improving the present situation" was possibility. Effectively the death-knell for any idea of "internationalising" of the city as required by the Partition resolution.

Reliable sources reported that the Irgun, possibly in tandem with the Stern Gang, intended to carry out a campaign of terrorism against British officials in Europe, including London. This would be in "reprisal" for the detention of Jewish immgrants in Cyprus.

Jamal Husseini, vice-chair of the Palestine Arab Higher Committee and chief delegate to the UN was recalled to Damascus for talks on the formation of a new "Government for the whole of Palestine." This was seen as an important change in the Arab League's view of the situation.

Previously King Abdullah's ambition to take over the Arab areas of Palestine had blocked any move to form a local government. The Arab League had now rejected Abdullah's conciliatory approach to the Zionists in favour of "unyielding opposition." It was reckoned that greater numbers of Arab troops would be involved in the next phase of the war.

At the request of Israeli foreign minister, Moshe Sharett, a memorandum was drawn up outlining a plan to prevent the return of the Palestinian refugees. Submitted on the 5 August, it recommended "pulling down Arab houses", a propaganda campaign to get the Zionist view of events to "local and possibly foreign journalists" and the drawing up of a plan for "the settlement of refugees in Arab lands." This programme was immediately approved by Sharett.[6]

August 6

With sniping continuing in Jerusalem, it was announced by the office of Count Bernadotte that all proposals for the future of Jerusalem had been dropped.

Beirut's reply to the invitation to attend peace talks was brief "We do not recognise the existence of a Jewish state and will not speak with terrorists." Cairo newspapers described the idea as "unthinkable." King Abdullah replied "I am concerned to-day only with the problem of those who were kicked out of their homes - our Arab refugees - and that is a problem that blocks every just and moderate solution."

Britain's representative at the UN, Sir Alexander Cadogan, replied point-by-point to a letter from the Israeli representative circulated the previous week. The letter tried to justify the kidnapping the five British employees of the electricity company in Jerusalem. The reply exposed the extent to which the provisional government was prepared to lie in order to justify the actions of the terrorist Irgun.

The reply rejected the assertion that the men had been arrested in their homes. They had been abducted either in the power station or the house opposite - all of which were under the protection of the UN truce commission flag. Added was the comment that the authority for the Israeli position lay with the Irgun and that it was not acceptable that "more regard should be paid to the word of a lawless, terroristic society than to the testimony of the truce commission . ."

Rejected also was the Israeli catch-all of "military security". The abduction had taken place on 16 July. It was not until nine days later that this part of Jerusalem was declared "occupied territory."

August 7

The Times published a comment on the actions of the "Israelite Government" arguing that it appeared to be oblivious of the immense moral effect which even a small token return of refugees would have on Arab public opinion. It found it difficult to understand the provisional Government's insistence that the problem should only be regarded from the viewpoint of military necessity and expediency.

It further reported that in the opinion of the mediator's advisers, that when it came to the problem of refugees, Israel could not be completely absolved from responsibility. Many Arabs had fled because they feared that they would suffer the same fate as the inhabitants of Deir Yassin, who were massacred by a "dissident" group of the Irgun Zvei Leumi early this year. The massacre it was noted, was intended as a demonstration of "Irgun strength and ruthlessness."

Even at this juncture the concept of blaming the victim for their plight was apparent. The reference to a "dissident group" demonstrates that the nature of the Irgun appeared not to be fully understood. And while Deir Yassin certainly has its place in the Palestinian experience as one of the reasons behind the mass exodus of the Palestinian people from their land, more than thirty years were to pass before the full terror was revealed, confirming the personal accounts of the eventual 750 000 refugees.

August 8

Typhoid was reported amongst the estimated 100 000 refugees sheltering in the hills between Nablus and Ramallah. There was a grave danger of spreading disease due to lack of water and under-nourishment. Eye disease was prevalent, affecting 90% of the children. Where there was water, there was a dense population of refugees - increasing the risk of epidemics.

The truce observers began using a small aircraft to monitor violations in Jerusalem. There were daily reports of small-arms fire, shelling and mortar fire. It was announced that the Irgun, while objecting to the proclamation of the city as "occupied territory" and the appointment of a military governor, would, never-the-less, obey the orders of the military governor. However they would maintain their "independent military formations" but would coordinate their activities with those of the army.

With the truce being broken every day, it was regarded that both sides were taking advantage of the undermanned observer force. Belgium had provided its full complement of 50. Both France and the US had provided under half of each of the promised 125 observers. Communications and transport equipment was poor with no radio communication between observer forces in the south and total reliance throughout Palestine on 30 mechanically unsound US jeeps from an army surplus dump in Greece.

It was reported that the water pumping station at Latrun had been declared a no-mans-land by both the warring sides.
Israel accused the Arab Legion of bringing 200 reinforcements from Transjordan into Jericho.

August 9

With the arrival of the first diplomatic representative of a major power to take up his post in Israel (Pavel Gershev of the Soviet Union),The Scotsman dwelt on the Russian and Communist influence within Israel. Here the popular sentiment was pro-Russian, partially arising from Soviet support at the UN with the caveat that "communism of the type practised in Russia has strictly limited appeal."

The Communist Party in Israel was small though very active. It maintained contact with Arab Communists and advocated Jewish-Arab cooperation. The large number of East European immigrants gave a further impetus to a pro-Russian bias, but with little love for Soviet ideology and methods.

Further support lay in the left wing of the Labour group and the right wing opposition Revisionist party, the Irgun and Stern Gang - all influenced by Russian support at the UN.
There was the realisation that Soviet support was more conditioned by its antipathy towards the Western Powers rather than a love for Zionism. The supply of arms and military equipment from Eastern Europe had a large bearing on the sympathetic attitude to that bloc of countries. It was widely understood that the Irgun and Stern Gang had long had unofficial contact with Soviet representatives.

Anti-British feeling still prevailed with the U.S. policy on Palestine being a source of disillusionment. In the case of the latter, with one eye on the material support received, the criticism was muted.

Count Bernadotte issued additional instructions which emphasised that since the truce was imposed by the Security Council, no one side could break the truce by claiming self-defence. A report from the mediator about "rumours of impending *coups* by irregular elements" was interpreted as referring to the Irgun.

Immigration of 600 000 European Jews into Palestine began, at a projected rate of 10 000 per month. Plans for 800 000 Jews in Muslim countries were being made. Transport costs of all immigration schemes were to be met by the American Joint Distribution Committee.

August 10

The Arab League rejected Israel's conditional invitation to open peace negotiations with regard to Palestine. They refused to recognise the existence of a "Jewish State".

A reply to the acting Secretary-General of the UN's enquiry concerning Jewish and Palestinian refugees was given by Jamal Husseini of the Palestine Arab delegation to the UN. The following points were made:

1] The problem of Jewish refugees in Europe has no relevance to the Palestine problem and, in this context, should not be considered by the Security Council.

2] The number of displaced Arabs and refugees exceeds 550 000, of which 300 000 had sought refuge in other Arab countries.

3] Jewish refugees in Cyprus are illegal immigrants (with most of those remaining being able-bodied young men purposely picked from militarily trained groups), trying to land in Palestine during the mandate. Their case has no relation to Palestine. They should be returned to their country of origin or port of embarkation.

The mediator, Count Bernadotte, announced stricter supervision of the "uneasy Jerusalem truce" accompanied by the threat to refer further to the Security Council if the situation did not improve. The military activity was such that it could not be attributed solely to infringements by "irregulars."

The Irgun and members of "Fighters for the Freedom of Israel"demonstrated against the mediator's presence in Jerusalem.

Three of the five British employees of the Jerusalem Electric Corporation, kidnapped by the Irgun were released. The remaining two abductees faced charges based on the British emergency regulations. (Author's note - regulations which are still in force in Israel and the occupied territories to the present day and used, when convenient, against those Palestinians under occupation.)

At a meeting between the mediator and Israel's foreign minister, the former expressed his frustration in terms of Israel "driving a hard bargain" and its "stock was dropping." The chauvinistic and racist response was to the effect that Syria and Iraq had vast potential for absorbing refugees. The minister argued that in the long run it was in the interests of "all concerned" that the Arab minority in the State of Israel should be a small one.[7]

August 11

The situation was reported to be "delicate." Whereas only four days ago the members of the mediator's staff were confidently stating that the end of the war was nigh, the situation had changed. This was due to two factors:

1] Haj Amin el Husseini, Mufti of Jerusalem and Head of the Arab Higher Committee had sent out a call to arms. The moment was opportune with hopes of returning home, now that a truce was in place, remaining unfulfilled for the Palestinian refugees. His intention to raise an army of 20 000 Palestinians gained many recruits along with training, small arms and ammunition supplied by Syria, Lebanon and Egypt.

Despite the calibre of the Palestinian fighters, judged to better than their neighbours, it was felt that their success would be no better than previous irregulars -the blame being laid at the door of the Palestinian Arab Higher Committee.

2] The behaviour of the Zionists which, to quote a member of Bernadotte's staff was "insolent, arrogant and deceitful." Predictably, they would apply pressure when the Arab side showed signs of willingness to negotiate. They applied the tactic of just asking a little bit more than previously agreed - a tactic well honed when negotiating with the British.

Worse was the "increasingly uncompromising behaviour" of the Irgun and Stern Gang. Despite protests from the government of being unable to control these "dissident" groups, many believed otherwise - it was more a matter of convenience to make this claim while the terrorists went about their business. They were responsible for the continuation of fighting in Jerusalem and along the Jerusalem Tel-Aviv road. It was they who were still "requisitioning" Palestinian Arab property, preventing the return of the refugees mainly, it was thought, because they would have to give up the houses, shops and land they had expropriated and looted.[8]

[Author's note: While this last comment reflects what was experienced "on the ground" in Palestine, the policy and practice simultaneously being hammered out in the Zionist corridors of power, would suggest that the terrorists were an integral and accepted cog of the Zionist "expand and conquer" machine.]

While the Arab protagonists accepted a proposal from the mediator that as from 7am, 13 Friday August, neither side should return fire from the other side in Jerusalem, a reply was still awaited from the Israelis. With the city suffering one of the "noisiest" nights - mortars and guns - since the second truce began four weeks previously, Bernadotte was clearly exasperated. "I am not joking . . . I am not at all satisfied with the situation in Jerusalem. There's not only sniping, but also machine-gun, mortar and artillery fire. There is much shooting early in the morning, and from the observers' reports it is my opinion that the initiative comes from the Jews, although they say the Arabs started it."[8]

In his first declaration of a violation of the truce, the mediator directed that Israeli troops who occupied the villages of Ajanjul and Buweira in the Latrun area - after the truce - should withdraw by noon the following day. Bernadotte and his staff visited the area and arranged for the return of the villages' 400 residents who had been living by the roadside - despite Israeli protests that the occupation had taken place before the truce.

The Arab League informed the mediator's HQ of 28 Palestinian villagers burned alive by Zionist forces. "This occurred during the present cease-fire. I possess the names of 14 victims and also the name of an eye-witness" reported Azzam Pasha. [Note: Truce observers failed to find any sign of the bodies.]

August 12

Two large explosions followed by fire destroyed the Latrun pumping station which supplied Zionist occupied West Jerusalem. Twelve hours earlier Count Bernadotte had visited the building and assured Zionist officials that the water supply, which had been cut off for four months, would be speedily resumed. The incident was considered a blow to Bernadotte and his staff who, at the best of times, were unpopular anyway with the Zionists.

The immediate reaction of the UN was to blame the Arab Legion since the pumping station was located within an area under the Legion's jurisdiction but guarded by UN personnel. However, it was reported that Arab irregulars had been seen in the area shortly before the explosions. One consequence was that the mediator agreed to a rearrangement of the boundary line in the Latrun area. Another was that the Israelis disregarded the mediator's instructions and refused to allow the residents of Ajanjul and Buweira to return to their villages.

Israel formally proposed to Count Bernadotte an exchange of prisoners of war. It was estimated that the Zionist forces held about 5 000 prisoners, with the Arabs holding about 850 Jewish Zionists.

August 13

It was reported that about 4 000 "Exodus Jews" who had been brought to Germany following an earlier abortive attempt to enter Palestine had fled their British zone camp in Berlin. Assisted by the American-Jewish Relief Commission, they reached the American zone where exit permits were issued. It was believed that Palestine via Marseilles was their eventual destination.

With the Israelis refusing to accept the "no return fire" request from the mediator a request was sent for more truce observers to be sent to Jerusalem. Outside the southern walls of the Old City, at Zion Hill, and at Deir Abutor to the west, heavy fighting was reported. Israeli sources indicated that an Arab Legion attack had been repulsed with one Israeli soldier killed and 12 wounded.

The Israeli government asked the UN to fix "an early time limit for the present truce by which either peace must be concluded or the invading armies leave, on the understanding that, failing either, the Israeli government would be free to seek a way out of the impasse by its own actions."

August 14

Israel's OC Operations Yardin wrote to foreign minister Shertok "Because of the spread of diseases among the Arab refugees, I propose that [we] declare a quarantine on all our conquered areas. We will thus be able to more strongly oppose the demand for the return of Arab refugees and all infiltration by Arabs [back] into the abandoned villages - in addition to our opposition [to a return] on understandable military and political grounds."[9]

August 15

With Zionist settlements being established in the Jerusalem "corridor", it was announced by Ben Gurion that the boundaries laid down by the United Nations could no longer be considered permanent.

The sporadic sniping in Jerusalem, a feature since the beginning of the truce, was in the increase with heavy mortar exchanges reported. The

Israelis accused the Arab Legion of taking up positions in no-man's-land. Concurrently, the military governor of the Zionist occupied section of the city, Dr Bernard Joseph, announced that the provisional government would have to annex the city and its "corridor" to the coastal plain. The decision to form a 27 member "advisory council" to administer the Zionist occupied section of the city was also announced.

The British foreign office denied the earlier Israeli claim of providing military equipment (search lights and electrical instruments) to the Egyptian forces.

Under American escort, 355 Jewish Zionist immigrants arrived at Marseilles, from Munich, en route to Palestine. In the past few weeks 3 000 immigrants had departed from French ports to Palestine.

Kibbutz Nordiya was established at Khirbet Beit Lid in the Coastal Plain.

August 16

The two remaining abducted officials of the Jerusalem Electric Corporation were charged on 12 counts including "spotting" for the Arabs and passing the information by radio to Jerusalem's Old City. In addition, one of the officials was accused of complicity in the bombing of Ben Yehuda Street in February, when 50 people were killed. These charges were brought by the police who asked that the session be held in "secret" in order that the prosecution witnesses could testify "more freely." [Author's note: A variant of this is still practised by Israel to this day when it comes to the prosecution of Palestinian detainees. In many cases, the accused and their lawyers are not allowed to see the evidence - usually on the pretext of "security."]

An Israeli army liason officer was shot dead by an Arab sniper while escorting the US Consul-General through "Jewish lines" on the northern Jerusalem front.

All 4 500 "Exodus Jews" interned in the British sector in Berlin had now been smuggled into Palestine "in driblets", according to a spokesman from an "unofficial" immigration organisation.

Count Bernadotte launched an appeal to all member states of the UN to help the "300 000 Arabs and Jews" made refugees by the fighting. Offers included £7 500 from Belgian religious bodies for "Christian Arabs" which one report identified as the Nazareth Christian Arabs. At this juncture only a £100 000 financial contribution from Britain had been forthcoming.

Sir Raphael Cilento, director of the social activities division of the UN, after a tour of the affected areas reported that 64% of the Palestinian refugees "are bedded on a sharing basis" with 15% in tents and the rest living in the open, under trees. The ever present fear of typhoid, typhus and other disease was raised with the stated intention of having a programme of inoculation well underway before October when the cold and winter rainfall will "severely aggravate conditions."

As part of their continuing activities of harassing local villagers and bedouin tribes, the villages in the Kaufakha - al Muharraqa area in the Negev were raided by the Negev Brigade, with the villagers expelled and their villages destroyed. "The villages' inhabitants and [bedouin] concentrations in the area were dispersed and expelled. A number of houses were blown up. Al Muharraqa and the houses of Sheikh Ukbi . . were mined."[10] The truce was, of course, ignored with "military" reasons cited.

August 17

A communique from Amman gave details of a Zionist attack on Deir Abutor in southern Jerusalem. Supported by tanks, armoured cars, artillery mounted on lorries and automatic weapons the Zionist force was allowed to cross into no-man's land before the Arab Legion attacked. Initially they captured and occupied Government House which, since 14 May, had been the HQ of the International Red Cross under the Red Cross flag. By the end of the day it had been re-possessed by the Red Cross.

The communique spoke of the Zionists being thrown back with "several hundred casualties", armoured cars and a variety of arms and munitions were captured with the Legion occupying the positions from which the attack had been launched.

Amman reported that the Zionists had attempted to disguise themselves in United Nations uniforms, pretending to be UN observers, and had opened fire when they entered Arab positions. An Israeli communique blamed the Arabs for the fire directed at the Red Cross building. Fighting continued throughout Jerusalem with continuous small arms fire occasionally interrupted by mortars and light artillery.

Count Bernadotte reported to the Security Council, effectively retracting the earlier claim that the truce observers were confident that the destruction of the water pumping station at Latrun had been the act of Arab irregulars. They were now unsure as to who was responsible.[Author's note: Keep in mind that the blowing up of the pump station gave the Israelis the pretext for ignoring a rare direct instruction from the mediator to allow some 400 residents from two neighbouring villages to return to their homes. It gave the Israelis an opportunity to criticise the UN "laxity" in protecting the station. In the event, the Jewish residents of the Zionist occupied section of the city were not too discomfited by this action in that an emergency pipe-line was soon in place].

No opinion was given as to the responsibility of the continuing hostilities in Jerusalem. Although the report made clear that the Zionists had been the "more aggressive party" since the start of the Second Truce and had only consented with reluctance to the mediator's request that neither side should open or return fire in Jerusalem.

The Times made a pertinent observation with regard to Israeli strategy at this point in the conflict.

The letter to the Security Council wanting a time limit to the truce within which peace must be achieved or military action would be resumed, had only been circulated to the Press, not the members of the Security Council. This was felt to be a disarming tactic, to mute any criticism of Israeli aggressiveness and violations of the truce, by pointing out the extent to which Israel felt disadvantaged by the truce.

Already signs of a world community willing to turn a blind eye to Israel's hostile actions, in order to avoid criticising the nascent state, were emerging. The report stated that some delegations, including the British, were most concerned at the turn of events in Palestine and at indications that the Zionist forces were receiving, among other armaments, large numbers of aircraft "but exploration of a situation which may involve the Jews in responsibility for fighting, even in the Holy City, is not a task that some other delegations can approach with relish."

Count Bernadotte appealed directly to US Secretary of State, Marshall, for emergency supplies to help the 330 000 Palestinian Arab and 7 000 Jewish refugees threatening to form "a sudden human disaster comparable to an earthquake or a tidal wave." Successful mediation, he said, depended upon a solution to this problem.

With winter approaching, the situation was "desperate", death threatened many. Of the refugees, 30% were children under five years of age; over 10% were pregnant or nursing mothers " . . almost entirely without food except for small supplies of flour."[11]

Dr Paul Mohn, a representative of the mediator, spoke with Israel's foreign minister Sharett concerning the occupation and destruction of Arab villages, warning that a "bad impression" would be made on public opinion if it was known that the intent was to ensure that the refugees could not return. He pointed out to Sharett that "on certain occasions Israeli armoured cars had encircled Arab villages in which the population was living peacefully and after herding the male inhabitants together had taken those of military age to concentration camps."[12]

The first issue of the Israeli pound, equal in value to the Palestine pound and British pound sterling, appeared.

The quality of the evidence against the two remaining British abductees started to become apparent in court. One Irgun terrorist claimed that one of the defendants was a fascist because he had found a document displaying swastika in his possession. The document turned out to be a 1925 issue savings certificate which displayed, as part of its design, a swastika. Not the reverse swastika, the Nazi emblem.

August 18

The US, France and Belgium decided to send more truce observers to "critical Palestine spots." The US was consulting with various US government agencies to see what could be done to answer the mediator's appeal for assistance to the refugees.

In the Security Council, the US warned both parties that neither had the right to break the truce, in reference to the Israeli letter (yet to be received by the Council) and threats that continuing military action in Jerusalem would entitle the Zionists to respond as they thought appropriate.The truce could only be terminated by the Security Council, he said.

Another avowed pro-Zionist state, Canada, agreed with the US, pointing out that neither side was entitled to assume freedom of action in response to alleged violations of the truce by the other.

The Syrian delegate expressed disapproval of speeches which said so much about the "iniquity of the fighting" and so little about the "300 000 Arab refugees lying out in the desert while Jews swarmed into Palestine to take their homes."[13]

With Israel's delegation expressing sympathy for the plight of the refugees, but absolving the state of any responsibility, Israel's Aubrey Eban urged a peace conference between the two sides, while the Soviet Union attacked Britain for alleged collusion with the Arab armies.

Shelling and sniping continued in Jerusalem with truce observers, ever protective of their own lives, apportioning blame to both sides. This accusation was vigorously denied by the Zionist forces, as it applied to themselves. One accused the UN observers of being "really too acquiescent to the Arabs."

Four spying charges against the remaining two kidnapped Britons were withdrawn for lack of evidence. Eight charges remained plus the additional charge of complicity in the Ben Yehuda Street bombing against one of the accused.

Kibbutz Yiftah was established on the lands of Blida in the Galilee area.

At a high-level meeting of Ben Gurion, his foreign minister, finance minister and others including Yosef Weitz of the Jewish National Fund (members of Mapam were not invited principally for their 'departure from reality and their ideological hallucinations'[6]) the problem of Palestinian Arab refugees and ways to prevent their return was discussed. A variety of views were presented at this meeting: the need to destroy Arab villages, settle Zionist Jews in the other villages and cultivate Arab land; others spoke of the need to buy land, some opposed the destruction of villages, reservations about settling Jews in Arab houses was evident for at least one member of the meeting.

Ben Gurion observed that it was best that as many Arabs as possible did not return.[14]

The meeting also discussed the question of Arab property, with one Israeli intelligence officer suggesting that refugees should be compensated for property they were forced to leave behind. The paymaster would be American Jews since "American Jewry's yearly income is 11 billion dollars."[15] One participant observed that Arabs in Israel would be forced to prove their right to their own property. Ben Gurion posed the question "Would it not be possible to exchange Arabs for Jews?", which attracted the approval of Minorities Minister Belchor Shitrit.[15]

These discussions were reinforced by actions on the ground. On the same day Yigael Yadin, OC Operations, issued an order which stated ". . . that we are not interested in Arab inhabitants [in Israel] and their return [to Israeli territory] must be prevented at all costs."[16]

August 19

The Security Council, in response to the almost desperate concerns of Count Bernadotte, adopted a multi-paragraph resolution essentially outlining the responsibilities of the warring parties in Palestine with regard to the truce. The Ukraine abstained while Russia (which took the position that there would be no Arab refugee problem if Britain had not incited the Arabs against the Partition scheme), Syria and Colombia declined to support differing sections. Britain, America, Canada, and France introduced the resolution.

Count Bernadotte complained of lack of observers and transport. He was concerned over the mounting tensions and the difficulty in apportioning blame for truce violations. He felt that further deterioration in the situation in Jerusalem could lead to a general resumption of hostilities.

A second and official Transfer Committee was appointed by Ben Gurion towards the end of August. However, on this day, renewed orders went out to Israeli army units to ensure that refugees did not return. There was a general agreement, by those who formed the Committee, as to the means:- destruction of villages, settlement of other villages and, on "abandoned" lands, the cultivation of Arab fields, purchase and expropriation of Arab lands, use of propaganda to persuade refugees that they would not be allowed back.

August 20

The provisional government of Israel informed the Security Council that it would apply for membership of the UN. Apparently Israel was waiting for a more opportune moment since Bernadotte had reported that both parties were "deliberately ignoring the authority of the United Nations." Israel, it was stated, was qualified for membership "since it is a State, peace- loving and ready to accept and abide by the obligations of the Charter."

The two remaining Britons kidnapped by the Irgun were both charged with complicity in the Ben Yehuda Street explosion of 22 January. The examining magistrate stated that he was happy with the veracity of the evidence from the 14 witnesses. However Press reports were of the opinion that the some "evidence" took the form of vituperation against Britain and British subjects. Within the local media the accused were condemned as spies and traitors because of their nationality.

Most vitriolic were religious and terrorist organisations, with the latter threatening to kill the three who were released should they return to Jerusalem. They stated that they would not allow the remaining two to "escape from justice."

An agreement was reached between the warring parties that the Arab Legion would replace irregulars in Jerusalem with an equal number of Legionnaires in an attempt to avoid "sniping and uncontrolled action."

The Jewish National Fund submitted a plan whereby the village of 'Amqa near Acre would be the site of a Zionist settlement. 'Amqa itself had experienced hostilities throughout July, into the second truce. The following year the settlement of 'Amqa was built on village land.

The plan included a further 31 settlements to be built on land now under the ownership of the JNF, land acquired by whatever means by the "State" and Arab owned land. As ever the pseudo-conscience of the left-wing of the Zionist movement prevailed - settlement on Arab land was to be on sites where there was sufficient surplus land to accommodate and maintain the original residents, should they return. How this conscience had to be squared with the fact that several of the proposed sites had yet to be conquered and "cleansed" of their inhabitants was never explained. It did, however, give a clear indication that with or without a truce in place, further hostilities were to be initiated.

In the end the 32 settlements were to occupy 30 000 acres of land of which under 6 000 acres was Jewish owned. All but five of the sites lay outside the Partition borders.

In the Jerusalem corridor Kibbutz Mishmar-David was built on the land of Khulda, Tal- Shahar on Khirbet Beit Far, Kibbutz Harel on Beit Jiz, Taoz on Beit Susin, Kibbutz Tzor'a on Sar'a, Beit Meir and Shoresh on Beit Mahsir/Saris, Kesalon on Kasala and Giv'at Yearim/Eitanim on Khirbet Deir 'Amr.

In the Lydda-Ramleh area Bnei Atarot, Mahane Yisrael, Be'erot Yizhak all on the land of Wilhema, Beit Nehemia on Al Haditha, Gimzo on Khirbet Zakariya/Jimzu, Mishmar-Ayalon and Kfar Bin-Nun on Al Kunaisiya/Al Qubab.

In the northern approaches to the Negev, Tirosh on Amuriya, Kibbutz Revadim on Al Kheima, Segula and Nahala on Barqusiya-Summeil, Kibbutz Gal-on on Zeita, Revaha on Hatta, Otzem or Komenemiut on Karatiya, Zerah'ya/Shafir on Jaladiya and Meishar/Asoret/ Zekher-Dov/Shdeima/Kfar Mordechai on Bash-shit.

In upper Western Galilee, Ahihud/Kibbutz Yas'ur on Al Birwa, Kafir Yasif/Amqa/Abu Sinan on Amqa, Ein Ya'akov/Kibbutz Ga'aton on Khirbet Shifiya, Goren on Khirbet Jalil, Shlomi on Al Bassa, Kibbutz Lohamei Hagetaot/Regba on As Sumeiriya and a settlement on the land of I'ribbin on the Lebanese border.

In Eastern Galilee, settlements were established on the lands of Nimrin and Eilabun.[17]

Ben Gurion was warned that the US was contemplating measures on the refugee question that Israel would find not to her liking. This followed a report from Israel's representative in Washington of "American public opinion gradually being undermined . . . . All hostile forces unite in publicising and shedding crocodile tears regarding plight [of] Arab refugees."[18]

US Secretary of State, Mr Marshall, informed Count Bernadotte that the State Department was working with other Government agencies to determine what could be done as quickly and practically as possible to alleviate the refugee problem in the Near East.

August 22

An "authoritative Jewish reaction" to the Security Council's demand for continuing observation of the truce was printed in the Palestine Post. Major military operations seemed unlikely in the near future since Israel's position - militarily and politically - was regarded as strong. Any initiative had to come from the Security Council and the mediator. If Israel was not satisfied with the action taken by the United Nations, she would decide her own course of action.

August 23

The Scotsman reported that caution was being exercised by Israel with regard to truce violations. Whereas Israel's actions had been guided less by international repercussions and more by territorial gains, military successes and Arab "discomfiture" there was a concern that Israel's "legality" with regard to the truce observance could be compromised.

Her action in trying to seize the International Red Cross HQ at the former British Government House had proved to be more than embarrassing, despite protests at the Red Cross allegedly handing over Israeli troops to an Arab patrol. Such actions could eventually work against Israel's interests, provoking a cessation of flow of dollars from the US. Apparently instructions had been passed to Colonel Dayan "an energetic and aggressive officer", now operating in Jerusalem, to exercise caution. Previously, Dayan's "positive" policy of making the most of every Arab alleged "provocation" had not been discouraged.

The media reported on a decision that Iraq and Transjordan had agreed to merge their armies into one "to coordinate military operations in liberating Palestine."

August 24

It was reported that "indirect contact" between the Żionists and Arab representatives had existed for some time. This followed a speech given by Israel's foreign minister, Moshe Shertok, at a Zionist Council meeting where he made reference to"contact with certain Arab States." Apparently the comment surprised his officials and were regarded as an attempt to prod Count Bernadotte in the direction of direct negotiations - something which had been resisted to date.

Speculation was rife with regard to the identity of the Arab state. Transjordan was the first guess for the reasons that it was widely understood that if it were not for his commitments to the Arab League, King Abdullah would have already sought a settlement. In addition, the Zionists and Transjordan were already in negotiations between 29 November and 15 May.[18] Other unconfirmed reports indicated that Israel was willing to recognise King Abdullah as ruler of the "Arab areas of Palestine" and to allow an unspecified number of refugees home if the occupied area of Jerusalem, the corridor to the sea and area west of Jenin were all ceded to Israel.

A four day operation commenced with the Givati Brigade mounting Operation Nikayon (Cleansing) in the coastal area west of Yibna. The objective was to "cleanse" the area of Palestinian communities perceived to be hostile or potentially hostile - in other words, remove all the remaining indigenous population. These included the villagers in the area, any bedouin encampments and refugees.The orders were to destroy any armed force "and to expel all unarmed [persons] from [the area]." In fact, according to Giv'ati intelligence sources, few Arabs were found.[10]

August 25

With the belief that the main obstacle to a settlement between Zionist and Arab was the continuing immigration of Jewish males of military age to Palestine, the mediator requested that no more males of military age should be allowed to enter after 2 September . Apparently an unstated threshold percentage figure relating all immigrants to those of military age, stipulated by the Security Council, had been reached.

As far as the Israelis were concerned such a request was simply "Bernadotte being pro-Arab again."

August 26

"Peace talks" in Paris - believed to be a continuation of discussions conducted between King Abdullah's representatives and Mrs Golda Myerson, just before the end of the mandate, were reported to have broken off. Apparently Israel's conditions on the internationalisation of Jerusalem (already stipulated in the partition resolution) were unacceptable. These included Israel holding on to the "New City" and the corridor already held by Israel, and part of the "Arab triangle."

In exchange, Israel promised to recognise King Abdullah's sovereignty over the "rest of Arab Palestine" and promised "financial and moral" aid in resettling Palestinian refugees in Arab states. These were refused as a basis for discussion by the Arab representatives.

Meanwhile talks resumed between Israeli foreign minister Moshe Shertok and Count Bernadotte regarding the restriction on Zionist immigrant males. It appeared that the increase in this immigration, particularly over the past two months, represented a violation of the truce in that it gave Israel a military advantage. With the number of observers allocated to keep watch over ports able to be counted on one hand, it was reckoned that thousands had landed unobserved.

In the vicinity of Jerusalem mortar firing and sniping had increased, leading to speculation that a break down of the truce in the city was imminent. Colonel Dayan accused the UN observers of "lax supervision" on the Arab side and "over zealous" with regard to the Zionist side. The Israelis alleged in excess of 50 truce violations in Jerusalem over the past three days with an Israeli communique stating that the Arabs had shelled various Zionist held districts of Jerusalem during the night with no reported casualties.

With in excess of 500 000 Palestinian refugees demanding the right to return to their homes, Israel's minister of immigration was facing severe criticism for his planned scheme for the future immigration of Jewish "displaced persons" from Europe. The rate of admission had been fixed at 100 000 persons per year for 10 years. Critics demanded unrestricted immigration and the abolition of visas or immigration permits for entering Israel.

August 27

Issa Nakhler of the Palestine Arab Higher Committee told a London press conference that the Arabs would never accept the "Jewish State" in Palestine as a fait accompli. "We shall not rest until this mock Jewish State is finished. We are determined, if necessary, to fight the Jews for 100 years." He pointed out that Britain and America should think carefully about the motives of Russia in supporting the Zionists in Palestine. Sixty per cent of the Jewish Zionists who had entered Palestine since the war, he claimed, were of Slav origin.

Jerusalem was the focus of military action which threatened to bring the truce to the brink. It developed into a major gun duel, with shells crashing into various parts of the town with the outer suburbs of southern Jerusalem bearing the brunt. The Israeli shelling was concentrated on Egyptian batteries near Bethlehem.

It was left to the UN truce observers to make an early start to their day in order to find who started this latest violation. The observers ordered the Israeli forces to withdraw from positions held along the northern (Iraq) front accompanied by the threat of Security Council action if they failed to comply.

Jerusalem's power station was blown up at night, allegedly by Arab irregulars, according to a report from Amman.

August 29

Conflicting reports emerged of the shooting dead of two French truce observers who arrived by plane at Gaza. Some said the plane was shot down; others said the white painted plane with UN markings was landing when bullets raked the side of the plane and front wind shield. One report placed the blame on a breakdown of communications and non-receipt of a landing notice from Haifa HQ.

Count Bernadotte's, Chief of Staff, General Lundstrom, was of "the very strong opinion" that the men had been shot as they left the plane since a flight engineer had found no sign of blood inside the plane. Eventually a message from the mediator's office confirmed that the plane had been flying without clearance, in the wrong air corridor, over an Egyptian occupied area.

The Egyptian Defence Minister had expressed his regrets at the death of the observers.

At the end of Operation Cleansing in the Yibna area, units of the Giv'ati Brigade blew up stone houses and torched the huts in the village of 'Arab Suqrir (whose fate was first outlined on a Haganah operational proposal of 11 January when it was recommended that "The village should be destroyed completely and some males from the same village should be murdered"[19]) and "ten Arabs who tried to escape were killed."[10]

The settlement of Udim, in Wadi Faliq, was established - probably on non-Jewish owned land.

August 30

The skyline of Bethlehem was lit up as Egyptian and other Arab gunners pounded the Zionist suburbs of Jerusalem. Mortar positions in the Old City were reported to have heavily bombarded the north-western part of the city. Fighting on Mount Zion was reported to be seriously damaging ancient shrines.

With the Irgun already accepting the authority of the miltary governor of Israeli occupied sector of Jerusalem it was reported that the Stern Gang operatives in the city were negotiating terms for amalgamating with the Israeli army.

August 31

Despite being ordered by the mediator's representatives to withdraw from the Red Cross zone near the former Government House in East Jerusalem, neither party had done so. In the city an American consular official was wounded by Arab snipers. A Jewish labourer was shot dead at the same place where the American consul-general had been killed three months earlier. A family of five were seriously injured in northern Jerusalem. Once again The Times' article was attributed to "a Zionist Correspondent."

Notes

1 Benny Morris, *The birth of the Palestinian refugee problem, 1947-49*, p.168
2 Norman Finkelstein, *Myths, Old and New*,(Journal of Palestine Studies, Autumn 1991) p.88
3 Michael Palumbo, *The Palestinian Catastrophe*, p.149-150
4 *ibid* p.149
5 The Times 5/8/48
6 Palumbo, p.156
7 Morris, p.147
8 The Scotsman 12/8/48
9 Morris, p.140
10 *ibid* p.215
11 The Scotsman 18/8/48
12 Palumbo, p.143
13 The Times 19/8/48
14 Benny Morris, *Falsifying the Record*, (JoPS, Spring 1995) p.49
15 Palumbo, p.157
16 Benny Morris, *Operation Hiram Revisited: A Correction*, (JoPS, Winter 1999) p.71
17 Benny Morris, *The birth of the Palestinian refugee problem, 1947-48* p.184/5
18 The Scotsman 25/8/48
19 Walid Khalidi, *All that Remains*, p.80

September

It would be an offence against the principles of elemental justice if these innocent victims of the conflict were denied the right to return to their homes while Jewish immigrants flow into Palestine

Count Folke Bernadotte, UN Mediator

During the Second Truce the Israeli army continued to destroy abandoned villages, usually for "military" reasons. In the Negev the armies of Israel and Egypt stumbled through an uneasy truce with a few Zionist colonies virtually besieged behind the Egyptian lines. The raiding war, with villagers expelled and their villages destroyed, continued throughout this period.

Sometimes the demolition of the villages would encounter local opposition from nearby kibbutzim. In the south it is on record that several kibbutzim supported the cause of the village of Huj near the Gaza Strip, a traditionally friendly village, where the villagers had been expelled eastwards on 31 May.

In the case of Danna, a village in the north whose residents were expelled on 28 May, its demolition was under way by September, despite criticism from a local kibbutz leader. When the protest reached government level, Ben Gurion denied permission was ever given with an investigation promised. Whatever the outcome, the villagers were never allowed to return and so this particular village, like many, many others, was doomed.

However Huj was to prove to be a textook example of Israeli policy and Zionist intent in ensuring that Palestinians did not return to their homes, regardless of the circumstances.

During September, with the Truce holding and the vicinity of their village being hostility free, the villagers of Huj appealed to Israel to be allowed to return. As the appeal made its way through the various bureaucracies it was acknowledged that the villagers had been "loyal collaborators", "they had not fled but had been expelled", and had an appeal which merited "special treatment." One department, the Middle East Affairs Department, in view "of the commonly held opinion that an injustice had been done" was prepared to allow them to return to Israeli held territory, not necessarily to their own village, rather an "abandoned" village. This recommendation was a qualified one in that its proposers would only support it as long as there was no danger of it being regarded as a precedent.

The Minority Affairs Ministry was critical of this reservation pointing out that there had been a Cabinet decision against wholesale return of the Palestinians as long as the war continued. However they also supported the appeal, going along with the suggestion that the villagers should be re-located elsewhere other than their village which was near the front lines.

Both recommendations were turned down by the defence authorities and the villagers of Huj were never allowed back to their village and their land.[1]

The conscience of Yitzhak Avira, a former Haganah Intelligence Service officer and member of Kibbutz Ashdot Yaakov in the Jordan Valley, came to the fore when he protested against the continuing destruction of villages and the policy and practice towards the Arabs in general

> "recently a view has come to prevail amongst us that the Arabs are nothing. 'Every Arab is a murderer,' 'all of them should be slaughtered,' 'all the villages that are conquered should be burned' . . . I . . . see a danger in the prevalence of an attitude that everything of theirs should be murdered, destroyed and made to vanish."
>
> The reply sought to justify the genocide which was being perpetrated:
>
> "War is complicated and lacking in sentimentality. If the commanders believe that by destruction, murder and human suffering they will reach their goals more quickly - I would not stand in their way. If we do not hurry up and do [things] - our enemies will do these things to us."[2]

Sometimes the position would appear contradictory. During September pressure grew from the kibbutzim in Beisan Valley to demolish and level a group of nearby villages - Al Bira, Al Hamidiya, Kaukab al Hawa and Jabbul. At the same time criticism was levelled at the destruction of villages more distant - Na'ara, At Taiyiba, Danna, Al Murassas, Yubla and Kafra where the view was taken that these villages were cooperative and might be prepared to share their land with neighbouring settlements.

The kibbutzim with a conscience were, however, the exception. The vast majority favoured the destruction which was being wreaked throughout Palestine. Some kibbutz demanded, and would themselves carry out, the destruction of neighbouring villages for their own selfish reasons.

September was the month that saw the start of the occupation of Palestinian owned houses in Jaffa by newly arrived Jewish Zionist immigrants. Both in Haifa and Jaffa, these illegal acts were characterised by confusion, verging on anarchy.

Impatient with living in schools and other public buildings, the empty Arab districts were invaded and houses seized. In Jaffa "invasion and counter-invasion" took place presumably meaning that the immigrants fought amongst themselves over the loot. "Invaders" callously evicted Arabs from their own houses if it took their fancy. Some houses were allocated to those with the right "connections."[3]

General Elimelech Avner enquired of Ben Gurion with regard to the settlement of immigrants in Ramleh. It was opposed, at that point in time, for political reasons.

From September into October, in coordination with the Office of the Custodian for Abandoned (Absentee) Property, tens of thousands of acres of Palestinian owned land, deemed to be "abandoned" were leased to Israeli settlements and farmers. The leases were for the duration of one year since the authorities wanted the option of redistributing this booty, should it remain in Jewish Israeli hands, at a later date.

September 1

UN Chief of Staff in Palestine, General Lundstroen warned all parties, particularly the Egyptians, that if the "neutralisation of the Red Cross area" in Jerusalem was not effected by the next day, it would be regarded as a serious truce violation. The Security Council would be informed. The Lebanon and Syria appeared to be the only two parties to the conflict respecting the truce.

Count Bernadotte expressed optimism with regard to the situation in Palestine.

September 2

It was reported that Arab and Israeli had agreed to a cease fire in Jerusalem. A meeting was to take place in no-man's-land to the south of the city. Attempts would be made to obtain agreement for the widening of the neutral Red Cross area.

Syria reported heavy Israeli casualties following a counter-attack on Zionist forces trying to occupy strategic points on the Syria-Lebanon front.

America protested to Czechoslovakia concerning illegal shipments of planes and arms to Israel. American citizens were involved. Despite the mediator's request that the immigration of military aged Jewish immigrants should cease, over 1 000 arrived at a camp near Tel Aviv.

In general, it was reported, the flow of immigrants of all categories was on the increase. Friction between Israel's US representative in Washington and the State Department was unavoidable when the US refused to allow Jewish male immigrants of military age to leave from areas under its control in Germany and Austria. Count Bernadotte was also insisting, it was alleged, that the names of prospective immigrants should be submitted to him for prior approval.

The Israeli Attorney-General finally filed charges against the remaining two abducted Britons. Four of the six charges were made under the Official Secrets Act and referred to conspiracy to collect information of use to the state's enemies.

September 3

It was reported that, as a result of British-American pressure the terrorist Irgun was to disband and merge with the "Israelite" army. The hope was expressed that a similar agreement would be made with the Stern Gang. "We have decided to give in to avoid useless civil war" said a Jerusalem member of the Irgun's High Command. The Irgun members were now going to enter the political arena under the banner of "Freedom Party" with the agenda of fighting for a Zionist state on both sides of the River Jordan. The considerable funds at the disposal of the Irgun, mainly from the United States, would be used to fund the Party's programme.

The freighter *Mala*, reported to be carrying munitions and arms, arrived in Haifa with Zionist refugees. Most had tried to land in Palestine earlier on the *Exodus*, but had been deported to the British zone in Germany.

September 5

The prime ministers and foreign ministers of the member states of the Arab League met in Alexandria to discuss the situation in Palestine. Renewed fighting was expected.

September 6

Israel's spokesman at the Security Council, Major Aubrey Eban, intimated that Israel wanted immediate peace talks with the Arabs. The mediator arrived in Alexandria to try to gauge the intention of the Arab states.

Egyptian guns were reported to have opened fire on the Jerusalem suburb of Ramat Rachel.

September 7

Israeli sources blamed the Arab Legion and Egyptian forces for the predawn battle which ended the five day "truce within a truce." Gun and mortar duels raged across various sectors in Jerusalem. About 530 Jews were reported injured in the battle, with mortars and 25 pounder artillery guns used.

The mediator announced that "for the moment" he was fully satisfied with the truce situation in Palestine. Apparently a "general agreement" was reached with the Secretary-General of the Arab League, Azzam Pasha, on the problem of Palestinian refugees. The Arab position was that no peace settlement would be discussed until all refugees from Palestine were allowed to return to their homes.

With the newspaper of the Stern Gang threatening to declare a war of assassination against UN officers in Israel, the Israeli Cabinet met to formulate its attitude to the immigration issue before the mediator arrived for his last tour of Tel- Aviv before preparing his report for the Security Council.

Paraguay issued a decree recognising the State of Israel.

September 8

In an operation which, it was openly acknowledged, would have been impossible to carry out inside the Zionist occupied part of Jerusalem, 15 members of the Stern Gang - including some leaders from Jerusalem - were arrested by Israeli troops and policemen. Arms, ammunition and machinery for printing forged documents were seized. With the imminent visit of the mediator, gone - at least for the time being - was the policy of co-operation with the Stern Gang in the hope that they would soon disperse to various army units.

The gathering had been convened to consider details of a campaign of terrorism should the mediator continue on his present course of action with regard to limiting particular categories of Jewish Zionist immigrants. It followed threats, printed in the terrorists's newspaper *Mivrak*, that UN observers in Palestine, and the British anywhere, would be attacked if the former stopped immigration from Europe and the latter refused to release those detained in Cyprus.

Bernadotte announced that the Arabs had agreed to withdraw from "strong positions" south of Jerusalem. This did not include holy sites covered by demilitarisation plans. Israel rejected the mediator's proposals to extend the present demilitarisation of Jerusalem.

It was announced that the Irgun's Freedom Party had merged with the Revisionists, with former Irgunists gaining control of the party. The agenda of the new party remained the same - a "Jewish State" on both sides of the River Jordan.

Transjordan took the first steps to separate its currency from that of

Palestine.

September 9

The Secretary-General of the Arab League suggested to Count Bernadotte that Jaffa and Haifa should be placed under UN control to help towards a partial solution of the refugee problem. This would allow nearly 200 000 refugees to return to their homes. The added bonus would be that with Haifa under UN control, the oil pipeline could be reopened.

September 10

The Scotsman carried a feature on the views of the Arab League on the current situation following attempts by the Arab states to reorganise their forces in Palestine and to better coordinate their actions at the UN. The Arabs were were not satisfied that the Israelis intended to observe the truce anywhere in Palestine. The feeling was that further military action was needed to establish enough confidence for them to consider a political settlement. The second truce had operated as much to their disadvantage as had the first.

Illegal immigration and import of arms for the Israelis had not been stopped. On several occasions Zionist forces had seized demilitarised points - actions which supported the mediator's view that only an armed international police force could succeed in demilitarising Jerusalem. The mediator's explanation of the Israeli truce violations fell largely on deaf ears with Arab confidence in a settlement steadily decreasing. Recognition of the Israeli state was not on the agenda. Any breach of the precarious truce could lead to an Arab attack on all fronts.

On the refugee issue, relief only sufficient for immediate needs had been procured.

Kibbutz Gazit was established on the land of At Tira in Eastern Galilee.

Golda Myerson presented her credentials at the Kremlin.

September 12

As the "so-called truce" entered its ninth week, The Times "Zionist correspondent" reported the deaths of eight people in "Jewish Jerusalem" following the shelling of the northern part of the city by the Arab Legion. Arab irregulars were reported, by the same source, to have attacked a girls' agricultural training farm in the recently demilitarized zone near Government House. Of Israeli depredations against the Arabs, there was no mention.

Two members of the Russian diplomatic mission to Israel arrived in that part of occupied Jerusalem controlled by Israel to take charge of Russian church properties.

With regard to the return of Palestinian refugees, Israel's Cabinet approved the instructions to their delegation at the UN General Assembly. Without making any reference to Israel's willingness or intention to allow back any proportion of refugees the instructions said "No return before the end of the war save for individual cases; a final solution to the refugee problem as part of a general settlement when peace comes. In informal conversations, the delegation will explain that it were better that the problem be solved by settling the refugees in the neighbouring countries."

September 13

The Special Correspondent for The Scotsman highlighted a new danger which had appeared in the Middle East - that of "loosely-formed association of Arab terrorists gangs of hot-headed xenophobic young men who have sworn to rid their countries of all Westerners . . particularly of British and Americans." Businessmen and reporters with contact in the Jewish community were considered to be particularly at risk.

"The backbone of this new Arab terrorist organisation is provided by young Palestinian Arabs. They have seen their country overrun by the Jews and have lost everything they possessed - homes, property, money, jobs; they have nothing further to lose. They feel they have been let down by the British and the Americans, by the United Nations, and also, to some extent, by the other Arab countries. They now realise that there is a grave danger that the present situation in Palestine, with the Jews in total possession of the best part of the country, will be generally recognised and legalised. They know they cannot fight openly and as an army. But they intend to carry on the fight underground . ."

" . . it is indeed on the analogy of the Jewish terrorists that these same Arab gangs will be formed. And with the same purpose. 'By their outrages in Palestine, Irgun and the Stern drove out the British. Now we will use the same methods to drive the British and the Americans out of the entire Middle East' " a young Arab nationalist observed.

Many had jumped on the band-wagon, espousing the cause of the exiled Palestinian for their own reasons. "The men behind the gangs mean business - and they know their jobs. Many of them, like their counterparts amongst the Jewish terrorists, were trained by British experts in sabotage and tough tactics during the war."

The village of al-'Abbasiyya, east of Jaffa, which first attracted attention on December 13th 1947 (the Jewish holy day of Chanukka) when an attack by the terrorist Irgun left seven adults and children dead, was the subject of discussion at a meeting of the Israeli Cabinet. Ben Gurion, on behalf of General Zvi Ayalon, the commander of the Central Front, asked for permission to destroy the village since, by this time, the Ministerial Committee for Abandoned Property had to approve such requests. Indications are that it was refused, for ten days later a recommendation was made that Zionist immigrants should settle in the Palestinian owned houses - or those that were still standing.

A similar request was made for the destruction of al Safiriyya near Jaffa (granted),Beit Nabala, al Qubab and Qula near Ramleh (decisions not stated but presumed granted). However, as before, the requests were made by Ben Gurion on behalf of the commanding officer, General Zvi Ayalon. Care was taken by Ben Gurion not to have his own name associated with the requests.

Eventually 14 villages were named for at least partial demolition: As Safiriya, Al Haditha, 'innaba, Daniyal, Jimzu, Kafr 'Ana, Al Yahudia, Barfiliya, Al Barriya, Al Qubab, Beit Nabala, Deir Tarif, At Tira, Qula.[4]

Count Bernadotte ordered Israel to allow the villagers from Jaba, Ijzim and Ein Ghazal (who had been expelled during July) to return in order to rebuild both their shattered homes and their shattered lives. Israel refused to comply with the order.

September 14

A number of enquiries were reported to be underway in connection with the disappearance of former RAF aircraft from Britain. In the latest incident, a Halifax was believed to have sunk in the Mediterranean some time in July.

September 15

The military governor of West Jerusalem, Dov Joseph, reported on the housing situation in that part of the city. With 5 000 incomers requiring housing, many broke into empty Palestinian property. Others wanted to improve their conditions and so targeted the deserted and more spacious Arab homes. Israeli officers and soldiers were amongst the offenders, with some looking for additional property to rent. [And by early 1950 these acts of theft were legitimised when the housing authorities authorised almost all squatters, soldier and civilian, to stay in the houses they had stolen.][5]

By mid-September, the looting in West Jerusalem had become institutionalised with the authorities admitting that they were powerless to do anything. A barbed-wire fence was erected around the Baq'a neighbourhood of the city, where those Palestinians remaining in West Jerusalem were concentrated and, in the evenings, under curfew.

The imprisoned Palestinians were preyed upon by Israeli thieves. Groups of Israeli soldiers would burst into Palestinian houses on the pretext of searching for "hidden arms and Arabs" while stealing and extorting from the residents. [It was not until November 1949 that the Baq'a Palestinians were allowed out of their "concentration camp." This was followed by the confiscation of the houses by the Israeli Custodian of Absentee Property whereby many Palestinian owners were regarded as tenants and forced to pay rent to the state of Israel][5].

The two abducted Britons on trial for alleged espionage and assisting the Arabs appeared in a Jerusalem District Court. Both pleaded not guilty.

September 16

Count Bernadotte completed his report in which he strongly supported the right of the refugees to return to their own homes "at the earliest practical date." The report recognised that no "just and complete" settlement was possible if the right of return was not recognised.

"It would be an offence against the principles of elemental justice if these innocent victims of the conflict were denied the right to return to their homes while Jewish immigrants flow into Palestine and, indeed, at least offer the threat of permanent replacement of the Arab refugees."

With increasing Zionist immigration into Palestine very much a reality, with the destruction of so many villages, the report recognised the complexity of the situation: "It must not be supposed that the establishment of the right of refugees to return . . . provides solution of the problem. The vast majority of the refugees may no longer have homes to return to and their re-establishment in the State of Israel presents an economic and social problem of special complexity."

The ninety page report proposed that Jerusalem should be internationalised; the Negev and Lydda-Ramleh would be part of an Arab state which would include Transjordan and the eventual West Bank. The entire Galilee area, including those parts still in Arab hands, would be given to

Israel. The report reaffirmed the cause of the Palestinian exodus "as a result of the conflict in Palestine almost the whole of the Arab population fled or was expelled from the area under Jewish occupation." A significant omission was reference to orders by Arab leaders to the Palestinians to quit their homes - the excuse, favoured by Zionists and their apologists, which no matter how false, somehow absolves them from responsibility.

The report made it quite clear that the mediator was aware of the wide-scale pillaging and destruction of Arab homes and property. He noted "numerous reports from reliable sources of large-scale looting, pillage and plundering and destruction of villages without apparent military necessity." He was insistent in reaffirming Israeli liability "to restore private property to its Arab owners and to indemnify those owners of property wantonly destroyed."

The political and military establishments within Israel appeared to be at variance with each other as regards the intent of the Arab forces. The latter was reported to be of the view that the Arab forces were preparing for an attack. Intelligence reports stated that re-equipping, reinforcing and improving positions indicated the imminence of an attack. The former took the opposite interpretation of events.

The mediator's military adviser, General Lundstrom, advised Israel's foreign minister that any military movement was in preparation for the onset of winter and for ensuring readiness in the event of Zionist forces undertaking unilateral military action. The Israeli response was to complain that the UN observers were not doing their job properly.

September 17

Count Bernadotte arrived at the small Arab airport of Kalandia, to the north of Jerusalem. He met an Arab Legion brigadier for about an hour in Ramallah. Two loud explosions shook the area resulting, it was later found out, from Israeli actions in the Mount Zion sector.

He disregarded Chief of Staff General Lundstrom's advice that his unarmed motorcade should not pass from Arab into Zionist zones since it was common practice for the Israelis to fire on vehicles making this journey. He wanted to take the same risks as his observers. This he did when his motor was fired upon from the direction of Hadassah Hospital on Mount Scopus.

Following lunch with the governor of the Zionist occupied part of Jerusalem, he proceeded to inspect various UN and Red Cross facilities in this sector of the city. In the Qatamon quarter the three UN vehicles, clearly identified as such, were flagged down by a group of men wearing the uniform associated with the Israeli army. One of the men sprayed bullets at point blank range at the mediator. Both he and Colonel Serot of France, who had vainly tried to shield the Count with his body, were shot dead.

Despite promises of "diligent and unrelenting pursuit" of those responsible for the assassination by Colonel Moshe Dayan, and the rounding up of the 'usual suspects' on the orders of Ben Gurion, no real effort was made. Claims of responsibility by a fictitious terrorist group fooled no one. The Stern Gang was held responsible but no effort made to prove it. Those responsible for the planning and execution of the assassination were never brought to justice, in spite of the fact that some later revealed their involvement.

Seventeen years after the death of Count Bernadotte, a biographer of Ben Gurion approached the former premier with name of one of Bernadotte's possible assassins. It turned out that the named person, Yehoshua Cohen, was a friend of Ben Gurion. On being questioned by Ben Gurion, Cohen confessed to being one of the assassins. There was no question of Ben Gurion being appalled by the action of this former terrorist. No question of Cohen being exposed or put on trial in an international court. They grew closer, united by friendship and a common secret.[6]

Principal amongst Cohen's co-conspirators was Yitzhak Ysenitsky, later to be known as Yitzhak Shamir. In common with his fellow conspirators and murderers, this act of assassination of a diplomat who had done so much to help those who had suffered during the Second World War and those who were now suffering at the hands of some of the victims of this war, Shamir's career in public and political life in Israel was never adversely affected.

The background of terrorism against Palestinian civilians has never been a barrier to acceptance within the Israeli military establishment or, indeed, Israeli society.And this acceptance reached the highest echelons of politics and society. Shamir's service as Foreign Minister, under the former Irgun terrorist boss, Menachem Begin as Prime Minister of Israel, was followed by his ascendency to power in the same post.

Yet Shamir, was one of triumverate who headed the Stern Gang at the time of Count Bernadotte's assassination. It was his casting vote that decided the mediator's fate.[6]

[The life and work of Count Folke Bernadotte, in the end, seemed to count for nothing in the eyes of the international community. Those in positions of responsibility must answer for the inaction in bringing the murderers to justice - and for subsequent events in Palestine. Maybe, with hindsight, the provisional government of Israel had the correct perspective of the situation when it was insensitive enough to submit a bill to the UN for 150 Israeli pounds to cover the cost of the post-mortem and embalming of the peace mediator. This for an act of murder carried out by Israeli citizens in an area under Israeli jurisdiction[8].]

Dr Ralph Bunche, chief of the UN Palestine secretariat, assumed complete charge of the "Holy Land mission."

Commandant of the Transjordan army, Brigadier JB Glubb, issued a statement before the news of Bernadotte's death. Referring to the interests of Russia in the Middle East he commented that "Israel seems to be able to make the best of both worlds. The large financial subsidies which she receives from America she spends on buying arms from Russia and her satellites."

Referring to Britain the point is made that "Although Britain has evacuated Palestine, she cannot disclaim all responsibility. After all it was she who inaugarated the policy which has brought Palestine to this desperate pass."[9]

September 18

In Acre, following a period of caution deemed necessary because of the presence of some 5 000 Palestinians who had remained, the Custodian for Absentee Property along with Ben Gurion took the decision to settle immigrant Jews in the city.

By 22 November there were some 2 000 settlers in Acre.[10]

September 19

The Israeli cabinet approved emergency laws banning membership of, and providing assistance to, Jewish Zionist terrorist groups. A curfew on the Zionist occupied section of Jerusalem was lifted, with raids, searches and questioning continuing. The Stern Gang HQ in the Talbieh district of the city was raided with scores of people, including teenagers, rounded up. Included in the round-up was Norman Nahum Nimri who worked in an intelligence branch of the British army HQ, as a specialist on Arab affairs while, at the same time, holding a top-ranking post in the Stern Gang.

Interrogations appeared to have been superficial since detainees were already being pressed into service in the Israeli army and dispersed. While the Stern Gang denied all responsibility for the murder of Bernadotte, blaming it on a splinter group called the "Fatherland Front", members of the terrorist group were reported to be seeking out any witnesses to the assassination - ostensibly to see if they had recognised the killers.

Dr Bunche, now in charge of the UN mission in Palestine, placed responsibility for the mediator's death squarely at the door of the Israeli government. Referring to "prejudicial and unfounded statements" concerning truce supervision at an earlier press conference, he felt that they could have encouraged the callous attack on Count Bernadotte.

In Jerusalem, an Israeli report said that Ein Shemer airport was shelled by Arab forces. An armoured car attack nearby was repulsed. Arab sappers had laid explosive devices against the wall of Notre Dame Hospice, an Israeli forward position, damaging the wall and injuring two soldiers. Israeli positions on Mount Zion were shelled.

The government of Panama cancelled the registration of 10 planes involved in the shipping of illegal arms, pilots and mechanics beween Czechoslovakia and the Arab states.

September 20

Count Bernadotte's report on his mediation efforts, where "reason and persuasion" had failed, was published. He believed that the time had come for the General Assembly to take firm action. At this point such action, he felt, would not be "forcibly resisted."

The report suggested that the present truce be replaced by a formal peace, or at least an armistice demobilising armed forces on both sides. Frontiers should be delimited by a boundaries commission under the authority of the UN. Haifa should be declared a free port and Lydda a free airport. Jerusalem should be placed under effective UN control, the Holy places protected with free access to all. A special conciliation commission should be set up by the UN.

A list of basic premises was given. These included "A Jewish State called Israel exists in Palestine, and there are no sound reasons for assuming that it will not continue to do so." He added that "the rights of innocent people, uprooted from their homes, to return to them should be affirmed and made effective, with assurance of adequate compensation for the property of those who may choose not to return."

International guarantees with regard to boundaries and human rights should be stressed. It was acknowledged that implementation of the proposals would not be easy but he felt that both sides would agree "however reluctantly" to any reasonable settlement carrying the stamp of the UN. He continues "What is indispensable is that the General Assembly take a firm position on the political aspects of the problem in the light of all the circumstances since its last session, and that its resolution be so reasonable as to discourage any attempt to thwart it and to defy the Security Council order by the use of armed force. I do not conclude that the problem of Palestine is insoluble by peaceful means, or that a basis for agreement cannot ultimately be found. But the conclusion is inescapable that at some juncture vital decisions will have to be made by the General Assembly if a peaceful settlement is to be achieved. I am firmly convinced, after the most careful appraisal, that this juncture has now been reached."[11]

Extra guards were in place around the US Consulate following reports that the US Consul-General, Mr John Macdonald, was next on the terrorists' list.

The Stern Gang was outlawed by the Israeli provisional government and declared an "illegal organisation."

King Abdullah of TransJordan told the Arab League that he would oppose the establishment of a Palestine Arab Government. Should it be recognised ". . it would mean that the Arab League had accomplished partition, which it fought against."

September 21

The round up of Stern Gang members continued but with no confirmation of the numbers involved. Estimates ranged from 300 to 400.

The Irgun accepted the 24 hour ultimatum to disband all its armed forces, give up its weapons and instruct its members, believed to number 2 000, to report for recruitment into the Israeli army. An Irgun spokesman, in attacking the provisional government for its action, said that the terms had been accepted "In principle . . . to prevent civil war and unnecessary bloodshed." It was pointed out that Ben Gurion had yet to face his first democratic election. "They will learn then that a regime founded on lies and the fist is destined to be short-lived" was the rather ironic comment from this terrorist organisation.

There was a bonus for the Irgun members. This was the promise that the government would not act against them for terrorist actions committed before the proclamation of the Zionist state on 14 May.

The settlement of Barriya Bet was established on the land of Al Barriya, southeast of Ramleh. However it was reported that the settlers abandoned the site for "lack of motivation" apparently preferring "the seeming comforts of town."[12]

September 22

An Israeli convoy escorting UN observers was ambushed in the Latrun area. Four deaths were reported, three of which were reported to be Jewish, one American. The Arab Legion denied Israeli accusations of responsibility, placing the blame on the actions of "irregulars."

The Arab Higher Committee announced the formation of a "Palestine Government" in Gaza.

The Scotsman correspondent, Clare Hollingworth, reported on the situation facing the refugees - spread between those parts of Palestine under Arab control and neighbouring Arab countries. They left their homes in fear and now lived in "destitution and utter misery."

With winter approaching, and in the absence of large-scale assistance, tens of thousands could die.The gap between the temperatures for nine months of the year, and those of the remaining three, is considerable. Palestinians are more organised for the nine months, even apart from the fact that, for many refugees, the few belongings with which they fled had been long discarded.

Any thought of returning home had been long dispelled by the oft repeated Israeli radio broadcasts informing them that they would not be allowed to return to their homes and property. As winter closed in, those refugees in the cold areas were expected to descend to the warmer Jordan Valley where the small town of Jericho would bear the brunt. If this had to happen, the town would be totally overwhelmed. Tens of thousands of distressed and destitute refugees could be expected to arrive. Given the best will and organisation in the world, the Arab states - who do not always have enough to satisfy the needs of their own people - will not be able to cope.

The refugee camps were considered to be "hotbeds of discontent", with people "let down" first by the British and then by the Arab League. Middle class refugees - those who had lost jobs, homes, property and personal wealth - were felt to be particularly prone to heightened grievances. Not helped by the fact that Britain had failed to make arrangements for payments of salaries, gratuities and pensions, many were in possession of cheques issued by the Government of Palestine upon banks whose doors had closed before the cheques were signed.

It was from the ranks of those educated and formerly well-off refugees that "the leaders of Arab terrorist gangs will come - are indeed coming."

The article concluded with a bitter comment from Azzam Pasha of the Arab League "that he did not expect the great Christian Powers to do anything for Moslem Arab refugees; he had thought, however, that they might have made at least some effort to help thousands of homeless Christian Arabs who had been forced to flee by the Jewish terror."

September 23

A passenger plane, from Beirut to Amman, carrying the Daily Telegraph and The Scotsman correspondent, David Woodford together with John Nixon, the BBC correspondent in the Middle East, was shot down by an Israeli plane over Tiberias. The two correspondents and an Arab passenger were killed as they jumped out of the plane on its approach to the crash landing.

Reports indicated that the Israeli plane had pursued the stricken plane for about 18 miles until it crashed. Iraqi Army HQ said the Israeli plane was showing a Red Cross and so avoided "interference." The passenger plane was apparently following a route fixed by UN observers and painted orange to identify it as a passenger plane.

The provisional government of Israel rejected the territorial proposals in Count Bernadotte's report. The right to consider Jerusalem "as part of Israel" was claimed. The issue of the recognition of the Palestinian right of return was simply ignored. Meanwhile, senior Israeli diplomats, Michael Comay met with Bernadotte's successor, Ralph Bunche and two of his aides, in Haifa for a two day deliberation on the question of the return of the refugees.

A recommendation was made to the Military Government Committee to settle new immigrants in "abandoned" villages, in the Arab owned houses. Initially selected were the villages of 'Aqir, Sarafand al Kharab, Beit Dajan, Al Yahudiya, Zarnuqa, Kafr 'Ana and Abu Kishk - all in the Tel Aviv/Ramleh area.

September 24

Midya Height, six miles from Lydda, was reported to have changed hands twice during the day following fighting between the Israelis and the Arab Legion. The Israeli road which bypassed the Latrun was under constant shell-fire as was the Arab supply route in this sector, the Latrun-Ramallah highway.

September 26

Dr Bunche, acting mediator, called on Israel and the Arab Legion to cease fire on all fronts and restore the status quo as it existed before the second truce. This appeal took place as fighting erupted in various sectors, particularly Jerusalem and al Midiar. Machine gun fire intruded into a one minute silence at a memorial service for the slain mediator.

Ramallah radio severely criticised the mediator's proposals, blaming the Arab states for trusting Britain. "You have sold us for American dollars" was the accusation levelled at Britain.

No progress was reported in the search for Count Bernadotte's murderers. A "curious blanket of silence" had been drawn over the investigations. For some reason the government had been counting on a public willing to assist in catching members of a terrorist organisation with which many had sympathy and were willing to support.

The "stringent" measures against terrorist groups, announced by the provisional government, failed to materialise. The majority of the Stern Gang, including its leaders, were still at large. Dissolution of the Irgun turned out to be a tactical compromise. The organisation still existed, albeit under the guise of the "Freedom Movement" and under the same "fanatical leader, Menachem Beigin."

The General Council of the International Refugee Organisation decided that they could not give aid to the 300 000 refugees in Palestine. It was felt that its present resources were inadequate to cope.

In its first comment since the plane crash which killed the three passengers, the Israelis said an investigation was in process. The Soviet news agency, Tass, said that it had been "authorised to deny as utterly false" the report that a Soviet Yak fighter in Israeli hands had brought down the aircraft.

Earlier, in reply to a question regarding the fate of the Palestinian civilian population should the Israeli army overrun populated areas, Ben Gurion's answer had been "vague and misleading." He was now, however, forthright when he addressed the Cabinet on the same issue. Should fighting be renewed in the north, the Galilee, he had been assured by his generals, would become "clean" and "empty" of Arabs.[13]

On this day, Ben Gurion also met with Yosef Weitz where the latter raised the question of Palestinian refugees in northern Galilee, an area still held by the Arab Liberation Army. Weitz painted a scenario where if these refugees were to be joined by those in Syria and Lebanon and the area was then to transfer to Israeli rule - as envisaged under Bernadotte's plan - then there would be a great many refugees to be absorbed by Israel.

The solution, as proposed by Weitz, was to "harass" those refugees and others in the Faluja area into moving into the Lebanon and territory held by Transjordan. Such a policy would be effected by Weitz's Transfer Committee with financial inducements being offered to Syrian and Lebanese gendarmerie in order to procure their assistance.

According to Weitz, Ben Gurion took note of his proposal and "promised to act in accordance with it."[14]

Kibbutz Hagoshrim was established next to the "abandoned" village of Khisas.

September 27

The Israeli delegation to the UN General Assembly was apprised of the result of the recent meeting with Bunche in Haifa.The murdered mediator's commitment to securing the recognition of the refugees' right of return was reaffirmed, however the subjective views of this particular group of interlocutors was allowed to prevail. Apparently "they were all of the opinion that for the most part the Arabs did not want to go back and live under Jewish domination." The Palestinian middle-class "exiles" were deemed to be unenthusiastic about returning to their homeland and once the villagers returned, they would no doubt "drift off again when they saw some of the things that were alleged to be going on in Israel, such as destruction of villages and taking over of the land."

In support of this position the thoughts of Count Bernadotte were resurrected. Apparently he had retreated from his original position of a general return of refugees and was prepared to argue for a partial return on political and humanitarian grounds. The burden of solving the refugee problem was to be placed on surrounding Arab states.[15]

While this position was never stated in the mediator's report, the idea of a mass return was successsfully put on the back-burner. Zionism was very much in the ascendancy.

It was reported that the Arab delegation to the UN General Assembly had been instructed to oppose Count Bernadotte's proposals and to reject any compromise which did not provide for an independent free Arab State for Palestine.

Brigadier General William Riley accused Transjordan Arab forces of the responsibility for firing on the Israeli convoy in company with UN observers five days earlier. The death of four Jewish escort personnel was described as a "massacre".

Meanwhile the provisional government of Israel gave its version of the shooting down of the civilian plane which killed 3 people, including two journalists. Apparently an Arab aircraft, similar to the one shot down, had been making daily reconnaissance flights, daily for two weeks, over the area. On the day of the shooting, an aircraft , identified as Arab, was observed flying back and forward over the Israeli lines in the Safad area. The plane was alleged to have ignored the approved international signals for it to land. When it tried to fly away it was shot down.

The settlement of Beit Meir was established at Beit Mahsir in the Jerusalem corridor.

September 28

Israeli press and media made a return to commenting on the need to resort to force of arms now that the murder of Count Bernadotte was receding into the past. In what The Scotsman referred to as "an obviously inspired Press campaign" the media, while accusing British policy in the Middle East as having "sinister anti-Jewish motives", condemned Count Bernadotte's proposals. The line taken was that the proposals were an attempt to sacrifice Israel in a new "Munich" under the cover of international tension.

September 29

One of the two Britons on trial for espionage was acquitted because of the lack of evidence.

The Moscow journal, New Times, claimed that British Intelligence operatives may have assassinated Count Bernadotte. Possibly part of a plot to free Britain's hands at the UN General Assembly and to discredit Israel.

The first meeting of the UN Political and Security Commission helped to put a few more nails into the coffin of Palestine's immediate future. With Britain accusing the Russians, with the support of Yugoslavia, of trying to use the committee for propaganda purposes, the agenda was finally fixed after three hours of wrangling. Palestine was third out of six items.

Hector McNeil, the British representative, who had argued that "No topic is so urgent as the maintenance of peace." registered his disapproval by reflecting that the poor land of Palestine would suffer while the committee was subject to weeks of propaganda (concerning atomic energy and arms reduction, the first two items on the agenda).

September 30

Nathan Friedman Yellin, leader of the Stern Gang and successor to its founder, Abrahem Stern, was arrested in Haifa. Yellin had disappeared the day before the Count was assassinated: His operations commander, Matatiahu Shmulevitz, was also arrested. Both were in possession of a variety of forged and other documents and were believed to be awaiting to leave the country.

The Scotsman reported that some of the documents found linked the terrorists' chain of command to Moscow. A diplomatic source stated that six "mysterious" visas were issued by an Eastern European Government consulate in Jerusalem the day after the mediator was murdered.

Apart from these two arrested, the other 250 Sternists arrested were reported to be of little importance within the organisation. The £5 000 reward offered for information leading to the arrest of the murderers was in no danger of being claimed.

Four military courts had been set up but apparently the prisoners had refused to be interrogated - except those who claimed wrongful arrest. The prisoners were reported as being "defiant, abusive and are imbued with a strong gang spirit." In Jaffa gaol, with its steel doors and bars torn off the walls, the military police guards were reported to be "obviously afraid" of the Stern prisoners and not able to control them. So much so that The Times correspondent was refused access.

Around this date, and into the first few days of October, two 'clearing' operations were launched by the Yiftach Brigade's 3rd Battalion and a unit of the 1st Battalion affecting the area defined by Kibbutz Tze'elim, Mishmar Hanegev and al 'Imara. It was alleged that "enemy civilians . . had begun a partisan operation blowing up the water pipeline, mining the road and hitting our people." "All the Arabs were expelled," their livestock 'confiscated' and the village wells blown up.[16]

The settlement of Ameilim was established on the land of Abu Shusha, southeast of Ramleh.

Notes

1 Benny Morris, *The birth of the Palestinian refugee problem, 1947-49*, p.152
2 *ibid* p.166
3 *ibid* p.191
4 *ibid* p.165
5 Nathan Krystall, *The De-Arabisation of West Jerusalem 1947-50* (JoPS, Winter 1998) p.16
6 Michael Bar-Zohar, *Ben Gurion*, p.181
7 Amitzur Ilan, *Bernadotte in Palestine,1948* (Middle East International 3/8/90)
8 Michael Palumbo, *The Palestinian Catastrophe*, p.160
9 The Scotsman 20/10/48
10 Morris, p.192
11 The Scotsman 21/10/48
12 Walid Khalidi, *All that Remains*, p.363
13 Morris, p.218

14 Benny Morris, *Falsifying the Record*, p.52 (Journal of Palestine Studies, Spring, 1995)
15 Benny Morris, *The birth of the Palestinian refugee problem, 1947-49*, p.153
16 *ibid* p.214

October

This is something that determines the character of a nation . . . . Jews too have committed Nazi acts.

Aharon Zisling, Israeli Minister of Agriculture

In the United Nations, Israel adopted the position that the murdered mediator's report did not even provide a basis for discussion. However, as subsequently emerged, she had no desire to seek peace. With an army of 70 000, plans were prepared to expand the boundaries of the new state by force of arms. And the coming offensives were to be more brutal than previously.

To the north, in the Galilee, and in southern Palestine, towns and villages which were prepared to surrender peacefully were subjected to Israeli criminal brutality. The reasons were various. It was no longer sufficient, as had previously happened in the Galilee, for Jewish dignitaries to whisper in the ear of their Palestinian Arab counterpart in order to stimulate an outflow of humanity from the villages before the Zionists arrived. Many who had fled then thought that they would be returning soon. By October, they realised that if they left their homes it would be for good.

With the Upper Galilee now home to many refugees from Acre, Safed and other towns, the realisation that you should resist expulsion and not give way to terror tactics was reinforced. In addition the treatment and condition of refugees in Palestine and the Arab states was widely known and did not make pleasant reading.

Yet, the Israelis wanted "Arab free" land.

Two operations to help achieve this objective were carried out simultaneously. Operation Yoav (initially named Operation Ten Plagues) in the south and Operation ha-Har in the southern part of the Jerusalem corridor. In the latter Operation, the intention was to denude the villages of their inhabitants to widen the corridor connecting Jerusalem to the territory occupied in the Hebron hills. Thousands of people were eventually "displaced." Shelter was sought by refugees in neighbouring valleys and caves until further expulsions by Israeli forces moved them on.

Patrols were sent out to the Hebron hills to keep the fleeing Palestinian civilians on the move, to ensure that they made no attempt to return to their land and their hilltop villages. One account was given in a Palmach report by a woman soldier "Aviva R":

"Scattered in the gulley, sitting in craters and caves....[were] dozens of

> refugees..... .We surprised them. A cry of fear cut through the air..... . They began to praise us and dispense compliments about the Jewish army, the State of Israel. With what obsequiousness! Old men bowing, genuflecting, kissing our feet and begging for mercy; young men standing with bowed heads and helpless .... . We tried to persuade them to flee towards Hebron. We fired several shots in the air - and the people [ie the refugees] were indifferent. 'Better that we die here than return [to Egyptian-held territory] to die at the hands of the Egyptians.' We fired again. No one moved. Tiredness and hunger deprived them of any will to live and of any human dignity. These are the Arabs of the Hebron Hills, and is it possible that this youngster, or that man, shed the blood of the 35 or looted the Etzion bloc - but can one take revenge here? You can fight against people of your own worth, but against this 'human dust?' We turned back and returned [to our base] ... That evening for the first time during the whole war I felt I was tired. My soul had grown weary of this war."[1]

Another undated account, but referring to the same period came from a farmer, Mahmoud Abu Ghayyon, whose village lay in the path of an Israeli attack. When the attack started most people were in the village mosque.

> "The Jews entered the mosque and slaughtered without mercy 100-150 people including old people, women and children. . . . Some twenty to thirty families sought shelter in a cave. The Jews found them there and shot them all." One woman, left for dead amongst the pile of bodies, survived.[2]

The dehumanising of the Palestinian villager is very much evident in these accounts. With such an attitude, the blitz on the Palestinian civilian population, the subsequent atrocities committed against them, all must have been second nature for too many Israeli soldiers.

With no documentary evidence available showing that Operation Yoav's commander and OC Southern Command, Yigal Allon, issued expulsion orders, Israeli historian Benny Morris postulated " . . it is quite possible that he indicated his wishes in pre-battle tete-a-tetes with his officers"[3]

In the closing months of 1948, the nature of the Israeli war-machine changed. With telling impact it deployed a small number of tanks, bombers and fighting bombers with strafing capacity together with a lot of field artillery. Although not particularly accurate, the rural villages bearing the brunt of the attacks were not prepared for the offensives - neither psychologically nor with defensive structures in place.

The end result was that the villagers under attack were either expelled or fled in the face of the impending attack. This change in tactic coincided with a shift in the thinking with regard to the fate of the emptied villages. Renovation, for the purpose of housing Jewish immigrants, rather than destruction, began to dominate the strategic thinking of the founders of the state of Israel.

October 1

In the Negev small bedouin encampments and villages, east of the line from Al Imara to Ze'elim, were blown up or burned during the first days of October.

October 2

The Scotsman's Special Correspondent gave an overview of the place of the Stern Gang and terrorism in the Israeli state, arguing that it was a matter of changing the outlook of considerable sections of the population. It was not simply a matter of distributing the terrorist members about the armed forces. It was a psychological problem.The "philosophy of terrorism" induced during the mandate days had to adapt and change to the new conditions. The government was no longer the enemy.

Apparently there was "genuine surprise" that the Jewish police were prepared to arrest other Jews, in contrast to the view that a Jew always protects any "hunted Jew." It was widely acknowledged that until the arrest of Yellin and his lieutenant the two to three hundred Stern Gang members arrested were small fry, consisting of large numbers of teenage boys and girls.

In echoes of more recent times, when Israeli prime minister Yitzhak Rabin was murdered by an Israeli right-wing zealot, the point was made that there was still a group of "pathological fanatics" at large who believed, for example, that the death of Ben Gurion could save "the Jewish people." Threats were still being made by the Stern Gang against members of the government, foreigners and UN observers. The American Consul-General had stopped his habit of taking his daughter for an evening walk.

The article comes to the interesting conclusion that one way of eradicating this acknowledged pro-terrorist sentiment in Israeli society would be the inclusion of "Jewish Jerusalem" in Israel. In other words, it would seem that the answer was to give the terrorists and their sympathisers all that they wanted.

October 3

For the first time the Stern Gang admitted responsibility for the assassination of Count Folke Bernadotte. Further threats were made to "all other foreigners in Palestine who impede and try to govern Israel."

Palestine's Chief Rabbi, Dr Isaac Halevy Herzog, on the day of the Jewish New Year said, in his broadcast, "Dissension, internal conflict, and lack of public discipline will act as rot in our young state."

Israel stated that she will oppose any UN plan to separate the Negev in southern Palestine from the other territory controlled by Israel. Four UN observers came under Egyptian fire as they inspected former Zionist held positions near the de-militarised Government House south of Jerusalem.

October 6

Israeli foreign minister, Moshe Shertok, said that the Bernadotte report on Palestine was unacceptable. He did not believe that the whole of Jerusalem should be internationalised. The "modern" part occupied by Israel should be incorporated within the Israeli state. Having occupied the Galilee, it was now considered indispensable to Israel and it was no substitute for the Negev.

It was reported that six of the seven Arab League states were expected to recognise the new Palestine Arab Government over the weekend. Trans-jordan was one of those still witholding recognition. A "supreme appeal to United Nations delegations for a Palestine solution based on wisdom, justice and peace" was issued by all Arab delegations. The statement call-ed for a single sovereign state, without partition, as the only solution.

The sole remaining Briton abducted on various charges had the charge of conspiracy to blow up Ben Yehuda Street on 22 February dropped.

Operation Ten Plagues, against the Egyptians in Southern Palestine, was approved by Ben Gurion at an Israeli Cabinet meeting.

October 7

Sir Raphael Cilento of the UN Palestine Relief Organisation said he was "greatly disturbed" by the conditions of the Palestinian refugees. With the onset of winter the conditions had worsened, particularly in the north. He gave a figure of 650 000 refugees in need. Surprise was expressed that the International Refugee Organisation had made no effort to organise aid for the refugees.

Already there were outbreaks of smallpox among the refugees in Syria and Lebanon.Typhoid, dysentry and malaria were widespread. Measles followed by pneumonia was taking a large toll of lives among the children.

Under the headline " 'Comedy' Prison in Jaffa", The Scotsman's Special Correspondent described the travesty of prison life in "Ben Gurion's Bastille." With uncertainty concerning the number detained (after all the prison had an "emigration office") - about 190, including 25 women and girls with about 50 prisoners aged between 14 and 17 - the prisoners considered themselves not so much as in prison, but under a siege imposed by Ben Gurion. The Stern Gang prisoners moved about freely. No door or bar in the cell windows remained intact.

The unhindered communal life, under the eye of tommy gun toting guards, was not regarded as that of criminals. They considered that no offences had been committed so they refused to answer questions when interrogated. When the prison had been smashed up it was regarded as the start of the storming of Ben Gurion's Bastille. In the meantime various education programmes were in the offing. In the evening there was Jewish folk dancing where the gaolers provided the music and participated in the dancing.

October 8

Frederick William Sylvester, an employee of the Jerusalem Electricity Corporation, the last Briton abducted by the Irgun, was sentenced by an Israeli district court to seven years imprisonment on three charges of espionage.The sentence, which apparently surprised "even the most virulently anti-British elements", was given for transmitting, on Sylvester's own admission, information to the British Consulate that shells aimed at the power station were well off their mark and that the station was still functioning.

While admitting that the possession of the transmitter was no secret - apparently it was only the Israeli authorities who were not aware of its existence - the judge quoted from the annals of famous British espionage cases. "To the amazement of the public" he concluded by citing the Nuremberg judgements for similar offences.

Kibbutz Ga'aton was established was established on the land of Khirbet Shifiya in Western Galilee.

October 9

Stern Gang prisoners seized control of Jaffa Prison. It was reported that 187 prisoners escaped. Those who remained, about 80 men and women, gained control of the prison. They were reported to have "forcibly entertained" their gaolers to coffee and beer in a neighbouring cafe, gone for a swim in the sea and held a press conference in the prison compound.

October 10

With further arrests made of the Stern Gang's so-called "Fatherland Front", which claimed responsibility for Bernadotte's assassination, security was stepped up around the HQ of the UN observer teams and the US Consulate. Places of entertainment were placed out of bounds to all UN personnel, most of whom were Americans. In Haifa details were released of 14 alleged truce violations. Ten involved the shooting of UN personnel. Of the 14, six were ascribed to Zionist actions, the rest were laid at the door of the Arabs.

The suburbs of "Jewish Jerusalem" were shelled in the morning. Egyptian planes were reported to have bombed three colonial settlements in the Negev during attacks which started two day previously.The Israelis challenged the UN authority when it informed the UN truce supervisory board that it would not accept its decisions on truce violations unless Israeli army representatives were first allowed to answer the charges.

The British delegation to the UN expressed concern, shared by other delegates, at the apparent lack of interest by the Security Council in reports from Palestine of alleged truce violations.

Of the Stern Gang prisoners who escaped from Jaffa Prison, 40 were reported to be still at large. The whole episode, on the one hand, had all the elements of a farce. The mass of troops and police called into find the escapees actually prevented some from returning.They were not allowed through the cordon because they did not have the necessary pass with which to enter a prohibited area. This followed a seven hour period immediately prior to the break-out when the Israeli army, which formed the cordon, had still not approached the prison. On the streets outside the prison, the more "lawabiding" Sternists were chatting to their friends.

On the other hand it was an excellent example of the way the then Israeli society and government tolerated those who took the law into their own hands, as long as the victims were not perceived to be a danger to Zionist interests or aspirations. Fifty years on we only have to compare the treatment of Palestinians alleged to be a danger to, or to have offended against, the interests of the Zionist state and those very few Israeli Jews who have ever appeared in court on charges related to the brutalisation or murder of any Palestinian, to see that things have not changed.

On this day, fifty years ago, a senior Israeli police official proclaimed to The Times Special Correspondent that the escape was not important. The authorities had not intended to detain the prisoners for long. It was unimportant if they took arms with them because they had plenty hidden away and "they would never shoot Jews, although they might kill non-Jews."

By this date the the Israeli Agricultural Ministry had formally leased or approved the leasing of 80 000 acres of "abandoned" land with approval awaited for a further 20 000 acres.

October 11

The New York Times reported that the village of Ijlil al Qibliyya, to the north of Acre, from which the villagers had fled on 3 April, was now an internment camp for Arab prisoners. It contained about 2 500 detainees. Apparently "not even the camp authorities are certain how many of [the prisoners] actually were soldiers in the Arab armies." However it was reported that all, except 250, were Palestinians exiled from their home village.

The settlement of Kesalon was established on the land of Kasla in the Jerusalem corridor.

October 12

The Special Correspondent of The Times wrote on the "Future of the Negeb" where aerial bombardment by the Egyptians and ground fighting was diminishing, with localised fighting dominating. Israeli military control of the area was reported to be superficial and the purpose of the recent offensive by the Egyptians was seen to be an attempt to clear the northern part of Israelis before the UN is brought in to adjudicate. The future of the area was further complicated, according to the article, by "dissension among the Arab states and the recent crystallisation of their individual territorial ambitions."

The article praised the "pioneering spirit" of the members of the left-wing Mapam party who were deemed to have established the "best agricultural settlements in Israel and most of those in the Negeb." Conveniently forgotten were the efforts of the indigenous Palestinian people whose land was in the process of being occupied. Who were being terrorised into fleeing the land they and their forebears had tilled for generations, in some cases stretching back to Biblical times. It was not always the desert that these Mapam members made "bloom", but existing cultivated land.

October 13

Four UN officers of the Special Investigating Team for the Negev, headed by Col Gerald De Greer, arrived to check on the status of any Arab civilians who might be left in villages occupied by the Israelis. "We emptied the villages where the population had a hostile attitude towards us." was the reply given to the question as to why the Israelis had expelled so many civilians.

The Team was unable to visit those villages where Israeli atrocities had been reported beacause they were, allegedly, blocked by minefields. The presence of these minefields around emptied villages was a feature of the Negev. "It's necessary to stop the Arab population from returning at night." was the reply given when asked why so many "abandoned" villages were surrounded by minefields.

As De Greer and his Team travelled to visit an Arab village supposedly intact and living peacefully under Israeli rule, the desolation of the area was apparent. Harvests were rotting on the vine; some villages had been demolished and others had new occupiers - Jewish Zionist immigrants; some new settlements had been established. Eventually the Team was shown, at a distance of about two kilometres, a tented village alleged to be Bedouin Arab encamped next to a settlement. A local UN observer later confirmed that the "villagers" in the tents had been Jewish immigrants.

In their report, the four investigators unanimously concluded that "lands have been taken quite unlawfully from the Arab population which was compelled to leave their villages."
It was noted that "we did not meet one Arab civilian." Force had been used to drive them out and force would be used to keep them out.

The investigators then moved into Egyptian held territory where about 175 000 refugees were living in all kinds of makeshift shelters, exposed to the elements. It was noted that child mortality rates were very high. The children were particularly vulnerable to exposure and the resulting sores. Many of the refugees had been driven from their homes in southern Palestine during the first truce at the end of June. They had been robbed of their land and cattle. The villagers had been "driven from their areas by Jewish mortar, machine gun and rifle fire. . . This Jewish action happened when no armed resistance was offered to their forces."[4]

October 14

With the imminent debate at committee stage on Bernadotte's proposals for Palestine, attempts were made by the Arab parties to have it postponed until after the presidential elections in the United States. The feeling was that such a postponement would be to their advantage.

In a joint resolution to the Security Council, Britain and China called upon the Arab and Israeli authorities in Palestine to cooperate fully with the UN observers and other truce supervision officers (since 11 June six had been killed and seven wounded). Sir Alexander Cadogan added "Elements in Palestine are seeking to eliminate the United Nations from the country altogether." The resolution also called upon the provisional Israeli government for an early report into its investigation of the murder of the mediator.

Sir Alexander, referring to statements from the Truce Commission, said that a deliberate campaign to discredit the UN and the Commission in the eyes of the Jewish community was being led by Dr Bernard Joseph, military governor of that part of Jerusalem occupied by the Israelis. It resembled the animosity raised against Count Bernadotte.

Israel responded, denying everything and alleging that terrorist activities were a legacy from British rule and that the truce worked to the advantage of the Arabs. In response, Syria pointed out that neither Europe nor America was permitted to export arms to Arab States, while Israel benefited from the hundreds of millions of dollars collected in the US and used to purchase armaments from Eastern and Central Europe. In addition, arms were received directly from America. Observers in Palestine knew of this but under the terms of their instructions could do nothing to stop it.

The Scotsman reported on a spate of burglaries, hold-ups and robbery with violence within the new state. Haifa and Tel Aviv were suffering from an epidemic of car theft. Blame was placed on soldiers on leave with the authorities being accused of reluctance to take action and the police slow to respond to appeals for help.

October 15

The meeting of the Political Committee at the UN was adjourned indefinitely. This followed a call by the acting mediator for the UN to set out its position on the "Seven Fundamental Issues." These included (1) permanent peace in Palestine (2) boundaries of the "Jewish State" (3) future of Jerusalem (4) disposition of Arab controlled areas (5) guarantees of rights for all inhabitants (6) repatriation and resettlement of Arab refugees (7) continuing involvement of the UN.

The Syrian delegate, Faris al Khoury attacked the acting mediator for his omissions and criticism of armed Arab involvement. There had been no mention of the "atrocious acts of the Jews committed against the Arab population." Under the mandate over 300 000 had been massacred or expelled." Great Britain had done nothing to protect these peaceful people." This is what had caused Arab intervention in Palestine.

However not a single member state on the committee was ready for a debate.

On the day that the UN met to start considering Bernadotte's proposals, the Israelis, with three and a half brigades deployed in the Negev, sent a convoy of 16 trucks to besieged settlements in the area. This was done safe in the knowledge that the local Egyptian forces would not allow the passage of the convoy, having announced that convoys would not be allowed to pass until the refugee villagers of the Negev were allowed to return home. Several lead vehicles burst into flames, with the blame levell-ed at the Egyptians. A subsequent UN report indicated that the Zionists had blown up their own trucks. However, this was then used as a pretext to launch savage attacks on dozens of villages. Operation Ten Plagues commenced, resulting in an exodus of tens of thousands of new and old refugees to the Hebron hills and the Gaza Strip.

In the following three weeks of hostilities, Count Bernadotte's proposal that the Negev be apportioned to the Palestinians in return for ceding Western Galilee to Israel, suffered a fatal blow.

Gaza, al-Majdal and Barbara were bombed and strafed by Israeli planes

October 16

Israeli forces made a second unsuccessful attempt (following an earlier attempt on 28 July) to capture the village of Iraq el Manshiya in the Gaza Strip. Before being beaten back by Egyptian forces, an armoured column stormed and "shot up" the village, killing some Egyptians.

October 17

Accompanied by air attacks, the Israeli navy shelled the Gaza Strip, precipitating further flight from the coastal communities. Hundreds were, according to reports, killed or injured near the railway station.

However, as usual, the media concentrated on military objectives and operations, not the effect on the terrorised Palestinian villager. Both Egyptian and Israeli rejected a UN demand for a cease-fire. Israeli planes attacked al Majdal, al Faluja in the northern Negev and al Arish on the Egyptian frontier. Convoys and infantry units were harassed by Israeli fighter-bombers. Egyptian spitfires were fighting back, shelling Zionist settlements to the east of Gaza.

The Israeli Palmach adopted guerrilla tactics behind Egyptian lines. with their forces capturing a "tactically important height", after heavy hand-to-hand fighting, somewhere in the Negev. The Egyptian counter attack was eventually driven off.

Israeli HQ insisted that the only purpose of this offensive was to keep open the road to the Negev, to enable food and other supplies to reach the settlements. It was not regarded as a resumption of the war with Egypt. With correspondents not allowed to enter the area it was believed that Israeli attacks were ranging far and wide, a battle for the Negev was in process, "which is certainly the covert intention of Israel" stated The Times.

The situation in Jerusalem district was reported to be deteriorating rapidly, with positions on Mount Zion changing hands several times over short periods. Both sides used large calibre mortars, resulting in the destruction of some buildings.

The French Consul-General complained of "brutal shelling" by the Arab Legion of the French Benedictine Church of the Dormition on Mount Zion.

October 18

Reports indicated that following quick, decisive attacks by Israeli motorised columns, the Egyptian front had crumbled, leaving a beleaguered bastion at Faluja in the Negev.Occasional shell bursts were the only "obstacle" to Israeli movement in the area. The Egyptians were now in an untenable position. With the Israelis having achieved there objective of relieving the settlements, any further Israeli aggression was viewed as "covert design to occupy the Negeb."

The occupation of the Negev was reported to be a priority for two reasons, communications and settling of immigrants. The northern Negev totalled about one million acres, about half of Palestine, and was considered to be a potential home to 250 000 Zionist immigrants over the next 10 years - once the area was "cleansed" of the indigenous Palestinians.

Although not prepared to order a cease-fire, Israel indicated that it was prepared to discuss with Egypt means of peacefully settling their basic "difficulties."

Following an earlier aerial and artillery bombardment which stimulated the exodus of many villagers, the village of Bayt Tima in the Gaza Strip was captured.

Operation ha-Har began with an attack on the Egyptian forces stationed west of Deir Aban, forcing them to retreat, leaving a string of villages in the Judean Hills at the mercy of the invaders. Thousands of local residents sought refuge in the Hebron hills. During this four day Operation (which was coordinated with Operation Yekev) care was taken not to engage the forces of the Arab Legion.

October 19

The Security Council passed a resolution calling for an immediate cessation of hostilities in the Negev with the warring parties returning to their original positions. Egypt accepted the resolution on the understanding that Israel did likewise. Israel rejected the cease-fire but agreed to negotiate. Apparently the Council was spurred into action by the concerns of Syria and Egypt who felt that, under American chairmanship, a "complacent" course of action would be taken with Israeli military action continuing.

Al Burayi, in the southern part of the Jerusalem corridor was captured around this date.

Kibbutz Tzova was established on the land of Suba in the Jerusalem corridor.

Israeli artillery shelled Gaza with the Israeli forces about five miles to the north-east of the city. The village of Hulayqat, in the Gaza Strip, was the scene of the "heaviest fighting" in the area. Despite heavy fighting between Israeli invader and Egyptian defender during the Second Truce, there were still some villagers remaining in their village. They apparently fled the impending hostilities. Hand-to-hand fighting was reported with 100 out of 600 Egyptian troops reported killed and a similar number captured.

Beit Jibrin, to the north of Hebron, was reported by The New York Times as being "added to the usual targets of the Israeli airforce for the first time" in their night raids. It continued, along with Faluja, Gaza, al Arish, and Beersheba to be "pummelled" by wave upon wave of aircraft, leading to what one Israeli historian described as "panic flight" from the village. Deir Nakhkhas was occupied at the same time.

Fighting broke out in other parts of Palestine with Jerusalem, Nablus and Tulkarm "particularly tense."

Commenting on the Israeli campaign, The Times drew attention to the intensity of the air operations as indicating the success of the Israelis in acquiring aircraft. As regards road transport, there was a sufficiency of appropriate vehicles since trucks and jeeps were not regarded as military equipment under the terms of the truce.

From this point onwards, Operations Yo'av and ha-Ḣar were both commanded by Yigal Allon "who in all his previous campaigns had left no Arab civilian communities in his wake."[5]

Despite the resolution passed by the Security Council requesting a cease-fire, to which the Egyptians gave their immediate agreement, the Israelis had further military conquests in mind. So the second wave of advances, lasting until 24 October, began. The Harel brigade captured a number of villages, with the population fleeing south towards Bethlehem and the Hebron hills.

October 20

With the Israelis in command of the main road into the Negev and in control of all the main heights, the government held a special session to consider the Security Council's demand for an immediate cease-fire. Reports indicated it had decided to hold out for the whole of the southern desert in any prospective political settlement of Palestine.The military situation had stiffened official resolve and the feeling was that the entire area could be in Israel's grasp as outlined in the original partition proposals.

Eventually the provisional government accepted, in principle, the order to cease fighting in the Negev.

Discussion of the question of Palestine and the Bernadotte report was postponed by the Political Committee of the General Assembly. The Soviet Union disagreed with the decision blaming it on the Americans who preferred to have it discussed after the forthcoming Presidential elections.

At the UN, the condition of the Palestinian refugees was updated. With a figure of 500 000 taken as being the number of refugees, their situation would be desperate within weeks. The resources on which they had been depending were running dry. The approach of winter gave added emphasis to the plight of the 95 000 living under trees without shelter of any kind and to the 120 000 without blankets. The need for clothing and shelter was immediate.

The village of Kawkaba which first encountered Zionist aggression in January was reported captured by the Israeli army. Situated in the Gaza Strip, its fortunes had fluctuated as the year progressed. In violation of the first truce it had been occupied on 14 June and re-captured by a mix of Saudi and Egyptian forces on 8 July. The residents probably left at various points in time, in response to the hostilities invited upon their village.

October 21

The Israeli provisional government claimed it was prepared to accept a cease-fire as long as the Egyptians, and the irregular fighters, accepted likewise. The Egyptian response had still not been received by the afternoon but observers reported that Israel was doing its utmost to delay calling a cease-fire until her objectives had been achieved.

The date of the capture of Deir Sunayd, scene of an earlier battle in May with the Egyptians , was approximate. It had suffered bombing by Israeli planes four or five days earlier and on this day, it was further "pummell-ed".

Al Majdal, in the south, was subject to both air and sea attack. Israeli intelligence reported that a "wave of fear" passed over the local inhabitants. Demonstrations took place in protest against the inability of the Egyptian army to protect the civilians.

The historical village of Hiribya, in the Gaza Strip, was established on a Canaanite site with clear indications of habitation in antiquity. During Operation Yo'av it was one of many subject to an aerial attack. Eventual capture was reckoned to have taken place at the end of the Operation in November.

The village of al Jura was also bombed by Israeli planes, with the villagers fleeing to safety in the Gaza Strip. Beit Wettif, which dominated the Faluja- Jerusalem road was captured.

The village of Beit 'Itab, in the Jerusalem corridor, was captured during Operation ha-Har. Identified with the town of Enadab in the 4th century AD, all that now remains are heaps of rubble along with the remains of a crusader castle.

Similarly occupied, in proximity to Beit 'Itab was the village of Deir al Shaykh. Some villagers had fled, others were expelled. Al Qabu, the site of Qobi during the Roman period, suffered the same fate when the Sixth Battalion of the Har'el Brigade invaded the village. The inhabitants either fled or were expelled. Ras Abu 'Ammar, Khirbat al 'Umur and Khirbat al Tannur suffered the same fate as the rest.

Three Battalions, drawn from three different Brigades, conquered Beersheba after a seven hour battle with most of the population, numbering thousands, being driven out to seek refuge in the Hebron hills. Extensive looting then followed. This followed a battle where the town's defences had been damaged by air raids. Before the final infantry assault, the Egyptian defenders had been bombed and strafed. This victory by the Israelis altered the whole strategic balance in southern Palestine.

The official report on this operation spoke of the Beersheba population being transferred to Egypt "at their own request." Ben Gurion knew differently, expressing his approval with the comment "Land with Arabs on it and land without Arabs on it are two very different types of land." He was, however, apparently annoyed by the looting and excessive brutality. His diary noted "the army failed to control its men."[6]

On this day Ben Gurion declared "The Arabs of the Land of Israel have only one function left to them - to run away."[7]

October 22

Gaza, the seat of the recently proclaimed "Arab Government for Palestine", was heavily bombed with Israeli troops pushing close by. Beit Hanoun was reported to be captured. The Egyptian forces were reported to be "badly mauled" with no lines of communication and cohesive command. It was announced that both sides had ordered their troops to obey the order for a cease-fire. By 3pm the Negev was "fairly quiet".

The Times concluded its report by observing the nature of this short military campaign. Commenting on the shortcomings of the Egyptian forces, apparently many officers surrendered voluntarily, it was only the Sudanese soldiers who fought well, with the other Arab states observing strict neutrality. Even a minor counter-offensive by the Arab Legion from Latrun would have seriously inconvenienced the Israelis. It concluded by stating "It is obvious that dissension among members of the Arab League is deeper than the most optimistic Israeli previously dared to imagine."

The New York Times reported on the situation on the southern front "Arab village after village lay deserted, some battered beyond repair and still burning where the Egyptians had held out. From all, however, whether destroyed or not, the Arabs had fled to the coastal strip still in Egyptian hands.[8]

Beit Nattif, to the north of Hebron, was captured by the Fourth Battalion of the Ha'rel Brigade. One report indicated that "the inhabitants fled for their lives" with another reporting "some light resistance." It was a strategically located village and victim of the stated aim to drive out refugees from nearby villages to the south.

In the same area, Ra'na fell into Israeli hands. Those residents who had not fled to the hills for safety, before the arrival of the occupiers, were expelled towards Hebron. Nearby Zikrin and 'Allar al Fawqa suffered the same fate.

In the north of Palestine, Operation Hiram pushed the Israelis forward along the line from the villages of al Nabi Yusha' to Manara thus extending Israeli control over the length of the Lebanese border. The villagers of al Nabi Yusha' fled or were expelled probably during hostilities in May.

The Arab Liberation Army stormed the hilltop of Sheikh 'Abbad which overlooked Kibbutz Manara. They then proceeded to fire on passing Israeli traffic.

October 23

The village of Deir al Dubban, north west of Hebron, was captured with the villagers either having fled or being expelled. Neighbouring Kudna, with a history dating back to Crusader times, suffered the same fate. Any remaining villagers were expelled.

Nine months after being attacked by the Haganah and the Palmach, the village of Zakariyya was revisited. The last link in the chain of conquest from the Jerusalem corridor to Israeli held part of the Hebron hills was forged. The villagers were not expelled at this point in time. They had to wait until January 1950 for this to happen, following a report from the Israeli Interior Ministry that "in the village there are many good houses, and it is possible to accommodate in them several hundred new immigrants."[9]

October 24

In southern Palestine the continuing military actions of the Israelis, in direct contravention of the recent cease-fire, prompted a meeting of the Security Council to be called. Confirmed by reports reaching the UN, the Israelis were still attacking on the Negev front. The Gaza-Madjal road was one target, with mines being laid in the wake of the attackers. UN observers were refused access by the Israelis to positions near Bethlehem where Egyptian forces had been attacked. Gaza port was under siege by two Israeli corvettes.

Attention switched to the northern front where the situation was described as "serious". A UN spokesman in Haifa reported that the border with the Lebanon was "aflame" with the Israelis launching attacks by land and air in Upper Galilee. The Israelis claimed that the Arabs had broken the truce when an armed convoy, on its way to a Zionist settlement near Manarah, was "badly mauled" by Arab irregular forces. This action of the Israelis was largely regarded as provocation, giving them the excuse to launch the offensive. They occupied two Arab-held heights, with the Arab Liberation Army and the Lebanese army holding on along the 15 mile front. At this juncture, according to The Times, there was nothing to suggest that this was no more than a "localised action."

Blida was shelled by Israeli artillery. It was also bombed as were Meisse, Djebel and Houle across the Lebanese border.

A dusk to dawn curfew was imposed on the Old City of Jerusalem in an attempt, it was believed, to stem the casualties from Israeli reprisal shelling.

Following a night raid on Beit Jibrin and Al Qubeiba, "panic flight" took place from the two villages. This was followed by flight from Tarqumiya which expected to be next in the line of attack. Around this time King Abdullah sent the Arab Legion to both Hebron and Bethlehem to prop up the Egyptian forces which were on the verge of collapse.

October 25

By this date only a few hundred people remained in Beersheba. These were mostly women, children and the sick. With the exception of 100 able bodied civilain men, the rest were expelled to Gaza. The men were deployed to clean the town up before being sent to a POW camp. The town, it soon emerged, was extensively looted by the occupying troops.

A graphic account of Beersheba, and the Negev in general, was given by The Times' own correspondent.

The report indicated that areas of the Negeb recently won by the Israeli army were now empty and silent except for army traffic. The Arab villages were deserted, with their "miserable houses" looted, and many burnt. The inhabitants, estimated to be about 20,000 - a number which had been swollen considerably by refugees from the north - had fled with no one knowing, or apparently caring, where they have gone.

It was obvious that most of them fled in panic, leaving behind the cloaks, sheepskins, and blankets so necessary if they were to survive the cold nights in the Hebron hills. The authorities in the Transjordan, where it was believed most of the refugees were wandering, would find it difficult to care for them, and it was hoped that the refugee relief section of the United Nations mission in Palestine would increase its efforts to help the victims.

In Beersheba itself, once a thriving centre of camel trading, a few inhabitants remained alongside members of the Israeli Army who were systematically looting the houses which survived the bombing. The article observed that it is perhaps a tacitly accepted rule of war that troops should make themselves "comfortable" at the expense of the vanquished, but it was difficult to excuse the behaviour of some, who ridiculed Islamic devotions in a desecrated mosque.

In this "pleasingly designed building" holy books had been torn and strewn over the floor. Israeli soldiers attempted to amuse their female compatriots by imitating the Iman's call to prayer. All this was in sharp contrast to the care taken by the Israeli Army to guarantee the sanctity of Christian holy places elsewhere, and to those correspondents who that very day had visited the Imperial war cemetry just outside the town. In spite of the difficulties under which they worked, the Arab caretakers, to the last, had obviously tended with care the graves of the British and Australian soldiers who died there in 1917.

The Scotsman commented on the Israeli draft constitution. It was said to be based on "two Bibles", the old Hebrew one and the UN partition resolution. The draft was described as "profoundly humanistic."

October 26

An emergency session of the Security Council, called for at the request of the Egyptians who were increasingly concerned at Israeli cease-fire violations, was adjourned. Reports were awaited from the acting mediator and his observers who were increasingly hindered from going about their business.

The Israeli foreign minister, Moshe Shertok, announced that Israel had no intention of withdrawing its forces to positions they held prior to recent hostilities. The Times report indicated sympathy with the Israeli position, arguing that the Egyptians had defied truce conditions which allowed for supplies reaching isolated settlements - an argument which ignored the fact that one of the reasons given by the Egyptians for their position was that the Israelis were refusing to allow Palestinian villagers to return to their homes.

October 27

The village of Beit Jibrin was eventually captured, although not destroyed immediately. Benny Morris observed that Ben Gurion may have been trying to put future historians off the scent when he inserted a small diary entry "Tonight our army entered Beit Jubrin . . Yigal asked [permission] to blow up some of the houses. I responded negatively."

Acting UN mediator, Ralph Bunche, accused the Israeli forces on the southern front of operating with a "prearranged plan" to permanently occupy the territory under their control. Israeli chief of operations, Col Yigal Yadin made light of this observation, commenting that probably American war plans contain a plan to capture Monaco.

Kibbutz Eretz-Ysrael and Gizo on the land of Beit Susin in the Jerusalem corridor were established. The settlement of Tal-Boqer (or Tal-Shahar) was established on the land of Khirbet Beit Far at the western end of the Jerusalem corridor. The Times, reporting on the establishment of three *kibbutzim* ("prefabricated huts") in the Jerusalem corridor, observed that work had began "reclaiming" the alleged "barren soil." One can only wonder how the Palestinian farmer managed to exist over the preceding centuries and why the *kibbutzim* were so keen to acquire this "barren soil."

What is undeniable was that the once thin Jerusalem corridor, linking the coastal plain to Jerusalem, had been fattened substantially with settlements consolidating the territorial gains.

It was estimated that up to 3 000 Egyptians were trapped in the Faluja "pocket" with a further considerable force of soldiers cut off in the Majdal region. With between 20 000 to 30 000 troops committed to the Negev, Egyptian casualties and prisoners were reckoned to be about 2 000 in number.

October 28

Ben Gurion announced that Israel would never withdraw from the Negev but wanted peace with Egypt.

The Security Council begun a debate over a joint British and Chinese resolution calling for an economic and diplomatic boycott of Israel and Egypt if both failed to return to their pre-truce lines in the Negev.

The British representative expressed concern that if the Zionists were allowed to remain in their present positions all the Council's actions in Palestine would be nullified to a great extent. The Israeli representative, with a touch of sarcasm but with no reported hint of irony or hypocrisy, stated that the Council and the mediator wanted to bestow upon the Egyptian forces the success they could not achieve themselves. They were to advance in front of the banner of the UN while the Israelis fragmented to their previous positions.

Arab spokesmen were quick to point out that the Zionists, in talking of Arab invasion of the Negev, overlooked another invasion which was carried out under the "complacent eyes" of the League of Nations which the UN was now being asked to endorse. There were no Jewish refugees but countless Arab refugees were fleeing for their lives.

The debate was adjourned to the following day.

Egyptian forces started to withdraw from forward positions in southern Palestine. Lack of food and water was felt to be a contributing factor. The

Times commented that for the first time the whole British Press had hailed Israel's victories and had not concealed its satisfaction at Egypt's defeat.

The third stage of Operation Yoav began in the Hebron foothills and along the coast. Once again expulsions and "panic flight" took place.

This was possibly the day that Dimra, in the Gaza Strip, was occupied. Since May, Dimra had been the home to many refugees from nearby Huj, whose residents had been, repeatedly, prevented from returning to their village. The historic town of Isdud, which ten days earlier had been subjected to Israeli air force bombing three days in succession, fell. The majority of the townspeople had earlier fled with the retreating Egyptian forces. About 300 remaining villagers had flown the white flag but were almost immediately expelled - despite an Israeli communique which would have its readers believe that the Israeli forces had entered the town at the request of a delegation from the townspeople.[10]

The nearby village of Hamama, home to a substantial number of refugees (particularly from Isdud) who had fled from previous military offensives, was also targeted. The remaining residents of the village, together with the refugees either, fled or were expelled when the Yiftach Brigade entered Hamama. Close to Hebron, al Qubayba, a village dating from the Crusader period, suffered the same fate. As in the case of many villages "cleansed" during this period, "panic flight" was given as a reason for its rapid depopulation. In the case of Khirbat Umm Burj, although it was occupied, some villagers remained.

The villages of Mirun and Tarshiha, near Safad in Upper Galilee, were bombed by three Israeli planes shortly before nightfall.

Operation Hiram, a three day blitz "to eliminate the Arab-held bulge descending into Galilee from Lebanon . ." commenced. Within sixty hours, tens of thousands, villagers and refugees, fled - mostly to Lebanon. Yosef Weitz of the JNF, on hearing of the start of the Operation wrote to General Yadin urging that the army expel the refugees from the newly conquered areas.[7]

The Archbishop of Galilee put a figure of 600 000 on the number of refugees from Palestine, located as follows: Lebanon 90 000; Syria 140 000; Transjordan 100 000; Judea 100 000; Samària 50 000; Egypt and the Negev 75 000; Arab Galilee 15 000; Iraq 15 000.

October 29

The Security Council adjourned indefinitely while a sub-comittee prepared a new draft of the resolution tabled by Britain and China. The previous day, the resolution - which threatened sanctions against Israel - had the support of the US. Today this support was withdrawn, according to informed sources, on the personal intervention of President Truman.

Washington denied the report.

President Truman, in an obvious bid to win the votes of the Jewish voters in New York went the farthest yet in support of Israel. In doing so he ignored the position of the US representative at the UN, Mr Marshall, who endorsed Count Bernadotte's plan - which would greatly reduce the land area claimed by Israel.

The first village to fall in Operation Hiram was Safsaf, near the Lebanese border. It was captured before dawn following a surprise three-pronged attack by two platoons of armoured cars and a tank company from the Seventh Brigade. With local Arab armies failing to assist, the local militia and ALA volunteers retreated to Lebanon. Most of the villagers suffered death or injury.

While the *History of the War of Independence* tried to tone down events at Safsaf, stating that the village "was occupied after a brief battle", Moshe Erem, in a report submitted to the Mapam Political Committee on 11 November listed the crimes committed by Israeli soldiers:

"52 men tied with a rope and dropped into a well and shot. 10 were killed. Women pleaded for mercy. Three cases of rape . . . a girl aged 14 was raped. Another four were killed."

Palestinian, Nafez Nazzal, was told by one survivor:

"As we lined up, a few Jewish soldiers ordered four girls to accompany them to carry water for the soldiers. Instead, they took them to our empty houses and raped them. About seventy of our men were blindfolded and shot to death, one after the other, in front of us. The soldiers took the bodies and threw them on the cement covering of the village's spring and dumped sand on them." Later, passing Israeli troops advised the remnants that they should forget what they had witnessed and could stay in their homes. However, they left their village.[11]

A massacre was also carried out at the nearby village of Jish and, along with that of Safsaf, is given as the reason for "panic flight" from other villages as the Seventh Brigade approached. However no detail is given of this massacre.

Al Dawayima was a village 18km to the west of Hebron. Like many others which were to be demolished by the Israelis it had Biblical significance, being tentatively identified with the Old Testament village of Bozqat or Bosqat.

On this day, it was visited by the 89th Battalion, part of the Eighth Brigade commanded by General Yitzhak Sadeh, founder of the Palmach (under the overall command of Yitzhak Rabin who was OC Operations of the Southern Front) at a time when Israel's domination of the area was no longer in dispute. By the time this unit left a little known massacre had been perpetrated. A massacre not carried out in the heat of the battle.

The Israeli daily *'Al ha-Mishmar* received the following report:

"The first [wave] of conquerors killed about 80 to 100 [male] Arabs, women and children.The children they killed by breaking their heads with sticks. There was not a house without dead . . . One commander ordered a sapper to put two old women in a certain house . . . and to blow up the house with them. The sapper refused. . . The commander then ordered his men to put in the old women and the evil deed was done. One soldier boasted that he had raped a woman and then shot her. One woman, with a newborn baby in her arms, was employed to clean the courtyard where the soldiers ate. She worked a day or two. In the end they shot her and her baby"

[Author's note:Israeli historian, Benny Morris, recorded that the account received by *'Al ha- Mishmar* was never published. It was decided that its publication would harm Israel and Mapam would be "lambasted" for it.]

In 1984 the Israeli daily *Hadashot* interviewed the village *mukhtar*. He recalled:

"The people fled, and everyone they saw in the houses, they shot and killed. They also killed people in the streets. . . . two tanks passed Darawish Mosque. About 75 old people were there, who had come early for Friday prayers . . . They were all killed."

The *mukhtar* said that about 35 families were hiding in caves outside the village, including some from the previously occupied village of al Qubayba. The Israeli forces discovered them:

"They told them to come out and get into line and start to walk. And as they started to walk, they were shot by machine guns from two sides . . We sent people there that night, who collected the bodies, and put them into a cistern, and buried them."

In 1984 the *mukhtar* paid a visit to the village site in the company of an Israeli journalist. His first visit since the massacre. He showed the journalist where his home had been and the cistern. Later the journalist returned with four labourers to excavate the cistern. They discovered several human bones, including three skulls - one was a child's. The excavation was stopped and the bones reburied.

Investigations into the massacre were launched but no findings ever published. They ended with the issuing of rules on treatment of Arab prisoners and, according to one report, a few soldiers were disciplined. Some investigations came to the conclusion that "many there are [former members of] the LHI [Stern Gang], Frenchmen, Moroccans, who tend to bad behaviour."

Ben Gurion, in his diary, referred briefly to "rumours" that the army had "slaughtered 70-80 people." Soldier eyewitnesses to these events concluded that "cultured officers . . . had turned into base murderers and this not in the heat of the battle . . .but out of a system of expulsion and destruction. The less Arabs remained - the better. This principle is the political motor for the expulsions and the atrocities."[12]

[In December, a general discussion of atrocities at ministerial level brought up the events at al Dawayima. Agricultural minister, Aharon Zisling, said "This is something that determines the character of the nation . . . Jews too have committed Nazi acts." He agreed with other ministers that, in order to preserve Israel's image, nothing should be admitted.[12]]

Although initially investigated by the Israeli government, the massacre was conveniently ignored and only vaguely reported. A one-man confidential ministerial investigation was authorised by prime minister David Ben Gurion. Attorney general, Hayim Moshe Shapira, was given the responsibility. To this day the Shapira report, which has been located in Israel's State Archives [Justice Ministry papers 21/1/0], remains a closely guarded secret. It did identify the perpetrator of the massacre as Isar Be'eri, former head of the Haganah intelligence section. [His leadership in the massacre and previous involvement in giving the order to murder, in cold blood, a refugee named 'Ali Qasim never impeded his career. He rose to be head of the Mossad in the 1960s[12]] Thirty six years later the Hebrew newspaper *Hadashot* published two articles (24 & 26 August 1984) on the tragedy. Then testimony of Israeli soldiers who had participated began to emerge into the public domain.

About 10 miles from Hebron, the area around the village of Deir Nakhkhas was one of the first to suffer the after-shock of the massacre at al Dawayima. A massive exodus of the inhabitants was reported.

The Druze village of Mughar, near Tiberias, "surrendered" around this date. The residents of nearby al Mansura probably fled their village. The villagers of Tarshiha feared retribution from approaching Israeli forces because of their history of resistance earlier in the year. Once the village had been "softened" by aerial strikes and a prolonged shelling, most of the village's Muslims and ALA forces fled. The village's Christian residents, in the main, were allowed to stay.

October 30

The village of Sa'sa' was to experience a second massacre, the first being during February when ten houses were blown up and "tens" of people killed.

On this occasion, the New York Times reported that several hundred defenders had been killed with a few hundred taken prisoner. Another report spoke of a thousand white flags being raised, an "offering" being prepared for the invaders - all prior to the death or expulsion of the villagers. The Haganah description of the operation said that there had been no resistance, the village had been taken with ease. And Israel Galili, former head of Haganah National Staff said that acts of "mass murder" had been committed.

Detailed accounts of the massacre have never been given but Moshe Carmel, Commander of the Northern Front, witnessed an incident shortly after the occupation of the village "I saw suddenly by the roadside a tall man, bent over, scraping with his fingernails in the hard, rocky soil. I stopped. I saw a small hollow in the ground, dug out by hand, with fingernails, under an olive tree. The man laid down the body of a baby who had died in the arms of his mother, and covered it with soil and small stones."[13]

Later, near Tarshiha, Carmel came across a 16 year old youth "sitting by the roadside, naked as the day he was born and smiling at our passing car." He recorded how some Israeli soldiers regarded the columns of refugees with astonishment and "great sadness." One unit ate no food that day because all the food sent by the company kitchen was given to the refugees.[14]

North of Acre, Deir al Qasi and Tarshiha were both captured.The villagers were not expelled during the attack. However, Israeli cabinet discussions on 9 January 1949 sealed the villagers' fate when it was decided to "encourage introducing *olim* (Jewish Zionist immigrants) into all the abandoned villages in the Galilee."[15] The villagers of Kafr 'Inan, likewise, were not expelled immediately following the capture of their village. Despite excuses from Israel's Bechor Shitrit, the Minority Affairs minister, that increasing numbers of Palestinians together with "infiltration" could mean the need to "conquer the Galilee anew", their eviction did not take place until February.

The village of Suhmata, with its roots going back to the Byzantine period (cAD555), put up some resistance against the conquerors. There is no information with regard to the fate of the villagers. It was common, however, for "punishment" to be meted out to those who resisted . This usually took the form of expulsion into Lebanon.

'Alma (or Alme in Crusader times), about 4km from the Lebanese border in Upper Galilee was another village where the residents, despite massacres nearby, decided to stay put. Since they had not resisted occupation, they were not to be "punished" However they were, eventually, "uprooted and expelled."

The village of Dayshum was reported to be empty when units of the Seventh Brigade arrived. It was surmised that news of massacres, carried out by the same Brigade, had probably stimulated their flight. The same reason was given for the depopulation of Fara and al Ras al Ahmar villages, as the Seventh Brigade advanced through Upper Galilee, with the villagers probably fleeing to Lebanon. In the case of the "cleansed" al Ras al Ahmar, it was renamed Kerem Ben Zimra and by May of the following year was ready to receive new Jewish Zionist immigrants.

Al Farradiyya, on the Nazareth-Safad road, did not suffer a direct attack and many of its residents remained in the village unscathed. However, as with other villages in a similar situation, moves were afoot to remove them. This happened in February of 1949 following, amongst other factors, the deliberations of the Committee for Transferring Arabs from Place to Place. Here it was decided to evict the remaining 261 inhabitants from al Farradiyya (and Kafr 'Inan).[16]

A very cryptic report was given of atrocities at the village of Jish by Moshe Erem:

"Rings [cut off with?] knives. Jiz [should be Jish]-a woman and baby killed. Another 11 [killed?] The kibbutzim are participating in the looting . Ear-rings are torn off with ears . ."[17]

Eventually this particular incident of massacre and vicious thievery reached the Knesset where an Arab member noted "When the people who were robbed insisted on being given receipts, they were taken to a remote place and shot dead. . . The finger of one of the dead had been cut off to remove a ring."

One of Ben Gurion's trusted military advisers, Fred Grunich, revealed that of the atrocities he had observed, one was "the horror of the seizure of the Arab village of Jish including the massacre of civilians."[18]

At Ghabbatiyya, the New York Times reported that several hundred of the Arab Liberation Army's area garrison had been killed, with hundreds taken prisoner. The village was occupied at the same time. The village of Sabalan was occupied, possibly by units of the Golani Brigade as they advanced to the north-west. The village of Ar Rama was captured by Golani units. Any surviving villagers in Marus, which had been partially "emptied" during hostilities in May, were probably expelled by the Seventh Brigade.

Situated in the Upper Galilee mountains, next to the Lebanese border, the village of Saliha was subjected to the terror of the Seventh Brigade. At a meeting of Mapam party officials, Moshe Erem reported the massacre of 94 people who had been herded into a house and blown up with the building.[19]

The village of Mirun, according to the *History of the War of Independence*, resisted to the extent that it was initially bypassed. Following the massacre at Safsaf, the village fell to the occupiers "after most of the enemy company defending it had been wiped out."[20] Indications were that it was "depopulated" as a punishment for resisting occupation.

When the village of Majd al Kurum was occupied, about one-third of the population had already fled. A few days later about another 60 families fled following the execution of 12 village men in the square by the occupying troops.[21]

The Christian Maronite village of Eilabun was occupied by units of the Golani Brigade. No resistance was given. White and yellow flags of submission had been hung out and the conquerors were met by four priests. However the severed heads of two Israeli soldiers were found in one of the houses. The villagers were then ordered to assemble in the village square, in the process of which one villager was killed and another wounded by the soldiers.

"Then the commander selected 12 youngsters and sent them to another place, then he ordered that the assembled inhabitants be led to Maghar and the priest asked him to leave the women and babies and to take only the men, but he refused, and led the assembled inhabitants - some 800 in number - to Maghar preceded by military vehicles . . .

He himself stayed on with another two soldiers until they killed the 12 youngsters in the streets of the village and then they joined the army going to Maghar . . . When they reached Kafr 'Inan they were joined by an armoured car that fired upon them . . . killing one of the old men, Sam'an ash Shufani, 60 years old and injuring three women . . . At Farradiya [the soldiers] robbed the inhabitants of IL500 and the women of their jewellery and took 42 youngsters and sent them to a detention camp, and the rest . . . to the Lebanese border. Imagine how then the babies screamed and the cries of the pregnant and weaning women."

Hundreds fled to nearby gulleys, caves and villages and some later infiltraed back to their village. The village itself had been looted - furniture, livestock and other movable property had been carted off by the Israelis. The churches had been desecrated.

The death of the two Israeli soldiers was found to be the responsibility of an ALA sergeant. There followed various appeals for the villagers to be allowed to return and, eventually, the following November, hundreds were allowed to return.[22]

October 31

In two days of fighting - proclaimed by the UN Mission in Haifa as being "a serious breach of the truce" - the Israelis claimed complete control of northern Palestine, having seized control of 300 square miles of Upper Galilee. While the media reported on the fight against "Fawzi el Kawkji, the guerilla leader and adventurer", decades were to pass before the reality of this last day in October were revealed.

The eventual disclosures put paid to the excuse that the military operation was in self-defence, that it was only a response to the desultory attacks by Kawkji's "Muslim irregulars and Yugoslav, Polish and German adventurers" on the solitary colony of Manarah.

While a cease-fire had been ordered for 4pm, the Israelis waited until they had realised their objectives and eventually honoured it at 11am the following day. At this juncture it was reckoned that only three Arab forces could be counted as effective. The Syrians, to the south of Lake Hula; the Iraqis (following a recent change of government) in the Nablus-Tulkarm - Jenin triangle. And the Arab Legion, described by The Times as "a formidable force, disciplined, unbeaten and unprovocative."

In the Security Council a new draft was drawn up on military positions in the Negev, stipulating withdrawal of forces. The possibility of sanctions was retained - with the French, the Soviet Union and the US expressing their opposition.

"A wave of cynical opinion" was saying that the Bernadotte plan would be abandoned. Perhaps influenced by the impact that the impending US presidential elections was having on the resolve to address the Palestine question, the Security Council sub-committee had put off writing its report on the new draft. Any decision was now way into the future. Even the committee looking at the refugees was reported to have suffered a "retarding influence" thanks to the forthcoming elections.

A number of villages were captured at the end of Operation Hiram, but with no clear date given. Al Malikiyya was one such. Between May and October it exchanged hands five times. Although fortified, it was attacked under cover of the Israeli airforce and occupied. Any remaining villagers probably fled.

Mi'ilya was deserted by most of its residents having, during the previous months, fought alongside the Arab Liberation Army. In a rare show of "compassion", the local Israeli commander allowed the residents of this Christian village to return.

The village of Ar Rama was re-entered and its almost 1 000 villagers expelled under threat of death. One refugee gave an account "The people in Ar Rama were ordered to assemble at the centre of the village. A Jewish soldier stood on top of the rise and addressed us. He ordered the Druse present . . to go back to their homes . . Then he ordered the rest of us to leave to Lebanon."[23] [Note: Newspapers were reporting on the presence of "Druse cavalry" fighting alongside Israeli forces.]

The previous day the mukhtars of al Bi'na and Deir al Assad had travelled to Birwa to implement their surrender. Now, during the morning, Israeli forces entered the villages, ordered all the villagers to a field between the two villages where 100 rifles were surrendered:

"the Jews grouped us with the other villagers, separating us from our women. We remained all day in the village courtyard . . we were thirsty and hungry." recounted one refugee. Two villagers were taken aside and shot. [Another account speaks of some men asking to go to the well to bring back water. At the well they were shot dead. UN observers described the murders as 'wanton slaying without provocation.']

The refugees were robbed of their valuables. About 200 men were 'selected' and driven off (to a POW camp?):

"It was almost night . . Al Bi'na mukhtar asked the Jews to permit us to stay overnight . . rather than travel at night with our old men, women and children. The Jews rejected the mukhtar's request and gave us (ie the refugees) half an hour to leave . . When half an hour passed, the Jews began to shoot in the air . . they injured my nine-year old son in the knee . . We were terrified, the road was full of people in every direction you looked."

The young men who had been driven away ended up in concentration camps along with others from villages in Upper Galilee. Stripped of all their belongings, denied food and subjected to frequent interrogations and beatings, they were eventually released near the Arab lines at Lajjun. Shots fired over their heads forced them over the lines into Arab held territory.

When challenged by a UN observer over the treatment and expulsion of the young men, the Israeli commander at Lajjun denied that any such acts had taken place. Unconvinced, the observer reported "Regardless of the denial I believe it did happen."[24]

Qadas, steeped in history going back to the first millenium, was another village which changed hands in the course of events. It was occupied about the same time as al Malikiyya. Likewise the village of al Sammu'i, which was wholly or partially evacuated in May, was occupied. The village defenders apparently put up a fight since it was used, by Israel's foreign affairs ministry, as an example of a village which resisted and was therefore "depopulated."

An oral report exists of a massacre of villagers from 'Arab al Mawasi, near Tiberias at the end of October. Israeli soldiers rounded up 15 men, took them to the nearby village of Eilabun and shot them. Two pretended to be dead. However the soldiers returned and shot each of them again, in the head. Only one survived.[25]

[This oral version of events was eventually confirmed when the Israeli Defence Forces Archive report 1096/1949/65 was open to researchers. It confirmed the massacre under soldiers commanded by Lt Z Kleinman and platoon OC Haim Hayun of the 103 Battalion. The report was dated 2 November 1948[26]:

On this day two squads accompanied by the battalion armoured squad arrived at'Arab al-Mawasi (or Khirbet Wa'ra al-Sauda, eight kilometres to the east of Eilabun].The adult males were assembled and seven rifles collected. At this point a separate patrol discovered the remains of two Israeli soldiers killed in previous military action. They were headless.

"The men set fire to the Arabs' houses and returned to base with 19 Arab adult males. At the base the men [ie captives] were sorted out and those who took part in hostile actions against our army were identified, and they were sent under command of Haim [Hayun] to a place that had been determined and there they liquidated [*ve'sham huslu*] 14 of the adult males. The rest are being transferred to a prisoner-of-war camp."

Ben Gurion recorded Operation Hiram's success in the Upper Galilee by noting that of the 50 000 to 60 000 population (refugees and residents) prior to 29 October about half were in the Lebanon. The army later estimated that only about 12 000 to 15 000 remained.

Discrimination on the basis of religion played a part. In mixed villages where resistance was encountered the Christians, by and large, stayed put while the Muslims fled or were expelled. Druse and Circassian villagers put up no resistance.[27]

At the end of Operation Hiram, participating units were ordered to extend their control along the length of the border with Lebanon. The village of 'Arab al Samniyya along with other villages such as Iqrit and Tarbikha was probably occupied on this date. Evidence points towards the expulsion of its people on the pretext of creating a "security" border.

This creation of a northern border strip, free of Arabs, was at the forefront of the expulsions of the residents of Iqrit and Tarbikha, a policy which was approved by the General Staff of the Israeli army in the second week of November.

In the case of Iqrit, the residents were told that their eviction would be temporary and they would be allowed to return. The regional commander, Ya'acov Kara, ordered the villagers to take few supplies. They would be gone for no longer than 15 days. A few young people were left behind to guard the homes. They were eventually ordered to leave with the homes being looted shortly after. Some were trucked to Lebanon, others (126 families amounting to 616 people) to the nearby "cleansed" village of al Rama.

At the end of October, Israeli forces beseiged the "Faluja pocket" in the Gaza Strip where an Egyptian army brigade and about 3 140 Palestinian civilians held out until February 1949. Then the pocket was handed over to Israel under the terms of the Israeli- Egyptian armistice. The Egyptians departed as did a small number of the Palestinians.

Within days the the local Israeli army unit intimidated the population, in breach of the terms of the armistice, into leaving by 21 April. UN observers reported beatings, robbery and attempted rape. Israeli foreign minister, Moshe Sharrett personally reprimanded the chief of staff for the acts committed against the Palestininian population and acknowledged that the army was conducting "a 'whispering propaganda' campaign among the Arabs, threatening them with attacks and acts of vengeance by the army, which the civilian authorities will be powerless to prevent. There is no doubt that there is a calculated action aimed at increasing the number of those going to the Hebron hills as if of there own free will, and if possible, to bring about the evacuation of the whole civilian population of [the pocket]."

The outrage expressed by Israeli officials was regarded by Israeli historian, Benny Morris, as false. The intention being to mislead the international community about Israel's actions. Ben Gurion probably gave his approval to the actions. However it gave a cautionary lesson to Palestinians elsewhere, particularly in the Galilee, where the same tactics had less success.[28]

On this last day of October, Moshe Carmel, OC of the Northern Front radioed all his brigade and district commanders:

"Do all in your power to clear quickly and immediately from the areas conquered all hostile elements in accordance with the orders issues. The inhabitants should be assisted to leave the conquered areas.[29]"

History records that this message was interpreted as an order to expel the civilian population.

Commenting on Carmel's orders to his commanders, Major Yitzhak Moda'i wrote:

". . . it is clear that our forces in the Galilee did not act with restraint . . Although . . . operational orders for Operation Hiram make no mention of the local population [and its prospective treatment], all were aware of General Staff/Operations stand on this score.[30]"

Notes

1 Benny Morris, *The birth of the Palestinian refugee problem, 1947-49*, p.221
2 Michael Palumbo, *The Palestinian Catastrophe*, p.xii
3 Walid Khalidi, *All that Remains*, p.226
4 Palumbo, p.vii-ix
5 Morris, p.219
6 Palumbo. p.xi
7 Morris, p.218
8 Khalidi, p.94

9 *ibid*, p.226
10 *ibid* p.112
11 *ibid* p.491 (See: Journal of Palestine Studies, Winter 1999, p.76, Note 12 for clarification)
Palumbo, p.168
12 Nur Masalha, *Recent Hebrew and Israeli Sources for the Palestinian* Exodus, (JoPS , Autumn 1988)
13 Khalidi, p.497
14 Morris, p.231
15 Khalidi, p.13
16 *ibid* p.449
17 Morris, p.230 (See Appendix to Note 11 above)
18 Palumbo, p.171
19 Khalidi, p.492 (See Appendix to Note 11 above)
20 Khalidi, p.477
21 Morris, p.228
22 Morris, p229
23 Morris, p.227
24 Morris, p. 228
Palumbo, p.169
25 Khalidi, p.546
26 Benny Morris, *Operation Hiram Revisted: A Correction*, (JoPS, Winter 1999) p.76
27 Benny Morris, *The birth of the Palestinian refugee problem, 1947-49*, p.225
28 Khalidi, p.96
29 Benny Morris, *Operation Hiram Revisted: A Correction*, (JoPS, Winter 1999) p.70
30 *ibid* p.71

November

They abandon the villages of their birth and that of their ancestors and go into exile . . . . . women, children, babies, donkeys - everything moves, in silence and grief, northwards, without looking to right or left.

Moshe Carmel, OC Northern Front

During this period the political and strategic aims of the Israeli state fused. The former required as few as possible of the indigenous Palestinian Arab residing within the boundaries of the new state. In addition, empty houses were required for the new immigrants. The latter aimed at "Arab-less" boundaries with the surrounding Arab states. It was the Israeli army which was to effect the policy, with the politicians giving their approval after the event.

At the start of the month Israel's finance minister, Kaplan, complained about the reported destruction of Arab villages following their capture and "cleansing" in upper central Galilee. With about 20 000 Zionist immigrants already living in tents, he observed "Every possibility of accommodating [immigrants] must be exploited and a general order must be issued to the army not to destroy houses without a reason."[1]

By mid-November the Gaza Strip's refugee population had jumped from about the 100 000 mark, prior to the launch of Operation Yoav, to about 230 000. According to the UN Refugee Relief Project the condition of the refugees "def[ies] description . . . Almost all of them are living in the open . . . [and are] receiving no regular rations of food . . . There are no sanitary facilities . . . and conditions of horrifying filth exist."[2] Blame was laid at the door of the Egyptian Army and the Arab Higher Refugee Council.

Throughout the month the Israeli military carried out raids on the "cleansed " villages of Upper Galilee. These were empty or half-empty, with the purpose of the raids being to expel so-called "returnees" or "infiltrators." In other words, Palestinians trying to return to their homeland and villages, now under Israeli control, encountered forced deportation.

These raids followed a census carried out during the month where those not registered during the census, did not have an ID card or military pass, were considered to be "absentees." No matter the reason for your absence during the census, if you were discovered without the appropriate documentation you were regarded as "illegal" on your own land and faced expulsion. A continuation of the ethnic cleansing of Palestine.

During the following year, Moshe Carmel, officer in command of the Northern Front, detailed some of what he witnessed:

> "They abandon the villages of their birth and that of their ancestors and go into exile . . . women, children, babies, donkeys - everything moves, in silence and grief, northwards, without looking to right or left. Wife does not find her husband and child does not find his father . . . no one knows the goal of his trek. Many possessions are scattered by the paths; the more the refugees walk, the more tired they grow - and they throw away what they had tried to save on their way into exile. Suddenly, every object seems to them petty, superfluous, unimportant as against the chasing fear and the urge to save life and limb."[3]

November 1

The Arab Legion permitted convoys to pass through its lines to supply the demilitarised zone on Mount Scopus - including the Hebrew University and Hadassah Hospital.

Israeli forces refused to withdraw from their positions in Lebanese territory as requested by the UN. With reports of an impending Israeli offensive near the Syrian border, UN observers took up their positions in the area.

Resistance was met by the invading Israeli forces at Suhmata village in Upper Galilee. Following its capture, UN observers found that villages in the area were deserted and "reported the extensive looting of villages and the carrying away of goats, sheep and mules by the Israeli forces. . . The looting appeared to the observers to have been systematic, army trucks being used. The situation has created a new influx of refugees into Lebanon."[4]

Israeli historian Benny Morris recorded that, in early November, dozens of refugees were confronted by a platoon from the Har'el Brigade near the village of Khirbat al Lawz a few miles to the west of Jerusalem. The Israelis ordered the refugees to leave Israeli held territory and stole their livestock at the same time.

November 2

The Bedouin village of 'Arab al-Mawasi was the site of a little known massacre of 14 Bedouin Arab males at the hands of members of 103rd Battalion in Eastern Galilee during Operation Hiram. [See 31 October for details].

The black-out enforced in the Israeli occupied sector of Jerusalem was lifted as the provisional Israeli government met for the second day with members of the Jewish Agency to discuss the "sharing of duties between the state and the Zionist movement."

In the Negev, Israel wanted to bring about demographic changes - the less Palestinian Arabs the better. Israeli officials met with Bedouin chiefs with the aim of getting a voluntary agreement for the departure of most of the tribes "far into the desert or into Transjordan."

November 3

A British-Chinese resolution was presented to the Security Council. It was designed to restore the truce in the Negev and establish a committee to consider sanctions which might be applied in the event of non-compliance.

Egyptian troops trapped in the "Faluja pocket" in the northern Negev were foiled by the Israelis in their attempt to break out. They were believed to be seriously short of food, water and medical supplies. Their approach to the Israelis, to be allowed to withdraw, had been turned down the previous week.

The sole remaining Briton, of those abducted earlier by the Stern Gang, appealed to the Israeli Supreme Court against his seven year sentence for espionage.

General Yigal Allon, Operations Commander, cabled the commander of the Eighth Brigade, General Sadeh, to check rumours that the 89th Battalion had "killed many tens of prisoners on the day of the conquest of Ad Dawayima."

November 4

The Security Council, meeting in Paris, adopted the Sino-British resolution. It had been watered down by the US but still held out the prospect of sanctions and armed intervention. The Ukraine voted against with the Soviet Union abstaining.

It was reported that the Egyptian forces were retreating along the beach from Majdal, with Beit Hanoun waiting to fall into Israeli hands. The Israelis apparently made no effort to impede the withdrawal. With the latter poised to fill the vacuum left by Egyptian retreat, it was noted that this changed the balance of power and "makes the debates in Paris more unreal."

The Arab League informed the UN of the raid on al Dawayima where the Zionist forces had "ruthlessly massacred Arab women, children and old people, thus perpetrating barbarities rivalling in horror those committed by the Nazis." Britain proposed that Security Council "sanctions" envisaged for the Negev should be extended to other areas.

The villagers of Barbara near Gaza were either expelled or fled prior to the capture of the village.This followed, two weeks earlier, bombing and strafing by Israeli planes and being subjected to military activity in the area which, according to Israeli intelligence, caused "despair among the local inhabitants". The same fate was suffered by the villagers of neighbouring Beit Jirja, Ni'ilya, al Jiyya, and al Jura. In the case of the town of al Majd- [pop 9 910 in 1944], only about 2 000 people remained. According to Benny Morris the expulsion order was never executed and looting was not carried out.

On the civilian population of the coastal towns, it was observed "Our airforce had made a tremendous impact. It was a surprise for them to see squadrons of Jewish aircraft rule the skies."[2] This "impact" resulted in terrorised Palestinian civilians fleeing for refuge to the dunes and beaches. The glee and pride with which the Israeli aircraft was regarded was only matched by the total silence on the condition of the fleeing Palestinian residents.

November 5

The Egyptian forces were reported to have withdrawn as far as Gaza, giving them domination over a 12 mile coastal strip of Southern Palestine - the Gaza Strip.

The Scotsman printed an article arguing for "reorientation" of British policy in Palestine. With the U.S. presidential elections out of the way, the time was right for direct American-British talks.

The article spared no punches when it came to 'Zionist inspired morality' with regard to Palestine and its people. "In the inevitable conflict for the possession of Palestine or the larger part of it, both Arab and Jews had an irrefutable moral case, the Arab case being one of possession, the Jewish case based on dire-need. With nothing to choose between the parties from the point of view of justice . . . the only question for America and Britain to decide was which side was more likely to win . . and therefore more deserving of support in terms of hard-boiled *realpolitik* . . . The time has now come for Britain to accept the judgement of fact and reorientate her Middle Eastern policy accordingly."

The article could have been written by Ben Gurion himself.

The Ministerial Committee for Abandoned Property discussed the possibility of settling new immigrants in the town of Ramleh since "the country is in a bad way in connection with the continuing arrival of new immigrants. Every possibility of accommodation should be exploited and the army should be given a general instruction not to destroy houses without cause . ."[5]

A platoon from the Harel Brigade raided to the south of Beit Nattif and the village of al Jaba which bordered with Transjordan. At Khirbet Umm al Lauz dozens of refugees were found moving in the wrong direction - westwards. They were then forced out of Israeli held territory with their livestock being stolen. Al Jaba had 15 houses blown up.

Initial reports indicated that the refugees did not respond to threats. They refused to move eastwards, with some asking to be allowed to stay under Israeli rule. Constant raids, patrols together with sniper fire soon persuaded them otherwise.

November 6

A week after the atrocities carried out at neighbouring al Dawayima, a platoon from the Ha'rel Brigade found about 150 villagers still defying all the odds and remaining in their village of Khirbat Umm Burj. About 100 were expelled, with injuries being sustained by the refugees.

Yosef Nahmani, director of the Jewish National Fund in Eastern Galilee, recorded the recent events in his diary. This followed a tour of the area where the representative of the Minority Affairs Ministry, Immanuel Friedman, briefed him on "the cruel acts of our soldiers."

"In Safsaf, after . . . the inhabitants had raised a white flag, the [soldiers] collected and separated the men and women, tied the hands of fifty-six *fellahin* [peasants] and shot and killed them and buried them in a pit. Also, they raped several women . . . At Eilaboun and Farradiya the soldiers had been greeted with white flags and rich food, and afterwards had ordered the villagers to leave, with their women and children. When the [villagers] had begun to argue . . . [the soldiers] had opened fire and after some thirty people were killed, had begun to lead the rest [towards Lebanon] . . . in Salhila, where a white flag had been raised[,] . . . they had killed about sixty-seventy men and women. Where did they come by such a measure of cruelty, like Nazis? . . .Is there no more humane a way of expelling the inhabitants than by such methods . . ?

It is worth noting that when Yosef Weitz published a commemorative (and sanitised) volume based on Nahmani's diaries and papers, the above account was omitted.[6]

November 7

General Riley, the UN chief of staff in Haifa, arrived in Paris to report on the situation in Palestine. He was reported to have informed the acting-mediator that it was hopeless to try and restore the positions held on 14 October. The truce had outlived its usefulness and so sanctions to impose the truce were a non-starter. He was of the opinion that the Israelis could dominate the whole country if they so wished. Direct negotiations between Israel and the Arab states was the only practicable solution.

He was in favour of reducing the corps of UN observers to a handful in readiness for a more permanent state of affairs.

It was reported that the U.S. complained to Czechoslovakia on 25 July concerning the shipment of substantial quantities of arms and supplies to Israel. An Israeli air force deserter had given details of the supply route which, he alleged, had tacit approval of the Soviet Union. Soviet personnel were also alleged to be working with the Israelis. To date an "evasive" reply had been received from the Czech government.

The New York Times reported that Israeli forces had occupied 15 Lebanese villages, some as much as 10km inside Lebanese territory. The London Times gave a similar report, adding that the Arab villages in Galilee were found to be deserted with signs of systematic looting. "Goats, sheep and mules have been carried off in army trucks, and a new flight of refugees into the Lebanon is in progress."

At a meeting of the Israeli Cabinet, the subject of the October atrocities surfaced and criticism of the soldiers' conduct was aired. A ministerial committee of inquiry was established to investigate "the army's deeds in the conquered territories." It was reported that only prime minister Ben Gurion and foreign minister Shertok appeared not to have been "shocked" by what was heard.[7]

The ministerial committee, dubbed the "Committee of Three", eventually encountered evasiveness, delays and silence from army commanders.

November 8

Dr Ralph Bunche, the acting mediator, issued an official retraction of the statements attributed to General Riley with regard to the situation in Palestine. Every effort would be made to carry out the instructions of the Security Council.

The editor of the Mapam newspaper, *Al Hamishmer*, received a graphic account of the atrocities committed at Al Dawayima. The decision is taken not to publish it.

During this second week of November, "clearing" operations were in action along the border with Lebanon. The village of Suruh was one of the casualties. There is no record of what happened to the villagers. It was clear, however, that in the following weeks, the Israeli forces re-visited the "cleansed" villages to ensure that villagers had not returned to claim their homes, their land and their heritage.

Tarbikha was another casualty of this operation. Despite the villagers putting up no resistance to the invading Israelis, the residents were expelled for "military" reasons.

Meanwhile the Israelis were planning a £65 000 000 scheme, to be 75% financed by "American Jewry", to empty Europes's Displaced Persons camps of 100 000 Jews together with another 40 000 from eastern Europe. Already 80 000 settlers had been absorbed during the first six months of Israel's existence.

Israel's immigration minister, Moshe Shapira, was openly planning to use the homes of the expelled Palestinians. Up to 30 000 rooms, after repairs, would be available to accommodate 75 000 settlers. Compensation, he said, would be worked out in the "peace settlement." No mention, of course, that the Palestinians may want their own homes back.[8]

November 9

At the Security Council, the acting mediator proposed an armistice with the separation of Israeli and Arab forces by broad demilitarised zones. Implicit in this suggestion was the postponing of an open meeting to act on the British move to extend the "sanctions" resolution to cover the events in Galilee.

Britain denied Israeli accusations that British troops and arms had been supplied to Transjordan.

Following a successful six month defence of the strategically placed police station of the village of 'Iraq Suwaydan by Egyptian troops, the Israelis launched a blitz on the position. It was first bombed by a B-17 Flying Fortress and two fighter aircraft. This was followed by a sustained artillery bombardment "unequalled at any other time [during the war]", armour and infantry attack. According to the History of the Haganah the Israeli attackers "had never before seen such firepower aimed at a single target." Not surprisingly, the defenders surrendered.

Two truce observers appeared on the scene in the company of Israeli liason officers. The former were arrested when they refused to leave the scene of the battle. Initially the observers had been refused access close to the military action because the Israeli liason officer had deemed it too dangerous. They had been arrested when observing from a nearby village.

This action was described by the UN as a "deliberate attempt to thwart effective truce supervision and a flagrant violation of the Security Council's resolution of October 19th."[9]

November 10

The Israeli Cabinet met to discuss the army's behaviour during recent successful offensives. Agricultural minister Aharon Zisling was quoted as saying "Jews too have committed Nazi acts." Ben Gurion inserted a diary entry concerning "rumours" that the Israeli army had slaughtered 70-80 people at al Dawayima.

Moshe Carmel, OC of the Northern Front gave a somewhat "gentler" order to his troops when he said " . . .(B) [The troops] should continue to assist [in the departure of] the inhabitants wishing to leave the areas conquered by us. This is urgent and must be carried out swiftly. (C) A strip five kilometres deep behind the border between us and Lebanon must be kept empty of [Arab] inhabitants."[10]

Following the attack on the police station the previous day, the Israelis reported that the Egyptian forces had withdrawn from the village of 'Iraq Suwaydan and nearby Beit 'Affa. Nothing was said of any remaining villagers.

The second day of fighting was reported in the Jordan Valley. In the Negev fighting was also reported. Heavy artillery fire was heard in the Faluja area, with two groups of Egyptian soldiers surrendering to the Israelis.

November 11

Ben Gurion said that "a new reality" had been created in Palestine and that the provisional government was no longer bound by the partition resolution of 29 November 1947. With a view to future immigration (20 000 arrived the previous month, not the expected 10 000), The Times reported that the provisional government was looking with "covetous intent" on the Arab held areas in central Palestine where, at present, there was no fighting. It observed that despite Ben Gurion's disclosure that talks were taking place between Israel and the Arab states, central Palestine will certainly not change hands as a result of these talks.

At a meeting of the Political Committee of the left-wing Mapam, a briefing was given which confirmed some of the atrocities committed during the past few weeks. General Yisrael Galili blamed Stern Gang members, Frenchmen and Morrocans "who are prone to such grave behaviour" in reference to the massacre at al Dawayima.

Moshe Erem reported:

"52 men [in Safaf] tied with a rope and dropped into a well and shot. 10 were killed. Women pleaded for mercy. [There were] 3 cases of rape . . A girl aged 14 was raped. Another 4 were killed."At Jish "a women and her baby were killed. Another 11 [were killed?]." At Sa'sa, where the whole village was expelled, there was "mass murder a thousand[?] lifted white flags [and] a sacrifice was offered [to welcome] the army."

At Saliha "94 . . were blown up with a house."

The Seventh Brigade was singled out for condemnation. In general the atrocities were mostly committed against the members of the Muslim communities.[11]

The meeting revealed the thinking behind some of members of the committee. The party executives were asked not to use the phrase "Nazi actions". The parallels were obviously too close for comfort. It was asserted that there was "no connection" between the atrocities and the expulsions of Arabs.[7]

The difficulty experienced by UN observers in ascertaining the truth behind massacres and atrocities is well illustrated by the account of the UN team sent to investigate the murder of nine villagers, including two women, in the village of Majd al Kurum. Various teams had been sent to the village. However on this occasion the team included a Belgian officer by the name of Pallemans, who was fluent in Arabic but who decided not to inf orm the Israeli escort of this fact.

With the Israeli liason officer acting as an interpreter it became obvious that the truth was not being told. The villagers' complaint that they had no food and were not allowed to work in their fields was relayed to the effect that the villagers were well fed and content.

Despite Israeli refusal, on the insistence of Pallemans, photographs of the blown up houses were taken. The body of one of the Arab victims was exhumed in spite of the obvious Israeli disapproval. It became clear that the villagers who had returned to Majd al Kurum had been subjected to a continuing Israeli reign of terror. If they attempted to go to their fields they were shot at, robbed and beaten by Israeli soldiers. They had been warned not to give any testimony about present or past atrocities.

Pallemans' report eventually concluded "there is no doubt about these murders." The main fear of the villagers was that if they had to give information to the UN observer team "the Jews may commit further acts of violence." The report was signed by two American, two French and one Belgian UN observer.[12]

November 12

The Scotsman printed a feature on the Druze "National Army" which had been fighting alongside Israeli troops in the Galilee. Most were from the Jebel Druze in Syria who had "adopted Israel." It was claimed that the Israeli desire for "independence" fitted in with the Druze ambition for autonomy. Their persecution in Syria identified them with the Jews. And "since the Jews have been a minority as we are they think they will treat us better" according to one Druze officer.

November 13

Ben Gurion disclosed, without mentioning any names, that discussions were taking place with two Arab states and proclaimed that with "wise guidance" from America the Palestine "problem" could be settled in four weeks. He said that the Israeli troops would not abandon the Negev unless "physically forced to do so" by UN troops.

Britain was singled out as the perceived main obstacle to peace in the area. With no hint of irony Ben Gurion went on to proclaim "If the United Nations means anything at all it must mean two things: a sense of reality and a sense of justice. Any orders for sanctions would ignore these two conditions."[13]

The Christian village of Kafr Bir'im in Upper Galilee, with its population of about 1 000, suffered the same fate as neighbouring Iqrit some two weeks earlier. The residents of this "friendly" village were given 48 hours to move 5 km to the north. Despite the fact that they were led to believe that it was a temporary move, they camped out in their fields in freezing conditions. In the following days seven babies died of the cold. The villagers were eventually moved to the Muslim Quarter of nearby "cleansed" village of Jish

The fate of the villagers of Bir'im (or Biram) and Iqrit has been described, for those Israelis with conscience, as "a stain on the forehead of Israeli democracy". The events leading to the expulsions, the human tragedy which overtook the villagers is well documented in "Blood Brothers" by Fr Elias Chacour. The author, a priest in the Melkite Church, was a young boy when he and his family were expelled.

It has always been acknowledged that the two Christian communities of Iqrit and Biram were regarded as friendly towards Israel. They had been told they could return home once the fighting ceased. A promise which has never been honoured. And yet the villagers have never stopped fighting for the return to their land.

On 28 July, 1951 the Israeli High Court affirmed the villagers' right to return to their villages. Yet on Christmas Eve of that year the army demolished every house in Iqrit, leaving only the church standing.

Elias Chacour outlined a similar fate for Biram. Early in December when the village elders handed the court order to the Israeli officer in command, they were told it would take time to pull out. Return on Christmas Day was the reply.

In a joyous mood the villagers arrived at the top of the hill overlooking Biram. They were met by the sight of Israeli tanks, bulldozers and other military equipment. On command, the tank shells slammed into every building. After five minutes the bulldozers took over. Not even the church was left standing.

Every four years, around election time, the account of the villages usually reach the Israeli newspapers. The villagers even supported the first government of former Irgun leader, Menachem Begin, because of personal promise to return them to their village. A promise which a committee headed by Ariel Sharon decided to negate.

During the 1992 elections, the Israeli Labour Party adopted the cause of the two villages. Villagers who carried out protests in the vicinity of their land were harassed and attacked by local settlers who had started to cultivate the village land. In 1996 the government offered a compensation package (land elsewhere and a new village) which discriminated between family members. It was rejected.

In March 1998 the Israeli High Court gave the Israeli government three months to make a decision as to why the villagers from Iqrit should not be allowed back to their village. If the state failed to produce an answer, another hearing would take place in July. Apparently the Court stated that Cabinet deliberations on the matter cannot go on indefinitely[14].

November 14

Israel received instructions from the Dr Bunche, acting mediator, to withdraw Israeli forces in the Negev behind provisional demarcation lines to be established by 19 November. In effect, the northern Negev would be transformed into a no-man's-land or neutral zone.

Doubt was expressed as to Israel's willingness to adhere to them, with the spokesman repeating the refrain that the instructions lacked the "basic elements of reality, reason and justice, and was bound to damage the prestige of the United Nations." Britain was regarded as the villain of the piece.

By night-fall the Egyptians had accepted Bunche's proposals.

November 15

Following a week of secret discussions the Security Council met in Paris to consider the British proposal for extending the requirements of its Negev resolution to the recent Israeli military operations in northern Palestine. In the event, the prior discussions had brought about "a distinct change of attitude" towards the question of Palestine. A Canadian proposal to establish armistice lines in the various sectors as a first move towards a permanent peace found favour, with Britain waiving priority for her motion to extend sanctions.

Within the General Assembly, the political committee at last embarked upon its debate of the Bernadotte report which, by then, was nearly two months old. Israel's foreign minister, Moshe Shertok, set out the Israeli argument by claiming that the report was not a basis for discussion. Valid territorial settlement rested, he claimed, only on the partition resolution of 29 November 1947.

The Balfour Declaration of 1917 was invoked and used to assert that the Zionist Jews had been promised a "national home" of 44 740 square miles. When Transjordan had been taken away, the area shrunk to about 10 000 square miles. By 1947 this had been reduced to give about 6 350 square miles. This was later reduced to 5 579 square miles [Author's note: keep in mind that of this area and the property established thereon, only about 7% was Jewish owned at the time of partition.] The assassinated mediator now wanted this further reduced to 2 124 square miles it was claimed.

The statement then argued for Israeli sovereignty over, and access to, various chunks of Palestinian land.

The Negev was essential for future colonisation and immigration. The chemical wealth of the Dead Sea should not fall into Arab hands. The Gulf of Aquaba was Israel's "gateway to the eastern seas." Haifa port and Lydda airport could not be considered "free." Modern "Jewish Jerusalem" was claimed (with international custody of the holy places in the city conceded) as was the "strip" connecting it with the "Jewish state."

Then came the claims which were to be rehearsed and repeated throughout the coming decades. The Palestinian refugees had not been driven out by the Zionists. Not only had the Arabs started the fighting but they had arranged the "evacuation", sometimes with British help. Throughout, alleged British connivance with the Arabs was emphasised.

The terror and military campaigns which historians later revealed were given no mention. Instead the image of mass-migration, a familiar feature of modern history, was allowed to obscure the harsh reality of genocide. Quite simply, it was argued, the Arabs had brought about their situation by their folly and short-sightedness. The victims had only themselves to blame.

November 16

At the Security Council the Canadian armistice plan was adopted. Britain dropped its motion to extend "sanctions" to the Negev. A Syrian attempt at a similar amendment was roundly defeated. Israel "applauded the central purpose of the new resolution to move from truce to peace." Already the media was referring to the conquered and occupied Palestinian land as "its (ie Israel's) territory."

In the Political Committee the Arab position was not to accept either partition or the Bernadotte report. Neither provided a basis for peace or harmony. How could the Arabs be asked to desist from fighting when the most fertile part of their land had been taken from them? Arab proposals, including one to refer the whole matter to the International Court of Justice, had never been considered.

The Egyptians objected, pointing out that the Arabs and the UN were being faced with a *fait accompli*. "The Jews occupied the land, brought in a few prefabricated houses which they called a settlement and then rushed up troops to protect it, with the result that hundreds of thousands of the lawful people of Palestine were being driven systematically from their homes, and systematically put to death."

Attention was drawn to events in Bethlehem and Nazareth and to the "anti-Christian strain of Zionism." Galilee was being systematically pillaged according to reports from UN observers.

The Arab League met in Cairo where discussion of relief measures for the refugees was followed by decisions on the situation in Palestine: Arabs will never agree to partition; Britain and the US should not think that they can win Israeli gratitude by trying to persuade the Arabs that their case is hopeless; an all-Palestine Government at Gaza is to be the symbol of

Palestinian independence and resistance to Israel and is to be supported by all Arabs.

The US Consulate General reported to the US government, quoting Arab sources on the atrocities at Al Dawayima. A figure of between 500 - 1 000 people killed was given.

On the border with Lebanon, the village of al Nabi Rubin was one of the villages referred to by Moshe Carmel, the commanding officer of the Northern Front, when he reported to Ben Gurion that the army "had been forced for military reasons . . . to expel the villages on the border." In the case of al Nabi Rubin, the villagers were forcibly expelled into Lebanon.

Carmel was ready to "freeze the situation" whereby there would be no more expulsions and nobody allowed to return.

By this date about 100 Zionist immigrant families had settled in Arab properties in Ramleh. Another 500 to 600 families arrived in the months to follow.

The Israeli Supreme Court freed the last remaining abductee of the Stern Gang, Frederick Sylvester, jailed for seven years on charges of espionage. There was no evidence to support the three charges.

November 17

Arab members of the UN Political Committee continued to express their implacable hostility to the Bernadotte proposals. Faris Bey el Khoury, the Syrian delegate made the speech of the day, accusing Britain of bias.

During the mandate the Jewish Zionists had been allowed to amass arms which citizens in no other country would be allowed to possess. Meanwhile the Arabs in Palestine had not been allowed arms "not even a knife" and anyone found with a revolver was condemned to death. By what rights had the Zionists proclaimed a sovereign state? In all the 14 districts of Palestine they were not in a majority except in Tel Aviv, but the United Nations had preferred to work for political, rather than legal, ends.

Within the Israeli Cabinet, Ben Gurion was accused by the agricutural minister, Aharon Zisling of having ignored "Jewish behaviour" towards the Arabs for over half a year. He was accused of pleading ignorance and of deflecting criticism of the army. It was agreed that, outwardly, to preserve its "good name", Israel must admit nothing. The matter of the atrocities, however, must be thoroughly investigated.

In the end evasiveness was still apparent. One member of the

"Committee of Three" resigned. It was then disbanded with Ben Gurion given the task of investigating "the charges concerning the army's behaviour towards the Arabs in the Galilee and in the South." This task was eventually passed on to three army officers.[15]

November 18

At the Political Committee of the UN, Britain introduced a resolution calling on the General Assembly to accept and take steps to apply the conclusions of the Bernadotte report. The American silence on the matter apparently spread "infectiously" throughout the committee.

The speech pointed out that under the Bernadotte proposals the Zionists would be getting a very high percentage of good land in Palestine and the Palestinian Arabs would be left with nearly 100% of the poor and useless land. It was Britain's view that it was not too high a price for the Negev to be returned to the Palestinian Arabs in return for central and western Galilee.

Israel announced its welcome for the armistice proposals of the Security Council if they would lead the way from truce to peace. The provisional government stalled on the question of withdrawing troops from the Negev.

Ya'akov Shimoni, acting director of the Israeli foreign ministry Middle East Affairs Department wrote to Walter Eytan, director general of the foreign ministry:

> "Our advice [to the army] and our view [ie, the view of the Middle East Affairs Department of the Foreign Ministry] which were not acted upon, are certainly clear to you: We asked that [the army] make an effort during the conquest that no Arab inhabitants remain in the Galilee and certainly that no refugees from other places remain there . . ."[16]

Sixteen Bedouin chiefs formally presented a request that they be allowed to stay in Israel. With the fear that Israeli settlement and agricultural interests could be sacrificed, Yosef Weitz of the JNF, proposed that if the area was not be "cleansed" of the Bedouin, it would be better that they were concentrated in a limited area reserved for this purpose.

In late November, Yosef Nahmani of the Jewish National Fund, lamented that "the army continues to destroy villages in the Galilee, which we are interested in [settling][1]

November 20

Kibbutz Revadim was established on the land of Al Kheima at the western end of the Jerusalem corridor.

November 21

A preliminary statement from the U.S indicated a marked divergence from the British position on the Bernadotte proposals. While it supported the boundaries of Israel as set out in the partition resolution, any modifications should only be made if acceptable to Israel. No mention was made of the views or desires of the dispossessed Palestinians. No mention was made of those who were sacrificed to make the emerging Israel a reality.

The rather contradictory and ironic view, in light of the support given to the partition resolution, was expressed that the UN should not devise a blueprint for Palestine. The parties should be left with the burden of peaceful adjustment.

With Britain observing that the imbalance of the military situation placed the Arabs under "duress", the scene was set for fifty years later. Let the Israelis and Palestinians sit together around a table to hammer out a peace agreement. Never mind that the table would seat two very much unequal partners with the U.S., as usual, adopting a position of professed neutrality while leaning on the weaker party to accommodate Israel's every whim.

November 22

At the Political Committee of the UN, the Soviet Union rejected the Bernadotte proposals out of hand and supported Israeli claims in the Negev. Henry Cattan of the Arab Higher Commitee made a scathing attack on the partition plan and Bernadotte's proposals.

No people, he said, could agree to be dominated by a foreign minority brought into their midst against their will nor to have their homeland dismembered for the sake of the illegal claims by such a minority. Politically, historically, and economically, Palestine was one entity, one homeland, in which population, ownership, and economy were inextricably linked. From the economic aspect partition did violence to every sense of justice.

The Zionist Jews were to be given all that was best in the country. With Zionist Jews owning only 7% of the territory, it was proposed to give them all the best agricultural land, including all the citrus groves, 53% of which was Arab owned. "In the proposed Arab area" he observed, "there will be nothing to produce, nothing to export, nothing to live on."

Canada, in giving support to the British resolution, told the Committee that the Israelis could "not have it both ways." Israel could not have all the territory given to it by the partition plan and also all the territory it had taken by force.

November 23

America made sweeping amendments to the British resolution supporting Bernadotte's proposals, arguing that they "strengthened" the British proposals. A sentiment that convinced nobody within the British delegation.

The amendments sought to delete the British clause endorsing the specific conclusions of Count Bernadotte, while strengthening references to partition. Much to Israel's satisfaction, greater emphasis was placed on direct negotiations.

Australia was, in Israel's eyes, the darling of the day. A resolution was tabled which not only promoted the idea of local "arrangements" as opposed to an "imposed" plan but called for Israel's admission into the United Nations.

Fourteen alleged members of the Stern Gang, including an "important" member of the Gang, escaped from prison. The police stated that they intended to make no special effort to apprehend the escapees and said that 173 suspects had been released.

November 24

Syria warned that Western Europe might have its Middle Eastern oil supplies halted if they voted for the Palestine partition plan in forthcoming UN debates.

The Israeli Cabinet gave retrospective approval to the "cleansing" of the boundary with Lebanon. Ben Gurion gave his approval for the return, from Lebanon, of the refugees from the Christian village of Biram - but not to their own village. Some were eventually forced to remain in Lebanon due, it was said, for lack of transport.

Yosef Weitz and others immediately started to plan new settlements along the border strip. Within months Biram's land was parcelled out to various settlements.

Ben Gurion met with his top Arab affairs and military advisers to hammer out policy with regard to the Bedouin in the Negev. The views of Allon prevailed and became official policy five days later. This resulted, in early 1949, with the forced concentration of thousands of Bedouin to an area east of Beersheba.

November 25

A revised British resolution on Palestine was presented to the Political Committee. Emphasis was still given to Bernadotte's proposals and it clearly stated the objections to the Arab parties having to negotiate a settlement while under duress. This, it was argued, would result in an imposed settlement

Dr Bunche expressed optimism that, with the truce not being able to hold out much longer, a settlement was the closest it had ever been. He declared that the General Assembly must give unequivocal decisions on seven points:

1] affirmation of the existence of the state of Israel and its admission to the United Nations
2] the parties must negotiate
3] establish a conciliation commision
4] guidelines for the commission, particularly over allocation of territory
5] affirmation of the rights of the Arab refugees to return home
6] the future of Jerusalem on the basis of international status with maximum local autonomy for Arab and Jew
7] international guarantees for the boundaries

The Soviet Union introduced a motion calling for the immediate withdrawal from Palestine of foreign military personnel. This was seen to bolster a previous position where the Soviets did not want the Negev handed back to the Palestinian owners.

The Jewish Agency reported that out of the 92 000 Jewish immigrants who had arrived over the past 11 months, 35 000 had been settled in "abandoned" Arab villages and cities. Thirty thousand wooden dwelling units were under construction. A new town was planned for the Negev, with immigrants being directed to Beersheba.[17]

November 26

The U.S. informed the Political Committee that it was unable to accept the essential clauses of the revised British proposals.

Syria proposed the establishment of a five member commission which would prepare for the creation of a single Palestine State on the basis of cantonisation or federation with wide autonomous privileges.

Israel replied to the earlier armistice proposals, with eagerness expressed for entering into direct negotiations, although it was prepared to negotiate through the UN if necessary.

November 28

The UN reported that negotiations had started to bring about a "complete and effective cease fire" for Jerusalem. The Israelis informed the UN observers' chief of staff that unless the Egyptians entered into armistice negotiations she would would feel free to revise her attitude to the Egyptian forces trapped in the Faluja pocket in the northern Negev. This was regarded as a thinly disguised threat to resume hostilities in the area.

Ten members of the Stern Gang tried to seize control of the radio station in Tel Aviv. It was thought they intended to broadcast a political speech.

An open letter of protest was signed by three prominent New York clergymen - Roman Catholic, Protestant and Jewish - against a $50 per head fund raising dinner in honour of Menachem Begin, terrorist leader of the Irgun. The Irgun was described as a "terroristic band" whose acts horrified Zionist supporters, and which had apparently been repudiated by the Israeli authorities. As a "totalitarian-minded group" it was described as reactionary and compared with the "fanatical" Moslem Brotherhood with its funds raised from gullible Americans and used to buy arms from Soviet Russia.[18]

November 29

This first anniversary of the partition resolution passed with little celebration. Ben Gurion used the occasion to repeat an earlier statement that Israel was no longer bound by the letter of the resolution and there would be no peace and security until the Negev and the Galilee were settled by Jewish immigrants.

At the United Nations, Israel formally applied for membership stating that from the day it is admitted the obligations of the Charter would be honoured. British sources indicated the government's position that Israel should not be admitted until the final boundaries of a partitioned Palestine were outlined.

In the Political Committee, attention turned to debating six resolutions placed before it. The Syrian resolution apart, all were based on the partition plan of the previous year.

November 30

At the UN Political Committee, Britain and America moved closer to agreement when Britain withdrew the paragraph of her resolution which called on the General Assembly to endorse the Bernadotte report. This included the proposal to give the Negev back to the Arabs with the Israeli state acquiring Western Galilee. Territorial adjustment between the two parties would be based on reciprocity reached by negotiation.

In Jerusalem the Arab and Israeli commanders agreed upon cease fire arrangements.

A plan for the construction of 96 settlements - to fill the "vacuum"created by the recent Arab "exodus" was presented by the Jewish Agency's Settlement Department to the Ministerial Committee for Abandoned Property. It proposed 40 settlements in Upper Galilee, 8 in the Jerusalem corridor, 18 in the northern Negev and its approaches, 22 in central Negev and 8 along the Mediterranean coast. The proposals urged that "Wherever conditions make it necessary, the new settlement should be established [on the site of] the existing [Arab] village."[19]

Notes

1 Benny Morris, *The birth of the Palestinian refugee problem, 1947-49*, p.169
2 *ibid* p.224
3 *ibid* p.231
4 Walid Khalidi, *All that Remains*, p.6
5 Morris, p.192
6 Benny Morris, *Falsifying the Record*, p.55 (Journal of Palestine Studies, Spring 1995)
7 Benny Morris, *The birth of the Palestinian refugee problem, 1947-49*, p.232
8 The Scotsman 10/11/48
9 Khalidi, p.109
10 Benny Morris, *Operation Hiram Revisited: A Correction*, (JoPS, Winter 1999) p.71
11 Benny Morris, *The birth of the Palestinian refugee problem, 1947-49*, p.130
12 Michael Palumbo, *The Palestinian Catastrophe*, p.172
13 The Scotsman, 14/11/48
14 Elias Chacour, *Blood Brothers*
The Jerusalem Times 27/3/98
Challenge No.35 Jan-Feb 1996(A Jerusalem Magazine on the Israeli-Palestinian Conflict)
15 Morris, p.233
16 Benny Morris, *Operation Hiram Revisited: A Correction*, (JoPS, Winter 1999) p.69
17 The Times 26/11/48
18 The Times 29/11/48
19 Benny Morris, *The birth of the Palestinian refugee problem, 1947-49* p.188

December

We will not allow the Arabs back.

David Ben Gurion, Prime Minister of Israel.

In the Galilee, during the month of December and into January 1949, pressure increased for further expulsions of remaining villagers and of those who had infiltrated back to their homes. If the latter was not halted Israel, it was said, would have to "conquer the Galilee anew." Semi-empty villages were a magnet to those returning Palestinian villagers, with the "danger" of a permanent increase in Israel's Arab population. In addition, Israeli settlements wanted the land of these half-empty villages.

Yosef Weitz of the Jewish National Fund visited the village of al Zib, to the north of Acre, and noted that it had been "completely levelled." He further observed "I now wonder if it was good that it was destroyed and would not have been greater revenge had we now settled Jews in the village houses."[1]

During this month the Israelis approved the settlement of 3 000 Jewish immigrants in the Palestinian houses in al Majdal (to be re-named Ashkelon) in the south. By this point in time there was a gradual change in the practice of outright expulsion to one of eviction from one site to another. However it was to be 1951 before the remaining 1 500 or so remaining Palestinian residents in al Majdal were convinced that it was in their "interests" to move into exile in the Gaza Strip.

With the end of 1948 approaching, it was apparent - as far as the media was concerned - that the traumas of the year were fast losing their news value with regard to Palestine. The plight of about 750 000 dispossessed and devastated people, exposed to harsh winter conditions with very little food or shelter, rarely featured.

December 1

The U.S. accepted Britain's modified proposals on Palestine while they were rejected by Israel. The proposals called for a conciliation committee to assist the negotiations between the parties. They were also considered to be a compromise between the original partition plan and Bernadotte's proposals.

Israel rejected the giving of "Arab Palestine" to Transjordan and the proposal for an international regime for all Jerusalem. Both Egypt and Syria repeated their demand that the whole question of Palestine should be submitted to the International Court of Justice

The settlement of Bustal Hagalil was established on the land of As Sumeiriya.

December 2

Britain rejected an American attempt to secure Israel's admission to the United Nations. The Israeli application was described as "both premature and rather doubtful." At the UN Political Committee the British-American proposals on Palestine were defeated. The proposal for a conciliation commission was accepted but its functions were disputed.

December 3

The UN Political Committee rejected the last of Count Bernadotte's recommendations - to join the remaining Arab parts of Palestine to Transjordan. A three-man conciliation committee was given the responsibility for the future of Palestine, with a vague mandate to "persuade Jews and Arabs to agree on all the controversial issues that have torn the Holy Land apart."

The remnants of the British-American proposal included;

1] an international regime for "Greater Jerusalem" to include several famous religious shrines

2] a UN Commissioner for the Holy City

3] demilitarisation of Jerusalem under direction of the UN Security Council

4] maximum autonomy for Arab and Jewish Local Authorities

The Syrian government resigned following disturbances throughout the country in response to events in Palestine.

December 5

Arab delegates to the UN expressed bitter disappointment at the British resolution on Palestine which, after passing through the Political Committee, was "unrecognisable". The Egyptian delegate observed that the only paragraph in favour of the Arabs was that providing for the return of Arab refugees "at the earliest possible date." And even these advantages were considered illusory.

In contrast, Israel's supporters were described as being "highly satisfied."

"Public enemy number two" during the British mandate, Nathan Friedman Yellin, appeared in court in Acre accused of being a member of the outlawed Stern Gang, along with his lieutenant. Yellin, who succeeded Abraham Stern following his death at the hands of the British police in 1942, was caught trying to flee Palestine shortly after the murder of Count Bernadotte.

The Ministerial Committee for Abandoned Property approved the settlement of Beersheba. With the army objecting, Ben Gurion intervened and ordered the military to free half the town for "civilian purposes".

December 7

For the first time since the end of the mandate, news correspondents were allowed to cross Israeli lines into the Arab-held Old City of Jerusalem. Surprisingly little damage was reported. Those areas which had suffered most were those which had been the focus of military activity. The Latrun Monastery was severely damaged as was the Jewish Quarter of the Old City, which had been the setting for some of the fiercest fighting.

A plan for 41 new settlements to fill the vacuum left by the fleeing Palestinians in Upper Galilee, the Negev and Mediterranean coast was endorsed by the directorate of the Jewish National Fund. The stipulation was made that land be set aside for returning Arabs. Opposition was expressed against the original proposals that the settlements be established on existing village sites, some of which were still inhabited.

Kibbutz Mishmar-David and Hever Hakvutzot was established on the land of Khulda towards the west of the Jerusalem corridor, along with Kibbutz Me'uhad at Sar'a.

December 8

Britain warned the UN of Israeli incursions over the Transjordan border. She warned that she might have to take action under the treaty obligations with Transjordan.

The acting mediator gave both Egyptians and Israelis 48 hours to stop fighting in Palestine or the issue would be brought before the Security Council. Resolutions being breached were those of 4 November (ordering Arabs and Israelis in the Negev to withdraw from certain positions) and that of 16 November which called for immediate armistice negotiations.

December 11

The Israelis carried out one of their "security checks" in the Wadi Nisnas area of Haifa. The Ministry of Minorities and the police were looking for Palestinians who had "infiltrated" back to their homes. About 300 so-called "illegals" were arrested. Some were deported across the "borders" of the state of Israel. Others were detained for investigation. With a clear cut aim of not allowing the indigenous Arab population to grow in Haifa, the Palestinian population lived in constant fear of these raids[2].

The UN General Assembly passed Resolution 194 which called for the return of Palestinian refugees to their homes and reaffirmed the separate status of Jerusalem. In reaction, Israel stepped up settlement activity.

December 12

An agreement was reached between Israeli and Arab commanders to open the road to Bethlehem, controlled by both Arab and Israeli, for Christmas.

Following months of deliberation, the Emergency Regulations Relating to Absentees Property were published. They gave the Agricultural Ministry control or possession of those leased lands designated as "Abandoned Lands."

December 13

Following a meeting and the decisions of the Arab Congress in Jericho, both Houses of the Transjordan parliament unanimously endorsed a Cabinet decision to annex the Arab areas of Palestine under the sovereignty of King Abdullah. Egypt and Syria disowned the Arab Congress. Syria asked Transjordan that no action should be taken on Palestine. Saudi Arabia regarded the Jericho resolution as invalid.

December 14

The Scotsman printed an article on the "Rivalry of Kings" which highlighted the tensions between the various Arab states and, in particular, the decisions facing King Abdullah of Transjordan. Should he remain faithful to the views of the Arab League on Palestine? Should he risk the ire of the members of the League by annexing that part of Palestine which his troops, together with some Iraqis, had saved from the Israelis ? And, by doing so, admit the existence of the state of Israel.

The article dwelt upon the intertwined relationships between the various kingdoms, with King Abdullah being viewed as a "realist." If he does not take over the remnants of Arab Palestine, the Israelis will do it for him. In addition there is Abdullah's relation with Britain where he is largely regarded as the tool of the British Imperialists. His life was regarded as "prone to attack by fanatics as was that of Count Bernadotte."

December 15

The Committee for Transferring Arabs from Place to Place deliberated on the proposals from a Major Sulz that the inhabitants of Farradiya, Kufr I'nan near Safad and Saffuriya near Nazareth be moved. The proposals were endorsed but not implemented immediately.

In reaction to the passing of UN Resolution 194 four days earlier, particularly its failure to include Jerusalem within the state of Israel, the military governor of Jerusalem, Dov Joseph ordered the immediate expansion of Jewish housing areas into empty Palestinian property. The first to be settled was close to the Mamilla commercial centre.

December 17

A motion proposing Israel's membership of the UN was rejected by two votes in the Security Council. Britain abstained, rejecting the U.S. argument that to support the application would support the work of the Conciliation Commission in Palestine. A Syrian resolution to ask the International Court of Justice at The Hague to give an opinion on the question was rejected.

The Security Council refused to discuss an Egyptian appeal for urgent action on an Israeli breach of the truce in the Negev. The Soviet Union and America argued that they should wait for a report from the acting mediator before looking at the actions of Israeli forces against Egyptian troops trapped at Faluja.

The Jewish Agency treasurer, Israel Goldstein, revealed that in the year following 29 November 1947, the date of the partition resolution, 101 000 Zionist immigrants had arrived in Palestine. An average of 1 000 per month was now expected, with some 1 500 000 coming from Europe and "Muslim lands" over the next five years.

Before the start of Operation Horev in southern Palestine, General Allon issued an appendix to operational orders. In setting out guideleines for the treatment of captured Arab soldiers and the conquered civilian population, reference was made to the "dreadful incidents" that had occurred in the past.

The guidelines included injunctions to take prisoners where possible, not to kill them. . . . "unjustified killing of civilians will be regarded as murder . . . Torture of placid civilians will be dealt with sharply; Arab populations must not be expelled except with special permission from the Front Battle HQ."[3]

Units of the Alexandroni Brigade attacked the village, 'Iraq al-Manhiyya, only to be driven back by Egyptian forces. The village remained within the "Faluja pocket" until the Armistice of February 1949 finally sealed its fate.

December 18

Yosef Weitz of the Jewish Agency asked Ben Gurion whether, in the planning of settlements, "suplus land" should be set aside for possible refugee return. The reply was in the negative. "Not along the borders, and in each village we will take back everything, as per our settlement needs. We will not allow the Arabs back."[4]

Towards the end of December, the 1948 Absentees Property Regulations were set in motion to solve the problem of leasing non-Jewish owned land. Why not sell the so-called abandoned land to the Jewish National Fund? Thus earning the state large sums of money while avoiding the problems of managing the purloined land. The JNF could then lease the land out to settlements.

It was around this period that, following a lifting of the ban by Ben Gurion on Jewish settlement in Lydda, immigrants began to occupy Palestinian owned homes in the town. Likewise in Jerusalem, a mass movement of immigrants started, commencing with the settlement of some 150 families in the Palestinian village of 'Ein Karim to the west of Jerusalem.

December 21

Reports indicated that an Iraqi delegation had failed to persuade King Abdullah to renounce his plan for "unifying" the remainder of Arab Palestine with Transjordan. Egypt, in particular was seen to be particularly vexed over the issue, with Abdullah's appointment of his choice of Mufti for Jerusalem not exactly designed to extinguish the flames. Egypt was reported to be re-arming itself, making some of the armaments available to those Palestinians who still held an allegiance to the old Mufti.

December 23

The UN headquarters in Haifa reported an Israeli combined air, sea and land offensive against the Egyptians based in Gaza and strongholds in the Negev. Heavy artillery, mortar and air bombardment was reported. The Egyptians trapped at Faluja were targeted. Blackouts were imposed in Tel Aviv and the Israeli held areas as Egyptian tanks, under air cover, attacked Nirim settlement.

This outbreak of hostilities was considered to be the Israeli response to Egypt's refusal to proceed with armistice talks " . . with a view to defending its territory and hastening the conclusion of peace."[5]

Ben Gurion sent a Christmas message to all "Israeli Christian citizens" - the majority of whom were Palestinian Arabs - wishing them a joyous holiday, prosperity and happiness.

With Ben Gurion believing that the Gaza Strip, and its burgeoning refugee population, was about to fall into Israeli hands, he instructed General Avner to take severe measures to protect the inhabitants of the Gaza Strip. Expulsions were to be avoided.[3]

On the same day Ben Gurion gave instructions with regard to the arriving immigrants, or *olim*. The absorption organisations were to send "ten thousand *olim*" to the Galilee villages.However, opposition was expressed to this instruction within the Mapam movement, with one opponent, Pinhas Ger of Kibbutz Ma'anit arguing "- - we never thought of settling a Jewish *oleh* in the house of the expelled Arab. It is the right of the Arabs who were expelled or fled to return to the Land of Israel."

As Benny Morris observed, this opposition may have been motivated by the growing antagonism to the competition that the private *moshavim*, to which the *olim* were being directed, presented to the ideological *kibbutzim*. However the debate was brought to a conclusion the following month when, by majority vote, the Israeli Cabinet supported Ben Gurion "to encourage introducing *olim* into all the abandoned villages in the Galilee."[6]

December 24

Whereas, thousands had always set out to attend the evening service in Bethlehem's Church of the Nativity, only a few score pilgrims set out. For a parallel, according to The Scotsman, you had to go back to the twelvth century when Saladin beat the Crusaders and barred the traditional pilgrimage road.

The Egyptian commander in Gaza reported that Israel had bombed towns packed with refugees and a refugee camp. Some 165 000 refugees were at the mercy of aerial and mortar bombardment. Ten men women and children were seen by one correspondent lying severely wounded in a Red Crescent hospital. An eight year old refugee boy from Ramleh died from his wounds in the same hospital. Six other civilian deaths were reported by doctors and other witnesses resulting from bombs dropped on Gaza and

Khan Yunis.

The Security Council put off a debate, at the request of the USSR, on the renewed hostilities until a report was received from the acting mediator.

Canada announced its recognition of the provisional government of Israel.

December 26

Reports continued to give accounts of fighting between Israeli and Egyptian forces in the Negev. Hostilities were concentrated at the frontline positions, Gaza and to the south.

December 27

"I have no knowledge of any incidents which could be claimed as a provocation for the fighting in the Negeb. . . In view of all the above circumstances I must report to the Security Council my inability to supervise effectively the truce in the Negeb, since U.N. observers are being refused access to the area on the Israeli side, and since the Government of Israel feels bound to reserve its freedom of action."[7]

So observed acting mediator, Dr Bunche, in his report to the Security Council which laid the blame for the outbreak of hostilities squarely at Israel's door. Israel had expelled all UN observers from their posts alongside Israeli forces and had then undertaken unilateral military action.

Egypt's delegate to the UN warned that Israel was trying to present the Security Council with an accomplished fact by occupying the Negev.

December 28

Egypt complained to the UN Truce Supervisory Board that Israeli troops had opened a "full-scale attack" in the Negev. The Faluja "pocket", Bir Asluj to the south of Beersheba and, on the Egyptian border, Auja el Hafir had all borne the brunt of the attack. Thousands of Palestinian refugees were on the move again, fleeing Gaza.

There were reports and counter reports that Gaza had been captured, that it had been cut off and isolated from the other Egyptian positions.

Meanwhile the Security Council, meeting in Paris, prevaricated and put off for 24 hours any decision on the events unfolding in the Negev. The "intransigent attitude assumed by the Israeli authorities on the situation at El Faluja" which Dr Bunche blamed for preventing progress on implementing the Security Council resolution of 16 November was debated.

Syria apart, Britain was the only member in any apparent hurry to do something to stop the fighting in the Negev.The Council's Negev sub-committee had yet to report back and the three nations of the Conciliation Committee had yet to appoint their representatives. Once again Britain was prepared to argue for sanctions, pointing out during the May truce she had been prepared to support sanction orders against the Arab states if they had stepped out of line.

Israel argued that the armistice resolution had priority over the truce order and unless Egypt agreed to open armistice talks Israel could not be bound over by the truce agreement. Britain regarded the situation facing the Security Council as serious, putting to test the authority of the UN in Palestine. The situation in the Negev was not a simple breach of a truce but a clear attempt to present the UN with a *fait accompli*.

December 29

With Israeli forces reported to have crossed the Egyptian-Palestine frontier speculation was voiced that Britain would have to invoke the Anglo-Egyptian Mutual Aid Treaty. However it was assumed that the Israelis had acted in "error". The continuing military operations in the Negev was described by an Israeli spokesman as "mopping up operations taking place in Israeli territory."

The UN Security Council adopted the British resolution which called on both sides to implement without delay the truce regulations for the Negev ordered on 4 November. The U.S. found itself alongside the Eastern bloc countries when it decided to abstain. It was noted that the position of America on the Palestine question was in marked contrast to its stance on the Dutch breach of the truce in Indonesia. In this latter case, the U.S. was responsible for the convening of the Security Council to discuss the matter.

The attitude of the Arab states was one of weary disillusionment with the United Nations.While talking was taking place, the situation in the Negev could easily be out of control by the time the Security Council next met on 6 January.

Britain rejected the Israeli contention that the fighting was taking place within the "national" territory of Israel. Gaza and Khan Yunis were Arab under the partition resolution. Likewise, Faluja and Beersheba - from which the Israelis had refused to evacuate despite an order from the acting mediator - had been awarded to the Palestinians under partition.

December 30

Israel said that she had yet to receive the Security Council's resolution calling for an immediate cease-fire. Once the text of the resolution was known, Israel would give it consideration.

Fighting in southern Palestine was still going on, with less intensity but over a wider area. It was reported that two Egyptian planes were shot down by Israeli planes over "Jewish territory."

And so ended 1948.

As far as the Palestinian people were concerned, it was the year of treachery of the international community, as represented by the will of the United Nations, towards their rights. A treachery which resulted in the dispossession of about 750 000 people of their land.

It started with the aftermath of the terrorist Irgun attack in Haifa. It ended with the completion of the ethnic cleansing of northern and southern Palestine, euphemistically referred to as "mopping up" operations. These ensured that as much of Palestine as possible was acquired by Israel. Acquisitions which, in spite of many UN resolutions, Israel never intended to relinquish. In this she was abetted by the inaction and perceived self-interests of the major powers of the day.

To this day the Palestinian people continue to fight for their rights.

However December 31, 1948 did not see the end of the expulsions for the Palestinian Arab.

In January 1949, the remaining villagers of the village of Saffuriya, near Nazareth, were evicted. The village land, long coveted by neighbouring kibbutzim, was apportioned amongst these interested parties.

The following month, under the pretext of "security, law and order" the remaining villagers of Farradiya and Kafr I'nan, near Safad, were expelled. The villagers of Al Ghabisiya in Western Galilee suffered the same fate. This type of action continued into the 1950s.

During January 1949, eleven new colonial settlements were established to help in the consolidation of the Israeli state's claim to the newly conquered areas in Western Galilee, the Jerusalem corridor and Lydda-Ramleh district.

On 28 January 1949 the terms of purchase of 250 000 acres of stolen Palestinian owned land, by the Jewish National Fund from the state of Israel, was agreed. In the following months much of the land was leased, mostly to new settlements

On 24 February, 1949 the Israel-Egypt General Armistice Agreement was signed. Within days the Israelis had breached the conditions of the agreement which guaranteed the safety and property of those civilians remaining in the villages of Al Faluja and Iraq al Manshiya - albeit under curfews and restrictions imposed by the Israeli Military Government rule.

UN observers on the spot complained that "Arab civilians . . at Al Faluja have been beaten and robbed by Israeli soldiers and . . . there have been some cases of attempted rape."

The tactic of "whispering campaigns", threatening attacks and acts of vengeance, was put to good effect. This together with Israeli troops "firing promiscuously" at helpless civilians resulted in about 2 400 terror stricken people seeking refuge around the UN observers. All wanted to go to safety in Transjordan-held Hebron.

While some Israelis conveniently labelled the UN reports as "exaggerated" others, like foreign minister Sharett, felt the the army's action questioned Israel's "sincerity as a partner to an international agreement." In the end, the position seemed to be one of feigned outrage while blaming unruly local commanders together with local initiatives.

On 30 March 1949 the Israeli-Jordanian Armistice Agreement was signed. This involved the cession of land to Israel. Known as the Little Triangle, this land housed a population of 12 000 Palestinian Arabs in about fifteen villages. In exchange, Israel gave its approval to Jordan's annexation of what was to become the West Bank. On top of this, with the withdrawal of Iraqi forces from Palestine, there was the threat of military action if King Abdullah did not agree to the transfer.

This latter action, it was feared, would precipitate the flight of a further 15 000 refugees. After all, Israeli intelligence reported in mid-April that the Arabs "live in great fear of our 'barbarity' and it would take little inducement to persuade them to abandon their lands."

On the 1 June, 24 hours after the signing of the Armistice Agreement, the Israelis evicted some of the local population in the Little Triangle to make way for new Zionist settlements[8]. However the cession of Palestinian territory to Israel did not, this time, result in wholesale expulsion of the population. Moshe Sharett commented a couple of months later"This time . . . the Arabs learned the lesson; they are not running away. It is not possible in every place to arrange what some of our boys engineered in Faluja [where] they chased away the Arabs after we signed an . . international commitment . ."

The one exception took place on the night of 27 June 1949 when up to 1 500 refugees living around Baqa al Gharbiya were "forcefully and brutally" expelled. Israel argued that the armistice agreement only protected local residents, not refugees temporarily sheltering in the ceded area. This action was investigated by the Armistice Commission and, when its judgement was in the balance, Israel threatened that if forced to take back the refugees, the refugees "would regret it."

By June 1950 the Israeli side of the armistice line with Transjordan had been cleared of a small shifting population of frightened refugees. Semi-intact villages had been levelled or occupied by Zionist immigrants. The remaining Palestinian residents of the village of Zakariya and the town of Al Majdal were expelled.[9]

Negotiations with Lebanon started on 1 March 1949 and together with Syria, lasted until July. In the case of the former, it was not perceived as a threat. Syria was, however, obliged to withdraw its forces and agree to a demilitarised zone being established around the river Jordan. This last creation was to be a cause of friction between Syria and Israel for the about the next 20 years.

Notes

1 Walid Khalidi, *All that Remains*, p.37
2 Michael Palumbo, *The Palestinian Catastrophe*, p.151
3 Benny Morris, *The birth of the Palestinian refugee problem, 1947-49*, p. 234
4 *ibid* p.186
5 The Scotsman 24/12/48
6 Morris, p.194
7 The Scotsman 28/12/48
8 Ilan Pappe,*The making of the Arab-Israeli Conflict 1947-1951*, p.190
9 Morris, detail extracted from Chapter 8

Appendix

The immediate aftermath of the Partition Resolution

December 1947

With the passing of the Partition Resolution on 29 November 1947, areas of Palestine were submerged in spontaneous chaos and violence as the Arab population demonstrated against the partition of their homeland. Particularly affected were those urban centres where there was a mixed Arab-Jewish population. For the unfortunate Arab or Jew who, in the absence of a police or army patrol, accidently stumbled into an angry group or sniper from the opposing community, the outcome was death or serious injury.

Tuesday, 2 December, was the start of a three-day strike called by the Arab Higher Committee in protest against the division of Palestine. It was the signal for widespread Arab violence to erupt. An 18 hour curfew was imposed on Jerusalem in the aftermath of shooting, looting and arson which affected 50 Jewish shops. In retaliation, Jewish youths, professing to be members of the Irgun, burned down a cinema they presumed to be Arab owned. In reality, it was part owned by relatives of the Zionist leader, Dr Chaim Wiezmann. In "no-man's land" between Jewish Tel-Aviv and Arab Jaffa shooting was reported

Ten thousand members, men and women, of the "semi-illegal" Jewish National Defence Force, the Haganah, were mobilised by night-fall to help "maintain order." The Jewish National Council in Jerusalem issued a "peace plea" in leaflets written in Arabic. They accused the Palestine police of "calculated indifference" in the face of Palestinian Arab rioters and demonstrators.

The Scotsman's Special Correspondent's overview of the day's events highlighted aspects of the evolving situation within Palestine, and how the events were perceived and reported in the media.

Already a considerable number of Arab families in towns of mixed Arab-Jewish population had fled to safer areas. Likewise Jewish residents moved into established Jewish quarters and formed "security zones" with promise of protection from the Haganah. Arab villages and tribes close to Zionist settlement colonies were reported to have given formal assurances to the colonies of their "peaceful and cooperative intentions."

The Moslem Brotherhood was reported to have many "efficient rabblerousers" in Palestine, while the Arab Higher Committee was dominated by the "extremist Husseini family" the head of which was the Mufti of Jerusalem, the leader of the Arab Rebellion in the 'thirties.

Conflict over dominance in Palestine, which was to blight any effective resistance against Zionist incursion into the land, was highlighted, as was the absence of any effective leadership on behalf of Palestine's Arabs. While the Mufti was believed to be trying to persuade the government of Syria to send troops to Palestine, he and his Palestine Party were reported to be afraid of the ambitions of King Abdullah of Transjordan.

In the US, the Hebrew Commitee for National Liberation appealed for surplus army equipment to be made available to the Zionist forces in Palestine. At the international level, within the US, serious consideration was given to the political considerations arising from the spiralling levels of inter-communal violence within Palestine. As with the concerns of some the Arab governments, it was not so much the future of Palestine and its people, more with how to ensure that your rivals did not get any advantages. Within the American political establishment, any possible involvement of the UN Security Council was a matter of worry as this could give the Soviet Union an opportunity to send troops to Palestine.

As the first week of December progressed it was the areas of mixed Jewish-Arab residents that dominated the news, with Palestinian Arab action and Jewish Zionist reaction. In particular, Jerusalem, the northern port town of Haifa and the border between Tel-Aviv and Jaffa featured in the news reports. The mix of roof top sniping, tommy guns, grenades, burning torches and use of the more basic "stick" by the protagonists brought about an inevitable increase in deaths and injuries

On 4 December the Acting Chief Rabbi in Britain, the Rev Dayan Lazarus took issue with the then Archbishop of York, Dr Garbett, when his letter to the Press Association was printed in the press. The former condemned the comment in Dr Garbett's Diocesan letter that "We cannot rely on the Jewish State giving adequate protection, or showing impartial justice to Christians and Arabs."

While this statement certainly displayed ignorance with regard to the existence of those members of the human race who were both Palestinian Arab **and** Christian, it was not this that bothered the Rev Dayan Lazarus. His concern focused on the alleged hatred being preached by the Archbishop and was of the view that "The Jews of all people know the terrible results of intolerance towards themselves. They are the last who would practice it towards others."

By the end of the first week, the conflict in Palestine, a five mile long "battle front" illuminated by raging fires, was centred on the border between Tel-Aviv and Jaffa with the "battle of the orange groves" stretching to Salameh village. The death total was quoted as 25 Jews and 22 Arabs in the first week following the passing of the Partition Resolution.

On 8 December, Arab forces carried out a concerted attack on Hatikvah, at the south east corner of Tel-Aviv, using small bombs and machine guns. Haganah forces were rushed to the area and later criticised the Irgun for spreading panic amongst the population. There were no Jewish deaths reported. On the same day it was announced that the Mandate authorities would take advantage of the Zionist offer to maintain law and order within the Jewish community. This allowed for the withdrawal of British and Arab police from designated areas, to be used in mixed areas.

The conflict reached new heights on 11 December, resulting in the death of 13 Jews and 12 Arabs by the end of the day. Jerusalem was reported to have been raked by bombs and bullets, with the "Moslem flag" flying above the ancient synagogue in the Old City. Fighting took place throughout the day in the winding alleys.

Two Haganah lorries were ambushed near Bethlehem resulting in the death of nine Zionists. In the Negev Desert, five more were killed. The Haganah launched a "vicious" counter-attack in Haifa. Street fighting, described as "whirlpools of violence", featured in the mixed areas with gangs of youths attacking, beating or stabbing the single individual they happen to come across. Under such an onslaught, the mixed areas were described as "disintegrating into rigid cantonments." This, despite an appeal from the mixed Arab-Jewish Municipal Council in Haifa for a cessation of the violent disturbances and a similar plea from the mayors of Tel-Aviv and Jaffa.

In Jerusalem, mobilisation of the Zionist forces continued apace. In an interesting observation, The Scotsman's correspondent pointed out that the Haganah patrols usually included one female who carried the arms. In such situations it was then the girl who was arrested for carrying arms (and released within a couple of weeks) because the Zionists could not afford to lose their trained men.

On 14 December the violent clashes took a new turn when Jewish settlement police, while escorting a convoy, were reported to have flung hand grenades and fired into the Royal Engineer's dump near Lydda. On guard duty were the Arab Legion from Transjordan who returned fire, killing 14 Settlement police and wounding ten others. At nearby Ramle, Arab raiders attacked an Arab police training depot, escaping with rifles, Bren guns, Sten guns and quantities of ammunition.

By the end of this weekend, a further 58 people were reported killed, bringing the total dead, since partition, to 238.

There then followed, throughout Palestine, a lull in the violence. Not, it was observed, because there had been any significant change in the situation. Less people, it seemed, were prepared to show themselves in the streets as victims. There was little sign of compromise between the two sides although the Jewish Agency still maintained "a stubborn and meaningless facade of good-will towards the Arabs."

By this point, more Arabs and Jews had been killed and, for the first time, there was now sign of Arab military organisation. By and large the Arab forces were reported to be composed of the more "excitable" youth, with little discipline. This contrasted with the Haganah which was largely composed of ex-Servicemen from the British forces.

Safad City became the focus for "communal" fighting. It followed an admission by the Haganah that its forces were responsible for the death of five young children when an Arab house was demolished in the city. The Zionists alleged that the house had been the centre of "Arab violence" and described the deaths as "very unfortunate."

Christmas brought no respite to Palestine. Fighting in the north of Palestine caused the death of 13 Jews, with scores wounded. Fighting flared along the Mediterranean coastal plain. Rooftop sniping was reported in Haifa with the death of 14 Arabs and three Jews reported on Mount Carmel. The border between Tel-Aviv and Jaffa was, once again, the centre of fierce fighting. Zionist supply convoys were under increasing attack. The conflict spread into new areas of Palestine, including Tiberias on the shores of the Sea of Galilee.

On the 26 December, the Stern Gang demonstrated its particular brand of "patriotism" by stealing four lorry loads of textiles from a Tel-Aviv warehouse. Increasingly, Britons, both civilian and military, featured amongst the casualties.

As the end of the year approached, serious clashes took place in the Arab-Jewish quarter of Romena, Jerusalem. Assailants, believed to be members of the Stern Gang, bombed a petrol station and raked a cafe with gun fire. In central Palestine further train robberies took place, believed to be carried out by Arab armed guerrillas intent on building up supplies.

It was reported that two Panamanian registered ships passed through the Bosphorus carrying nearly 12 000 illegal Jewish immigrants destined for Palestine. The British navy boarded the *29 November* in the Mediterranean and escorted its cargo of illegal immigrants to Haifa.

On 29 December, one month to the day from the passing of the Partition Resolution, Palestine witnessed one of the worst incidents in its recent troubled history. At Damascus Gate in Jerusalem, a six gallon barrel bomb was rolled out of a green, Jewish owned taxi, towards a lunch time queue of men, women and children waiting for a bus to Haifa. As the taxi sped away it sprayed the crowd with machine gun fire.Within seconds, the area was a mass of flames and hysteria. Bodies lay everywhere in the aftermath of an incident described as the worst since the start of the present troubles.

The taxi was eventually stopped, one occupant stabbed to death and the other reluctantly handed over to the police. The Irgun admitted reponsibility, claiming that Damascus gate was a meeting point for Arab "gangsters", during a day described as having the heaviest death-toll since 30 November - 18 people dead including three British policeman and one soldier. Elsewhere the Irgun was busy, attacking the Arab Legion and an army camp, escaping with military supplies from the latter.

On 30 December, the previous day's atrocity was surpassed when, in Haifa, the efforts to arrange a truce between Jew and Arab were shattered. At 10.20am two bombs were flung from a passing car at a queue of about 100 Arab workers looking for employment at Consolidated Oil Refineries. Six Arabs were killed and 42 reported wounded. However such was the outrage at this act of terrorism, following hard on the heels of the previous day's incident, that the 2 000 Arab employees at the refinery went on the rampage.

This resulted in 41 Jewish deaths, with seven injuries. Three hundred escaped the attack by locking themselves into rooms. It was the heaviest loss of life since the King David Hotel was blown up by Zionist terrorists.

Throughout the day, the Stern Gang attacked two British policemen, killing one and seriously injuring another on Jaffa Road. A British policeman was killed by Arab sniper fire while escorting a Jewish funeral at the Mount of Olives. Another was seriously injured, along with two Jewish fatalities at the same funeral. An attack on Katamon power station left Jerusalem in the dark.

Towards the end of the year it was reported that the Zionist terrorist groups were recruiting in Austria. Individuals posing as businessmen and journalists were visiting the camps holding the displaced persons. Several East European countries, particularly Bulgaria and Romania, were reported to be more open in their assistance of illegal Jewish immigrant traffic.

The last day of 1947 was a precursor of the fate which was soon to overtake many a village in Palestine. On the outskirts of Haifa the village of Balad al-Shaykh, with its cemetry containing the tomb of Shaykh 'Izz al-Din al-Qassam - famed for his resistance against the British occupation of Palestine and whose death triggered the 1936 revolt against the British, was targeted by the Haganah.

The *History of the Haganah* records that a force of 170 men from the Palmach had orders to "encircle the village, harm the largest possible number of men, damage property, and refrain from attacking women and children." The end result was a massacre of more than 60 villagers, including women and children. Several dozen houses were reported destroyed. The action was supposedly in retaliation for the killing of Jewish oil refinery workers the previous day, allegedly by men from the village.(*All that Remains*, p.154)

Collated from The Scotsman, December 1947

Map 1

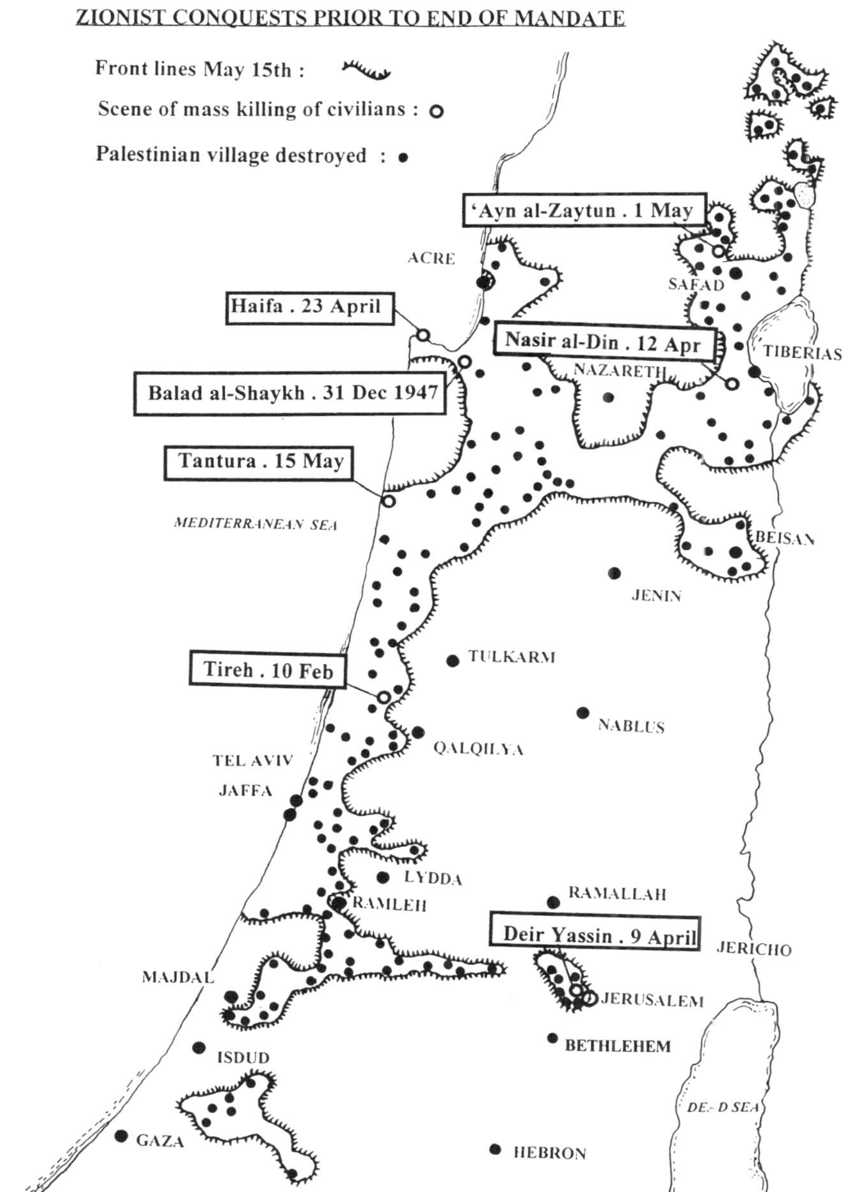
ZIONIST CONQUESTS PRIOR TO END OF MANDATE
Front lines May 15th :
Scene of mass killing of civilians :
Palestinian village destroyed :
'Ayn al-Zaytun . 1 May
ACRE
SAFAD
Haifa . 23 April
Nasir al-Din . 12 Apr
TIBERIAS
NAZARETH
Balad al-Shaykh . 31 Dec 1947
Tantura . 15 May
MEDITERRANEAN SEA
BEISAN
JENIN
TULKARM
Tireh . 10 Feb
NABLUS
QALQILYA
TEL AVIV
JAFFA
LYDDA
RAMALLAH
RAMLEH
Deir Yassin . 9 April
JERICHO
MAJDAL
JERUSALEM
BETHLEHEM
ISDUD
GAZA
HEBRON

Map 2

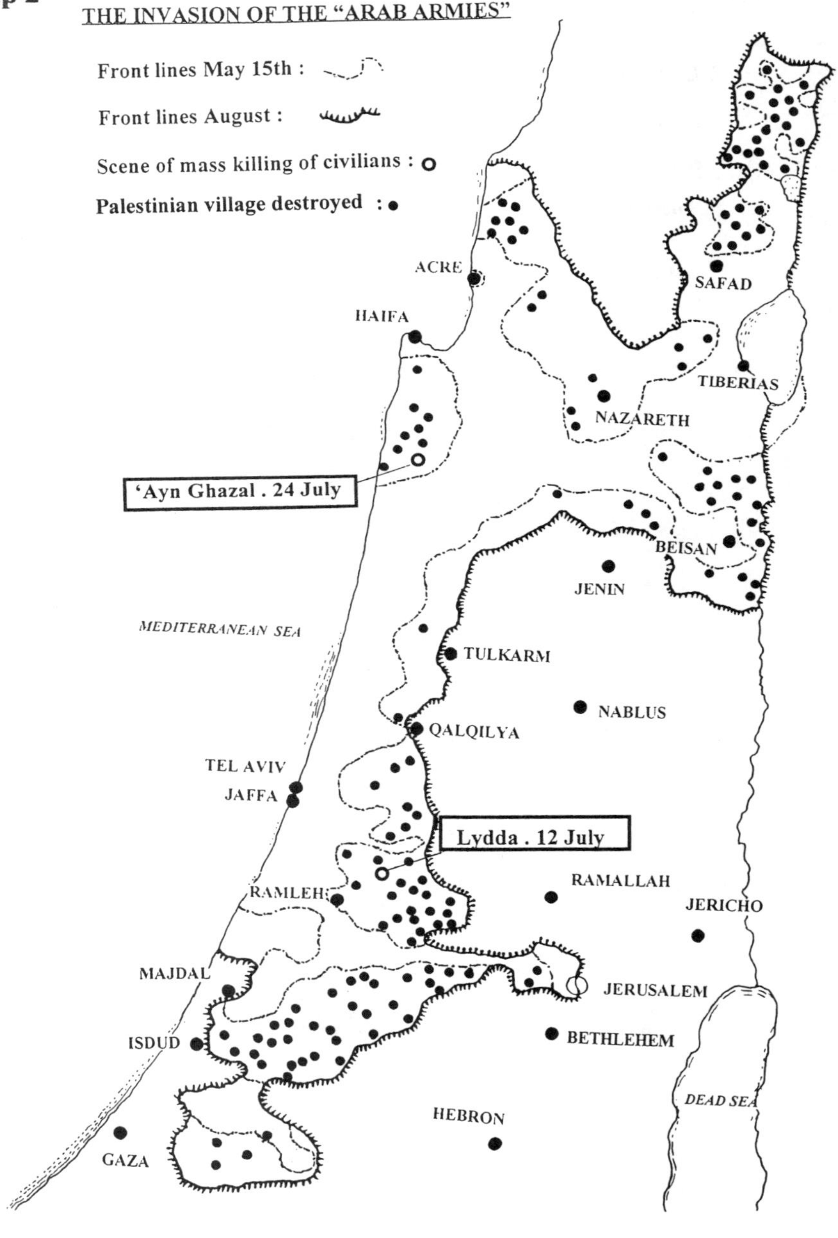
THE INVASION OF THE "ARAB ARMIES"
Front lines May 15th :
Front lines August :
Scene of mass killing of civilians :
Palestinian village destroyed :
ACRE
HAIFA
SAFAD
TIBERIAS
NAZARETH
'Ayn Ghazal . 24 July
BEISAN
JENIN
MEDITERRANEAN SEA
TULKARM
NABLUS
QALQILYA
TEL AVIV
JAFFA
Lydda . 12 July
RAMLEH
RAMALLAH
JERICHO
MAJDAL
JERUSALEM
ISDUD
BETHLEHEM
DEAD SEA
HEBRON
GAZA

Map 3

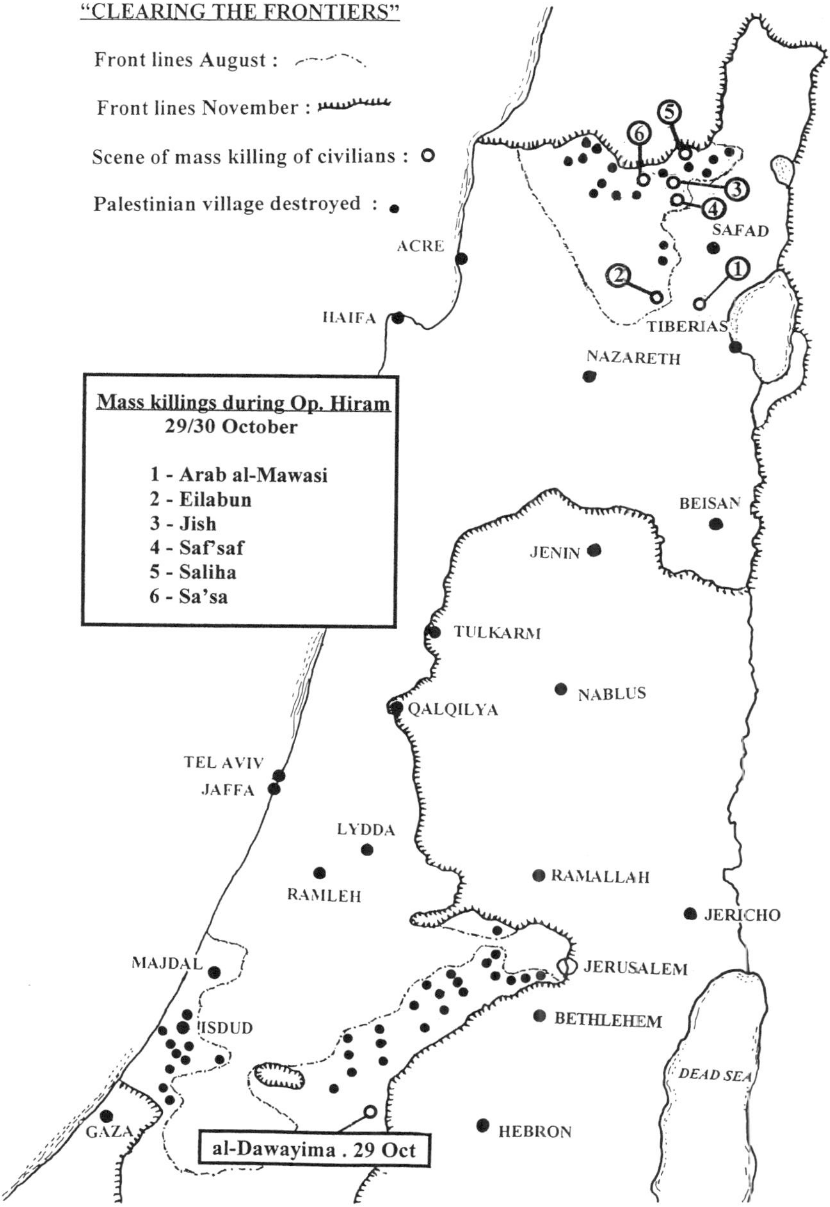
"CLEARING THE FRONTIERS"
Front lines August :
Front lines November :
Scene of mass killing of civilians :
Palestinian village destroyed :
Mass killings during Op. Hiram
29/30 October
1 - Arab al-Mawasi
2 - Eilabun
3 - Jish
4 - Saf'saf
5 - Saliha
6 - Sa'sa
ACRE
HAIFA
SAFAD
TIBERIAS
NAZARETH
BEISAN
JENIN
TULKARM
NABLUS
QALQILYA
TEL AVIV
JAFFA
LYDDA
RAMLEH
RAMALLAH
JERICHO
MAJDAL
JERUSALEM
ISDUD
BETHLEHEM
DEAD SEA
GAZA
HEBRON
al-Dawayima . 29 Oct